The Secrets of Hegemony

Tai-Yoo Kim · Daeryoon Kim

The Secrets of Hegemony

Springer

Tai-Yoo Kim
College of Engineering
Seoul National University
Seoul
Korea (Republic of)

Daeryoon Kim
School of Undergraduate Studies
Daegu Gyeongbuk Institute of Science & Technology
Daegu
Korea (Republic of)

ISBN 978-981-10-4414-4 ISBN 978-981-10-4416-8 (eBook)
DOI 10.1007/978-981-10-4416-8

Library of Congress Control Number: 2017935387

Printed on acid-free paper

This Springer imprint is published by Springer Nature
The registered company is Springer Nature Singapore Pte Ltd.
The registered company address is: 152 Beach Road, #21-01/04 Gateway East, Singapore 189721, Singapore

This book is dedicated to Jungnyeo Chang
for her commitment and love

Tai-Yoo Kim

For Jayoung, Chaewon, and Joowon
with love

Daeryoon Kim

Preface

The rise and fall of nations and states has always been a topic of keen interest in the fields of history, economics, political science, and other parts of the social sciences. This interest most likely results from the topic's direct connection to economic abundance, which we could describe as a prerequisite for happiness, an absolute value that humans seek. Even without relying on Marxist theory, it is undeniable that human history is a series of conflicts and compromises made at the least to provide sustenance and beyond that to increase material prosperity.

To be sure, there have also been exceptional individuals who have given up the fierce battle for victory and the exhausting struggle for progress and contented themselves with their lot. But are we really sure that their lives were better than the material and spiritual abundance that is generally enjoyed in the developed world? Whether because it is our fate to compete over limited resources or our nature to always compare our lives to others, most nations and states, along with the individuals of which they consist, have dedicated themselves to the struggle to attain abundance. Despite the importance of the rise and fall of nations and states, no sound theory of national development is to be found that can consistently explain the economic growth that sustains such abundance or beyond that to guarantee that the developed and developing worlds will escape from the trap of recurring recessions and low growth so that they can grow and flourish together.

I published my own theory about this issue a few years ago in *Economic Growth: The New Perspectives for Theory and Policy* (Springer Publishing, 2014). This book represents the synthesis of my intellectual journey: studying engineering in university, changing directions to economics in graduate school, and spending half my life as an economist. At the same time, I also wanted to determine how accurately the theory of economic growth I outlined in this book could predict the future.

The decision I made after much deliberation was to undertake the study of history. Just as economic theories are commonly tested through real-world data that we accumulated over time, so it seemed to me that a careful study of history could allow me to test my hypothesis about the basic principles of national development in the laboratory of history. *The Secrets of Hegemony* is the culmination of this goal, as well as of my studies over the past few years.

Thus, my desire was not only to review the past (in this book, the time stretching from the Spanish Empire to the USA following World War II) but also to forecast the future through those past events. With any luck, I thought, I could also unlock the secret to accelerating economic growth, which could continue to increase human happiness.

But history consists of as many fragments as the stars filling the night sky, and they do not by themselves link to the future (or the past or even the present, for that matter). The fragments of history do not fit neatly together like the pieces of a jigsaw puzzle to form the picture on the box cover. The diverse facts and phenomena that constitute the history of human civilization sometimes point toward new pictures and places because of chance happenings, bizarre changes, and the will of visionaries. Thus, as long as I was trying to sail across the vast ocean of history without a theory of economic growth to serve as my compass, it was very naïve of me to expect that I would ever reach my destination, which is to say, the future.

My theory of economic growth largely divides the economic growth models that appear in human history into two categories: economic growth that diminishes over time and economic growth that accelerates over time. I located the first of these categories in agricultural societies, and the second in commercial and industrial societies. The difference between the two categories of economic growth (diminishing and accelerating) is not quantitative but qualitative; that it, it has to do with the fundamental nature of societies. This means that there is a wide gulf between these two kinds of economic society.

That is why the first society examined in this book is the Spanish Empire. While most scholars categorize the Spanish Empire as a commercial society, I argue that the rise and fall of the Spanish Empire follows the same course as agricultural empires of the past such as the Roman Empire. The Spanish Empire went into decline, after all, because its economic system never managed to overcome the limitations of diminishing growth. On the other hand, it was the advent of societies with accelerating economic growth based on commerce and industry (which first appeared in the Netherlands and which was perfected in Great Britain) that prefigured modern civilization and represented a crucial turning point in human history. If not for the accomplishments of the Netherlands and Britain, the human race might never have aroused from the slumbers of agricultural society, which is characterized by stagnant growth and income and consequently by a static population and life span. This suggests the breadth of the gulf between these two economic societies.

My repeated emphasis on contrary outcomes in the agricultural society of Spain, the commercial society of the Netherlands, and the industrial society of Britain results from my belief that most standard academic theories about economic growth have committed the error of regarding the transition from agricultural society to industrial society as being the result of linear and inevitable historical development, or in other words of continuous and gradual evolution.

While we will address this view in detail in this book, a decelerating society and an accelerating society cannot in theory be consecutive, nor does this accord with the historical facts. Furthermore, industrialization was not the natural outcome of the evolution of agricultural society—rather, it was the product of grafting industrial capitalism onto agricultural society. This can be said not only of the USA, which dominated the global economy for one century after the Commercial Revolution in the Netherlands and the Industrial Revolution in Britain, but also of Germany and Japan; of South Korea and Taiwan, which are now halfway there; and of all the developing countries, including China, which has recently become the factory of the world.

I emphasize this point because I am concerned about the recent tendency for people seeking solutions to the problems we face today and a vision for our future to turn to agricultural society, which met its demise long ago, and to the classics, which are agricultural society's intellectual heritage. It is of course admirable to use the classics to reflect upon one's life and to cultivate wisdom for what lies ahead. But this reactionary tendency must not lead us to ignore the harsh reality of agricultural society and to wrongly idealize it as the place that is no place—that is to say, utopia. Indeed, agricultural society was a time when the average human life expectancy was less than half of what it is today, a time of rampant famine, disease, and violence. It was a time when people's material conditions left them vulnerable to starvation and nakedness, a time when the bonds of social status prevented most slaves and peasants from rising above the lot of livestock who could talk.

On the other hand, the countless technological innovations made as industrial society matured and particularly our technological achievements over the past three centuries of accelerating growth eclipse the combined progress of the past three thousand years (or perhaps even thirty thousand years). The industrial technology that Aldous Huxley parodied in *Brave New World* has instead served as a springboard for humanity to move toward an even braver world.

If we accept the argument that human ideologies and cultures are the product of specific social conditions, we must admit that there is a profound gap between the values that dominate agricultural society and the values that dominate industrial society. It is imprudent and even irresponsible to subjectively judge the results of today's industrial civilization, which is based on rationalism and technology, according to the outmoded ideologies and values of agricultural society. Such an assessment does nothing to help us address the grave challenges that we face, including our polluted environment and the wealth gap between countries.

To use a fanciful expression, this way of thinking is rather like looking for insights about how evolution will transform the human body by skipping over Homo sapiens and the great apes and going back to the age of the dinosaurs. Put another way, it is as futile as trying to derive the primary colors from black and white or trying to find a three-dimensional body in a two-dimensional surface. We must be extremely cautious about such efforts, since they are not only foolish and wasteful, but may also lead intellectuals who are seriously concerned about the future of human civilization and leaders who will determine the future of their nations to devise the wrong solutions for the wrong problems.

To conclude, I would like to make a few remarks about the results of this collaborative project between an economist and a historian. If the offspring of a male lion and a female tiger is called a liger, then the fusion of economics and history may be called economic history. When the first hybrid generation has characteristics that are superior to both parents, biologists call this "hybrid vigor"; the opposite case is called "hybrid weakness." Let us set aside for now the question of whether economic history exhibits hybrid vigor or hybrid weakness, academically speaking, compared to the fields of economics and history. Nearly, all books of economic history until now have been written by people studying the history of economic activity, and hardly, any of them have been written (as this one has) through vigorous debate between an economist and a historian. By combining the scholarly strengths of economists and historians, this book maximizes the academic "hybrid vigor" of economics and history, which I expect will further increase its credibility.

My co-author Daeryoon Kim is a principled historian. As we were discussing and writing this book, Daeryoon always maintained a critical attitude about my ideas, and he was sure to bring to my attention historical facts that were needed to fill in the picture that I was painting. While he does not yet agree with every aspect of the theory of economic growth underlying this book or the message that this theory has for the history of civilization, our energetic debates gave me a chance to encounter and to study the new field of history. For that, I am grateful.

In fact, this book has a hidden author, too. During her work as a teaching assistant, Bogang Jun dedicated herself to laying the foundation and building the basic framework of this book as if she had been writing it herself. Even though she was unable to bring this book to completion because of an opportunity to study overseas, traces of her work can be detected throughout. I hope that my cherished student Bogang will move on to even greater academic achievements and eventually publish a book that expands upon—and improves upon—this one.

Many people's encouragement, support, and assistance went into the publication of this book. First, I would also like to thank William Achauer, a senior editor at Springer, for his affectionate care and his immense help during the publication of this book. Second, a great amount of research (including what appears in this book) was made possible by a grant from the National Research Foundation of Korea for "A Theoretical and Empirical Study on the Development of Human Civilizations and Economic Growth: Understanding the Roles of Science and Technology through an Interdisciplinary Approach" (project number: NRF-2010-0026178). I would like to express my gratitude to the anonymous reviewers who worked with the foundation on our research, as well as the foundation's staff and its president, Lee Seung-jong. The exceptional consideration and care of the staff at Seoul National University Press, including Kwak Jin-hui and its director, Kim Jong-seo, guided this book down the path to publication.

I would like to dedicate this book to the memory of my father Kim Yong-hoe and my mother Park Sun-seon, who sowed the seeds of my soul and body and raised me with correct principles and abundant love.

Seoul, Korea (Republic of) Tai-Yoo Kim

Prologue

History shows us how countless states have gained and then lost hegemony. The captivating story of rise and fall can be found both in ancient and modern times, and both in the West and the East: from Athens and Rome to Great Britain and the USA, and from the Qin Dynasty and the Han Dynasty to Japan and China.

It is hard not to feel curious about how these states have seized—and then surrendered—their hegemony. This curiosity is prompted by the ferocious rivalry between states that has caused a series of global conflicts going as far back as the Seven Years' War and that continues today under the guise of globalization. This is a rivalry in which rich states attempt to consolidate and strengthen their current position while poor states try to catch up to the rich ones. This is surely one of the interests shared by all who live today, regardless of what country they call home.

This book was also inspired by such curiosity, by the question of what conditions have determined the rise and fall of the various civilizations that have adorned the history of mankind and of the states that have led those civilizations. In other words, what is the secret of hegemony? What is it that enables some states to achieve hegemony?

But first, what exactly is hegemony? Examining the word's etymological history, we find that it derives from the ancient Greek concept of *hegemon*. A *hegemon* was a powerful city-state such as Athens or Sparta that held sway over other city-states. In this sense, Athens was the hegemon of the Delian League, while Sparta was the hegemon of the Peloponnesian League.

While the first hegemons in the West can be found in ancient Greece, their East Asian counterparts are the Five Hegemons of the Spring and Autumn period in ancient China. These were five figures chosen to lead a league of feudal states formed when China's Zhou Dynasty entered a period of weakness: Duke Huan of Qi, Duke Wen of Jin, King Zhuang of Chu, King Helü of Wu, and King Goujian of Yu. The Five Hegemons exercised power over the other feudal states and their rulers, just as Athens and Sparta did in Greece. If power means influence and leadership that can be used to impose one's will on others, then hegemony can ultimately be seen as the power that one group exerts over another.

Thus, hegemony was originally a term that referred to the supreme leadership of one state in relation to other states, and we can call this the traditional definition of hegemony. According to *Dizionario di Politica*, published in Italy in 1976, the concept of hegemony was frequently used by nineteenth-century German historians such as Leopold von Ranke and Georg Dehio. For them, it was a key term in historical interpretation that was of equivalent importance to the concept of the balance of power. According to these historians, every state has an inherent tendency to seek to extend its power outside itself, and these efforts to achieve hegemony always threaten and destabilize the balance of power. Not only the city-states of ancient Greece but also the Italian duchies in the late Middle Ages and the early modern period and the European monarchies in the early modern period fought fiercely for regional hegemony.

To be sure, some historians have focused on the fact that the unceasing attempts to seize hegemony—ranging from the Holy Roman Empire under Charles V in the sixteenth century to Hitler's Germany in the twentieth century—have been frustrated time and time again as neighboring states have been forced to form alliances to maintain the balance of power. But considering that even this is just a temporary balance between highly unstable forces, the very tendency for cultures and powers to expand their power and to seek hegemony may be a fundamental part of the development of states and of human civilization. For similar reasons, history sometimes appears to be swinging between hegemony and balance of power with the perpetual motion of a pendulum.

The German historians mentioned above for the most part dealt with hegemony in terms of political and military superiority. In contrast, Italian historians such as Vincenzo Gioberti regarded hegemony from the perspective of culture and traditions rather than military power and tended to use it to mean moral and civic superiority. This was an important expansion of the concept of hegemony. Gioberti concluded that, while nineteenth-century Italy was weak on a political and military level, it possessed a clear moral and cultural superiority. Even inside Italy, he believed, Rome's status as the center of papal authority made it superior to Piedmont despite Piedmont's more powerful army. This was also the origin of the idea of unifying Italy around the hegemony of the pope. Of course, Italian history demonstrates the ultimate futility and failure of hegemony that is not grounded in economic and military power: Gioberti's ideas, known as Neo-Guelphism, foundered in the revolutionary maelstrom in 1848.

The concept of hegemony was further elaborated by the Marxists of the twentieth century. These scholars applied the concept not to the relationships between states but rather to the relationships between different social classes inside a single state. They regarded hegemony as the power of the ruling class to achieve control while simultaneously justifying that control. According to *Dizionario di Politica*, "Possessing institutionalized political power, the ruling class uses direct and indirect means of controlling information to propagate a comprehensive and self-justifying concept of the world that presents its rule as a natural and necessary thing that serves the interests of everyone." [1]

What is worth noting here is that the emphasis on presenting "its rule as a natural and necessary thing" falls not on physical force and coercion but rather on persuasion and consent. That is also why Italian Marxist theorist Antonio Gramsci fundamentally understood hegemony as the combination of force and consent but was more interested in the latter of the two. Gramsci focused not so much on the political elements of force and rule as on the intellectual and moral elements of persuasion and leadership. That is, control cannot last long without hegemony; indeed, without hegemony, it is impossible to seize control in the first place [2].

However, two important addendums should be made to Gramsci's concept of hegemony. The first is that this persuasion and consent must be accompanied by some degree of economic concessions and sacrifices on the part of the ruling class. These concessions and sacrifices need not be unilateral, however. The ruling class can use "gentle rule" based on persuasion and consent to maintain its overall hegemony while also minimizing the long-term cost of rule and gaining the maximum profits. The ruling class willingly makes economic concessions and sacrifices because its members bear in mind their long-term effectiveness.

The second addendum is that conflict can also arise inside the ruling class in regard to the manner of its rule. Multiple elite groups exist within the ruling class, and each elite group competes with the other elite groups. Such conflict between elite groups can break out for economic reasons, such as over their immediate interests, and they can also develop for political, moral, and ideological reasons, such as over the long-term prospects for improving their system of rule.

Indeed, scholars such as Richard Lachmann depart from the Marxists' emphasis on class conflict to argue that the conflict between elite groups can be an important, even decisive, factor in social change [3]. On a historical level, this is borne out by the conflict between the Court and Country Parties and between the Whigs and Tories in seventeenth-century England, or between the Federalists and the Antifederalists and between the Federalists and the Republicans in late eighteenth- and early nineteenth-century America. There is no need to reiterate how critically important these internal hegemonic conflicts were for the future development of both countries.

The concept of hegemony as we have defined it above can be applied to ancient Greece, where the word first appeared. During the Greco-Persian Wars, the Athenian navy played a decisive role in repulsing the Persians. But even though Persia had suffered a defeat, it remained a threat, which prompted the Greek city-states to form the Delian League under the lead of Athens. The member cities supported the league by donating money and warships.

But even after the Persian threat was eliminated in the Greek victory in the Battle of the Eurymedon in the early 460s BCE, Athens sought to maintain the league. It even used force to subjugate Thasos when that city tried to secede from the league. This showed that Athens had begun building an empire.

Athens' empire building consisted of policies that reflected the wishes of the class of Athenians known as the thetes. The thetes were paid a stipend to serve as sailors in the Athenian navy, and if they were to continue receiving that stipend, the navy had to be preserved. The dissolution of the Delian League might have meant the dissolution of the navy, too, which would have been a serious loss for the thetes. The political leaders of Athens were forced to heed the shifting public opinions of this class, which accounted for the majority of the citizens of Athens. This reflected the political need to persuade and pacify the public.

This point was not lost on Aristides, regarded as "a leader of the people," who advised that the riches brought in by Athens' imperial activity be used to maintain its hegemony. In *A Political History of Athenian Democracy*, Byeong-u Yang relates Aristides' recommendation as follows: "After that, when the nation had gained confidence and earned a great deal of wealth, he advised [the Athenians] to seize hegemony and to come out of the farms and live in the cities. He said they should all earn a living by going to war, defending the city, or attending to the affairs of state, so that they could defend their hegemony along with him." [4]

Even though Aristides remained on cordial terms with Cimon, who represented the wealthier Athenians, his recommendation was not completely accepted by the leaders of Athens. This is clearly demonstrated by the political struggle that broke out between the conservative Cimon and the reformer Ephialtes after Aristides left the political stage. It was the victory of the reformers in this struggle that opened the door for the Age of Pericles, the golden age of the Athenian Empire and of democratic government.

These historical facts are significant, not least because Aristides' recommendation makes clear that hegemony is not merely coercion backed by force but rather persuasion based on economic rewards. Leaders found it necessary to pay heed to the will of the people and to reflect it in their policies, if only so that they could maintain their leadership. And if they could not do that, they had to at least agitate or appease the public. This helps explain the appearance in Athens of the rabble-rousers known as *demagogos* (the origin of the English word "demagogue").

Aristides' recommendation is significant because it illustrates the close connection between hegemony in the relations between different states and hegemony within a single society. Paradoxically, Athens used the wealth that it plundered from other states to expand the basis of democracy at home, and the radicalization of its democracy pushed Athens to continue its empire building. From this, we can infer the existence of a mechanism by which hegemony abroad strengthens social unity at home and social unity at home supports hegemony abroad. We can also conclude that Athens' hegemony was what enabled the reformers led by Ephialtes and Pericles to emerge victorious from the conflict between elite groups.

In this book, we will be employing the concept of hegemony in the manner of Aristides. While our primary area of interest is the conditions under which a state gains and loses its hegemony in international relations, we must also remember that this is closely tied to the degree of domestic social unity. Acknowledging differences of type and degree, every society is based on a hierarchical relationship between the ruling class and the subject class. As such, the hegemony that the ruling class exerts over the subject class is a critical factor determining whether, and to what extent, that society achieves unity.

While there are a variety of ways in which the ruling class can exercise hegemony (as shown by the examples of Athens in the ancient world and Britain and the

USA in the modern world), no method of persuading and appeasing the masses is as reliable as economic rewards. The availability of this method, of course, depends on whether the society can adequately produce and appropriately distribute an economic surplus. Another critical variable affecting a state's future is the developmental agenda of the elite group that gains the upper hand in the conflict between elite groups. In short, the two domestic variables that determine whether international hegemony is possible are the developmental agenda of the dominant elite group and the formation of an effective and stable economic system that can produce the maximum economic surplus while distributing this surplus appropriately.

To be sure, economic methods and the economic system are not the only important aspects of how a state and its ruling class exercise hegemony. In a previously published book, we have already dealt with the extra-economic and noneconomic means and conditions that make hegemony possible [5]. In that book, we emphasized the importance of hegemony in the areas of politics, society, and culture—which is to say political hegemony, social resilience, and cultural vitality—that produce the wealth of a nation.

In this book, we will assume that a hegemonic power is not only among the wealthiest countries of the world but that it is also influential in the areas of politics, society, and culture. Given that assumption, we propose to concentrate on the methods of producing and distributing economic surplus (which concerns the economic conditions that enable a state to exercise hegemony) and on the economic systems that can serve as such methods.

While some may not agree that the question of economic systems is the most important issue facing human society, it can hardly be denied that this issue is one that every society must face and try to solve. Indeed, there is nothing so fundamental to human life as the economic question. Humans cannot be fully explained as *homo economicus*, but neither can humans survive without an economy. That is why the attempt to solve the economic question is one of the most important themes in the history of humanity.

By stressing the persuasive effect of economic rewards on the exercise of hegemony, Aristides' recommendation is also consistent with the stance taken by Gramsci, who was less interested in compulsion than in consent. This implies that changes in the total economic rewards that a society can distribute (that is, changes in the quality of economic growth) are bound to have an effect on how hegemony is exercised. In agricultural society (a zero-sum society in which economic growth decelerates and stagnates with the passage of time), the distributable surplus decreases, and hegemony is used to convince the members of society to make concessions and sacrifices and to gain their consent for this. But in industrial society (a positive-sum society in which economic growth accelerates), the distributable surplus continues to increase, and hegemony is used not to demand concessions and sacrifices but to emphasize the economic advantages enjoyed by all the members of that society.

The differences between the exercise of hegemony in agricultural society and industrial society are apparent in the social cohesiveness of the hegemonic state and in the strength of its hegemony. Compared to passive consent that is contingent on concessions and sacrifice, voluntary consent produced by distributing economic advantages is a much more effective—and powerful—guarantee of hegemony. While agricultural empires of the past depended upon passive consent and coercive power, mature industrial societies have exercised hegemony by producing voluntary consent through democratic systems and procedures, which has enabled them to maintain their domestic stability.

The emphasis on voluntary consent in the exercise of hegemony is also relevant to discussing the formation and transfer of hegemony in international relations. In agricultural societies, relations between states inevitably became a zero-sum game with those states squabbling over the limited surplus that is characteristic of a decelerating economic system. Ultimately, it was not easy for such a hegemonic power to persuade other societies to accept its international leadership.

Admittedly, the history of competition between agricultural and industrial societies since the early modern era shows the surplus of agricultural societies being appropriated by industrial societies. Even so, it has been possible to present the free trade on which these relationships depend as being complementary or even mutually beneficial. In addition, this has enabled the process of persuasion and consent to function to some extent even amid intense international competition. This is illustrated by Britain's advocacy of free trade and peace in international relations after it became a mature industrial society in the nineteenth century and by the United States' promotion of the ideology of the free market around the world once it gained an overwhelming economic and technological advantage after World War II.

This can be contrasted with Nazi Germany's attempt during World War II to expand its territory in the manner of past agricultural empires on the grounds of acquiring "Lebensraum" (meaning "living space") for the German people. But the Nazis were unable to win the consent of their neighbors, not least because of their repressive rule over the non-Aryan peoples that they conquered.

As this suggests, the most important condition for a state acquiring and maintaining hegemony (whether at home or abroad) is the ability of that state's economy to produce an adequate amount of economic surplus and to distribute it appropriately. In other words, hegemony depends upon a virtuous cycle in the economy. But when the economic system of the hegemonic state runs up against its inherent limitations or when that state's hegemony is threatened by other states, this incites social and international conflict and usually leads to war. For the hegemonic state, war is a way to resolve the problems of an economic system that has reached its limits; for the states that seek to challenge the hegemonic state, war is a way to destroy the hegemon's economic base while simultaneously boosting their own economies. That is how war became an economic tool for restoring the virtuous cycle in the economy.

But a state's defeat in war (or in another words the vicious cycle of war) nearly always leads to its decline and downfall. In this regard, war is not merely the continuation of politics, as Carl von Clausewitz said, but also the continuation of economics. As historian Paul Kennedy observed in his study of the rise and fall of great powers, "There is a very clear connection *in the long run* between an individual Great Power's economic rise and fall and its growth and decline as an important military power (or world empire)." [6]

As indicated above, the central point we will make in this book is that the most fundamental principle that makes hegemony possible is the virtuous cycle of war and the economy, and that this principle can be both neatly confirmed through theory and repeatedly observed in history. At this point, there is one more concept about which some further explanation is necessary. In this book, we will be using the term "empire" to refer to various hegemonic states throughout history: the Qin Dynasty in ancient China, Rome in the classical West, and Spain, the Netherlands, Britain, and the USA since the early modern period. This means that we will refer to agricultural states that achieved hegemony as agricultural empires, commercial states that achieved hegemony as commercial empires, and industrial states that achieved hegemony as industrial empires. Some readers may find themselves wondering about the aptness of this method of nomenclature and about the definition of "empire" as used in this book [7].

While "empire" has a number of meanings, the working definition that we will use is that an empire is a governing authority by which a ruling nation and the country they inhabit control the smaller nations or states around them [8]. To be sure, this kind of governing authority can take a variety of forms, and scholars have often distinguished between official and unofficial empires. According to this distinction, an official empire is one that uses hard power to control its subjects directly, while an unofficial empire uses soft power to control its subjects indirectly. An unofficial empire, that is, persuades and supports its subjects and gives them a model to emulate. In this latter case, some scholars prefer the term "hegemony" to "empire" [9]. History appears to show us a shift from official empires to unofficial empires, while on a political level, the power wielded by hegemonic states has seemed to be much more effective and legitimate than that of empires.

Nevertheless, all of these—official and unofficial empires, empire, and hegemony—belong to a larger category that can also be labeled "empire." Thus, there is no reason why we cannot refer to the hegemonic states of the past as empires. Indeed, it is only by referring to them as such that we can shed light on the close relationship between hegemony and empire. Indeed, if we view an empire as a polity that uses various means to enter a ruler–subject relationship with its neighbors, we can say that any state in history that has attempted to expand beyond its borders through the virtuous cycle of war and the economy is an empire, regardless of the success of its imperial ambitions.

For these reasons, in this book, we define an empire as a state that is structurally oriented toward expansion and that has achieved some degree of success in such expansion. Ultimately, we can say that a successful empire is a hegemonic power. In particular considering that international trade and international relations have become necessary conditions for a state's existence, growth, and development since the Industrial Revolution, the states commonly referred to as great powers are bound to be hegemonic powers as well.

In light of these considerations, we will be using the terms "empire," "hegemonic state," and "great power" synonymously. But it is important to remember that a developed country need not be an empire, hegemonic state, or great power. The concept of "developed country" has cultural, social, and political implications for the quality of life of individual members of that country, whereas the concepts of "empire," "hegemonic state," and "great power" generally refer to the total power of the state, including the size of the national economy and the strength of its armed forces. While it is true that most empires, hegemonic states, and great powers are developed countries, there are certainly examples of developed countries (Switzerland and Luxembourg come to mind) that are neither empires, hegemonic states, nor great powers. While such developed countries are also of great importance, it should be made clear before continuing that they are not the subject of this book.

In the vast sweep of history, countless hegemonic empires have fallen. These empires have sought peace and prosperity within the limits of their unique economic systems—whether agricultural, commercial, or industrial—or while valiantly attempting to transcend those limits. But history shows us that, in the end, empires always fall.

Is it possible to create a general theory of the rise and fall of empires? Gramsci once summed up political theory as he understood it in two basic principles of political theory (in language borrowed from Karl Marx). These principles are very significant: "No social formation disappears as long as the productive forces which have developed within it still find room for further forward movement" and "a society does not set itself tasks for whose solution the necessary conditions have not already been incubated." [10] But Gramsci warned his readers against adopting fatalistic or mechanistic interpretations of these principles.

This is an important warning. Indeed, some states have collapsed because of social fragmentation or military defeat despite having "room for further forward movement." There are others that have been compelled by outside forces to accept a new system when no solution was available to them. This merely illustrates the complexity of history.

Nevertheless, the potential to develop a state's productive capacity and the maturity of the conditions necessary to solve problems can serve as useful standards for interpreting history despite its complexity. And while the numerous historians involved in diachronic and comparative studies of history may not explicitly state it, these standards are quite naturally the assumptions implicit in their work.

Next, we need to explain how these standards are specifically applied in this book. Each economic society and each hegemonic empire have been able to continue developing inside the limits of their potential for the virtuous cycle of war and the economy, a potential that is determined by their economic system. But ultimately, as long as peace is being maintained thanks to an empire's hegemony and prosperity, a new economic system is unlikely to appear. At the height of the *Pax Romana*, who could have predicted the Industrial Revolution?

Despite this, it is possible for a state and society to recombine existing internal factors or to incorporate new external factors to reorganize its economy into a new system. Examples of this can be seen in Britain, Germany, and Japan. Britain combined market elements with proto-industrial elements during its transition from an agricultural-commercial society to an industrial society, while the governments of Germany and Japan fabricated the elements of industrial society through industrial policies derived from the industrial experience of other countries.

Ultimately, this study represents the search for the structural limitations on the potential of each economic system (the limitations that have decided the rise and fall of numerous hegemonic empires) as well as the historical factors that are combined and created inside these limitations to enable the transition to a new system. And since our formula for hegemony includes both constants (the structural limitations) and variables (the historical factors), it is important to pay attention to both the constants and the variables. It would be futile to emphasize the historical factors without considering the structural limitations, and it would be close-minded to focus on structural limitations without taking historical factors into account.

But we must bear in mind that historical factors do not only include what is coincidental or accidental. To be sure, such factors are important. But when we talk about historical factors in this book, we speak of a variety of factors obscured by historical chance and uncertainty that are closely linked to the structural effects and limitations of economic systems and that function through them. The secret of hegemony consists of such structural limitations and historical factors, and it is our belief that cracking this code will point the way to a better future.

Despite these references to the secret of hegemony, we do not mean to suggest that we have gotten to the bottom of that secret. What we have done is carry out an exhaustive study of the rise and fall of several historical empires that have promised their people that hegemony would bring permanent peace and prosperity.

Long ago, the poet Dante Alighieri imagined the nations of the world being unified under a single empire. What was needed to guarantee the fulfillment of mankind's intellectual potential (*intellectus possibilis*), Dante said, was universal peace (*pax universalis*), and what was needed to guarantee universal peace was world government (*universale imperium*) [11]. Dante pinned his hopes on the Holy Roman Empire, but far from bringing world peace, that empire only became the source of strife and in the end failed to achieve imperial domination.

This brings to mind economist Joseph Schumpeter's observation that most civilizations have faded without fulfilling their original potential. Indeed, while countless books have been written about the secret of hegemony, they have focused so much on the historical facts concerning the rise and fall of hegemonic states that they have done more to illustrate hegemony's futility in the past than its potential for the future.

In light of history's lesson that all things must pass, it may be rash and inane to promise a new hegemony and economic system that could guarantee peaceful coexistence and shared development. Even so, Dante's dream of universal peace and world government brought us thinkers such as Jean-Jacques Rousseau and Immanuel Kant, and it remains a source for inspiration for future peace and prosperity.

While some aspects of this inspirational dream are unrealistic, it is also a force that drives us to create a better world for humanity, and it may be gradually perceived as a more realistic alternative, both in the industrial society of today and in the knowledge-based society of the future. If we possess the "intellectual potential" of which Dante spoke, we have both the duty and the responsibility to use his dream to inspire us to imagine a better future. And that, of course, is what Dante himself thought:

> All men [...] should especially concern themselves in laboring for posterity, in order that future generations may be enriched by their efforts, as they themselves were made rich by the efforts of generations past. For that man who is imbued with public teachings, but cares not to contribute something to the public good, is far in arrears of his duty, let him be assured [12].

References

1. Silvano Belligni, "Egemonia," *Dizionario di Politica*, eds. Norberto Bobbio and Nicola Matteucci (Torino, 1976), p. 361.
2. While it is true that Gramsci generally used the concept of hegemony in regard to class relations in a single state, he was aware of its wider applications. He said that, for a given class to exercise true hegemony, that class needed itself to become the state. In other words, a class perfected hegemony by becoming the state. The example that Gramsci provides is the Jacobins during the French Revolution at the end of the eighteenth century, but in fact, the ruling classes in the Netherlands and England between the sixteenth and eighteenth centuries vividly illustrate how a social class can perfect hegemony by becoming the state. In the Netherlands and England, the hegemonic classes that were synonymous with the state itself (which is to say the capitalistic merchant class in the Netherlands and the landed class in England) exercised unprecedented hegemony both domestically and internationally. In that sense, hegemony is a concept that can be applied to class relations and to international relations, as well as to both simultaneously. Antonio Gramsci, *Quaderni del carcere*, a cura di Valentino Gerratana (Torino, 1975), pp. 2029, 2289.
3. Richard Lachmann, *Capitalists in Spite of Themselves: Elite Conflict and Economic Transitions in Early Modern Europe* (Oxford, 2002), pp. 8–14.
4. Byeong-u Yang, *Atene Minju Jeongchisa* [A Political History of Athenian Democracy] (Seoul National University Publishing House, 1976), p. 66.
5. Tai-yoo Kim and Mun-seok Jang, *Gukbuui Jogeon: Gamsokhaneun Sahoeeseo Gasokhaneun Sahoero* [The Conditions for National Wealth: From a Decelerating Society to an Accelerating Society] (Seoul National University Press, 2012).
6. Paul Kennedy, *The Rise and Fall of the Great Powers: Economic Change and Military Conflict from 1500 to 2000* (New York, 1987), xxiii–xxiv. Emphasis is in the original.
7. On an etymological level, the word "empire" originally derives from the Latin word "imperare," which means "to give an order." Furthermore, the word "imperium" referred to the domain in which the *imperator* (that is, Rome's kings, consuls, tribunes, dictators, and, after Augustus, its emperors) could give orders and in which those orders held sway. These Roman traditions were passed down to the Westerners who traveled to Asia, and when they

encountered khans, sultans, shoguns, and others ruling vast areas in Asia, they understood them on their own terms as imperators. Ultimately, the terms “emperor” and “empire” came to be commonly used around the world. Timothy H. Parsons, *The Rule of Empires: Those Who Built Them, Those Who Endured Them, and Why They Always Fall* (Oxford, 2010), p. 9.

8. Yeong-seo Baek, *Dongasiaui Jiyeok Jilseo: Jegukeul Neomeo Gongdongchero* [The Regional Order in East Asia: From Empire to Community] (Changbi, 2005), p. 11.
9. Parsons, *The Rule of Empires*, p. 10.
10. Antonio Gramsci, *Okjung Sugo II: Cheolhak, Yeoksa, Munhwapyeon* [Prison Notebooks Volume 2: Philosophy, History, and Culture], trans. Sang-hun Lee (Keorum, 1993) p. 139.
11. Alighieri Dante, *Dante Jejeongron* [Dante’s *De Monarchia*], trans. Yeom Seong (Kyongsaewon, 2009). In particular, see the first volume of the book and explanatory notes (pp. 224–245).
12. Dante, *Dante Jejeongron* [Dante’s *De Monarchia*], p. 13. The English translation is by Aurelia Henry (Boston and New York: Houghton, Mifflin and Company, 1904), available online at http://oll.libertyfund.org/titles/2196.

Contents

Chapter 1
The Virtuous Cycle of War and the Economy: Theory and History

In our attempt to study historical examples of the virtuous (or vicious) cycle of war and the economy, we have rejected abstract generalizations. This is because the economic systems and methods of war that we encounter vary with changes in the environment and historical periods. But neither do we intend to scrutinize each individual historical incident or to merge the findings of history, economics, and other disparate fields of study. Instead, we mean to avoid being too general or too specific while categorizing the states and societies we find into types and examining the economic systems and methods of war for each of these types. This typological approach (which is admittedly rather eclectic) originates in the division of historical economic societies into agricultural societies, commercial societies, and industrial societies. This division is based on the fact that, in the end, all facets of human civilization and culture, including politics, society, and art, are ultimately rooted in and spring from the economy, which is to say the domains in which and the methods by which economic value and economic surplus are created.

Readers may wonder what standard we have used to determine which of these three types a given society falls into. The standards that are generally used are the percentages of the economically active population that work in agriculture, commerce, and industry, and the percentages of gross domestic product accounted for by these three sectors. But in this book, we will rely not on quantitative economic standards such as these but rather on a qualitative standard. The standard that we apply is the new concept of the acceleration and deceleration of economic growth that results from the differences in the methods, forms, and outcomes of value creation found when specific economic societies undergo simple reproduction or expansive reproduction.

Such qualitative differences are important. Regardless of quantitative standards, decelerating economies and accelerating economies have fundamentally different DNA, and those qualitative differences in their economies (or in other words their structural differences) determine their future economic performances. Viewed in light of our quantitative standard, agricultural society represents simple reproduction: it is a self-sufficient society consisting largely of peasants, and most of their

T.-Y. Kim and D. Kim, *The Secrets of Hegemony*,
DOI 10.1007/978-981-10-4416-8_1

production is used for self-consumption. Since production in such societies tends to decrease, there is no way to force individual peasants to increase production. Even if production does increase (during a bumper crop, for example), this is not an economic system in which surplus can be invested into new factors of production to expand production. This results in decelerating economic growth, meaning that the rate of increase of output relative to input gradually slows and finally stops.

Commercial society comes close to the kind of growth seen in industrial society in the sense that expansive reinvestment occurs through commercial profit (typically from trade in luxury goods) and capital accumulation. However, since the items being traded are generally agricultural products, this system is fundamentally based on agricultural society. In this regard, commercial society is located in a transitional period between agricultural society and industrial society, the period that served as the cradle of the Industrial Revolution.

Industrial society is one in which goods and services are produced by placing factors of production such as capital, labor, technology, raw materials, and energy into the artificial spaces of factories and corporations. The profit that is made here is accumulated as capital and invested in technological innovation, which enables the ongoing development of new products based on new technology. This is what enables industrial society to overcome the limits on growth in commercial society and ultimately initiate a virtuous cycle of expansive reproduction.

To be sure, production can decrease and growth can decelerate even in an industrial society, at least in the short term. But capital investment and technological innovation make it possible to supply mass-produced goods in bulk while new products derived from new technology create new demand. This leads to expansive equilibrium in market supply and demand, which in turn enables the economy to grow at an exponential rate. As a consequence, the Malthusian Trap that represented the limits of agricultural society was finally overcome with the advent of industrial society. Thus, industrial society represents an entirely new type of society in which there is accelerating growth.

In this book, we will look at the major hegemonic states that are located on what could be called the critical path in the development and evolution of human civilization moving through the agricultural society of Spain (not the best-known agricultural empire, but one that has some things in common with commercial society) to commercial societies with their system of expansive reinvestment and then to industrial societies with their system of expansive reproduction. In order to understand the secrets of success for the commercial and industrial hegemonic states, it is first necessary to understand the developmental principles (both theoretical and empirical) of agricultural society, commercial society, and industrial society. The development and evolution of each economic society in history is represented in the following figure.

Figure 1.1 shows the development of human civilized societies from primitive hunter-gatherer society to agricultural society and at last to industrial society. Through this developmental flowchart, we can see that agricultural society did not become industrial society directly, but rather that commercial society, a subcategory to agricultural society, evolved into industrial society by way of the Industrial

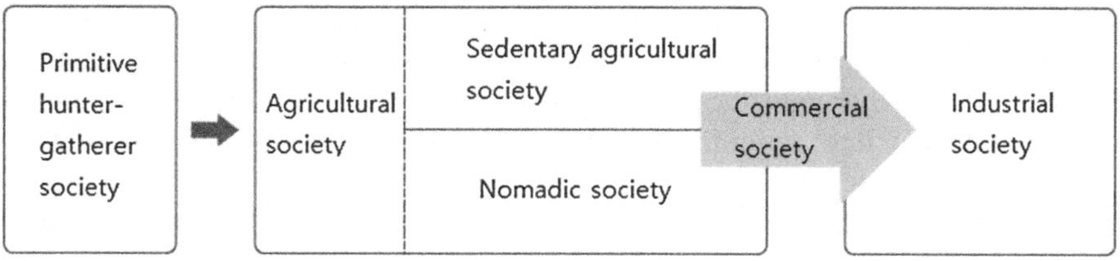

Fig. 1.1 The developmental path of economic societies

Revolution. Of course, we must bear in mind that more recently industrialized states skipped the phase of commercial society and transitioned directly to the phase of industrial society by adopting or imitating the Industrial Revolution experienced by the first states to industrialize.

War and the Economy in Agricultural Societies

It can be said that human civilization began with agriculture. The development of farming techniques about 7000 years ago gave humans the chance to live a new kind of life. People adopted a lifestyle of sedentary farming and left behind the exhausting practice of hunting and gathering, which had required following the animals they hunted in their seasonal migrations. Production in agricultural society generally relied on renewable biological resources, which is to say farm products, animal products, forestry products, and fishery products. This type of production also includes mineral products and handmade goods [1]. This made it possible for people to supply themselves with abundant food and materials through every season of the year, which caused the birth rate to increase and the infant mortality rate to sharply decline. The increasing population caused clans to expand into tribes and eventually those tribes to establish the earliest states. The establishment of states resulted in the development of all aspects of human civilization and culture, including politics, the economy, society, religion, and art. It is tempting to think that culture is an inherent part of agriculture, as the words themselves suggest.

At this point, some mention must be made of nomadic society, which is here included as a subcategory of agricultural society. In contrast with pastoralism, nomadism is a lifestyle whose practitioners not only raise livestock but also engage in trade and banditry while ranging over a wide area instead of remaining in one place. Because of their inherent mobility, nomadic societies maintained a complementary relationship with sedentary agricultural societies, trading with them or raiding them to acquire the food and necessities that the nomads lacked. Nomadic societies have had an immense influence on the course of history, which is perhaps best illustrated by the Mongol Empire. Over the course of his life, Mongol leader Genghis Khan conquered about 7.77 million km^2 of territory. Indeed, a considerable number of the dynasties that ruled China were descended from the nomadic nations to the north. In such cases, however, nomadic methods were very useful for conquering an empire, but they were not as useful for ruling it. While many scholars assume that nomadic methods were ineffective because nomadic nations were assimilated into agricultural nations, this focuses on the outcome without examining the cause.

One factor was that the ruling nation was outnumbered by the nations it ruled, but even more important was the fact that, in order to run the empire and collect taxes, the nomadic rulers were forced to adapt to the local style of production. When Genghis Khan tried to convert all the farmland in the conquered territory into the pastureland to which nomads were accustomed, Yelü Chucai (耶律楚材), one of the Mongol's retainers, managed to persuade him that it would be more effective to let the locals farm the land in their own way. This illustrates how nomadic peoples that conquered empires were compelled to adjust to local conditions. There are doubts about the exact role played by Yelü Chucai, but there can be no doubt that the nomadic kingdom of the Mongols adapted to its conquered territory and became an agricultural empire.

The Mongol Empire and other nomadic empires that spanned the continent of Asia controlled the Silk Road, which gave them a monopoly over trade between Asia and Europe and allowed them to accumulate a vast amount of commercial wealth. But overland trade on the Silk Road was hampered by the harsh terrain, and the return on investment from these caravans was much lower than for seafaring vessels. Furthermore, the prospects for developing maritime trade worsened after the Ming Dynasty was founded by the Hongwu Emperor. The emperor espoused agrarianism in an attempt to help the Han, a farming people, throw off the yoke of the nomadic peoples and to reassert their identity. The Ming Dynasty launched huge naval expeditions under Admiral Zheng He, but for reasons that still remain unclear it later lost its interest in the ocean. After issuing the Haijin, or the sea ban, which prohibited not just maritime trade but also the construction of large vessels, the Ming concentrated instead on fortifying the Great Wall. These historical developments illustrate how nomadic empires and agricultural empires had powerful beginnings and for a time exercised global hegemony but gradually began to decline, passing their hegemony on to the maritime commercial empires that rose after them. This suggests that the decline of nomadic and agricultural empires is due to inherent limitations in their unique economic systems.

Next, we will examine the characteristics of the economic system of agricultural society. Fundamentally, agricultural societies were self-sufficient. The majority of the food and materials produced in an agricultural society were intended for the consumption of the producers and their families. As a result, pure agricultural societies were mostly composed of families of peasants. In such societies, economies of scale were not an option. Although there was some surplus production in agricultural societies (used to trade for necessities such as salt and farming implements and to pay taxes to the government either in cash or in kind), it was much smaller than the portion consumed by the producers. Theodore Schultz has argued that expansive equilibrium could not be achieved in agricultural production regardless of how rationally the peasants (the typical type of farmers in agricultural societies) worked to improve production. The reason, Schultz said, was that the uncertainty of agricultural production and the chronically low income earned by farmers created a tendency to avoid risk by not investing in technological development [2].

Needless to say, this does not mean that no technological developments occurred in agricultural societies. Indeed, there were noteworthy technological advancements in expanding irrigation facilities, making new iron tools, domesticating livestock, inventing the three-field system of crop rotation, applying fertilizer, and developing new seeds. At the time, these were significant advancements that radically increased agricultural productivity. But considering that agricultural societies lasted for thousands of years, the overall speed of technological development was extremely slow. This is especially true if we compare it with industrial societies, which have achieved rapid technological progress in a few centuries. This slow speed of technological development was the primary reason for diminishing production and decelerating growth in agricultural societies. Decelerating growth implies stagnation, and decelerating growth and stagnation reflect the structural limitations of the system of simple reproduction.

Thus, agricultural society was characterized by a tendency for production output to increase at a slower rate than labor input, and this tendency gave peasants a reason not to actively attempt to innovate technology or to invest in increasing surplus production. Even when technological developments increased agricultural output, causing the price of crops to fall, revenues continued to fall, too. The problem was that the actual consumption of crops did not change, since they are a necessity good of which the same amount is always consumed regardless of changing prices. And even when the actual scale of production increased because of external factors such as new varieties, climate change, or the cultivation of new farmland, agricultural societies had neither the technology needed for long-term storage of surplus output nor the economic structure in which reinvestment could occur. As such, increasing production ultimately led to the Malthusian Trap. This is the origin of the phrase the "treadmill effect," describing how agricultural society consists of the repetition of simple reproduction, rather like a treadmill [3]. These observations about agricultural society show how it is based on the system of simple reproduction, in which output diminishes and growth decelerates.

In the end, the system of simple reproduction, which is to say the lack of surplus production, is itself a vicious cycle of the economy. Consequently, the only way to increase the national wealth on limited farmland was through finding technical ways of increasing production, such as launching a state-managed irrigation project, supplying better iron farming implements, or improving husbandry techniques. But because of the structural characteristics of agricultural society, even these methods had a very limited effect. In agricultural society, there could be a short-lived increase in production, but production output did not increase proportionally to the resources invested into it, and there was also a limit on the potential growth of supply and demand. Thus, the easy option for the leaders of an agricultural society was to raise taxes on the peasants, who were forced to increase their production. In order to survive, the peasants had to produce enough surplus to cover the amount plundered from them in the form of taxes.

While plunder of this sort did serve to increase production, extortionate tax hikes and natural disasters such as poor harvests also caused the peasants to revolt or to abandon their farms and become vagrants. Moral considerations aside, the monarch who looted the peasants and the peasants who revolted against the monarch can both be regarded as having acted rationally (at least from their own perspective). In other words, under an agricultural system, both the monarch and the peasants were only attempting to maximize their own utility and satisfaction. But none of these methods were able to fundamentally resolve the problem, namely that growth was limited by diminishing agricultural production. The system of simple reproduction in agricultural society that we have just examined is represented in the Fig. 1.2.

In an agricultural society, the monarch or ruling elite looked outside their borders to acquire new territory as a way of prevailing over the natural stagnation in agricultural production shown in Fig. 1.2. Since agricultural output is generally proportional to the area of farmland, acquiring more farmland and peasants from other states was an easier and more reliable method than attempting to increase agricultural production that was already at its limits. That was the only approach that would satisfy these rulers' desire to have and enjoy more possessions. Indeed, since expanding territory through wars of conquest was agricultural empires' only practical means of increasing aggregate production, these empires were essentially massive war machines. Their behavior followed a cycle: each time that aggregate production became stagnant, they would wage a new war to increase aggregate production. As a result, agricultural economies grew in stages (see Fig. 1.3).

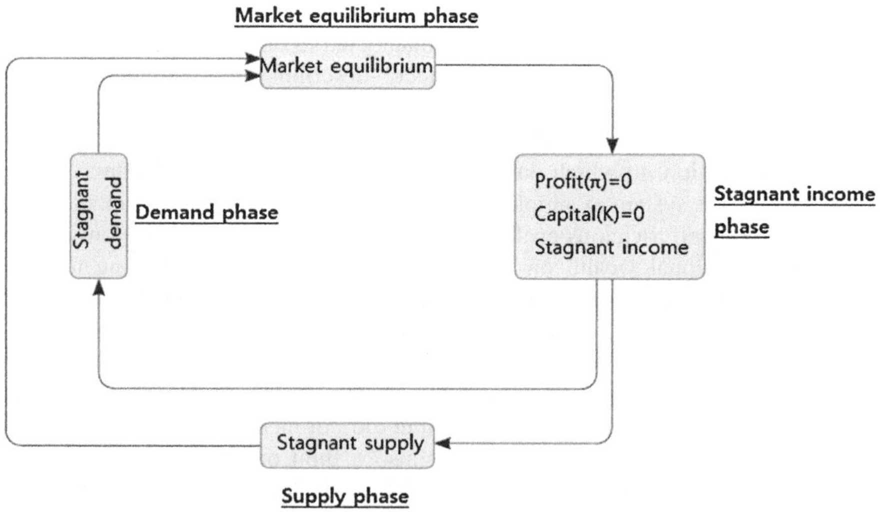

Fig. 1.2 The system of simple reproduction in agricultural society

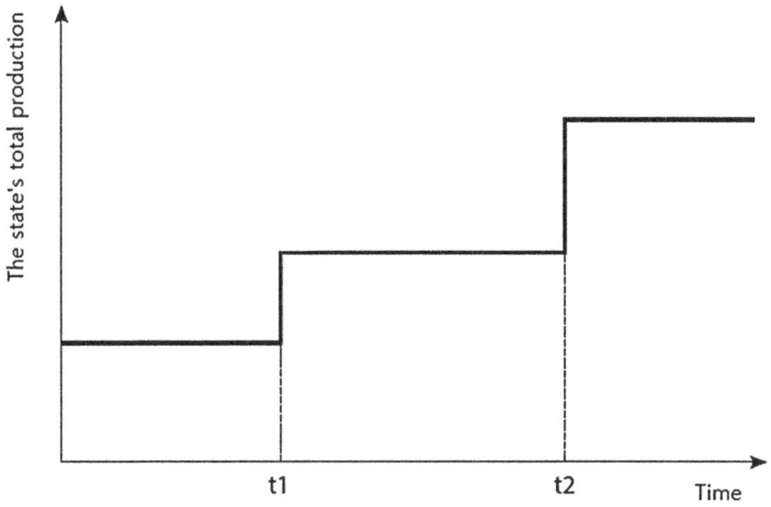

Fig. 1.3 Trends in the virtuous cycle of war and the economy in agricultural society

This cycle of growth continued until geographical constraints prevented the empire from expanding any further, after which point growth stagnated in the unified empire. This marked the beginning of the empire's decline and prefigured its fall. Since agricultural societies are compelled to expand for structural reasons, successful agricultural states took the form of empires. This also represents the process by which states developed in agricultural society's virtuous cycle of war and the economy. This process is examined in Fig. 1.3. Here, an agricultural society whose economy has stagnated initiates a war of conquest at time *t*1 to bring about a single leap in aggregate production. When the society's economy stagnates once more at time *t*2, it uses another war of conquest to achieve another leap in aggregate production.

The typical cycle of expansion in agricultural society was as follows. First, the state raised taxes to acquire military provisions and armaments; next, it waged a war of conquest to gain more farmland and subjects; finally, it used the spoils of war and tax revenues to fund an even bigger war of conquest. To be sure, military defeat meant the loss of territory and wealth and led to the decline of the state. This was because war (which was the only growth engine for agricultural societies with their stagnant economic growth) was in the end only a zero-sum game in which wealth was transferred from the vanquished to the victors.

While raising an army and acquiring the weapons and supplies it needed was an important aspect of war, victory typically depended on fighting ability. Supplies could be bought using the state's tax revenues or purchased by the soldiers themselves; weapons could be produced in much the same way as farming implements; horses used on farms and ranches could be appropriated as warhorses; and an army could be raised with relative ease by drafting peasants or hiring mercenaries. More difficult to acquire were soldiers whose occupational experience lent itself to military applications and a well-trained and organized army. Discrepancies in these two areas often made the difference on the battlefield. An example of the former is the outstanding horsemanship of the Mongol army, which was perfected in their nomadic lifestyle. An example of the latter is the discipline of the Roman legions, which was forged in rigorous training.

States seeking to conquer territory typically waged war on their immediate neighbors. This strategy is expressed in the Chinese phrase *yuan jiao jin gong* (远交近攻), which means befriending distant states and attacking those nearby. But this was the basic foreign policy and defense strategy for successful agricultural states not only in Asia but also in Europe. The states that successfully practiced this strategy can be described as agricultural empires because of their expansionist tendency.

In China, the *yuan jiao jin gong* strategy originated in the state of Qin, a classical example of an agricultural empire. Of the seven warring states that rose from the ashes of China's Eastern Zhou Dynasty, Qin had the poorest soil and was thus the least suited for agriculture. But if we recall that development in agricultural societies is fueled by wars of conquest, Qin's low agricultural productivity ironically propelled its rise as an agricultural empire. The peasants came to realize that war was more profitable than farming.

In the West, Rome serves as a paradigm of such an agricultural empire. Rome's approach was similar to the *yuan jiao jin gong* strategy of the Qin Dynasty: it began by conquering the small tribes around it, eventually unifying the Italian peninsula and using this as a springboard for building its empire. Roman peasants would work on their farms until war came, when they would join their heavy infantry units and go into battle. This was how Rome, a state that had barely supported itself on pastoralism and agriculture in an inhospitable environment, assembled the killing machine known as the Roman legion and went on to create the largest agricultural empire in European history.

There is no denying that Qin and Rome were the most successful agricultural empires in human history. What is interesting is that successful agricultural empires continued to appear in China even after the fall of Qin, whereas no European agricultural empire ever managed to repeat the success of Rome. After the fall of the Roman Empire, Europe was divided into a patchwork of minor states and kingdoms, but this turned out to be a blessing in disguise. It was in the ruins of this empire that the seeds of the Commercial Revolution were planted and the Industrial Revolution took root. This is how Europe rose to be the center of industrial civilization in the early modern era and how it ultimately acquired global hegemony. In contrast, China's agricultural civilization can be seen as having suffered a relative decline because of the accelerating development (and predation) of Europe's commercial and then industrial civilization.

But the crucial point here is that the critical path in the development of human civilization toward the industrial society of the present day is to be found not in the history of the successful development of agricultural society in China, but rather in the history of the failure to develop agricultural society in Europe. To be sure, Japan and South Korea have achieved (and China is in the process of achieving) industrialization on a speed and scale so impressive that it has shocked the world. This is a testament to these countries' attempts to learn from the developmental experiences and methods of early industrialized states. Regardless, since the agricultural empires of China parted ways with the critical path of history after the Qing Dynasty, they do not fall within the scope of this book, which as we have said is an attempt to explain shifts in global hegemony [4].

War and the Economy in Commercial Society

The transfer of global hegemony from one country to another began in earnest with the emergence of commercial society. The Spanish Empire (1469–1716) was part of the transition from traditional agricultural society to commercial society, which would give rise to industrial civilization in the early modern period. Since Spain (and to a lesser extent Portugal) were the maritime powers that discovered sea routes to the New World and Asia and ushered in the Age of Discovery, they are often regarded as commercial empires. In the words of historian Timothy Parsons, Spain was "the world's first truly global imperial state." This language underscores the fact that Spain's maritime expansion and subsequent exploration and conquest of huge sections of Asia and the Americas made it the first state in history to control land not only on other continents linked by land routes but also on continents across the ocean. Spain ruled a vast empire that stretched from western and central Europe to the Americas and across the Pacific Ocean to the Philippines.

But Spain never managed to centralize the administration of its empire, partly because of the sprawling transportation and communication network of its agricultural society and partly because of the ceaseless strife inside Europe. For reasons such as these, Spain assigned viceroys to rule the lands it had conquered overseas and gave them considerable autonomy, a practice that Parsons described as "empire by franchise" [5]. This was similar to the practices of the agricultural and nomadic empires in the continent of Eurasia. But these aspects of the Spanish Empire clearly revealed its imperial limitations. Even though Spain advanced overseas unlike the land-based agricultural empires that had preceded it and even though its maritime activities marked the dawn of its commercial society by enabling trade in luxuries, Spain remained encumbered by the traditions and economic systems of agricultural empires. In this sense, Spain can be seen as Europe's last agricultural empire.

There is diverse evidence to support the assertion that Spain was not a commercial empire but an agricultural one. First, the manner of Spain's formation as a nation mirrors how agricultural empires generally develop. The Spanish Empire's expansion—symbolized by the Reconquista—is typical of agricultural societies, which tended to expand through wars of conquest in the virtuous cycle of war and the economy (the fundamental principle of national development). The Reconquista generally refers to Spain's unification of the Iberian Peninsula by subduing the remaining Muslim states, but Spain's overseas expansion can be regarded as an extension of the Reconquista. Spain's expansion was not commercial in intent; that is, it was not intended to promote intermediary trade, as it would be in the Netherlands and England. Rather, this expansion was fundamentally motivated by the religious zeal of Spain's Catholics and by the desire of the rulers of this agricultural society to expand their land holdings. This point is made clear by the fact that Spain's focus in the Americas was on running plantations and mines.

Second, Spain's development represents the typical pattern of agricultural economies, which rely upon the diminishing output of farms and mines. Even though Spain collected an immense amount of silver and gold from the New World —amounting to around 74% of global silver production—it invested this in ranching and low-quality wool production instead of in domestic manufacturing. Thus, Spain exported wool and other raw materials and imported products that it paid for using gold and silver from the New World. Third, Spain also resembled an agricultural empire in its national policy. One example was Spain's expulsion of the Jews and Moriscos (Muslims who had converted to Christianity), many of whom were engaged in trade or industry. Another was a Spanish law that required merchants to receive a royal permit before engaging in trade. Such policies weakened trade and industry in the empire. Fourth, Spain's wars were also characteristic of agricultural society. Spain remained embroiled in pointless and unprofitable wars that it thought were required to preserve the legacy of the Holy Roman Empire [6].

The fact that Spain was more of an agricultural empire than a commercial empire also suggests that commercial society is a transitional phase between agricultural society and industrial society. We will need to clarify what exactly we mean by the word "transitional," however. This does not mean that commercial society simply falls between agricultural society and industrial society. Commercial society is based on a distinct economic system that is ready to make the shift to industrial society. It was in commercial society that the economy began to experience accelerating growth through the system of expansive reinvestment, and thus commercial society can be understood as the first capitalist society in the history of mankind.

In agricultural society, everything that is produced is consumed, but in capitalist commercial society, some is left over as profit. This is accumulated as commercial capital, which in turn is reinvested in commerce to make more profit. Profit increases demand by raising corporate and household income, which leads to an increasing supply of existing products or to the introduction of new products. The profit acquired through this method is again accumulated as capital, and the increase in supply and demand enables a new market equilibrium to become established and leads to a smooth succession of business cycles. This is the virtuous cycle of the economy in the system of expansive reinvestment in commercial society. This can be clearly distinguished from the system of simple reproduction in agricultural society, in which the same market equilibrium recurs without supply or demand increasing. The system of expansive reinvestment in commercial society is depicted in Fig. 1.4.

But even commercial societies eventually reached the limits of economic growth. On the supply side, the main reason was that the economy of commercial

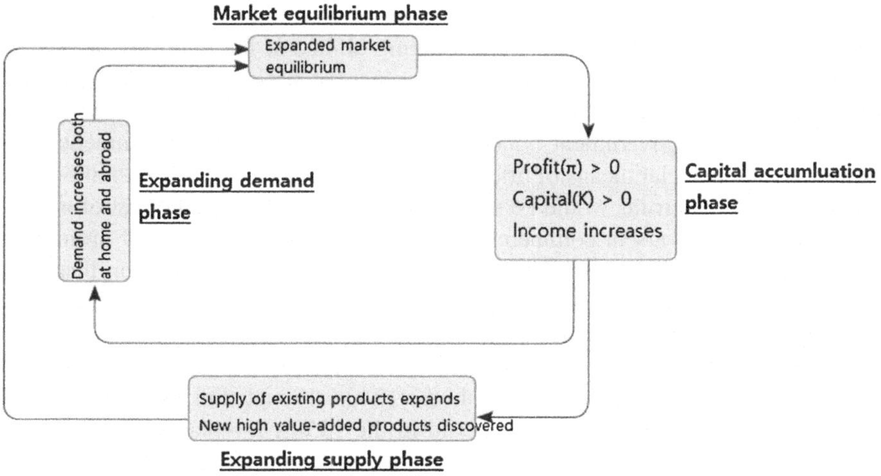

Fig. 1.4 The system of expansive reinvestment in commercial society

societies was based not on ongoing technological development but rather on trade in luxuries, which depended on specific agricultural products. This made it difficult to improve productivity or to develop new products. Furthermore, since commercial societies had to rely on wagons and sailing ships as their methods of transport, such trade was bound to have a weaker economic impact than in industrial societies, in which goods can be transported by railroads, steamships, and airplanes. On the demand side, there was fixed demand for trade in agricultural products and other necessity goods. Even with spices and other luxuries, once demand expanded from the wealthy to the public as a whole, there was no more room for growth.

For such reasons, the system of expansive reinvestment in commercial society was fundamentally limited: once it reached a certain point, it could not develop any further. Even worse, when the unexpected happened—when the transportation routes used for commerce were closed, when the supply of trading goods shrank, or when it became harder to find new trading goods—the virtuous cycle of the economy in commercial society was disrupted. This led to conflict between states to secure new transportation routes, markets, and products and was ultimately a sign that war was imminent.

War in commercial society was fundamentally different from war in agricultural society. Whereas agricultural wars were provoked by dynastic conflict or motivated by the desire to seize territory, commercial wars were fought to gain advantages in economic activity. And while minor skirmishes and wars of conquest were frequently fought in agricultural societies, war occurred less often (though still regularly) in commercial societies. These commercial wars, however, were much larger in scope than agricultural wars, and the economic benefits gained by the victors were much greater and lasted much longer.

Furthermore, while the outcome of war between agricultural societies was generally decided by the strength and fighting ability of the opposing armies, the most important factor in wars between commercial societies was their ability to raise funds to pay for the war. By then, war had become so costly that each warring state had to issue government bonds to cover the cost. These government bonds represented a financial means of bridging the chronological gap between the future, when commercial profits would be made, and the present, when the cost of war had to be paid. Since wars in commercial society generally protected and promoted a state's commercial interests while also enabling commercial expansion that could cover the cost of the next war, they can be regarded as having formed a kind of "military-commercial complex."

In the Netherlands, government bonds were part of a financial revolution that unfolded in the mid-sixteenth century. In the 1540s, the state linked the interest paid on long-term bonds to specific taxes, and in the 1550s, it replaced the mandatory bond system with a bond market as its means of raising money. The government was selling bonds that were guaranteed by nothing but the potential of future profits, and the high degree of uncertainty made them risky (and thus led to high discounts). Even so, the bonds sold because of the huge amount of expected profits. This shows that the economy in commercial society grew at an accelerating rate, unlikely the economy in agricultural society.

In the 1600s, when the Dutch Republic's future was unclear, the national debt was low and the interest rate was above 8%. But when the situation stabilized in the 1620s, the national debt rapidly increased and the interest rate dropped to 3%. This meant that the commercial society in the Netherlands had created a virtuous cycle, and that investors had a high degree of confidence in the massive profits that could be brought by victory in war. The fact that a small commercial state like the Netherlands could defeat a huge agricultural empire like Spain and emerge as a hegemonic power should be seen as deriving from the accelerating economic growth in commercial society, or in other words commercial society's economic superiority to agricultural society.

The rapid growth of commercial societies under this superior economic system coincided with the military revolution that Europe underwent in the sixteenth and seventeenth centuries. During this revolution, swords and spears made way for guns and cannons; armies swelled in size; tactics were transformed; and more attention was paid to discipline and training. One aspect of this "gunpowder revolution" worth noting was the clever idea of putting cannons on ships, as well as the technological superiority that made this possible. As a result, the traditional Mediterranean style of naval warfare, which largely consisted of ships ramming each other and boarding parties engaging in hand-to-hand combat, was replaced by the Atlantic style, in which ships traded fire from a distance. Such technological superiority—along with a providential storm—is what enabled the English fleet to defeat the "invincible" Spanish Armada.

Another major development was the appearance of massive armies. Whereas the Mongol armies had consisted of 30,000–40,000 mounted soldiers, the Spanish army under Charles V at the beginning of the sixteenth century was 150,000 strong, while the French army between 1701 and 1702 numbered 650,000. Thus, as armies became larger and formations more complicated, drills and discipline grew in importance. In particular, the adoption of the tactic of volley fire and the need for formations to wheel rapidly and in good order in response to enemy artillery fire made it necessary to standardize soldiers' movements and to regularize those movements through repeated drills. An excellent example was the drills introduced by Maurice of Nassau, stadtholder of the Netherlands. In the view of historian William H. McNeill, these drills were the means by which men from diverse places of birth were integrated into a tightly knit community based on obedience and respect, which he called a "New Leviathan" [7].

But it cost a great deal of money to maintain a strong fleet and its sailors along with forces to wage war on land both in peacetime and in war. In consequence, war spending ballooned until it took up an unprecedented share of the state budget. In a way, the emergence of states that relied on such huge budgets and fleets was at the very heart of the military revolution.

During the seventeenth century, the military is said to have accounted for 75% of government spending in France under Louis XIV, 85% in Russia under Peter the Great and 90% in England when the Civil War was raging. These figures tell us that states of this age were fearful war machines. Quite naturally, the outcome of war depended on how swiftly and efficiently a state could raise the great sums of money needed to wage war. It is in this sense that Europe's hegemony resulted from the development of the new financial techniques that enabled commercial societies to finance their wars and by the accelerating economic growth that ultimately underwrote those financial techniques. Or in other words, economic power dictated military power, and military power made possible hegemony.

As a result of the financial and military revolutions, England succeeded in establishing a strong and efficient "fiscal-military state" that rested on three governing institutions: the treasury, the excise, and the navy. Thanks to this, English was able to supplant the Netherlands as the global hegemonic power. While the conventional view is that England was a liberal country in which the state was weaker than civic society, the English state actually wielded even more power than the absolute monarchy in France [8]. And through the Civil War and the Glorious Revolution in the seventeenth century, England established the tradition of parliamentary sovereignty known as "king-in-parliament." This enabled the state to move beyond the past belief that sovereignty was invested in a person or in a dynasty and to become a modern nation-state that pursued the national interest under the newly created system of the national economy. This was how England was able to enter a period of unlimited commercial and colonial expansion according to the principles of capitalism and the nation-state—rather than the dynastic squabbling for territory in continental Europe that led to wars of succession and to political marriages between various royal families.

A powerful and aggressive state that successfully expands its overseas territory on the basis of such accelerating economic growth could certainly be described as a commercial empire, and two good examples of such empires are the Netherlands and England (later Britain) from the sixteenth to the eighteenth centuries. In a certain sense, these two states may have been the only ones that passed through a commercial phase while they were transitioning from agricultural society to industrial society. After all, the Industrial Revolution was what catapulted England from the system of expansive reinvestment in commercial society to the system of expansive reproduction in industrial society, but states that industrialized later imitated England's process of industrialization and moved directly from agricultural society to industrial society without passing through the phase of commercial society.

Historically speaking, the Netherlands was where the expansive reinvestment system of commercial society first appeared. While various geopolitical, economic, and religious factors no doubt played a role here, one of the most important was the Dutch people's political will and their courage to reject Spain's imperial rule and to choose the path of commercial development. The Dutch formed an economic community of interest around their resistance to Spain's oppressive taxes, and the resulting cohesiveness also propelled their revolt against Spain.

As for England, its status as an island nation gave it an advantage in trade on the Atlantic Ocean. Another important factor, however, was the political will of the ruling elite to install the Duke of Orange from the Netherlands as King William III, to embrace sophisticated commercial techniques, and to deliberately encourage maritime trade through national policies such as the Navigation Acts. Both of these states consciously created a variety of financial instruments in their pursuit of commercial development. The stock market in seventeenth-century Amsterdam brings to mind Wall Street in twentieth-century New York, while the Bank of England was an effective means of financing war, making it a crucial component of England's military-commercial complex.

The Netherlands and England were typical commercial societies in which the merchant classes wielded considerable economic and political influence. Both states had learned that the best way to increase tax revenue was facilitating the exponential increase of commercial profits, and they devoted considerable effort to setting up an optimal institutional environment in which individuals' property rights would be protected and in which they could freely engage in commercial activity. A commercial society was one in which commercial policy served as the foundation of national development, and the way to create the optimal environment for a commercial economy was waging war to seize maritime routes, gain commercial supremacy, and acquire colonies. Victory in such commercial wars was the result of the state and the people working together to maximize individuals' commercial profit and to increase the states' tax revenues and economic growth. The overlap between the goals of the people and the state was a crucial factor that enabled small commercial states to overtake huge agricultural empires both economically and militarily in their ascent as hegemonic powers [9].

Furthermore, the high profits that could be earned in commercial societies were fertile soil for the kind of entrepreneurs who were willing to take risks. It is no coincidence that it was in commercial societies that not only entrepreneurship but also capitalistic values and attitudes first appeared. Two relevant points here are that high returns are accompanied by high risks and that merchants who have accumulated a certain amount of wealth tend to look for secure investments to diversify their risk. In commercial societies, this conservative tendency was further encouraged by the observable fact that finding new high value-added products necessarily required traveling farther and taking on greater risks.

This was a clear warning sign that the system of expansive reinvestment in commercial society was losing its momentum. But there was an even more fundamental and inevitable limit on growth in commercial society. In industrial society, accumulated capital can be effectively used to develop new products through technological innovation, but this was not an option in commercial society. As a consequence, investors had no choice but to seek high profits from the existing products of agricultural society. This limit tells us that commercial societies ultimately failed to sever their ties with their agricultural past, despite at first exhibiting the bourgeois and capitalist tendencies of societies with accelerating growth.

One important factor contributing to the decline of commercial societies is that, when commercial capital could not be used to discover new products, it eventually was turned into financial capital or used in speculation. This soon brought about the decay of entrepreneurship and an aversion to enterprising economic activity. The difficulty of having to constantly look for new products to create new demand and the consequential structural constraints in commercial societies created incentives for merchants to invest in the commerce of competing countries, since this was an easier way to make money than taking on new challenges. This represented a shift away from the development of commercial capital and toward the expansion of financial capital and even toward the formation of the kind of speculative capital that caused economic bubbles. Ultimately, this foreshadowed the downfall of commercial empires.

When commercial capital was invested in spices and other agricultural products from overseas, the added value gained by trading these agricultural products more than compensated for the diminishing agricultural production and thus aided the commercial empire's economic growth. But when commercial capital was invested in the corporations and capital markets of that empire's commercial rivals, it only aided those rivals. And when those rival states had a geopolitical, economic, or military advantage, the outflow of commercial capital served to hasten the commercial empire's decline. In addition, capitalists who were fixated on short-term profits invested the capital they had accumulated into financial markets, triggering speculation and economic bubbles that brought on the empire's collapse. In this sense, we can say that the fall of commercial empires was fundamentally caused by the structural limits on commercial society.

This is clearly demonstrated by the fact that the Netherlands ultimately relinquished its hegemony to England and that it was in England where the Industrial Revolution took place, even though both the Netherlands and England were states that developed through commerce. As a commercial society, the Netherlands was completely dependent on importing agricultural products from overseas. When Dutch capitalists were unable to find profitable new investments for the great wealth they had earned through intermediary trade in spice and other high value-added products, they diverted it into the financial markets, investing it in real estate or in the Netherlands' rival England. They also invested this capital in speculative products such as tulip bulbs, which triggered economic bubbles and showed that there were definite limits on growth.

To be sure, the Dutch did try to find new engines for growth—by investing in the whaling industry and in sugar plantations in the Caribbean, for example—but none of these could provide an economic boost comparable to spices. Perhaps there simply was no other agricultural product that could be as profitable as black pepper had been. Even though tea created a significant amount of added value in Asian trade in the eighteenth century, the Netherlands failed to grasp the market conditions in China and Indonesia and ultimately was forced out of Asian trade.

But England was a commercial society in which not only intermediary trade of agricultural products but also domestic production made up a substantial amount of economic activity. In England, craft production of wool and other domestic agricultural products developed into a manufacturing industry through a phase of proto-industrialization, creating the conditions necessary for the system of expansive reinvestment to evolve into the system of expansive reproduction.

One important point is that England had gradually banned the export of wool as a raw material starting in the fourteenth century. Instead, it encouraged wool producers to export it in the form of intermediary or even final goods such as wool cloth, which was part of a policy of maximizing the added value of exports. While such industrial policies did not have an appreciable effect at the time, they prefigured the policies that would eventually usher in the Industrial Revolution and transform England into an industrial society. Furthermore, England remained aloof from the religious strife that troubled Europe in the sixteenth century and welcomed in many Protestant craftsmen and merchants seeking shelter from these wars, which provided England with the momentum it needed to become an industrial society. Since these refugees represented a class that possessed both capital and skills, they were invaluable human capital for England that laid the groundwork for its industrialization.

Of course, one interpretation is that England's use of the Navigation Acts to restrict Dutch trade with the New World and its suppression of Dutch resistance to this during the Anglo-Dutch Wars were the primary reasons that the Netherlands lost its hegemony. Undeniably, these incidents largely coincided with the period when hegemony was shifting from the Netherlands to England and indeed accelerated the handover of hegemony. But England had a comparative advantage (both quantitatively and qualitatively) to the Netherlands in Atlantic trade since England's trade was backed by domestic manufacturing, unlike the Netherlands' purer form of intermediary trade (entrepôt trade). This comparative advantage suggests that the transfer of hegemony from the Netherlands to England was an objective and indeed inevitable phenomenon that could not have been dictated by a few historical accidents.

One major implication of the development of the Netherlands and England described above is that a commercial society that failed to acquire the self-sustaining engine that is the system of expansive reproduction was bound to run into the limits on growth and to collapse, just as agricultural societies did. Even

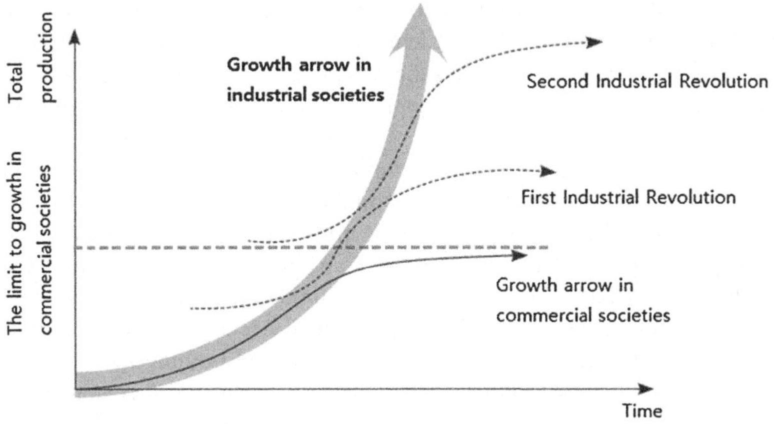

Fig. 1.5 Growth in commercial society and industrial society

though commercial society had its own distinct developmental principles (which we are calling the system of expansive reinvestment), it does not constitute a distinct economic society as agricultural society or industrial society do. Commercial society can even be seen as falling within the larger category of either agricultural society or industrial society. Our earlier statement that commercial society was a transitional phase should also be understood in this sense. Figure 1.5 contrasts the limits on growth in commercial societies with the continuous growth of industrial societies.

As can be seen in Fig. 1.5, commercial societies showed the same accelerating growth as industrial societies for a certain period of time, but they soon ran into the limits on growth. But the Industrial Revolution represented the transition to industrial society, which enabled them to transcend commercial society's limits on growth and achieve accelerating growth. When industrial societies reached the limits of the accelerating growth brought by the First Industrial Revolution, accelerating growth was sustained by the Second Industrial Revolution, and when that growth trend reached another limit, new products based on new technology once again created new demand, enabling the accelerating growth trend to continue. If a commercial society can be described as a society that lacks an independent growth engine because it relies on trade in existing agricultural products, an industrial society can be described as a society that is structurally equipped with the independent growth engine of technological innovation.

War and the Economy in Industrial Society

Industrial society is marked by expansive reproduction, leading to continuing expansion of the market equilibrium between supply and demand. As a result, earned profit is accumulated as capital, and accumulated capital is invested in production facilities and technological innovation, creating more demand and enabling mass production. The system of expansive reproduction has made it possible to temporarily escape from the Malthusian Trap that plagued agricultural societies—the fact that the food supply could not keep up with the growing population.

The reason we include the caveat "temporarily" even though the development of industrial society has enabled both the population and the economy to grow with increasing speed is because some scholars argue that not even industrial societies have completely escaped the Malthusian Trap. French historian Fernand Braudel argued that the decline in real wages was fundamentally the same before the Industrial Revolution as after it. If we still find it necessary to reduce the surplus population, Braudel said, the Industrial Revolution did nothing more than increase the limits of humanity's Malthusian potential [10]. But the fact that these limits were raised is itself significant. Indeed, the continuous growth of industrial societies has prevented demographic catastrophes such as the outbreak of bubonic plague that struck Europe in the fourteenth century, and it has provided adequate sustenance for the growing population.

Changes in the world population and per capita income during the industrial age (see Fig. 1.6) show that per capita income has increased exponentially even while industrial societies have continued to feed the exponentially increasing population. This implies that the total value created by industrial societies has theoretically increased at a rate that can be calculated by multiplying the exponential increase of the population by the exponential increase of income. In that sense, there is no reason not to declare the achievements of industrial societies in the areas of increasing production and creating value to be an escape from the Malthusian Trap.

The system of expansive reproduction in industrial society is similar in a number of respects to the system of expansive reinvestment in commercial society; indeed, it can be said that commercial society laid the foundation for industrial society. Industrial society and commercial society are similar insofar as both involve profit being accumulated as capital and higher income creating demand. But industrial society is fundamentally different from commercial society in the respect that technological innovation in industrial societies enabled supply to increase by leaps and bounds while the development of new products continued to create new demand. If commercial society was the first glider to soar through the air, industrial society was the airplane that could fly anywhere the pilot wished.

Generally speaking, there are three forces in industrial society as we have defined it that sustain the virtuous cycle of the economy. The first is entrepreneurship in the private sector; the second is a technological bent in society; and the third is industrial policy in the government. Of these three, the government's industrial policy is of particular importance. To understand why, we need look no further than England and other early industrialized states. Not only did these states have the conditions necessary for the Industrial Revolution such as coal and iron deposits, but the virtuous cycle created by the system of expansive reinvestment in commercial society led to the formation of entrepreneurship and the technological mindset. But when states that industrialized later (such as Germany,

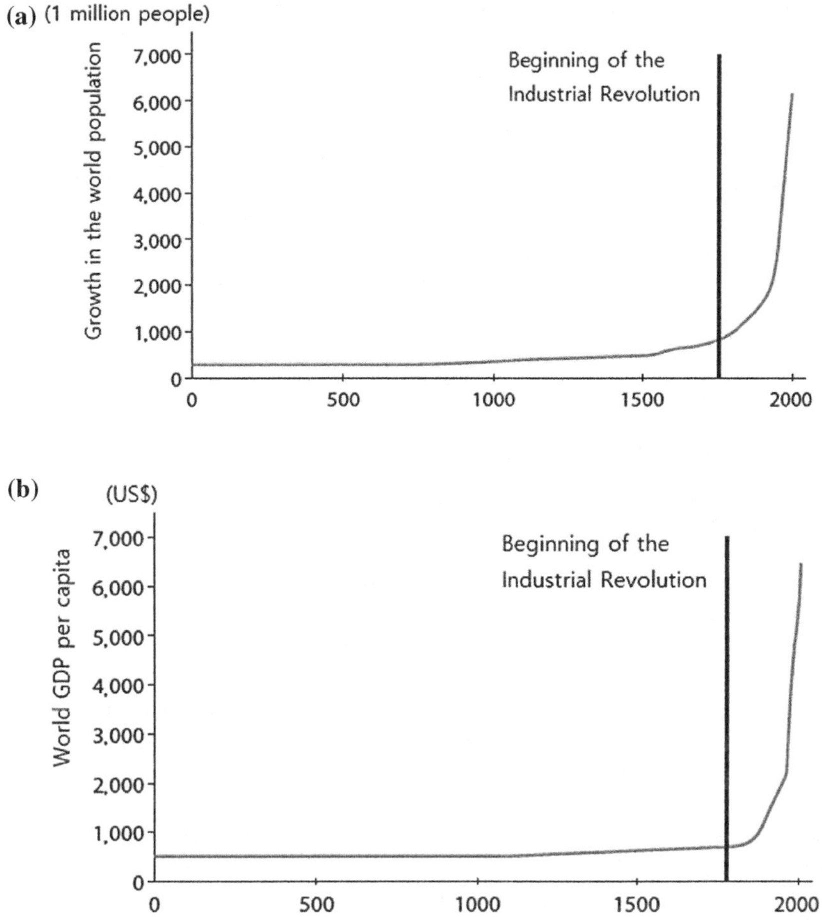

Fig. 1.6 Changing growth in the global population (*top*) and changing growth in per capita income (*bottom*). **a** *Source* M. Kremer, "Population growth and technological change: one million B.C. to 1990," *The Quarterly Journal of Economics*, 180:3 (1993), pp. 681–716. **b** *Source* OECD development centre, *The World Economy: A Millennial Perspective* (Paris, 2001); OECD development centre, *The World Economy: Historical Statistics* (Paris, 2003)

Japan, and South Korea) attempted to move directly from an agricultural economy to an industrial one, they had no choice but to artificially create such conditions through industrial policy. The system of expansive reproduction in industrial society is depicted in Fig. 1.7.

The system of expansive reproduction in industrial society can be basically defined as a cycle in which resources such as raw materials and energy are used to make new products based on new technology and then these products are sold on

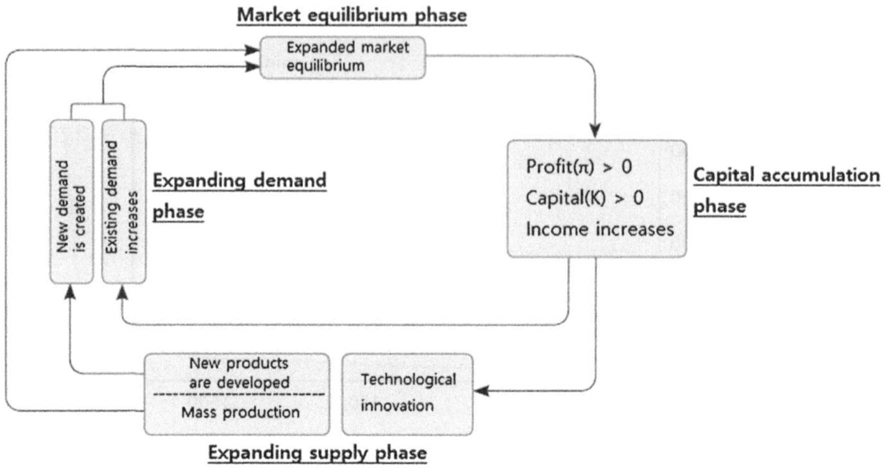

Fig. 1.7 The system of expansive reproduction in industrial society

the market for a profit. Accelerating economic growth requires a supply of resources that is at least as great as the level of domestic production and an export market that is at least as large as the domestic market. Consequently, industrialized states had no choice but to expand overseas.

At first, there was a complementary relationship between industrialized states and agricultural states. While conflicts occasionally broke out between them, the overwhelming economic and technological superiority of the industrialized states left no doubt about the outcome. But competition between industrialized states possessing comparable strength over the raw materials of agricultural states or over control of markets for their products eventually escalated into massive conflicts like the two world wars. That was because industrialized states were resource-dependent manufacturers of bulky products that constantly competed with each other in the global market over demand for a limited number of everyday goods such as clothing, electronics, and automobiles.

Furthermore, it is a generally acknowledged historical fact that the difficulty of technological innovation and the delay between supply and demand for new products causes capitalistic industrialized states to encounter periodic economic crises. At such times, industrial societies have tended to try to overcome these crises through war, just as agricultural and commercial societies before them. But whereas fighting ability decided the outcome of war in agricultural society and the ability to finance war was critical in commercial society, the factors that have shaped the face of war in industrial society have been industrial output and advanced technology. In industrial society, war came to approximate total war, and in total war, victory depends upon the ability to produce huge quantities of war supplies and to develop new weaponry.

In industrial warfare, even a strong army that is properly equipped and willing to fight has little hope of achieving victory unless it is supported by industrial output and advanced technology. This ushered in the age of the military-industrial complex, in which military power and industry merge into one [11]. Governments have also played a major role in wars during the industrial age. They have taken the lead in wartime production, often setting up command economies. Russian revolutionary Vladimir Lenin even regarded the German economy during World War I as a sort of state socialism. In industrial society, therefore, the government, army, and industry form a trinity.

The characteristics of industrial war have been observed in numerous wars since the nineteenth century. During the American Civil War, the industrialized Northern states of the Union had a military advantage thanks to their industrial output and advanced technology, both of which were superior to the agricultural Southern states of the Confederacy. Compared to the Confederacy, Union factories rolled out eight times the iron, 17 times the textiles, 25 times the artillery pieces, and 32 times the small arms. In 1860, there were six times more manufacturing concerns in the North than in the South; the state of Pennsylvania alone produced 15 times as much pig iron as all the Southern states combined; and the manufacturing output of the state of New York far exceeded the combined output of Virginia and three other Southern states [12].

It is also widely acknowledged that Prussian supremacy in the Austro-Prussian War in 1866 was made possible by the breech-loading steel cannons and rifles produced at Krupp, as well as by the railroads. To be sure, Prussia's victory in the Franco-Prussian War in 1870 cannot be wholly attributed to its technological edge, since France also had breech-loading rifles and early machine guns. What decided victory in this war was not the Prussian army's technological advantage but rather the strategic and tactical acumen of its general staff. While the Prussian army's artillery pieces were inferior to those of the French, Prussian innovations in how to deploy those pieces and in how to maneuver infantry formations under French shelling gave them the victory. As historian William H. McNeill observed, "The Prussian capacity to learn from deficiencies in their past performance was, perhaps, the master key to their dazzling succession of victories. The application of reason and intelligence to the waging of war was not in the least new in nineteenth-century Europe" [13].

But what are industry and technology if not a synthesis of "reason and intelligence"? During the wars fought in Europe in the twentieth century, the military advantage conferred by industrial output and advanced technology became virtually absolute. In World War II, for example, victory was contingent on air power, and the United States produced aircraft at a rate seven times greater than Japan and 15 times greater than Germany. And as military historians have frequently observed, the Soviet Union's ability to produce thousands of T-34 tanks was of crucial importance to defeating the Nazis. In that sense, while the United States and Soviet Union may have lost individual battles in the early phase of the war, their latent industrial potential essentially predicted their eventual victory.

Such considerations indicate that industrial societies also achieved accelerating economic growth through the virtuous cycle of war and the economy based on the system of expansive reproduction that we have already examined. This cycle is

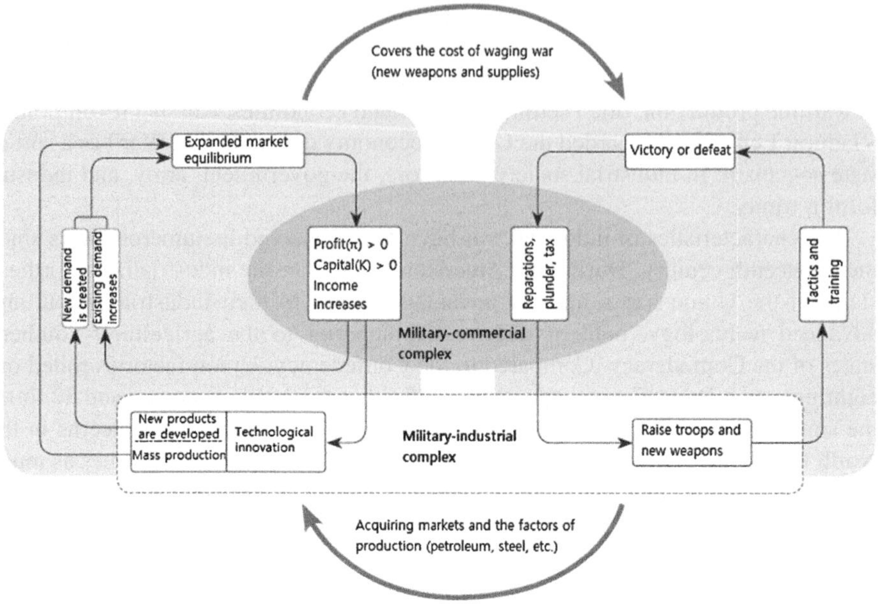

Fig. 1.8 Flowchart of the system of expansive reproduction and the cycle of war in industrial society

summarized in Fig. 1.8. The left side of this figure depicts the system of expansive reproduction in industrial society, while the right side depicts the virtuous (or vicious) cycle of war and the economy that is shared by agricultural society, commercial society, and industrial society. But since the system of expansive reproduction includes the system of expansive reinvestment, we have depicted the military-commercial complex of commercial society alongside the military-industrial complex of industrial society, making it possible to see at a glance the economic cycle of these two types of society and the cycle of war to which it is linked.

There is a sense in which war was an inherent part of the transition from agricultural society to industrial society. The murderous potential of industrial warfare has had tragic consequences for the human race, but such wars were an inevitable result of the expansionist tendencies of industrial societies and their system of expansive reproduction. This made it more urgent than ever before to set up global government, international institutions, or at least regional arrangements to prevent war by arbitrating international conflicts. But such institutions either did not exist or were not given the authority they needed to arbitrate such conflicts. This made it impossible to prevent wars between the industrial powers, and once such wars began, they escalated into devastating struggles that covered the entire globe.

As a general rule, the decline of a state (whether an agricultural society, commercial society, or industrial society) results from its departure from the virtuous cycle of war and the economy. There are two main causes of such a departure, the first of which is the stagnation of economic growth. The virtuous cycle of the economy can grind to a halt in agricultural states because of diminishing production, in commercial states because of a lack of new products, and in industrialized states because of market saturation and a shortage of raw materials. When the virtuous cycle of the economy runs into such obstacles, the state resorts to the extraordinary measure of war in an attempt to restore that virtuous cycle. When such a war ends in defeat, it often leads to the collapse of the state in question.

The second cause of such decline is unproductive wars. As we have already seen, Paul Kennedy argued that economic decline is the result of a state spending more money on a war than it makes from winning it. Kennedy summarized the situation in Britain during World War II as follows: "The blunt fact was that in securing a victorious outcome to the war the British had severely overstrained themselves, running down their gold and dollar reserves, wearing out their domestic machinery, and (despite an extraordinary mobilization of their resources and population) becoming increasingly dependent upon American munitions, shipping, foodstuffs, and other supplies to stay in the fighting" [14]. This was how Britain's hegemony was transferred to the United States.

But Kennedy's argument has its limitations. In short, it is only applicable to agricultural societies, in which war is a negative sum game because of the destruction and slaughter it brings. While his argument makes sense when applied to England's predicament during World War II, it does little to explain the economic rise of Germany and Japan following their defeat in the same war. This implies that Kennedy did not adequately understand the function of war in industrial society.

The fundamental reason that Britain lost its hegemony was not so much that it had "overstrained" itself as that it had failed to rely upon its own industrial capacity to produce its war materiel. Britain instead relied upon the United States for its war supplies while devoting all its energy to costly battles (paralleling war in agricultural society). This explains how Germany and Japan, which produced all their war supplies domestically, were able to rise from the ashes of defeat to become economic powers after the war despite having squandered more of their strength and having suffered more destruction than Britain. The three states that produced the most military materiel, developed the most industrial technology, and trained the most skilled workers in the total war of World War II were the United States, Germany, and Japan, in that order, and in the postwar period these same states emerged as the three strongest economic powers, also in that order. The lesson here is that war in industrial societies (at least in the long run) is a positive sum game.

Let's examine what happens when a state with an inferior economic system and a state with a superior economic system (an agricultural state and a commercial state, or an agricultural state and an industrialized state, for example) confront each other in the international arena. When a decelerating economy and an accelerating economy remain in a complementary relationship, they ultimately undergo economic divergence. The divergence between agricultural economies, commercial economies, and industrial economies is the natural consequence of their different rates of economic growth, and military clashes between states with different kinds of economies result in rapid divergence between winners and losers. Agricultural states cannot raise money to finance a war as quickly as commercial states, while both agricultural states and commercial states eventually succumb to industrialized states' superior ability to manufacture weapons.

Even among industrialized states, the first states to industrialize accumulated more capital and acquired more technology than the states that industrialized later, and their relationship is much the same as that described above. To be sure, some late industrialized states have managed to catch up through resolute political will and effective government policy. But looking at history as a whole, there are very few examples of industrial latecomers overtaking industrial pioneers through ordinary economic activity in the global market.

Two exceptions to this trend are the industrial latecomers of Germany and Japan, which overtook England and France, both older industrialized states, after World War II despite their defeat in the war. This is an example of the phoenix effect, first observed by scholars such as A.F.K. Organski and later re-examined by Tai-Yoo Kim, one of the authors of this book. The concept was coined to explain unusual exceptions to the historical principle that victory in war is a necessary condition for economic development and prosperity [15]. Since the outcome of war in industrial society rests on industrial productive capacity, the typical postwar effect of victory or defeat was offset by the level of industrial technology that these states had acquired during the war. This industrial technology ended up having a greater effect on their economic growth than victory or defeat.

One point to note here is that, as these industrial societies matured, the phoenix effect began to transform into the virtuous cycle of industrial production and industrial technology. What this means is that agricultural and commercial states that had fallen out of the virtuous cycle of the economy fought wars in an attempt to return to that cycle, but industrialized states have been able to escape from the vicious cycle of the economy not through war but rather through a government policy of concentrating investment in industrial technology and R&D. This suggests that we have moved beyond the historical practice of using war to create the virtuous cycle of the economy and that we may be on the cusp of a new paradigm for civilization that could simultaneously accomplish the age-old dreams of lasting peace and continuous development.

Bearing in mind this system of expansive reproduction in industrial society, we should look a little closer at historical examples of industrial empires. Though England was a commercial empire like the Netherlands, England was able to sustain its economic advantage rather than declining after a short period of dominance as the Netherlands did because of its transformation into an industrial empire. This transformation was made possible by the Industrial Revolution, which took place in England (which had become Britain) sometime after the mid-eighteenth century.

Unlike the Netherland's system of expansive reinvestment, which was founded on intermediary trade, Britain's system of expansive reinvestment formed in such a way that a substantial portion of supply could be covered by domestic production. In Britain, the development of commerce brought an increase in the national income that caused domestic demand to grow, and the discovery of new high value-added products in Asia and the Americas caused trade to expand and domestic capital to accumulate steadily. And since the Atlantic trade enabled British manufacturers to export their products, the expansion of commerce also served to stimulate technological innovation. In this way, the development of the system of expansive reinvestment was accompanied by rapid technological innovation that led to new products based on new technology and created a large amount of new demand. That is how Britain began shifting toward the system of expansive reproduction around the mid-eighteenth century. By the nineteenth century, Britain was looking decidedly like an industrial society, with the economy accelerating under the system of expansive reproduction. At the heart of all these changes was the Industrial Revolution.

How should the Industrial Revolution be defined? According to the current scholarly consensus, the Industrial Revolution was a period of radical socio-economic change during which technological innovations enabled staple products to be manufactured and the economic structure shifted toward the system of expansive reproduction in industrial society. Because of the technological innovations during this period, new products began to appear more rapidly, production grew in scale, and new demand was created more quickly. It was this sort of new demand that made mass production possible. The system of expansive reproduction in industrial society that appeared during the Industrial Revolution refers to a system in which economic growth accelerates because of technological innovation based on mechanization and fossil fuels. This system could be described as the result of adding technological innovation in the supply sector to the virtuous cycle of the system of expansive reinvestment.

In that case, what were the necessary and sufficient conditions that enabled Britain to be the site of the Industrial Revolution? As we have previously mentioned, the system of expansive reinvestment in commercial society (which first developed in the Netherlands) was the necessary condition for the system of expansive reproduction in industrial society that appeared in the Industrial Revolution. That is, the system of expansive reinvestment that gradually became established and matured in Britain is what enabled both the Industrial Revolution and the system of expansive reproduction to emerge there. There are many indicators showing that the system of expansive reproduction developed and matured in Britain. These include the increase in overseas demand resulting from the Atlantic trade, the rise in income caused by commercial development, the increase in domestic demand in the wake of population growth, the formation of entrepreneurship through bold behavior in risky business areas and through creative technological development, the enthusiastic adoption of foreign technology, and the fall in energy prices.

The fact that the Netherlands was ultimately replaced as hegemon by Britain despite developing the system of expansive reinvestment earlier than Britain implies that the system of expansive reinvestment is a necessary condition, but not a sufficient condition, for developing a system of expansive reproduction. This prompts us to ask what sufficient conditions the Netherlands lacked but Britain possessed. First, Britain had abundant natural resources such as coal and iron. One leading scholar has defined the Industrial Revolution as the process of shifting from organic sources of energy to mineral sources, which suggests how critical mineral deposits were for the development of industrial society. Britain's mineral wealth satisfied this condition [16]. Second, Britain had been developing wool production and the woolen industry since the sixteenth and seventeenth centuries. The woolen industry in particular had grown steadily under the protection of the state. This manufacturing tradition would later provide an important technological foundation for the Industrial Revolution and would promote the development of the cotton industry, a leading sector during the Industrial Revolution.

In 1700, the British government banned the import of certain cotton fabrics from India that had been eroding the British market, and in 1721 it forbade the import of cotton fabric altogether. It imposed these bans at the request of woolen manufacturers, one of the most powerful manufacturing interests. But contrary to the hopes of the British wool fabric producers, these government regulations actually served to stimulate cotton fabric production inside Britain. Thus, consumer demand for cotton fabric and the British government's protectionist policy triggered technological innovation in the domestic cotton industry [17].

The third sufficient condition was Britain's victory in the Napoleonic Wars at the turn of the nineteenth century. During the eighteenth century, trade with North America was so important to Britain and to many states in continental Europe that people talked about the "Americanization" of trade and industry. But under Napoleon's Continental System, many continental states that could have become powerful rivals of Britain were forced out of trade with America. In other words, Napoleon's blockade of the continent and the Napoleonic Wars prevented the countries of Europe (except Britain) from engaging in foreign trade and led to a simultaneous decline in manufacturing. This essentially gave Britain a golden opportunity to take the economic lead [18].

Fourth and most important was the British government's policy of protecting industry and promoting technological innovation. Robert Walpole's customs reform of 1722 was designed to ease regulations on the import of raw materials and to limit the import of manufactured goods in order to protect and promote the export of British manufactured goods [19]. The patent system, industrial subsidies, and legal measures to prevent the outflow of technology also served to foster technological innovation. Throughout the entire Industrial Revolution—from its infancy until its maturity—it developed in line with the British government's industrial policy.

During the nineteenth century, Britain began to espouse free trade and liberalism in place of protectionism. This shift was plainly made possible by its technological and industrial advantage. Recognizing that its economy had become strong enough to thrive in an international system of free competition, Britain boldly set aside its traditional protectionist measures. This was a rational economic decision for Britain to make. It was equipped both with logical arguments that could persuade other European states that liberalism was a legitimate option and with a military (and in particular, a navy) strong enough to impose this system on non-European states. Viewed in this context, thinkers such as Adam Smith who had already preached the doctrine of free trade at the dawn of the Industrial Revolution were undeniably nationalists. Starting in the late eighteenth century, Britain had a competitive industrial advantage over other countries, and these thinkers were confident that Britain's advantage in this area meant that free trade would benefit it more than other states.

Indeed, there were growing demands in Britain (especially from cotton fabric producers) to liberalize restrictions on the supply of raw materials and the sale of products, since industry and trade, it was argued, were the source of national wealth. As the argument ran, free trade would allow other states to increase their income by exporting foodstuffs and raw materials to Britain, and those states could then use that income to import more British products. Ultimately, this argument appears to have reflected the desire to force Britain's rivals to devolve into agricultural states and to trap them in a subordinate position in their relationship with Britain [20]. The theory of comparative advantage, which was formulated around this time, was also grounded in the assumption that, since the British economy had accumulated a great amount of capital and technology during the Industrial Revolution, it could use free trade to continue to widen the gap with less-developed economies. This shows that Britain's industrialists had realized (at least tacitly) that, since agricultural societies are characterized by decelerating growth and industrial societies by accelerating growth, free trade could guarantee Britain's absolute economic advantage.

Needless to say, there was considerable resistance to the shift toward free trade and liberalism. As a consequence, even though liberalism started to gain influence in the mid-eighteenth century, it was not until the mid-nineteenth century that the Corn Laws and Navigation Acts were actually repealed, marking the transition to a system of free trade. The landed class was particularly opposed to free trade measures that would enable the cheap import of grain from overseas, driving down their profits. But manufacturers needed an abundant supply of cheap raw materials. Even more than that, they needed grain prices to fall so that they could lower workers' wages. This prompted fierce bickering between manufacturers and landowners.

As Britain made the transition to an industrial economy, an ever higher percentage of the population was engaged in industry. In consequence, Britain was faced with the practical need to provide more grain at a cheaper price, and British farmers could not meet this demand. That was how free trade and liberalism became the pillars of British government policy, beginning with the repeal of the Corn Laws in 1846. The adoption of free trade and liberalism was a rational economic choice for Britain to make at the time.

That was when Britain began to develop into an "empire of free trade," a system that is also known as unofficial imperialism. The object of Britain's free trade empire was not to gain control of new regions but rather to turn those regions into satellites of the British economy. This was regarded as the most cost-effective way of starting the virtuous cycle in the system of expansive reproduction. In addition, the ideology of liberalism was effectively used to convince Britain's rivals to do away with their own protectionist policies. It is also important to remember that

Britain prided itself on being a technological giant and that its empire of free trade was built on this overwhelming technological advantage [21]. In particular, the technology used to build basic infrastructure such as railroads, telegraph lines, and steam ships contributed decisively to England's expansion as a free trade empire.

During the 1870s, however, warning signs began to appear in the British economy. The British economy itself, of course, remained as strong as ever. But emerging economies such as the United States and Germany were close behind Britain. They had high growth rates driven by advanced technology, and this growth presented a threat to Britain's hegemony. The British began to take a defensive stance and used expressions such as "commercial invasion" and "industrial defeat" to refer to the emergence of these economic rivals [22]. As these rivals took the lead in the Second Industrial Revolution, they posed a challenge to Britain in new industries and in technological innovation.

That was how Britain's technological advantage, a critical aspect of its economic hegemony, began to crumble. Throughout the nineteenth century, Britain had depended on the products of the First Industrial Revolution (such as textiles and steel) for the majority of its exports. The United States and Germany, on the other hand, produced and exported the products of the Second Industrial Revolution (including petroleum, processed foods, electronic equipment, and steel) with the oversight of government agencies and with considerable assistance from government policy, which enabled them to create an enormous amount of new demand and to reap tremendous profits.

While the decline of Britain's hegemony can be partly attributed to its failure to adapt quickly enough to the Second Industrial Revolution, we must not ignore the harmful effect of the excessive flow of capital overseas. In order to sustain the virtuous cycle in the system of expansive reproduction, accumulated capital must be invested in the supply sector to create new technology and new products. But beginning in the mid-nineteenth century, investors moved capital out of Britain and into British rivals such as the United States, which only aided the United States' rise as an industrial power. Indeed, this phenomenon is reminiscent of how the Netherlands lost its commercial hegemony to Britain after a large amount of Dutch capital was invested in Britain and other countries.

To be sure, Britain's overseas investment helped it perpetuate the success of the railroads and other sectors from the First Industrial Revolution, and historians continue to discuss the extent to which such overseas investment harmed British industry. But there is no denying that massive overseas investment seriously hindered the growth of British industry. The fact is that the increase in overseas investment and the decrease in domestic investment basically coincided with the period when Britain was gradually losing its economic hegemony.

It does seem unlikely that Britain could have maintained its hegemony simply by investing domestic capital in domestic industry. Along with investing in domestic industry, another measure that was needed to maintain hegemony was for the government to adopt strong industrial policies. The governments of the United States and Germany had already used industrial policy to facilitate the growth of new industries in the areas of electricity and chemicals and to establish effective educational systems for these industries. But in Britain, the government had already focused its policy on free trade, and there was little movement in this new direction.

In addition, British industry was dominated by small family-owned companies, while in the United States and Germany, companies tended to be larger and run by professional managers, often enjoying a monopoly or oligopoly in a given market. The type of company common in England was obviously well-suited for light industries, which consisted of small companies staffed by skilled workers, but it was less appropriate for technology-dependent heavy industries. These were the main factors that made Britain's economy less competitive.

Despite these circumstances, Britain remained focused on exporting the products of the First Industrial Revolution to its colonial markets instead of building new industries to compete with its rivals in the global market. As a result, the genteel British elite turned away from entrepreneurship and put their money in the finance and service sectors. These sectors became a new source of wealth for the landed gentry, for whom industrial development had caused financial difficulties. From 1688 to 1850, a significant portion of wealth was earned from the land, but after 1850, wealth flowed from financial capital.

As the gentry (whose wealth was now based in the finance and service sectors) remained the ruling class in Britain, industrial development was neglected by British society. Given the mood at the time, even industrial capitalists began imitating the gentry after they acquired their wealth. Under the dominance of the gentry, British society became more conservative, and the enterprising and adventurous spirit of the past gave way to the pursuit of stability and short-term profits. For the same reasons, the British government also started adopting policies designed to maximize financial gain rather than to build new industries.

Even worse, as competition intensified in the global market, the British government clung to its policy of free trade even as it abandoned its industrial policy and ignored the appeals of industrialists. The reason was that liberalism implied a *laissez-faire* stance toward the free flow of capital, which profited Britain's financial elite as financial income increased. Thus, the decline of Britain's hegemony accelerated even as the United States and Germany jostled to position themselves as successors to that hegemony. The turning point was the outbreak of World War I.

In a certain sense, the story of how the British Empire lost its hegemony is the same as the story of how the United States acquired it. In a short period of time, the United States emerged as the most powerful hegemonic state in the history of mankind, a state whose hegemony extended over the entire world. Since there was no historical precedent for the United States' rise, it was once common for scholars to describe the United States as being exceptional. According to the idea of American exceptionalism, the United States not only was blessed with vast lands and mineral wealth but was also a "land of liberty" that was unconstrained by the inefficient traditions that had preceded capitalism. Such characteristics were what enabled the United States to achieve such astounding economic growth, these scholars said. There are a number of weaknesses to this argument, however. For one thing, states such as Russia, China, India, Brazil, and Argentina have possessed the same natural advantages of the United States without achieving the same development. For another, even the United States is plagued with a persistent social hierarchy and a variety of illiberal traditions.

Rather than through simplistic catchphrases such as the "land of liberty" or "land of opportunity," America's hegemony should be understood in the context of its transition through the three general patterns of economic development that are found in human history: the system of simple reproduction in agricultural society, the system of expansive reinvestment in commercial society, and the system of expansive reproduction in industrial society. Indeed, the story of American development into a historically unprecedented superpower—a story that can be traced through the colonial period, the Revolutionary War, the Civil War, and two World Wars—appears to be a well-balanced synthesis of successful applications of the virtuous cycle of war in the economy seen in agricultural societies such as Rome, commercial societies such as the Netherlands, and industrial societies such as Britain. Needless to say, these successes were made even more impressive by to the United States' exceptional advantages.

The United States' development can be traced back to the colonial period. During this period, the colonies were as economically diverse as they were politically fragmented. The plantation-based agriculture of Virginia and the other Southern Colonies developed alongside the subsistence farming, trade, and rudimentary manufacturing of the New England colonies to the north. The decisive factor in the economic development of the colonies was the growth of commerce (and shipbuilding), which flourished as part of Britain's system of expansive reinvestment. Guarded by Britain's Navigation Acts and its imperial might, the colonial economy reaped a considerable commercial windfall.

This symbiotic relationship between the British Empire and the colonies began to change during the Seven Years War. As the British government struggled financially during the war, it swapped its previous policy of "salutary neglect" for mercantilist interventionism. Britain's objective at the time was to prevent conflicts in North America that would further strain its finances while binding the colonies to the British economy and maximizing colonial revenue. To accomplish this, Britain began passing a series of economic regulations related to the colonies, starting with the Royal Proclamation of 1763, which prevented westward expansion, and the Sugar Act of 1764. This ignited political and then military conflict between Britain and the colonies, culminating in the colonists' victory and in the thirteen colonies' independence from the British Empire.

In some respects, this is similar to how the Netherlands wrested its independence from the Spanish Empire. In both cases, individual colonies or cities joined together to form an economic community of interest that resisted economic pressure from the colonial power. And in both cases, the colonies gained the victory as rebel armies that were little better than militias vanquished the professional soldiers of the hegemonic power of its age. In addition, the American colonies' dependence on commerce resembles the unique commercial economy developed by the Netherlands. In this respect, both the Netherlands and the United States gained their independence from colonial empires through the system of expansive reinvestment in commercial society.

Of course, independence gave rise to new problems. For the United States, victory in the Revolutionary War laid the foundation for a national economy, but it also meant separation from Britain's system of expansive reinvestment to which the colonies had hitherto enjoyed access. The future of the United States became even cloudier when it underwent a financial crisis caused by the long years of war. Facing such challenges, the fledgling country was rife with conflicting viewpoints about what direction it should take. One of these viewpoints was espoused by the Republicans (also called Democrat-Republicans), who wanted the states to remain autonomous and who supported agricultural development based on yeoman farmers and commercial development based on trade. Another viewpoint was expressed by the Federalists, who wanted to establish a powerful federal government and who supported industrial development. In short, the Republicans envisioned an agricultural empire with some characteristics of commercial society, while the Federalists had an industrial empire in mind.

When Alexander Hamilton and the Federalists took power in the 1790s, they believed that the survival of the new nation depended upon the establishment of a strong fiscal-military state like Britain. They supported the creation of a single domestic market that went beyond the borders of the individual states, the establishment of a strong and stable federal bank, the absolute sanctity of private property, and the promotion of policies designed to protect industry. In short, they thought that the new state they were framing would have to be strong and united to weather the storms of international relations and that the goal of these endeavors should be the development of an industrial empire.

But the Federalists' cause suffered a temporary setback when the Republicans took control and another conflict broke out with Britain. The Embargo Act of 1807 and the War of 1812 presented the young state with new challenges. In the short term, these incidents took a toll on the American economy, but in the long term, they cut off the supply of British manufactured goods, providing the conditions under which the American manufacturing industry could grow. This was the crucial moment when the United States began to shift from the system of expansive reinvestment, which was based on agriculture and commerce, to the system of expansive reproduction, which was based on the accumulation of capital and technological innovation in the manufacturing industry.

Even inside the Republican Party, a broad consensus had formed in favor of adopting a balanced approach to development and of fostering growth in the manufacturing sector. Based on this consensus, the vanguard of American manufacturers compensated for the crippling shortage of skilled workers by turning to mechanization. In order to supply consumers with cheaper products, manufacturers developed what came to be known as the American system of manufacturing, which was characterized by standardized technology and interchangeable parts. Such innovation enabled the United States to surpass the productivity of the British manufacturing sector.

But the onset of industrial society was mostly limited to the northern states. The American South continued to exhibit the characteristics of agricultural society, and its plantations relied on slave labor. This reflected the huge regional gap in respect to industrial structure, a gap that exacerbated discord between the two sides in political debates about whether trade should be free or protected and whether the slave system should be preserved or abolished. Northerners pursued an ideal industrial society in which free workers owned the fruits of their labor and in which talent provided a means to improve one's social status. But Southerners countered that Northern workers were worse off than the Southern slaves who were under the paternalistic care of their owners. To forestall the class conflict that they foresaw industrialization would bring, Southerners proposed returning to the stable hierarchical order of pre-industrial society. Just as in the debate between the Federalists and the Republicans, these opposing perspectives reflected a fundamental disagreement about how the United States ought to proceed. The question of which viewpoint would prevail was a crucial one that would determine the United States' future.

These two perspectives clashed in the American Civil War, which caused immense material destruction and horrendous loss of life, along with great harm to the American economy, at least in the short term. But the Union's victory in the war made it possible to bring every part of the United States into a national economy in the fullest sense of the word. Prior to this, there had never been a single domestic market. Before the war, the Southern economy had depended on plantation agriculture and slave labor, and it had developed along with the system of expansive reproduction in Europe (and especially Britain). But after the abolition of slavery and the introduction of a new economic system based on the relationship between free labor and capital, the South's relationship with the North was destined to change as well.

After the Civil War, the West developed in a manner that was similar to the South. The small farmers of the West were steeped in republicanism, and they became an important support base for the Republican Party, which had led the Union to victory in the Civil War. But as industrial capital and financial capital in the North began to dominate the Republican Party and the federal government after the war, the West became a center of activity in primary industries including oil drilling, gold mining, and large-scale corporate farming. Rapid improvement in transportation and communication technology after the Civil War turned the South and the West into a dynamo that drove Northern industry, serving both as the source of its raw materials and as the market for its products. As a result, the North went through a period of innovation in management and production and of capital investment on a scale large enough to fully realize the potential for the Second Industrial Revolution, while modern industrial corporations were established one after another. This ultimately perfected the system of expansive reproduction as a synthesis of mass production and mass consumption.

The virtuous cycle of the system of expansive reproduction cannot be maintained unless it is accompanied by a market that grows fast enough to accommodate continuing technological innovation and industrial output. In Britain, where the system of expansive reproduction was first established, the sprawling colonies of the British Empire served as a source of raw materials and as a market for products. But the United States was able to develop the system of expansive reproduction even without aggressive overseas expansion since the South and West played a similar role to the British colonies. The United States took full advantage of its vast domestic market as it developed the system of expansive reproduction. While the empires of Europe were preoccupied with the catastrophic conflict known as World War I, the United States overtook its European rivals to become the world's leading manufacturer.

The American decision to enter World War I in the war's final stage was a significant event that testified to the emergence of the United States as a hegemonic state, but the United States was not prepared to take on the international role that hegemony requires. This was demonstrated by the fact that, during the political and economic crisis that followed the war, the United States was reluctant to forfeit any of its rights as a creditor over the Allied Powers. Furthermore, when the capitalist system was in danger of collapse during the tumult of the Great Depression, the United States opted for isolationism instead of leading efforts to repair the global economic order. The country's industrial output had doubled after World War I, and its system of expansive reproduction entered a protracted slump during this chaotic time as demand plummeted both at home and abroad.

As we observed earlier, industrial development alone is not enough for a hegemonic state to maintain its status. The hegemonic state must also minimize the domestic social conflict caused by expanding industrial output while simultaneously engaging in the process of persuasion and consent, or in other words convincing the international community to acknowledge its hegemonic authority. In these terms, the United States' development into a true hegemonic power was made possible domestically through the New Deal and internationally through World War II. While the economic effects of the New Deal continue to be debated to this day, it is clear that the New Deal at least succeeded in mitigating social conflict by arranging for a more equal distribution of the economic benefits of the United States' system of expansive reproduction, which by that point had become highly sophisticated. The institutional strategies devised during the New Deal period to share the fruits of industrial development—including social welfare programs and compromises between labor and capital—became the engine that powered the system of expansive reproduction in the United States at least until the early 1970s.

World War II provided the United States with an opportunity to part ways with isolationism and to rebuild the global system in its own image. During the war, the American system of expansive reproduction in the United States came out of the long shadow of the Great Depression and experienced a surge in manufacturing output that was comparable to the Second Industrial Revolution. High-tech industries including the aircraft industry expanded with the help of wartime demand and industry-friendly government policy. Meanwhile, the American public's purchasing power, which rose rapidly during the wartime boom, created explosive growth in the manufacturing and service industries.

In this fashion, the United States acquired incredible economic power, and the way that it used this power after the war set the course of the postwar global order. This time, the United States acted in a manner that was quite different from its actions after World War I—it was beginning to embrace its status as an indubitable hegemonic state. The United States played a leading role in the establishment of the International Monetary Fund and the World Bank, and these two bodies helped secure the stability of the global economy by promoting international trade and persuading various states to establish and implement a flexible exchange-rate system. Various aid packages, including the Marshall Plan, helped accelerate the postwar recovery. The United States' efforts to reorganize the global economic order were based on the belief that sustaining the system of expansive reproduction would require the soundness not only of the American market, but of the global market as well.

Through its superior technology, industrial output, military strength, and political leadership on the international stage, the United States' global system of expansive reproduction continued to develop for more than a generation after 1945. Backed by substantial investment in R&D by the government and corporations, American multinational manufacturing firms brought forth a wealth of new technologies and products, and numerous countries that depended on American military might and financial aid provided cheap raw materials, a labor force, and big markets. But as we have seen with hegemonic states of the past, the United States' rivals were racing to surpass it even during the long period of postwar economic expansion when American power was at its zenith. Just as Britain in the late nineteenth century faced the challenge of recently industrialized states that had designed new strategies for development, so the United States also had to confront new challenges.

The United States faced a particularly strong challenge from Germany and Japan. Under American military protection, both of these states were able to dedicate themselves to postwar recovery and to economic growth. Since they had begun laying the technological foundation for the system of expansive reproduction during the second half of the nineteenth century and had reinforced it during World War I and II, they were able to achieve a level of economic growth that was much faster than other states. And while the United States' absolute industrial advantage eroded under relentless competition from these states and others like them, the United States was forced to spend more and more to maintain its hegemony (as Kennedy and numerous other commentators have observed).

This reflects the unique historical conditions of the Cold War and the astronomical rise in military spending caused by the rapid advancement of military technology, but it does not adequately explain the cracks that began to appear in the United States' system of expansive reproduction after the Vietnam War. If the United States had been able to create enough economic value to easily cover the cost of maintaining its military and of convincing other states to accept American hegemony, things would have turned out differently. But during this same period, the focus of the American economy was shifting away from the industrial sector, which was facing pressure from developing countries, and toward the financial sector (just like the Netherlands and Britain before it) instead of toward new industrial sectors such as the knowledge-based industry.

The study of history shows that there is a vital need to develop an economic system that can enable states to enjoy the virtuous cycle of the economy without having to rely on the virtuous cycle of war. Such a system (presuming that one exists) must be established so that the benefits of economic growth can be distributed as evenly as possible. Failure to do so means that our countries and societies will have to pay the price of regular strife at home and wars abroad. Even worse, the historical consequences of social discord and military defeat have been catastrophic, both materially and morally, as they inevitably lead to the collapse of the state and the end of hegemony. Thus, "sustainable" hegemony will only be possible when a new economic system has been established that is capable of maintaining economic peace and prosperity, both within domestic society and in the world at large.

Establishing such a new economic system requires the ability to reflect upon past shortcomings and to improve upon them, an ability that we observed in the Prussian Army earlier in this chapter. Or in other words, it requires an accurate understanding of how previous societies have dealt with war and peace, with times of plenty and times of crisis, which we can find in the treasury of knowledge and experience that we call history. Reading about the past often allows us to see the future. Since ancient times, people have forged their own history as they dreamed of future peace and prosperity. But that splendid dream has been distorted and disregarded, leading to the nightmare of economic crises, social upheavals and terrible wars. This can be attributed to human error and to chance events, as well as to the structural limitations inherent to agricultural society, commercial society, and industrial society and to the painfully slow and frequently interrupted evolution of those societies.

It is only when we apply our reason and intelligence to fully understand the role played by human fallibility, happenstance, and historical constraints (that is, the basic structural forces that pressure and limit human thought and action) that we will learn how to direct rational thought and action toward the principles of peace and prosperity. This is analogous to how understanding the laws of nature has expanded the scope of human freedom. Humans today must learn how to exploit our reason and intelligence not to prosecute war as the Prussian Army did but rather to create lasting peace and prosperity. Throughout human history, reason and intelligence have never stopped evolving, and they continue to evolve today. This also means that the new economic system of the future, the system that will able to provide lasting peace and prosperity, ought to and indeed cannot help but use the reason and intelligence handed down from previous societies, or in other words their accumulated capital and technology.

In the following chapters, we will examine commercial society and industrial society. These economic societies empowered reason and intelligence to such an extent that they disrupted domestic society and the international order, and they hint at the possibility of achieving peace and prosperity in the future. While the emphasis that this book places on economic systems may sound like economic determinism, our real objective is to help readers understand how economic systems develop so that they can make deliberate and informed choices about development and craft the right policies. That is to say, understanding the economic systems of the past motivates people to take action in the present. In fact, this point is what we are ultimately hoping to prove by writing this book. Proving this point will make clear that as dreamers of the future we are also the children of the past—and more precisely, of the past process of evolution.

References

1. Mineral products and handmade crafts are not themselves agricultural products. But since mineral products are an output from the primary sector of the economy just like agricultural products, they too are characterized by diminishing returns. In addition, people began tilling the earth around the same time that they started mining it. Handmade crafts involved modifying and combining agricultural products and mineral products to increase their utility and added value. As such, the productivity of these items can also be increased to a limited degree. But since the production of handmade crafts does not increase at an accelerating rate despite the technological innovation and mass production of industrial society, it can be categorized as a product of agricultural society.
2. Theodore W. Schultz, *Transforming Traditional Agriculture* (New Haven and London, 1964).
3. Richard A. Levins and Williard W. Cochrane, "The Treadmill Revisited," *Land Economics* 74:4 (November 1996), pp. 550–553.
4. The claim that the critical path in the development of human civilization runs through the developmental history of Europe may sound Eurocentric. The comparison of Western development to Asian stagnation and the observation that capitalism emerged not in Asia but in Europe are familiar subjects to students of economic history. For example, eminent American economic historian David Landes has made the explicitly Eurocentric argument that Europe's unique geography, cultural attitudes, and political and social organizations were factors that enabled its economic growth. Landes' conclusion was that the poor countries (of Asia) must learn from the rich countries (of Europe) and follow in their footsteps if they are to enjoy economic growth. But Landes' argument is only valid if we assume that the rich and poor states exist in a state of free competition. In other words, this argument does not take into account the international hierarchy imposed by European hegemony. In contrast with Landes, our starting point is acknowledging the existence of hegemonic states and an international hierarchy; our approach is examining the transfer of hegemony and changes in international relations; and our goal is attempting to deduce from this the principles by which individual states and human civilization as a whole have developed. Of course, it is undeniable that European states were the first to become industrial societies and that they have exercised global hegemony on this basis. That it is why it is not Eurocentric to acknowledge in our study of the principles of economic growth that the system of expansive reproduction inherent to industrial society came into being in Europe and has since spread around the world. Indeed, we intend to pay close attention to the decline of Western hegemony and the possibility of discovering new principles for the development of nations and of human civilization. David S. Landes, *The Wealth and Poverty of Nations: Why Some Are So Rich and Some So Poor* (New York, 1998).
5. Timothy H. Parsons, *The Rule of Empires: Those Who Built Them, Those Who Endured Them, and Why They Always Fail* (Oxford, 2010), pp. 111, 119.
6. This aspect is reminiscent of the theory of "military overstretch" proposed by Paul Kennedy, the theory that excessive expenditures exhaust the state's coffers and lead to the state's decline. But this theory only applies to agricultural empires. If a state is enjoying steady and endogenous technological advancement and capital accumulation (as in an industrial society), it is theoretically possible to reduce expenditures relative to production. And even if such a state runs out of money, it can raise the funds it needs to wage war through various financial products that are guaranteed by the huge profits the state is expected to earn in the future. The

limits of the military overstretch theory have been demonstrated by Germany and Japan since World War II. The modern history of these two states makes clear that a state defeated in war can rise again as an economic power. Thus, the fact that Spain declined between the sixteenth and eighteenth centuries because of the "military overstretch" of unprofitable wars and was unable to rise again is evidence that it was a typical agricultural empire. At any rate, we will return to this argument in the section that deals with war and the economy in industrial society.

7. William H. McNeill, *The Pursuit of Power* (Chicago, 1982), p. 133.
8. John Brewer, *The Sinews of Power: War, Money, and the English State, 1688–1783* (London, 1989).
9. In this sense, nationalism can be said to have first developed in the Netherlands and England between the sixteenth and eighteenth centuries. It was previously thought that nationalism was born in the turmoil of the French Revolution at the end of the eighteenth century, but the prevailing view in recent years has been that nationalism appeared earlier than that in the Netherlands and in England. This is the background for Philip S. Gorski's argument that nationalism developed as a political discourse during the period of the Dutch Revolt, a phenomenon that he called "early modern nationalism." Even Anthony D. Smith, one of the leading scholars of nationalism today, acknowledges that the ideology of nationalism appeared not in France but rather in the Netherlands and England in the early modern period. Indeed, the social networks that formed at English coffeehouses, pubs, and churches during the seventeenth and eighteenth centuries stimulated lively debates about the meaning of the wars being fought with the Netherlands and France and of the national interest that they were supposed to protect. There is no doubt that this keen understanding of the national interest was a domestic source of energy that propelled England to global hegemony. Philip S. Gorski, "The Mosaic Moment: An Early Modernist Critique of Modernist Theories of Nationalism," *The American Journal of Sociology* 105:5 (2000), pp. 1436–1438, 1458–1462; Anthony D. Smith, *The Cultural Foundations of Nations: Hierarchy, Covenant, and Republic* (Malden and Oxford, 2008), x.
10. Fernand Braudel, *Civilization & Capitalism 15th–18th Century, Vol. 3: The Perspective of the World*, trans. Siân Reynolds (New York, 1979), pp. 614–615.
11. The term "military-industrial complex" was originally coined after World War II to warn of the influence exercised by the political and financial interests shared by the defense industry, military leaders, and lawmakers. For this reason, the term's connotations tend to be negative or even conspiratorial. In this book, however, we have used the term in a broader and more neutral sense to signify the close reciprocal relationship between war and industry.
12. Paul Kennedy, *The Rise and Fall of the Great Powers: Change and Military Conflict from 1500 to 2000* (New York, 1987), p. 180.
13. McNeill, *Pursuit of Power*, pp. 251–252; the emphasis is ours.
14. Kennedy, *Rise and Fall*, p. 367.
15. A. F. K. Organski and Jacek Kugler, "The Costs of Major Wars: The Phoenix Factor," *The American Political Science Review*, Vol. 71, No. 4. (December 1977), pp. 1347–1366; Tai-Yoo Kim et al., "War, Peace, and Economic Growth: The Phoenix Factor Reexamined," mimeograph.
16. E. A. Wrigley, *Energy and the English Industrial Revolution* (Cambridge, 2010); for efforts to understand England's Industrial Revolution through the lens of world history, see R. Bin Wong, *China Transformed: Historical Change and the Limits of European Experience* (Ithaca, 1997) and Kenneth Pomeranz, *The Great Divergence: China, Europe, and the Making of the Modern World Economy* (Princeton, 2000).
17. Jan de Vries, *The Industrious Revolution: Consumer Behavior and the Household Economy, 1650 to the Present* (Cambridge, 2008), p. 137.
18. François Crouzet, "Wars, Blockade, and Economic Change in Europe, 1792–1815," *The Journal of Economic History* 24:4 (1964), pp. 567–588.
19. Charles H. Wilson, *England's Apprenticeship, 1603–1763* (London, 1971), pp. 267–269.

20. P. J. Cain and A. G. Hopkins, "The Political Economy of British Expansion Overseas, 1750–1914," *The Economic History Review,* Second Series, 33:4 (November 1980).
21. Robert Kubicek, "British Expansion, Empire and Technological Change," *The Oxford History of the British Empire vol. 3: The Nineteenth Century* (Oxford, 1999), p. 248.
22. Deirdre McCloskey, *Enterprise and Trade in Victorian Britain: Essays in Historical Economics* (London, 1981), p. 55.

Chapter 2
Spain: Agricultural Empire on the Waves

In 1492, the year that Christopher Columbus set out in search of the wealth of the Indies and the Christian kingdom of Prester John, Europe was little more than the western frontier of the Eurasian continent. At the time, Europe was inferior to the world of Islam and to East Asia in nearly every respect, including economic activity, cultural vitality, and political stability. There were still vestiges of the glory of classical Rome, but all efforts to resurrect that empire had failed.

But as the energy of the Italian cultural movement known as the Renaissance shows us, fifteenth century Europe was putting the political strife and economic backwardness of the past millennium behind it as it entered a new era. A great deal of time was needed for this recovery. Agricultural productivity had been improving since at least the ninth century, enabling long-distance trade to flourish and cities to be rebuilt. This new vitality was also the momentum behind the Crusades, which began in the late eleventh century. While the Crusaders failed in their goals of crushing the Muslims and regaining control of the Holy Land, Europe had made clear its intentions of being more than a global backwater. These intentions were demonstrated even more dramatically during the so-called Age of Discovery. The result was a horizontal expansion of the boundaries of world history and the formation of a vertical hierarchy in the world's political economy [1].

As the Medieval Period gave way to the Age of Discovery, the kingdoms of Europe rejected political decentralization and devoted themselves to building up the state by waging frequent wars with their neighbors. Wars in early modern Europe not only had to be fought differently—involving new types of weapons, forms of organization, and approaches to commanding units—but also demanded human and material resources on an unprecedented scale. This forced the various states of Europe to pay heed to issues like government finance and political economy. Meanwhile, there was also growing interest both in the distribution of resources inside states and in new resources and markets overseas. At this time, the countries of Europe were fundamentally agricultural societies, and they were unable to overcome the inherent limit on agricultural societies that we discussed in Chap. 1: namely, diminishing growth. Therefore, the only way for agricultural societies to

T.-Y. Kim and D. Kim, *The Secrets of Hegemony*,
DOI 10.1007/978-981-10-4416-8_2

escape from the Malthusian Trap, if only temporarily, was to increase their supply of land by acquiring more territory and to resolve the problem of overpopulation through migration.

From this perspective, it is no coincidence that Spain and Portugal were the states that ushered in the Age of Discovery. These two states' long rivalry with the Muslims on the Iberian Peninsula had taught them the importance of expanding their territory by conquering other states. In order for these new states to become strong, they also needed to overcome the geopolitical limitations of the Iberian Peninsula, which was surrounded by the sea on three sides and blocked by the Pyrenees mountains on the fourth. In that respect, Spain and Portugal's decision to expand into Asia and the Americas was an inevitable one made in response to the diminishing growth that limited agricultural society. As pioneers of the larger historical trend of expansion in early modern Europe, Spain and Portugal began looking beyond Europe earlier than their rivals. This enabled them to acquire immense wealth in Asia and the Americas and (in the case of Spain) a huge empire. But their dazzling success only lasted for a century. By the second half of the sixteenth century, the two states had entered a period of decline and were eventually pushed to the semi-periphery or periphery of the global economy [2].

There are two significant lessons we can learn from Spain and Portugal's intriguing historical experiences. First, they teach us why empires that depend upon the system of simple reproduction in agricultural society are unable to achieve accelerating economic growth. While Spain and Portugal were agricultural societies whose economic systems required continual territorial expansion, the frequent wars they fought to acquire more territory only prevented their accumulated wealth from being invested productively and incited prodigality and waste (not to mention causing huge amounts of money to be spent on military and political purposes). The eventual result was that their systems of production entered a vicious cycle.

The second lesson to learn from these states' experiences is a paradox: the rise and fall of Spain and Portugal provided other European states with the basis for the system of expansive reinvestment, complete with accelerating growth and accumulating capital. The new sea routes, markets, and resources opened up by Spain and Portugal lay the foundation for capital accumulation by the merchants and bankers of the Netherlands, Italy, and England; in later years, they would become the dynamo that would drive development not only in trade and finance but also in agriculture and industry. It is in this sense that Spain and Portugal provide a critical clue for understanding the rise of Europe and the transfer of hegemony in the global economy.

The Reconquista

As a branch of European history, the history of the Iberian Peninsula goes back to the days of the Roman Empire. By the time of Augustus, the peninsula had already become an important province in the empire, serving as Rome's breadbasket and as a source of its silver. This was also when the Spanish began raising sheep, an industry that would be one of the chief drivers of the Spanish economy during the early modern period. Under Roman rule, Roman culture was actively transmitted to Spain, and Christianity and Roman traditions put down deep roots on the peninsula. During the period of migration by Germanic tribes in the fourth century, the peninsula fell under the control of the Visigothic Kingdom. As a consequence, the region underwent a fusion of Roman culture and Germanic culture for several centuries after the dissolution of the Roman Empire, just as happened in other parts of Europe.

The next chapter in the history of the Iberian Peninsula began with the arrival of the Muslims. In 711, a Muslim army from Tangier landed at Gibraltar, taking advantage of a time of political division in the Visigothic Kingdom. The Muslims had a powerful army and an extensive trade network, enabling them to conquer most of the Iberian Peninsula by 720. Muslim states survived in the region for nearly seven centuries, until 1492. The campaign to reconquer the Iberian Peninsula by driving out the Muslims—which is known as the Reconquista—began the moment the Muslims landed. This centuries-long conflict had two legacies for the Iberian Peninsula in the early modern period. First, the new Christian states that emerged amid the struggle with the Muslims experimented with a variety of political systems and approaches to governance. Second, a shared religious identity took shape that transcended political differences. This identity was grounded in the sense that the Christian states on the Iberian Peninsula were a bulwark defending the Christian world from the forces of Islam.

That does not mean that the Reconquista period was time of constant conflict. Both in the areas under Muslim control and in the contested border areas, Muslims and Christians also engaged in cultural exchange and explored ways to coexist. Mosques were built where Christian cathedrals had once stood, and it was common for Christians to convert to Islam. Even Christians who did not convert used Arabic in their everyday lives, and Arabic translations of the Bible were published as well. In addition, the Spanish adopted advanced irrigation techniques and new crops such as rice and sugarcane from the Muslim world [3].

The conflicts and compromises between the two groups left a mark on the Reconquista, and the relationships between Christian and Muslim states shifted between partnerships, alliances, and rivalries. This trend becomes visible early in the eleventh century. Around this time, the unified Muslim polity on the peninsula disintegrated in a military coup and a fight for succession, resulting in a number of petty states called *taifas*. The Christian states in the north took advantage of the squabbling to absorb more territory to their south and to accumulate wealth by collecting tribute from the *taifas* in exchange for military assistance. As local conflicts increased, the activity of mercenaries increased as well. One of the most famous of these mercenaries—Rodrigo Díaz, better known as El Cid—even became the ruler of a city-state [4].

The main reason that the Reconquista continued for as long as it did can be found not in religious pretexts or political and cultural conflict and exchange, but rather in economic incentives. Just as in other parts of Europe, the Christian states in the northern half of the Iberian Peninsula had to deal with growing populations in the ninth and tenth centuries, along with the resulting shortage of food. These kingdoms were typical agricultural societies, and inside their borders they could find no solution for the fact that their farmland was insufficient to support population growth (unlike the Muslim states, which had developed cities and a trading network). As a result, these kingdoms concentrated their efforts on acquiring new territory. Indeed, this was the only choice available for agricultural society when it reached the limits of growth because of diminishing production.

This predicament prompted migration by the people of the Christian states. This migration began in Catalonia in the tenth century and spread to central Portugal in the twelfth and thirteenth centuries. While these migrations occasionally took place on the orders of the monarch, they were for the most part voluntary. Typically, they involved groups of Christians raiding and plundering Muslim settlements, which they would then declare to be the territory of their monarch. Such migrations entailed substantial risks, and a custom developed in which warriors would defend peasants and their new settlements in exchange for receiving labor and rent from them. This resulted in an aristocratic class of landowners. After migrants founded a new settlement and even after that settlement became established, they remained at risk of a Muslim counterattack. To counter this risk, landowners and peasants stayed close together in towns. As the pattern of migration repeated, an agricultural empire began to form in Spain that was rooted in the cycle of war and the economy.

As this suggests, the Reconquista was motivated by economic considerations, and particularly the effort to overcome the economic limits of agricultural society. It was only after the Reconquista had been underway for quite some time that its religious aspect began to be emphasized. An important incident reflecting this shift of emphasis occurred in the second half of the eleventh century, largely instigated by the Cluniac Order, which was already firmly established in the Kingdom of Castile and León, and the Cistercian Order, which arrived on the Iberian Peninsula later. Responding to the appeal of these orders, a force of 3000 knights from Italy, France, and Normandy marched into the Iberian Peninsula in 1064 and slaughtered some 6000 Muslims. This was nearly a century before Pope Urban II launched the First Crusade during the Council of Clermont. The ferocity of this "holy war" helped spread the idea that it was righteous to fight the enemies of the church, linking the Reconquista with the Crusades.

The Crusades provoked a response from the Moors that ultimately aided the Reconquista. In the early twelfth century, a reform movement arose in the Muslim states of North Africa in which reformers called for Muslims to unite against the ferocious assault of the Crusaders. When the formerly fragmented Islamic states began to join together, the desperate Christian states on the Iberian Peninsula were forced to work more closely together. This paid dividends, as was amply demonstrated by the decisive victory won by King Alfonso VIII of Castile in the Battle of Las Navas de Tolosa in 1212, with help from the kings of Navarre and Aragon. After this battle, the influence of the Moors rapidly weakened, and the Iberian Peninsula came under the control of the four Christian states of Castile, Aragon, Portugal, and Navarre [5].

But there is gap of more than two centuries between Alfonso VIII's victory in this battle and the Granada War, which was the final phase in the Reconquista. Why were the Christian states unable to maintain the advantage they gained in the early thirteenth century? Part of the answer is the fact that recapturing territory from the Muslims was not originally the sole purpose of the Reconquista. The Reconquista was connected with a colonization project that involved mass migrations and the establishment of new settlements. This project had picked up momentum since the tenth century because of the pressure of overpopulation, but by the end of the eleventh century, there were not enough peasants to work the land acquired during the preceding period of conquest and settlement. And in addition to the weakened economic incentives for the Reconquista, the Black Death, a pandemic that swept Europe in the mid-fourteenth century, further aggravated the labor shortage. The population level eventually returned to normal, but the Christian states on the Iberian Peninsula were too preoccupied with rebellions and other political turmoil to pay much attention to the Emirate of Granada, which was the surviving Muslim state on the peninsula. In this sense, the progress of the Reconquista was inextricably linked to the cycle of war and the economy that is inherent to agricultural society.

Therefore, the fact that the Christian states of Spain were able to launch a campaign to conquer Granada in the 1480s implies that they had overcome the political and economic crises of the previous century and had acquired the ability to enter a new era. The demographic and economic troubles of the mid-fourteenth century were turned around in the fifteenth century as the Crown of Castile saw its population double and its economy grow rapidly. The political chaos was also partially stabilized through the marriage of Ferdinand II of Aragon to Isabella I of Castile. The Crown of Castile was the strongest state on the Iberian Peninsula in terms of its population and territory, while the Crown of Aragon was a major maritime power on the Mediterranean Sea, and the two states' union brought about a new political order. Ferdinand and Isabella were bestowed the title of "Catholic monarchs" by the Pope, and under their rule the unified kingdom of Spain achieved religious unity by completing the Reconquista and laid the foundation for the Spanish Empire by opening up sea routes and conquering colonies [6].

Ferdinand and Isabella's marriage did not lead to the legal and administrative unification of the two kingdoms, however. Their marriage was only a union of dynasties, and Castile and Aragon retained their existing legal systems and institutions even after becoming a unified kingdom. This same approach was also taken when the Netherlands and the Italian republics were later incorporated into the Spanish Empire, producing what John Elliott, a leading scholar of Spanish history, has called a "composite monarchy." This approach was faster and easier than centralizing power and unifying administration through military conquest or other means. Respecting the institutions and customs of each region meant that there was less risk of inciting nationalist feelings, which made it possible to minimize the unrest that results from unification [7]. For the ruler, the greatest appeal of the "composite monarchy" model was its utility in recruiting local leaders into the new system. Ferdinand and Isabella mostly resided in Castile and left the rule of Aragon to a viceroy. The appointment of a viceroy gave the monarchs an opportunity to integrate the local elite into their system of rule.

But it was also because of this system that the differences between the two kingdoms grew stronger after their unification. The Crown of Aragon was composed of Valencia, Aragon, and Catalonia, and during the thirteenth and fourteenth centuries Catalonia had become an important maritime power in the Mediterranean that depended on exports of woven goods just like the other kingdoms on the Iberian Peninsula. Catalonian merchants competed successfully with Italians in the Levant trade, and the wealth that they accumulated enabled Barcelona and other cities to prosper [8].

In order to properly understand the history of unified Spain and the Spanish empire, we must take note of the system of governance and the political principles of the Crown of Aragon. In the thirteenth century, a representative body known as the Cortes began to convene in Aragon on a regular basis, and this body (along with the administrative councils that assisted it) served as a counterbalance to the monarch's power, including its authority to levy taxes. As this representative tradition took root, people began to view it as a sort of contract. That is, they came to regard the monarch's authority as deriving from a contract with his subjects and to assume that the monarch's rule should not overstep the bounds of this contract [9].

Thus, even though Aragon's economy was rooted in agriculture, its cities and merchants became relatively prosperous, and the Cortes, which represented those merchants' interests, grew in power. In Castile, on the other hand, power remained with the crown. To be sure, the contractual tradition was not absent in Castile, but it was overshadowed by the belief that the authority of the monarch was derived from god and that the monarch and his subjects constituted an organic community. In other words, Castile never developed the system of checks on the monarch that arose in Aragon (largely consisting of the Cortes and various standing councils).

This was partly due to economic circumstances. The economy of Castile was much more dependent on agriculture (and in particular sheep herding) than Aragon. Furthermore, the Reconquista had left a lasting mark on the kingdom's landowners, who were descended from the knights who had protected the peasants in exchange for gaining power over them. Those knights had focused more on breeding livestock and producing wool than on growing crops in order to minimize the damage from Muslim raids. In addition, the merino breed of sheep that was brought from North Africa to Spain in the early fourteenth century stimulated demand for Spanish wool, which further increased the power of the aristocrats who owned vast sections of land. Since Castile's landowning aristocrats exercised so much influence (both economic and extra-economic) and were given various privileges by the monarch including tax exemptions, they had little need for a representative body like the Cortes. As a result, the Cortes of Castile became a largely ceremonial legislature for the cities.

To be sure, if the monarchs had adopted a policy of suppressing the landowning aristocrats and protecting the peasants while simultaneously maximizing the influence of the urban bourgeoisie, things might have turned out somewhat differently. But instead, the monarchs of Castile were the last line of defense for a reinforced and reenergized aristocracy, as historian Perry Anderson argues [10]. Since the Castilian economy and the crown itself were largely dependent on sheep breeding and the wool trade, the "Catholic monarchs" and their descendants could not move directly to muzzle the aristocrats and foster the bourgeoisie.

The finances and tax scheme of the monarchs of Castile had already begun to take shape in the early thirteenth century. During the reign of Alfonso XI of Castile, the system reached maturity, including tariffs, the *alcabala* (a consumption and sales tax), the *servicio* (extraordinary grants), and the *tercias reales* (a two-ninths tax on the ecclesiastical tithe). The *alcabala* was particularly important, accounting for 90% of tax revenues in the mid-fourteenth century [11]. The indirect taxes and tariffs that constituted the tax base depended to a great deal on the wool and woolen fabric trade. Contributions were also made by the Mesta, an association of sheep raisers granted a royal charter in 1273, clearly demonstrating how important the wool industry and the wool trade were to Castile and to Spain as a whole. Such factors prevented Ferdinand and Isabella from adopting bold policies to consolidate their authority over the newly unified kingdom.

The kingdom that was instrumental in unifying Spain was not Aragon, with its sophisticated trade and powerful legislature, but rather Castile, with its traditional agricultural society—and this was a fact that would have a profound effect on Spain's future. Aragon's commercial foundation gradually eroded after the fourteenth century under continuing competition from Italian cities, and the kingdom's merchant class gradually became rentiers. During the same period, the people of Castile were eagerly seeking new lands to conquer and settle under the protection of the newly unified kingdom. When the unified kingdom conquered Granada in 1492, for example, 40,000 Castilians scrambled to migrate there. Under the unified kingdom, the Castilians were looking for new opportunities, just as their ancestors had done when they strove to conquer and plunder new lands in the hope of transcending the economic limits of agricultural society. This kind of opportunity came when Columbus set sail in 1492 [12].

Spain's Expansion Overseas

Spain's agricultural society had already begun expanding during the Reconquista, and now its expansion was oriented toward the larger world outside of Europe. Adam Smith once described the discovery of America and of the maritime route to the East Indies as the "two greatest and most important events recorded in the history of mankind," and both of those events began in Portugal and Spain [13]. Portugal was the earlier of the two states to turn its attention to sea routes. To be sure, Europeans had also been interested in the gold of Africa and the kingdom of Prester John prior to this. As evidence of this, we have the records of voyages to islands in the Atlantic Ocean by Genoese merchants in the late thirteenth century and by the Portuguese in the early fourteenth century. Even in the 1360s, soon after

Europe was devastated by the Black Death, the Portuguese and the Castilians vied for control of the Canary Islands.

But it was at the beginning of the fifteenth century that Spain and Portugal's maritime expansion began in earnest. After seizing Ceuta on the Strait of Gibraltar in 1415, the Portuguese moved into a number of Atlantic islands including Madeira and the Azores, and in 1500 they continued on to Greenland, Labrador, and Newfoundland. Even greater success came on the coast of Africa. In 1434, the Portuguese reached Cape Bojador, and after this they advanced to the Gulf of Guinea, the equator, and the Congo River. In 1488, they discovered the Cape of Good Hope, and in 1497, Vasco da Gama succeeded in sailing to India [14].

There is still debate among scholars about how Portugal—a small country on the fringe of Europe—was able to spearhead Europe's overseas expansion [15]. One factor that is frequently mentioned is Portugal's geography. Because of its long coastline and its proximity to the Atlantic Ocean and to Africa, scholars have said, the Portuguese were among the first to focus on the Atlantic Ocean. More recently, though, the emphasis has shifted from Portugal's geographical location to its position on the frontier between Europe and the Muslim world. As we have already mentioned, there was not only conflict but also various forms of economic and cultural exchange between Christians and Muslims, and Portugal used this exchange to accumulate commercial experience and wealth.

Since there was a long tradition of exchange between Muslims and the Mediterranean world, Portugal was also able to draw upon Mediterranean societies' knowledge and capital. It is well-known that capital provided by the merchants of Genoa and other Italian cities played an important role in Portugal's maritime expansion during its early period. Thus, scholars today think that the Portuguese not only used capital from the Mediterranean world but also acquired valuable technology and information, including navigational techniques, that were widely available in the Mediterranean at that time. In later days, Portugal is thought to have disseminated its own experience with navigating in the Atlantic Ocean to the people of other countries [16].

Portugal's maritime expansion was closely linked to religious fervor and the desire for commercial profit. This point is illustrated by the behavior of Prince Henry, called Henry the Navigator, who is frequently represented heroically in the history of Portugal's maritime expansion. While Henry is described as a prototypical Crusader who was devoted to spreading Christianity by crushing the Muslims in North Africa (and in Morocco in particular), his letters reveal a more commercial ambition: advancing into the interior of Africa in search of gold [17]. These ambitions were thwarted, however, by the Muslims' determined resistance.

After Henry's death, Portuguese merchants and adventurers established trading posts on the Atlantic coast of Africa and concentrated on acquiring luxury good such as gold, slaves, ivory, and malagueta pepper. As the volume of trade with this section of Africa increased, the Portuguese crown rescinded the monopolistic privileges it had given to certain individuals and instead put the Casa da Mina, located in Lisbon, in charge of registering merchant ships to Africa and of storing their trade goods. This was when the crown began to aggressively intervene in maritime activities [18].

Portugal's expansion appears to have greatly provoked the Spanish. The Castilians had been vying with the Portuguese over the Canary Islands since the mid-fourteenth century, and the strife between the two sides concluded with Portugal acknowledging Spain's control over the islands. On two occasions, in 1478 and 1482, Isabella dispatched military expeditions to complete the conquest. Spain's conquest of a chain of islands located about 80 kilometers from the continent of Africa and 1200 km from Spain both signaled that Spain had joined the competition over the seas and hinted at the form that Spain's colonial activity would take.

The conquest of the Canary Islands was initially directed not by the state but rather by merchants and adventurers. It was easier to conquer these islands than the Islamic trading cities, not only since they had a small indigenous population (less than 10,000 people) but also since they were located outside of the Muslim sphere of influence. During the 1450s, kidnapping the inhabitants of these islands and selling them as slaves in Spain was a booming business, while during the 1480s, merchants began to import dye and sugar from the islands. Some of the figures who aided and profited in these commercial matters were ministers of the queen [19].

The queen's officials were thus involved in the enterprises of merchants and adventurers, which culminated in the state officially annexing the territory and dividing the spoils among those who had taken part. When Isabella dispatched military expeditions to the Canary Islands, the cost was paid for out of the royal treasury and through a contract with a merchant's guild, and the distribution of land after the expedition was supervised by the crown. This sequence of events was similar to a custom during the Reconquista in which the crown made a contract (called a "capitulación") with the commanders of a military expedition and distributed the spoils of war and concessions for the new territory with those commanders. This custom was brought back into use when Spain began conquering territory overseas [20], and it was applied in the same way to Columbus's expedition. That was how the expansion of agricultural society known as the Reconquista spread across the Atlantic Ocean to America.

In the spring of 1492, Ferdinand and Isabella held a series of meetings with Columbus to negotiate the conditions of his expedition. Columbus made a number of demands in these negotiations: an aristocratic peerage; the titles of Admiral of the Ocean Sea, Governor-General, and Viceroy; the right to bequeath all of those privileges to his descendants; and the right to part of the tax revenues and proceeds from the expedition. That is to say, Columbus wanted to claim for his family all the new land conquered during the expedition as a sort of feudal fiefdom.

Surprisingly, Ferdinand and Isabella agreed to most of Columbus's demands, though this was because they did not initially expect much out of the voyage. When the voyage proved successful, however, the monarchs naturally enough had a change of heart. Looking for a pretext to revise their charter with Columbus, they ordered two legal reviews into Columbus's performance of the largely ceremonial duties of Governor-General. In the end, Columbus had to content himself with the title of Admiral of the Ocean Sea along with one-tenth of the produce of the new territory [21]. One reason the monarchs changed their mind was because they felt that Columbus had been given too many privileges. But a bigger reason was their concern that, if such a powerful aristocratic fiefdom was established in the colonies, it might threaten royal authority. Following this, Spain's colonies in the Americas belonged to the crown (at least legally speaking), which ensured that the territorial expansion of Spain's agricultural society could also take place in the Americas.

Thus, Ferdinand and Isabella's interest in maritime activity derived not from commercial profit but rather from the traditional strategy of maintaining and expanding the economic basis of agricultural society while strengthening the authority of the crown. It is only by bearing this in mind that we can understand the bizarre policies that the monarchs adopted in regard to the Jews and the Muslims. At the end of the fourteenth century, Jews who had converted to Catholicism, called *conversos,* were actively involved in public administration, the church, finance, and manual crafts. Even after Spain was unified, a considerable number of these *conversos* continued to hold powerful positions in the church and the bureaucracy. *Conversos* and unconverted Jews were also well-represented in the finance and handicraft industries. But this made the militant Catholics who had spread the ideology of the Reconquista concerned about the influence of the *conversos* and the Jews. In order to assuage such concerns and to achieve religious unity in the kingdom, Ferdinand and Isabella instituted a religious tribunal commonly known as the Spanish Inquisition. From the Inquisition's establishment in 1480 until 1492, around 3000 *conversos* were found guilty by the tribunal, and about 2000 of them were executed.

Despite these measures, suspicions that the *conversos* were being seduced by the Jews still in Spain did not die away, and there were frequent riots against the Jews. In 1492, Ferdinand and Isabella resorted to the extreme step of making it mandatory for the Jews to convert to Catholicism. The monarch assumed that most Jews would be baptized, but their assumption proved erroneous. The Jews—who had played such an important role in Spain's economy and politics—preferred banishment to conversion. Undeterred by this failure, Ferdinand and Isabella only expanded their persecution of non-Christians. In 1502, the monarchs issued a royal decree requiring all Muslims to convert, and in 1526 they began persecuting the converted Muslims, who were known as Moriscos. This continued until 1609, by which time around 300,000 Muslims and Moriscos are estimated to have left the Iberian Peninsula [22].

The reason that Ferdinand and Isabella carried out these measures despite the huge economic loss they entailed was because the monarchs believed that the only way to guarantee the future of the realm was by bolstering the royal authority in unified Spain, and especially in Castile. As a result of these measures, the political factionalism that had long plagued Castile was mitigated to some extent, stability was restored to Aragon after a period of economic decline, and political stability also aided the state's finances. By 1474, Castile's state revenue had decreased by nearly two-thirds during a period of extreme political instability. After the Catholic monarchs ascended the throne, however, the situation had greatly improved, and by

1504, state revenue had been restored to its 1406 level. Even during the reign of Ferdinand and Isabella, the sales tax and the contribution of the church accounted for 80% of regular crown revenue (of which eight-ninths came from the sales tax), and tariffs represented a significant portion as well. The crown had always had the authority to levy the sales tax without the consent of the Cortes. But even if this had not been the case, the Cortes was in no position to interfere, since its influence had waned considerably after Ferdinand and Isabella ascended the throne [23].

Considering that the population of Castile nearly doubled during the fifteenth century and that its economy was also growing rapidly, it could be surmised that increasing revenues did not place an onerous burden on the subjects of the kingdom [24]. But though Ferdinand and Isabella had consolidated the royal authority by resorting to extreme religious measures and though the crown's revenue had greatly increased, problems remained for the Spanish Empire. First of all, the issue of the landholding aristocrats had not been completely resolved. Not only were these aristocrats exempt from various taxes, including the *servicio*, but they also siphoned off a significant portion of the state revenue by levying taxes on their fief and by cutting deals with royal tax collectors. Furthermore, state revenue was being redistributed to the aristocrats in the form of salaries. For such reasons, the total income collected by aristocrats during the reign of Ferdinand and Isabella exceeded state revenue [25].

In contrast with the wealth of the landed aristocrats, the peasants who made up the bulk of the population continued to live in abject poverty, and there were no signs that their lot would improve. The rapid economic growth that began in Castile at the end of the fourteenth century depended upon sheep raising and wool and textile exports. This meant that the Castilian economy was closely tied to the economies of the Italian city-states and the Southern Netherlands, including Flanders. The profits from such trade went to the aristocrats, the sheep raisers in the Mesta, and the merchants in the coastal cities of Castile—but it did not improve living standards for the peasants who toiled to grow cereals.

Furthermore, the political unification of Spain did not move the country toward a unified market, and there were few changes in the structural factors that governed economic activity. Aside from a few cities, Spain remained divided into small regional markets, and there were no road improvements or other infrastructure projects that would stimulate the exchange of information and products [26]. More population growth under such conditions would only make life harder for the peasants, who were already in an economically vulnerable position. If the market was disrupted by weakening trade conditions or by external shocks such as wars, the plight of the peasants would get even worse.

On top of this, the method of governance in the unified kingdom of Spain was prone to exacerbate structural weaknesses in the state budget and the economy and to provoke serious conflicts both between and within regions. As we have already said, the unification of Spain began with the union of two royal families, and Ferdinand and Isabella did not seek to truly unify their kingdoms. As a consequence, the relations between the two monarchs and the subjects of their two kingdoms varied with the unique political cultures of those kingdoms. But other regions were also incorporated into the kingdom in the same manner, which frequently caused the Spanish monarchs to became embroiled in problems outside of the realm. This increased fiscal demand on the state, but no decision had been made about how to distribute this demand.

During the reign of the Catholic monarchs, Ferdinand (as king of the Crown of Aragon) had already increased the unified kingdom's expenditures as he meddled in the affairs of northern Italy. So in the 1490s, Spain had to begin issuing government bonds to cover the budget shortfall, despite higher tax receipts [27]. It was precisely because of such circumstances that bitter debate and conflict arose between different regions and even between the crown and other political factions in regard to who exactly would cover the increasing fiscal demand. The result was that the subjects of Castile had to shoulder a greater tax burden, since the crown had more authority there than in other regions [28].

Ferdinand and Isabella's union created a unified Christian kingdom on the Iberian Peninsula and laid the foundation for a vast empire that would eventually stretch across Europe, America, and Asia. Their union enabled Spain to emerge as a European power, and as their descendants continued to expand the empire's territory inside Europe, they would exercise enormous power over a trade network linking Europe, America, and Asia. At first blush, this new Spanish Empire appears to have satisfied all the requirements necessary to become an economic hegemon. Supported by unity on the Iberian Peninsula, conquests in Europe, and maritime expansion around the world, the empire seemingly represented a new economic system that combined the agriculture and industry of Europe, the commerce and industry that developed in Asia, and the raw materials and metal deposits of Africa and the Americas.

But during the reign of Ferdinand and Isabella, the Spanish Empire was unable to transcend the basic economic logic of agricultural society. Spain's conquest and settlement of colonies during this period merely replicated the dynamic of the Reconquista (seizing land and loot through wars of conquest), albeit under the control of more powerful monarchs. Ultimately, Spain failed to tie this dynamic to its domestic commercial and industrial activities. Furthermore, while Spain's persecution of the *conversos* and Moriscos may have helped achieve religious and ideological unity under the crown, it was a costly economic sacrifice. The result was that the economic activity of unified Spain was concentrated in primary industries like sheep raising.

As Spain attempted to build an empire on this shaky foundation and to meet the military and fiscal demands that imperial expansion required, life became even harder for the peasants who propped up agricultural society. In the end, there was no alternative that could have enabled the Spanish Empire to overcome the diminishing economic growth that limits agricultural society. But since the Spanish Empire still faced the challenges of insufficient land and a growing population, it focused once again on expanding its territory. These shortcomings of agricultural empires are clearly illustrated by the history of the Spanish Empire after the deaths of Ferdinand and Isabella.

The Not-So-Golden Age of the Agricultural Empire: From Charles V to Philip II

Isabella died in 1504, and after the regencies of Ferdinand (1504–1516) and Cisneros (1516–1517), the unified kingdom of Spain underwent another major change. With the coronation of Charles I—the son of Philip of the House of Hapsburg and Joanna, daughter of Ferdinand and Isabella—Spain merged with the kingdom of the Hapsburgs. After becoming king of Spain, Charles I paid exorbitant bribes to be elected Holy Roman Emperor (his title here being Charles V). This made him without doubt the most powerful monarch in Europe [29]. Charles ruled a world empire that included not only the Low Countries, parts of today's Germany and Australia, and the unified kingdom of Spain, but also Naples, Sicily, and vast colonies in the West Indies and the Americas.

It would seem obvious that Charles now exercised hegemony in Europe, considering that he controlled more than half of the territory of Western Europe, the population and wealth of those lands, and most importantly the supply of precious metals in the Americas. But possessing an empire was one thing, and running it something else entirely. Furthermore, it is unclear whether the empire was even economically beneficial for Spain. Immediately after the ascension of Charles, the people of Spain, and particularly those living in Castile, had their doubts about what exactly this sprawling empire meant to them, and whether they would get anything out of it, as historian Henry Kamen has observed [30].

Indeed, the first consequence this had for the Spanish people was that their monarch no longer resided solely in Spain. Even during the reign of Ferdinand and Isabella, the subjects of the Crown of Aragon had been dissatisfied with the fact that Ferdinand, their king, had to stay in Castile. But the changes brought by Charles' coronation were of a different magnitude altogether. Charles had not been born in Spain, and at first he could not even speak the language of Castile, which led him to surround himself with courtiers from the Low Countries and from the Hapsburg lands. Under these circumstances, the Castilians were concerned that their new king would care more about other parts of the empire than Castile while demanding that they remain loyal to the empire and make economic sacrifices. These concerns ultimately erupted in the Revolt of the Comuneros in 1520 [31]. While the revolt was put down before Charles returned to Castile, it foreshadowed the conflicts that would later erupt in various parts of the empire.

Charles only resided in Spain for 16 of his 40 years on the throne, since he had to spend most of his time on the battlefield or touring the various parts of the empire. Charles was confronted with a few fundamental problems—how was he supposed to rule the empire under such circumstances or to bind together his diverse imperial subjects—but he never found solutions to these problems. While his empire was so immense that it came close to the Christian ideal of the "universal monarchy," he regarded the various kingdoms that composed the empire in exactly the same way as Ferdinand and Isabella [32]. Charles also saw the empire as property that he had inherited. Therefore, the various kingdoms in that empire only established personal relationships with Charles while retaining their own institutions, laws, and customs. Essentially, the universality of this universal monarchy was buried under the unique characteristics of its constituent regions.

Of course, resolving the latent conflicts between the various kingdoms in the empire was an important task. To that end, Charles not only perpetuated the viceroy system but also set up various councils through which the political elites of each kingdom could serve as his ministers, and he used these elites to look into and attempt to address the troubles and grievances of each region. This strategy certainly had some success, considering that the empire continued to survive amid unceasing wars and a number of fiscal crises. But there were still two fundamental problems. In order to maintain the empire, Charles had to review and personally address petitions from all over the empire. Since this required an immense amount of time and effort, his success ultimately depended on his personal ability. In addition, these separate vertical relationships between emperor and kingdoms did not guarantee the integration of the various political systems inside the empire. That is to say, the people of Castile (who were in the unusual position of having Charles as both king and emperor) did not have a shared identity with the people of Sicily or the Netherlands, though they were all subjects of the Spanish Empire.

If peace had been maintained in the empire, this structural vulnerability might not have been a serious problem. But there was no guarantee of peace during the reign of Charles. Though Charles did not himself describe his vast empire as a "universal monarchy," the monarchs of kingdoms on his borders could not help feeling concerned about their safety. One such kingdom was France under the House of Valois. Given that France was almost entirely surrounded by the territory of the Spanish Empire, it was obliged to confront the Spanish Empire to escape from its predicament. Even before Charles ascended the throne, Spain and France were engaged in a power struggle for the Italian Peninsula. Caught between these two great powers, the petty states of Italy threw themselves into diplomatic and military machinations that plunged Europe into even greater confusion.

But those were not the only challenges that Charles faced. He could not afford to ignore the Ottoman Empire, which was looking to expand into Europe. Since the Ottomans were threatening the Italian city-states, Sicily, and Austria, Charles was forced to resist it to protect not only his own empire but also the larger Christian world. Complicating things even further was the Reformation, which led to conflict and then war with Protestant rulers. This eventually jeopardized religious unity within the Spanish Empire [33].

As the storm of war and religious strife continued to rage, Spain itself appeared peaceful. War did not visit the country, and there was no serious unrest involving the Protestants there. But Spain was stuck with the ballooning cost of running the empire. While Charles was fighting wars elsewhere in Europe, Castile had to remain on a war footing, raising armies and funds to support them.

Of course, Charles contended that his wars were ultimately in the interest of his Spanish subjects. The truth was that many Spaniards took part in Charles' struggle against "pagans and heretics" and had their taste of the glory of the Reconquista. As John Elliott has said, such experiences may have boosted the Spaniards' morale, but they came at an enormous social and economic cost. Aside from the fiscal burden and the human losses brought by these wars, they also had the effect of further entrenching Spanish aristocrats' glorification of militant Christianity and the wars of conquest based on the tradition of the Reconquista [34]. Even if the Spanish managed to endure these sacrifices, however, it was unclear whether they would be able to survive in the rapidly changing and expanding global economy of the sixteenth century.

One possible solution for the Spanish was their colonies in the New World. After the potential of Atlantic trade became clear following Columbus's voyages, Spain enacted a series of measures to monopolize commercial profit. The colonies in the Americas were made the possessions of the Castilian crown, and only Castilians were allowed to trade with the colonies. In 1503, the Casa de Contratación, a government trading house, was set up in Seville to regulate colonial merchant ships. This meant that all merchant ships on the Atlantic had to depart from Seville and return there again. But despite these measures, foreigners found ways (both legal and illegal) to take part in Atlantic trade, and for a time Charles even granted them permission to do so. Furthermore, Seville's monopoly remained a source of frustration until 1529, when several ports on the Atlantic coast were partially opened to Atlantic trade. But Seville's status as monopoly was confirmed in the 1530s, and it served as the center of Spain's Atlantic trade until Cádiz assumed that role in 1680.

While Castile was taking various measures to monopolize profit from trade on the Atlantic, Spaniards continued to explore, conquer, and settle the New World. Columbus's goals can be summarized as gold, spices, and the conversion of the Indians, but he did not find any gold mines or spices. All that Columbus brought back to Spain were a few kinds of tropical fruit, a small amount of precious metals, and some Indians. Spanish explorers after Columbus followed his example by plundering the natives' possessions and forcing them to find gold for them [35]. When the explorers had exhausted the potential of plundering (and massacring) the Indians on the Caribbean islands, they turned to the mainland. This represented a revival of the tradition of the Reconquista. The conquistadors (as the warring explorers were called) continued to take new territory and build new towns. Some had native workers look for gold, others grew crops on plantations to send to Spain, and still others began breeding the livestock they had brought with them. This process of conquest and settlement resulted in Cortés's defeat of the Aztec Empire in 1519 and Pizarro's victory over the Inca Empire in 1531. Early on during the period of conquest, the main items that Spain imported from the Americas were gold and agricultural products like indigo and cochineal. But with the discovery of silver deposits in the 1540s, trade on the Atlantic entered a new phase [36]. The silver mines that began operating at Potosí in 1545 and in Mexico in 1546 marked the beginning of the "silver cycle." As a result, 85 tons of silver a year were mined in the late 1540s, 150–160 tons a year between the 1550s and 1570s, and 280 tons a year in the late 1580s. Of this silver, 18 tons a year was brought to Spain in the 1540s, 94 tons a year in the 1560s, 112 tons a year in the 1570s, and no less than 271 tons a year in the 1590s [37]. Silver production was able to increase so rapidly in the New World because of the adoption of the silver amalgamation process and the effective use of the Inca empire's mandatory public service system, known as the *mit'a* [38]. The *mit'a* system in particular was a good fit for the Spanish conquistadors, who saw the silver that the Indians mined as being comparable to the spoils of war or the rent that Castilian aristocrats collected from the peasants who farmed their land. Since this silver was dug from the ground by Indian workers, it is fair to say that the true treasure of the Spanish Empire was the Indians' labor, as Timothy Parsons has observed [39].

The effect that the massive amount of silver mined in the Americas had on the economies of Spain and of Europe has typically been discussed in relation to the debate about the Price Revolution. This debate can be summed up as a theoretical and empirical reassessment of the classic study by Earl Hamilton. Hamilton argued that the American silver that flowed into Spain triggered inflation, causing the price of manufactured goods and cereals to increase faster than wages. This in turn resulted in the rapid accumulation of capital and the development of capitalism in Europe, Hamilton said. The conclusion reached in this long academic debate is that the chain of cause and effect between the influx of silver, the increase in the price of manufactured goods, and the accumulation of capital is not as simple as Hamilton thought. This conclusion also lends support to the view that the rising prices were actually caused by fluctuations in real economic factors including population and production [40]. For the purposes of this book, however, the mechanism of the Price Revolution and other such theoretical issues are not as important as the effect that the influx of silver had on the Spanish economy and its fiscal situation.

First of all, inflation was accompanied by a major decrease in Spanish wool exports and a reduction in the size of the sheep breeding industry after the 1550s. As a result, the landowners who had a vested interest in sheep breeding saw their incomes fall. These landowners then put more pressure on peasants in the form of higher rents, which further worsened income inequality. As wool production and the textile trade declined, overall trading conditions in Spain deteriorated. Traditionally, Spain had exported a few crops and raw materials such as wool from the primary industrial sector while importing its cereals and manufactured products. But as trade conditions worsened, the Spanish economy was saddled with a gradually increasing trade deficit. In contrast, the people who profited from the influx of silver bought more imported goods that had been manufactured overseas while using a substantial portion of their profits to invest in real estate or government bonds or to procure public office. As a consequence, productive investment did not increase. Because of these structural problems, the silver that flowed into Spain flowed out again to various parts of Europe [41].

Did Spain's American colonies help it resolve its trade deficit? As we will see later, the Netherlands and England earned massive profits by re-exporting manufactured goods and Asian products to their Atlantic colonies. These profits helped those states compensate for the chronic trade deficit that formed after they entered the highly developed Asian trading network and began importing spices and other luxury goods. Spain obviously also had a chance to trade with its American colonies in this manner. Furthermore, since the Spaniards who settled in the New World were pathologically averse to adapting to the local customs and material culture, they relied on imports for nearly all of the items that they consumed on a daily basis. This fact suggests that Castile had an opportunity to promote manufacturing and exports at home. Indeed, Castilians were well aware of this opportunity, which is why they quickly adopted a system similar to the Navigation Acts enacted by England. The Castilian system banned the colonies from producing anything that could compete with domestic producers, restricted the trading activities of foreign merchants, and made Seville the sole port of trade.

But since inflation prevented Spanish manufacturers from achieving price competitiveness, they were unable to satisfy the demand in the colonies. In addition, Spanish merchants could not compete with foreign merchants who could draw upon a commercial network and great amounts of capital and credit. Even worse, as silver production increased, Spanish merchants who lived in the Americas began to trade directly with merchants from other parts of Europe and Asia in defiance of domestic regulations. The inevitable result was that the profits earned by Spanish merchants and manufacturers in the American colonies gradually decreased [42]. In other words, the Spanish Empire failed to create a system that could maximize the potential of its American economies to become a source of raw materials and a commodity market. In the end, Spain's colonies proved to be little more than a launchpad for the growth of the commercial economy in the Netherlands, with its system of expansive reinvestment, and the first industrial economy in England, which succeeded in transitioning from the system of expansive reinvestment to the system of expansive reproduction.

The influx of silver also had a negative influence on the political system. Since we will be examining in more detail later how the influx of silver affected the fiscal affairs of Charles V and his descendants, at this point it will suffice to mention that the influx of silver strengthened the authority of the monarch at the expense of traditional representative bodies. A portion of the silver that was produced in the Americas was reserved for the monarch of Castile, which greatly assisted the crown's fiscal predicament. Not only did the silver pouring into the royal treasury improve the kingdom's cash flow, but it also provided Charles and the monarchs who came after him with collateral for issuing government bonds and for taking out loans from the great bankers of Europe.

The Cortes, the representative body that was supposed to check the royal authority, had absolutely no control over this crucial source of royal income. The Cortes of Castile had always been weaker than the representative bodies in the Crown of Aragon or other regions of the empire, and its authority was weakened even further by the appearance of a source of revenue that the monarch was free to use without its consent. This ultimately eroded the political influence of the merchants and the other urban commercial and manufacturing interests represented by the Cortes and forestalled the development of commercial society [43].

With the Cortes no longer functioning as an institutional check on the royal authority, Charles fought numerous wars. The greatest threat to the empire was France, a country that was rich in land, population, and resources. Charles was rivals with Francis I, the king of France, in the election for Holy Roman Emperor, and their rivalry continued for more than a generation after that historic election, or more precisely until 1559. Charles' election meant that France would spend many exhausting years trying to end its encirclement by a huge empire that included the kingdom of the Hapsburgs, Spain, and the Holy Roman Empire. But there were ways for France to turn this into a strategic advantage. For example, the French kings Francis I and Henry II managed to force Charles to fight simultaneous wars on three fronts—in Italy, the Netherlands, and Spain. Charles had to raise a multinational force to fight France in Italy and the Netherlands while also raising a Spanish army to protect Navarre and Catalonia.

Charles was generally successful in his wars with France. He beat back repeated French attacks on the Southern Netherlands, and he managed to add several key strategic positions in the northeast part of the Netherlands to his empire. Furthermore, his defense of Naples and Milan in Italy enabled him to extend the empire's sway over the neighboring states of Piacenza and Mantua. While Charles had to hand over Florence to the Medici family in Tuscany, he was able to exert control over several strategic positions on the Tuscan coast that he brought into Naples' sphere of influence. Charles also recruited Andrea Doria, a powerful figure in Genoa, in 1528, and used the fiefs of Naples and commercial privileges there to lure the ruling elite of Genoa to his side. This enabled Charles to secure Genoa's powerful fleet as well as long-term loans from the city's bankers. Thus, Spain largely regained its influence over the Italian Peninsula, which at the time was the wealthiest part of Europe.

But Charles' long wars with France prevented him from dealing with the other threats to the Spanish Empire. For example, the empire's eastern flank was exposed to the Ottoman Empire. During the fourteenth and fifteenth centuries, the Turks had pursued an expansionist policy. They subdued most of Hungary in 1526 and besieged the Austrian city of Vienna on two occasions, in 1529 and 1530. The Ottoman Empire had a huge population and abundant resources at its disposal, and Charles was hard-pressed to fight them and France at the same time. In the end, he was forced to end the conflict and agreed to a truce with the Ottomans in 1547.

At the same time, Charles also had to combat the Protestants reformers. Aside from being a devout Catholic, Charles firmly believed that he was obliged as Holy Roman Emperor to defend the church and Christendom. He thought that the German princes and free imperial cities that were participating in the Reformation were only interested in the Catholic Church's assets and incomes. While this gave Charles a clear rationale to attack the Protestants, he lacked the means to put his intentions and convictions into action. Therefore, he chose compromise instead of coercion (with the Peace of Augsburg in 1530 and the Diet of Regensburg in 1541). But despite these efforts, he was ultimately entangled in religious wars because of the uncooperative attitude of the Catholics and Protestants.

Charles' wars demanded a tremendous economic sacrifice [44]. As we noted earlier, there was no central body that Charles could use to govern the Spanish Empire, and fiscal responsibilities including tax collection followed the practices and customs of the empire's various regions and institutions. While we will not enter into a detailed discussion of the fiscal structure and conditions of each of these regions here, there are two points that merit our attention. First, Charles's ability to acquire the resources he needed to run the empire and prosecute its wars was determined by the degree of political power held by the various regions' representative bodies. Consequently, a greater fiscal burden fell on Castile than in Aragon or the Netherlands because the crown was relatively powerful in Castile, whereas the Cortes had the upper hand in Aragon and representative bodies had developed in various parts of the Netherlands.

Second, the subjects of each imperial region were vertically connected to their monarch (often through courtiers who spoke on their behalf), but since Charles regarded the empire in its entirety as his possession, he saw no problem with transferring income earned in one region to another. But redistributing income around the empire like this carried a considerable political cost. A good example was the Dutch Revolt, which was provoked because of just such redistribution. Nevertheless, income transfers and redistribution continued while Charles was on the throne, and the region that bore the brunt of it was Castile.

We have a fairly good understanding of the extent to which Castile contributed to the Spanish Empire's finances. In Castile's fiscal system, the crown's income can be divided roughly into regular taxes and extraordinary income and contributions. The greater part of these regular taxes consisted of the *alcabala*, the *tercias reales,* various consumption taxes, and tariffs, while extraordinary income included the *servicio*, the ecclesiastical contribution, and silver from the Americas. Even during the reign of Charles, the *alcabala* still made up the largest amount of budget revenue (between 40 and 45%), while the *servicio* and the ecclesiastical contribution increased to around 20% [45]. Through such sources of revenue, the crown's income is estimated to have increased fourfold between 1522 and 1560 [46]. According to another estimate that compares the crown's average yearly earnings in the 1520s and the 1540s, the income that Charles received from Castile (population of 6 million) was around 1.8 million ducats in the 1520s and 2.27 million ducats in the 1540s. During the same period, his income from Naples (population of 2.1 million) rose from 900,000 ducats to 2 million ducats, and his income from the Netherlands (population of 2.17 million) rose from 500,000 ducats to 730,000 ducats [47].

How much of Charles' revenue came from the silver that was shipped over from the Americas? First of all, the portion of the American silver output that was reserved for the king (called the *quinto real* and part of the crown's extraordinary income) only amounted to 40,000 ducats in the 1520s. By the 1540s, however, this had increased to 280,000 ducats, and it represented an increasingly large share of the crown's income after Charles. But there was also income derived from this silver that was not reflected in the crown's income. The crown forced individuals who brought silver from the Americas to use that silver to buy government bonds (called *juros*). This method was used with greater frequency later, when Spain's fiscal situation deteriorated. But the real value of the silver brought in from the American colonies cannot be gauged from its face value alone. Once the colonial silver began to flow into Spain, it provided the crown with a very attractive form of collateral for international bankers. This collateral enabled Charles to take out even bigger loans [48].

Charles had a truly astounding amount of debt. Between 1521 and 1555, Charles secured around 28 million ducats in loans from international bankers, with their payment guaranteed by Castile. Most of the bankers who provided these loans were foreigners. Around 64% of the 28 million ducats was loaned by seven German and Genoese banking families, while only 7% was loaned by Spaniards. Since this amount also includes outstanding debt from previous years, it is in fact unclear how much was taken out in additional loans each year [49]. Since this figure also omits bankers' fees, some have even estimated that the total amount of money that Castile had to repay was not 28 million ducats but 38 million ducats. Regardless, repaying this immense debt required Charles to go to extreme lengths, and he raised taxes and issued government bonds. By 1557, though, Spain had yet to pay 12 million ducats of the principal. Philip II ultimately resorted to the desperate measure of defaulting on these loans [50].

What kind of effect did the rapidly increasing fiscal burden have on the Castilian economy? At least until 1580, Spain's gross domestic product continued to increase (amid a time of general expansion in Europe and the global economy). Even taking inflation into account, one could conclude that the tax burden had not become too heavy for Castilians to bear [51]. But we must also pay heed to the troubling signs that are not reflected in these estimates. Since, as we have already said, Castile's social structure and political institutions did not mitigate but only aggravated the inequity of the tax burden, it is necessary to examine how the tax burden and real wages of farmers and other producers actually changed and what the situation was like during and after the reign of Philip II, who retained the fiscal system that Charles had used.

Another point to consider is that most of the loans (which were several times larger than the crown's average annual income) were provided by foreign bankers. In other words, Castile's finances were at the mercy of foreign bankers. To be sure, the amount of foreign debt was reduced considerably during Charles' reign, but what remained of the principal still amounted to more than six times Castile's yearly income. Given the increasing cost of running the empire (and fighting its wars) during Charles' reign, he inevitably became more dependent on foreign loans.

The Castilian fiscal structure had already become precarious, and during the reign of Philip II, who assumed the throne in 1556, this structure almost collapsed. Philip treated the Spanish Empire as his personal possession just as Charles had, and instead of reforming the empire's institutions, he depended during his rule on the personal relationships he had formed with the empire's various kingdoms.

Philip differed from Charles, however, in how he chose to manage these vertical personal relationships. Whereas Charles had maintained ties with the ruling elites of each region by traveling through the realm for almost his entire reign, Philip's approach was to remain at the center of the empire while observing and manipulating the events that were happening in it. This approach is symbolized by Philip's decision in 1561 to move his capital to the Castilian city of Madrid, which was virtually unknown at the time. While this made clear that Castile was the center of the empire, it simultaneously provoked concerns that the Castilians would gain a monopoly on the empire's management. This was a very troubling development for the ruling elites of other kingdoms in the empire who had hitherto maintained a close relationship with the emperor [52].

But this change does not seem to have been enough to shore up the empire's fiscal structure and consolidate the imperial rule. During Philip's reign, the empire had to confront the threat of England and a revolt in its own territory in addition to the existing challenges of France and the Ottoman Empire [53]. France was less of a problem for Spain after 1559, when the death of King Henry II plunged the country for nearly 40 years into a conflict between Catholics and Protestants that was nearly a civil war.

But Spain could not afford to let its guard down, and Philip kept a close watch on the conflict in France. On the one hand, if the Protestant Huguenots were victorious, they would pose a genuine threat to the Spanish Empire, which claimed to represent the Catholic faith. On the other hand, even if the Catholics ended up winning, there was no guarantee that they would maintain friendly relations with the Spanish Empire. After 1589, Philip meddled in French politics for nearly a decade by helping the French Catholics who were on good terms with him and encouraging them to keep fighting the Huguenots. When Huguenot leader Henry of Navarre (later Henry IV, king of France) seized power, Philip chose the more aggressive approach of invading France himself.

But France was not as severe a problem as the revolt that broke out in the Low Countries, which played a key economic role in the Spanish Empire. Since the Dutch Revolt and the subsequent war for independence will be discussed in Chap. 3 , for now we will only look briefly at how the revolt affected Philip's management of the empire. The revolt was caused by a combination of factors, but it is clear that the Dutch people's longstanding dissatisfaction about the economic and fiscal cost of defending the empire provoked conflict between the local elites and the imperial authorities.

The Dutch elites were disquieted by several changes that occurred after Philip came to the throne. First, important positions in the church and the government were being given not to the local nobility but rather to Philip's associates at his court in Brussels. Second, new dioceses were being established in what appeared to be an attempt to reorganize and strengthen the Catholic Church. The elites were also growing anxious that debate over the heresy laws and the rumored establishment of an inquisition in the Netherlands would incite conflict between Catholics and Protestants.

Under these circumstances, Philip decided to put down by force the local nobility who were questioning his policies. In 1576, he dispatched the Duke of Alba to govern the Low Countries in place of his half-sister Margaret of Parma, who had been a moderate governor, and he began to systematically oppress suspected heretics and the recalcitrant nobility [54]. The Duke of Alba managed to repel an army of mercenaries led by William of Orange, who had fled to Germany. But when Alba introduced a sales tax similar to the *alcabala*, it alienated not only the nobility but also the merchants and manufacturers who were in financial straits because of the recession of 1571 and 1572. As a result, the revolt engulfed the entire region. Political and religious conflict combined with frustration about fiscal policy to arouse long-dormant dissatisfaction with the empire. In the ensuing war, the empire under Philip II never managed to gain the advantage. Instead, steeply climbing military expenditures and frequent mutinies in Spanish armies caused the crisis to spread across the entire empire [55].

The Dutch Revolt lasted for nearly 80 years (and indeed is also known as the Eighty Years War). One of the main reasons that the revolt dragged on for so long is that Philip was unable to concentrate on the Dutch problem at the beginning of the war. The rebels' morale suffered a heavy blow when the Duke of Alba defeated forces led by William and Nassau in 1568. If Philip had recalled Alba at that point and visited the local nobility himself to restore his relationship with them while bringing resolution to the religious strife, the subsequent events would have played out much differently.

But in 1568, Philip was dealing with a personal tragedy—the loss of his son and only heir—and he also had to put down a revolt by the Moriscos in Granada. Until the early 1570s, Philip was distracted from the Netherlands by conflict with the Muslims in North Africa and in the Mediterranean. In keeping with Philip's belief that he was the guardian of the Catholic world, he established the Holy League with the Italian city-states to check the Muslims who were threatening Venice. In 1571, Philip led the Holy League to victory over the Muslims at the naval battle of Lepanto [56]. But this victory did not completely vanquish the Muslims, and Philip had to dedicate a substantial portion of the royal revenue to military action in the Mediterranean in 1572 as well. As long as Spain held to the vision of a "universal monarchy," it had no choice but to assume such responsibility.

Despite the fiscal strain caused by the Dutch Revolt and the conflict with the Ottoman Turks, Philip's wars continued. In 1580, he annexed Portugal. While he had assumed that this would ease his fiscal troubles and give him the advantage in Asian commerce, Portugal's commercial position in Asia had already been weakened by then. If anything, annexing Portugal did less to assist Spain's economy than to further strain the empire's already overextended budget by increasing the amount of empire that had to be defended [57].

But what was even more harmful was the conflict with England. Not only was English piracy (which began in earnest after Queen Elizabeth I took the throne) seriously damaging Spanish trade in the Atlantic, but Philip also believed that England was funding the Dutch rebels. Concluding that war with England was unavoidable, he began preparing for war in the early 1580s. After England learned about these preparations, it launched expeditions targeting strongholds such as Brill and allowed the ships of Francis Drake to raid not only Spanish colonies but also Spanish ports. Because of the strain on Spain's budget, it took Philip a long time to prepare for hostilities with England: his forces did not go to war until July 1588. The war ended in the crushing defeat of Spain's "invincible" armada because of tactical miscalculations, inferior weaponry and hostile weather conditions, including a severe storm. Philip sought to challenge England several more times after that, but it was already too late for the Spanish Empire to regain its supremacy on the sea.

Philip's foreign policy and wars only exacerbated the empire's already fragile fiscal situation. During the early part of his reign, Philip had to dedicate most of his regular income to paying the interest on state debt acquired by his predecessors, and he employed every possible means to increase such income. Toward this end, he imposed a tariff on wool exports, appropriated all the tariffs collected at the trading ports in northern Castile, and even made salt farms a royal monopoly [58]. But despite such efforts, Philip's regular income was insufficient to cover both the interest on the government loans and the rapidly increasing military costs. For example, 9 million ducats were transferred to the Flanders region between 1571 and 1575, when the Dutch Revolt was in full swing, to cover military expenditures. This amount exceeded by far the entire value of precious metals (4 million ducats) imported to Spain from the Americas during the same period [59].

The growing fiscal burden at last compelled Philip to turn to the Cortes of Castile for assistance. The Cortes had already gained control of the *alcabala* (which accounted for the greatest part of the state's revenue) in 1525. In contracts between the crown and the Cortes called *encabezamiento,* the Cortes guaranteed that the crown would receive a certain amount of yearly income for a certain period of time, with the cities collecting the *alcabala*. In 1573, Philip began asking the Cortes to increase the amount of the *encabezamiento*, and in 1575, he was granted an amount nearly three times greater than before.

This increase forced the cities that were collecting the *alcabala* to greatly increase their tax rate, which caused the contracting economy to shrink even further. The city of Medina del Campo, for example, had to raise the tax rate from the previous level of 1.2 to 10% after 1575. Along with Philip's third suspension of payments to creditors in 1575, this caused the collapse of the markets held in that city. Under such conditions, the *encabezamiento* of 1577 had to be reduced by more than 25%.

When it became impossible to further increase the regular income, Castile's royal finances came to rely more on extraordinary income [60]. What prevented Castile's fiscal collapse (at least for the time) was the precious metals flowing in from the Americas. Income from precious metals had only been 3.9 million ducats in 1571, but between 1581 and 1585 this increased to 9 million ducats, and between 1596 and 1600, toward the end of Philip's reign, it reached 13 million ducats [61]. But despite the influx of precious metals, the crown could not cover the cost of its continuing wars. In 1590, Philip reached out to the cities once again and persuaded them to implement the *millones*, a tax on basic foodstuffs. The cities agreed to provide 8 million ducats to the crown over the next six years, and they were allowed to decide for themselves how to raise that money. In 1596, the *millones* increased to 1.3 million ducats a year, and in 1600 a yearly tax of 3 million ducats was levied on meat and other consumer goods [62].

Despite his best efforts, Philip was obliged in 1596 to once more default on his payments. This placed Medina del Campo and other commercial centers on an irreversible path of decline [63]. According to fiscal reports drafted in 1598, when Philip III assumed the throne upon Philip II's death, the fiscal situation in Castile looked irremediable. These reports projected that there would be a budget deficit of

1.6 million ducats every year through 1603 and that the only hope was the precious metals being imported from the American colonies and extraordinary income such as ecclesiastical contributions.

But the influx of precious metals rapidly declined from their peak in 1600, and Philip III also had to ask the Cortes for help. When negotiations with the Cortes broke down, Castile suspended payments once more in 1607. The Spanish Empire was no longer able to raise the money it needed to wage war, and in 1609 it finally had to agree to a 12-year truce with the Netherlands. This truce looked like a chance for Castile and the Spanish Empire to improve their fiscal situation. But military spending did not fall as much as expected, and when war resumed in 1623, military spending increased at an even faster rate.

Around that time, the Spanish Empire managed to secure 12 million ducats' worth of loans from foreign bankers, but before long the bankers of Genoa, the most important source of foreign loans, cut off funding. After this, Spain explored every possible means of making up for the resulting shortfall—taxing the *juros*, devaluing the currency, and selling concessions—but such efforts brought few results. The crown even resorted to demanding contributions (euphemistically called "donations") from the cities. The crown's authority had already been compromised during several rounds of negotiations with the Cortes, and these measures weakened it even further while strengthening the political clout of the nobility and other members of the privileged classes [64].

Decline of the Agricultural Empire

The proximate cause for the irreparable deterioration of fiscal affairs in the Crown of Castile and the Spanish Empire as a whole was the rapid increase of military spending, but this does not fully explain why Spain could not finance its military activities. As we shall see in the next two chapters, the Netherlands and England reinforced their fiscal structure and enjoyed sustained economic development while supporting even greater military expenditures than the Spanish Empire.

Thus, to understand the weakened fiscal situation in the Spanish Empire, we must take a look at the economic circumstances that were supporting the empire's finances. Particular attention should be paid to the situation in Castile because, as we have previously observed, Castile played the most important role in the empire's finances and also because much is known about the economic situation there. After the 1590s, Castile's economy rapidly deteriorated: the population fell, the cities shrank, the manufacturing sector contracted, and overseas trade declined. While the Castilian crisis was part of what has been called the seventeenth century crisis, this crisis appears to have had an unusually severe impact on Castile and the rest of Spain [65].

During the sixteenth century, the Spanish economy grew rapidly despite a number of structural problems including an overdependence on exports of specific products, weaknesses in cereal cultivation, and the unfair tax burden. Spain's population increased from 6 million at the beginning of the sixteenth century to 8 million in the 1580s, and the population of the major cities swelled even faster. Seville, the center of Atlantic trade, became a large city of 100,000 people, while the population of the manufacturing hub of Córdoba grew by 83% between 1530 and 1587.

As prices increased overall, such population growth caused rents to rise and profits to grow while the markets became more vibrant. For these reasons, the manufacturing sector and foreign trade grew rapidly as well. Between the 1530s and the 1580s, urban centers of wool and silk production like Toledo, Granada, Segovia, and Córdoba remained competitive not only in the domestic market but also in the Portuguese, Italian, and American markets. Exports of wool (a traditional Spanish export product) remained brisk until the 1560s, while textile exports showed no clear signs of decline until 1610 [66]. Because the economy remained so vital, there was no serious socioeconomic crisis at least until the 1580s despite the rapidly increasing tax burden.

But growth started to slow in the 1590s. While the population had already begun to decline when the birth rate ebbed in the 1580s, the decisive drop came between 1599 and 1600 as a result of famine and an outbreak of plague. During this period, the population of Castile fell by about 10%, and it shrank several more times in subsequent years (1605–1607, 1615–1616, and 1647) because of plague and famine [67].

The population decline was particularly severe in industrial and commercial centers. Two good examples are Segovia and Toledo, centers of the textile industry that flourished in the late sixteenth century. Segovia's population fell from 25,000 in 1580 to less than half of that in the mid-seventeenth century, while Toledo's population was reduced from 60,000 in 1571 to 20,000 in 1631. Circumstances were similar at Medina del Campo, the site of Spain's most important regular market. In 1561, the city had a population of 15,000, but by 1626, this had fallen to 5373 [68]. The decline in urban populations represented not only the absolute population decrease caused by the plague but also growing migration prompted by the contraction of manufacturing and commerce. As a consequence, the population of Madrid, the new capital of Castile, soared between 1561 and 1630 (from 30,000 to 130,000) [69].

The crisis in the agricultural sector appears to have been the result of sixteenth century expansion. As the population grew in the sixteenth century, demand steadily increased for agricultural products such as cereals, olives, and grapes, which resulted in a massive expansion of cultivated land. Spain's predicament exemplified the limits of agricultural society. In agricultural society, production hardly ever increases because of technological advancements, so the typical way to raise production is through cultivating more land (by farming marginal land and converting woods and pastures into farms). But this upsets the balance between farms, woods, and pastures, which decreases the supply of livestock needed to till the fields and reduces productivity once again. In Spain, this was compounded by inclement weather conditions in the 1590s, reducing agricultural output even further. During the first half of the seventeenth century, agricultural production in Castile fell by more than 30%, and since per capita grain production did not increase as the population shrank, productivity remained stagnant as well [70].

This phenomenon appears to have been the result of the power dynamic between peasants and landowners shifting in favor of landowners. Because of the steep rise in rents and the increasing tax burden, more than 40% of peasants' income went to pay rents and taxes. As the burden on peasants grew heavier, more of them left the land, and big landowners steadily increased their holdings by buying up land and seizing public land for themselves. Demand for wool had fallen since the mid-sixteenth century because of the war in the Netherlands and the decline of the Spanish and Italian textile industries, but in the early seventeenth century, demand began to rebound as the wool fabric industry recovered in England and elsewhere. The big landowners responded by hurrying to convert the fields where they had had grown cereals into pastures. These trends combined to further intensify polarization in rural areas [71].

The manufacturing sector was in trouble with rising prices reducing its competitiveness and the growing fiscal burden reducing demand. There were other ways in which the government's deteriorating fiscal conditions had a negative impact on the manufacturing industry. As the crown suspended payments on its debts several times in the second half of the sixteenth century, the private sector also faced a credit crisis, and the copper coins that were put into circulation to resolve the liquidity crisis further destabilized the currency's value. The situation was made even worse by the fact that the continuing wars disrupted and destroyed trade networks.

Because of such factors, Spain's manufacturing centers lost the vitality they had enjoyed during the sixteenth century. Spain's wool fabric and silk fabric industries, which had been its most important manufacturing sectors, could not compete with the onslaught of the "new draperies" from England and the Netherlands in the early seventeenth century, while the iron industry in Spain's Basque region lost ground to Sweden's iron industry. Similar developments befell the shipbuilding industry. Shipbuilding grew in the American colonies and shipbuilders in other countries boosted their competitiveness until, by the mid-seventeenth century, hardly anyone was using warships that were built in Spain.

The Spanish Empire's economic crisis was worsened by changes in trade with its New World colonies. As we mentioned earlier, Spain was rescued from its grave fiscal crisis in the 1580s by the dramatic increase in the influx of precious metals from the Americas, but in the early seventeenth century, this trend was reversed. There are varying estimates of the exact amount of precious metals that flowed into Spain, but the general trend is clear. According to Hamilton, the volume of precious metal shipments fell by seven-eighths between 1601–1605 and 1656–1660, while Antonio Domínguez Ortiz believed that shipments decreased by about the same amount between 1621–1625 and 1661–1665 [72]. This trend is also illustrated by estimates of the tonnage of merchant vessels on the Atlantic Ocean. Tonnage decreased by 76% between 1611–1615 and 1656–1660, and then once again by 53% between 1656–1660 and 1706–1710 [73].

A combination of factors was behind the drop in New World trade. The decline in shipments of precious metals to Spain can be attributed to the following factors: falling productivity of mines in the Americas, more smuggling, and increasing shipments of precious metals to Asia on the Manila Galleons. The reduction in overall trade also appears to have been caused by several factors. Merchants from England and the Netherlands challenged Spain's monopoly on trade and actively took part in smuggling; local merchants in the colonies gained more influence as part of this process; and the colonies' demand for Spanish agricultural and manufacturing products decreased as their own agricultural and manufacturing output increased. Of course, another factor that should be mentioned is that Spain's manufacturing sector was unable to satisfy colonial demand because of its own decreasing competitiveness [74].

The Vicious Cycle of War and the Economy: The Historical Limits of the Agricultural Empire

Spain pioneered maritime expansion in early modern Europe and built a vast empire comparable to the Roman Empire, but it was never able to overcome the economic crisis that began in the late sixteenth century. Spain had once ruled more than half of continental Europe, but amid a vicious cycle of wars and fiscal crises, it voluntarily surrendered control of the Hapsburg lands of Austria and lost the northern part of the Low Countries, which would later become a hegemonic power in the global economy. While Spanish colonies in the New World had temporarily saved imperial finances, they eventually stopped being a source of precious metals. Instead, they began to pursue their economic independence by trading with Spain's rivals, states that threatened the empire's security.

Many years before, when the unified kingdom of Spain became an empire through its merger with the House of Hapsburg, the Spanish wondered whether the new empire would really improve their lives—and those fears were ultimately borne out. The empire that had originally been forged from the union of dynasties expanded through more royal matches and unending wars, but Spaniards' lives were impoverished more and more by the fiscal burden of that empire.

Before Spain's unification, the Crown of Aragon had been an important maritime power in the Mediterranean, but its merchants and manufacturers were reduced to rentiers by competition with merchants and manufacturers in Italy, the Low Countries, and Hapsburg-ruled Austria. Furthermore, the major landowners and merchants of Castile who depended upon sheep raising and wool exports could only watch as their economic livelihoods were determined by the merchants who controlled overseas trade. The plight of the peasants was even more pathetic. Land ownership became more polarized, taxes continued to rise, and new opportunities were nowhere to be found in the empire's far-flung lands.

At first glance, this may seem paradoxical. The Spanish Empire was originally devised to transcend the economic limits of agricultural society. As we have seen, the Reconquista was an attempt to overthrow the Muslims' long rule over the Iberian Peninsula and to rebuild a Christian kingdom, but it also offered a way out of the Malthusian Trap caused by the imbalance between land and population (or in other words, between diminishing agricultural production and increasing population).

In the same way, Spain's conquests in the New World also represented a desperate effort to overcome the country's geopolitical limitations and find new land to accommodate the surplus population. But while Spain succeeded at building a great empire, it failed to sustain its agricultural society, and it also failed to provide Spaniards with new land. The prodigious amount of precious metals that flowed from the Americas into Spain did not breathe new life into the Spanish economy. Instead, it was immediately dispersed among merchants, manufacturers, and financiers both in and out of the empire or squandered on consumption and on the conquest of new territory.

It seems as if the empire's extensive territory ought to have provided the resources, capital, and markets needed for productive activity. There are several reasons why the Spanish were unable to take full advantage of the economic opportunities that the empire offered. The fact that the empire originated from a union of royal families and that they never really consolidated their imperial rule can be seen as two of those reasons. Since the Spanish Empire was no more than a confederation of states loosely bound together in the person of the Spanish monarch, it was futile to expect the free movement of people and goods inside the empire or the economic development that could result from this.

But for a more fundamental cause, we must consider the fact that the agricultural society of Spain did not have the capacity to take advantage of the empire's economic opportunities. Spain's rulers thought of the empire as a kind of personal possession, and they understood imperial expansion solely as a means of exhibiting prestige and power—both their own and those of their house. Spain's aristocrats were predisposed to conquer rather than to accumulate and reinvest wealth because of their experience in the Reconquista. Their sole interest was acquiring land and treasure so that they could enjoy the idle lifestyle of the nobility rather than demean themselves by engaging in productive activity. Spain's merchants, manufacturers, and peasants lived in a typical agricultural society, which meant that they had never seen how the accumulation and reinvestment of capital could lead to the continuing creation of surplus. Even if the Spanish Empire had achieved a greater degree of internal unity, these classes could not have developed commercial agriculture and new commerce and manufacturing industries in order to take advantage of the opportunities afforded by the empire's massive market.

This was the tragedy of the Spanish agricultural empire. As an agricultural society with diminishing production and slowing economic growth, Spain was compelled to rush into military conflicts in order to acquire new territory and overcome the limits of its economic system. But the new territory gained through war was just a temporary solution. Production only diminished in the new territories, and the wars of conquest launched to compensate for this demanded even more government spending. In short, the vicious cycle of war and the economy had arrived. When states emerged that had a new economic system in which capital accumulation and reinvestment were sustained by commerce and manufacturing and when those states challenged the hegemony of this agricultural empire, Spain could not long resist them. The rise of the new maritime powers of the Netherlands and England forced Spain to confront this harsh reality.

In his analysis of the Americas under Spanish rule, historian Timothy Parsons described the Spanish empire that linked Europe, Asia, and the Americas as "the world's first truly global imperial state." [75] The Spanish Empire showed that advancements in transportation and communication spelled the end of empires that were limited to an unbroken stretch of land on a single continent (or two neighboring ones) and the beginning of a new kind of empire built of far-flung lands across the ocean.

But the first global maritime empire that appeared in the early modern period was a decentralized composite monarchy. Such a vast area of land was difficult to rule according to uniform principles. And even though Spain ruled a maritime empire, those rulers clung to the logic of an agricultural economy. The rise and fall of the Spanish Empire shows the tragic fate that awaits empires that are bound to the principles of the past amid a changing environment. Doubtless, the Spanish Empire during the reign of Charles V was as mighty as a tiger—but that tiger was helpless in the ocean. That is why we have described Spain as the agricultural empire on the waves.

References

1. Gyeong-cheol Ju, *Daehanghae Sidae: Haesaeng Paengchanggwa Geundae Segyeui Hyeongseong* [Age of Exploration: Maritime Expansion and the Formation of the Modern World] (Seoul University Press, 2008), p. 26.
2. Immanuel Wallerstein, *The Modern World-System I: Capitalist Agriculture and the Origins of the European World-Economy in the Sixteenth Century* (New York, 1974).
3. Raymond Carr, et al., *Seupeinsa* [Spain: A History] (Kachi Books, 2006), pp. 85–90; Anthony Pagden, *Worlds at War: The 2,500-Year Struggle between East and West* (New York, 2008), pp. 188ff.
4. Raymond Carr, et al., *Seupeinsa* [Spain: A History], pp. 95–98; David Levering Lewis, *God's Crucible: Islam and the Making of Europe, 570–1215* (New York, 2008), pp. 343–346.
5. Lewis, *God's Crucible*, p. 378.
6. William Maltby, *The Rise and Fall of the Spanish Empire* (London, 2009), pp. 13–15.
7. John Elliott, "A Europe of Composite Monarchies," *Past and Present* 137 (Nov. 1992), pp. 48–71.
8. Of the approximately 380,000 people living in Catalonia, 30% lived in towns or cities, and Barcelona grew to the size of 35,000 people, which made it a metropolis for the time. Farmers in Catalonia focused less on cultivating grains than on growing cash crops and raising sheep, and Catalonian merchants plied their wares from the Levant to Sicily, Genoa, and southern France. Beginning in the mid-fourteenth century, the cities of Catalonia became less competitive, as a result of no fewer than 10 epidemics that ravaged the region between 1348

and the mid-fifteenth century, war with Castile, and fluctuations in demand for wool fabric. See Alan Ryder, *The Wreck of Catalonia* (New York, 2007).
9. Elliott, *Imperial Spain 1469–1716* (Harmondsworth, 1970), pp. 24–25.
10. Perry Anderson, *Lineages of the Absolutist State* (London, 1974), especially chap. 4.
11. Miguel Angel Ladero Quesada, "Castile in the Middle Ages," Richard Bonney (ed.), *The Rise of the Fiscal State in Europe c. 1200–1815* (Oxford, 1999), pp. 177–178.
12. Henry Kamen, *Empire: How Spain Became a World Power 1492–1763* (New York, 2003), p. 21.
13. Adam Smith, *An Inquiry into the Nature and Causes of the Wealth of Nations*, R. H. Campbell and A. S. Skinner (eds.), 2 vols. (Oxford, 1976), 2:626.
14. A. J. R. Russell-Wood, *The Portuguese Empire, 1415–1808: A World on the Move* (Baltimore, 1998), p. 9.
15. In the early fifteenth century, Portugal had a population of about 1 million, which was one-fourth the size of Castile's population and just one-tenth of France's. The country also had little in the way of natural resources. Aside from wool, about the only product that Portugal had to offer was salt. Maritime activity cannot thrive without the support of advancements in shipbuilding, and here, too, Portugal was at a disadvantage. The country had far too little of the iron and lumber needed to build ships. Some scholars argue that political stability was what facilitated Portugal's expansion, focusing on the fact that there was no dynastic change in Portugal for around two centuries after the crown passed to the House of Aviz in 1385. But since there are countries in which rebellions and other political upheavals have only served to promote expansion, this does not seem to be the whole story. An explanation of Portugal's precocious overseas expansion can be found in Fernand Braudel, *Civilization & Capitalism* 15th–18th *Century Vol. 3: The Perspective of the World* (New York, 1984), pp. 138-143; Felipe Fernández-Armesto, *Pathfinders: A Global History of Exploration* (New York, 2006), pp. 118–119.
16. Russell-Wood, *The Portuguese Empire*, chap. 1.
17. Fernández-Armesto, *Pathfinders*, pp. 129–138.
18. A leading role in these reforms was played by the third son of John I, who is regarded as a major figure in establishing Portugal as a maritime kingdom.
19. John Elliott, *Empires of the Atlantic World* (New Haven, 2003), p. 18; Hugh Thomas, *Rivers of Gold: The Rise of the Spanish Empire from Columbus to Magellan* (New York, 2003), pp. 58–60.
20. Elliott, *Imperial Spain*, pp. 59-60.
21. Elliott, *Imperial Spain*, p. 61; Felipe Fernández-Armesto, *Columbus: And the Conquest of the Impossible* (London, 1974), pp. 43–45.
22. It is unclear how many of the 200,000 Jews in Spain left the country at this time. There are a range of estimates: around 100,000, between 120,000 and 150,000, and around 200,000. Whichever estimate we accept, this was clearly no small number, considering that the entire population of unified Spain at the time numbered about 6 million. Thomas, *Rivers of Gold*, pp. 78–84; Ralph Davis, *The Rise of the Atlantic Economies* (Ithaca, 1973), p. 60; Elliott, *Imperial Spain*, p. 110.
23. Quesada, "Castile in the Middle Ages," pp. 178, 182–183.
24. Carlos Álvarez-Nogal and Leandro Prados de la Escosura, "Searching for the Roots of Retardation: Spain in European Perspective, 1500–1850," *Universidad Carlos III de Madrid Working Papers in Economic History* (March 2007); Carlos Álvarez-Nogal and Leandro Prados de la Escosura, "The Rise and Fall of Spain (1270–1850)," *The Economic History Review* 66:1 (February 2013) pp. 1–37. It is our view that the Reconquista enabled Spain to largely avoid the Malthusian Trap that affected other parts of Europe. See pp. 18–20.
25. For the limited success of measures designed to check the power of the aristocracy, see Elliott, *Imperial Spain*, pp. 96-99; for the tax exemptions granted the aristocracy, see Quesada, "Castile in the Middle Ages," pp. 189–192.
26. Henry Kamen, *Spain, 1469–1714: A Society of Conflict*, 2nd ed. (London, 1991), p. 48.

27. The government bond, called the *juro*, paid a fixed rate of interest. The interest rate was initially 10% but later fell to 7.12%.
28. Regina Grafe and M. A. Irigoin, "Bargaining for Absolutism: A Spanish Path to Nation-State and Empire Building," *Hispanic American Historical Review* 88 (2008), pp. 173–209.
29. The bribes that Charles I gave to ensure his election as Holy Roman Emperor amounted to 850,000 florins.
30. Henry Kamen, "The Decline of Spain: A Historical Myth?" *Past and Present* 81 (November 1978), pp. 26–27.
31. Kamen, *Empire*, pp. 50–57; Elliott, *Imperial Spain*, pp. 144–159.
32. For Charles V's ambitions of a "universal monarchy," see Anthony Pagden, *Peoples and Empires* (New York, 2001), pp. 42-45. In regard to the empire's structure, Pagden says (on p. 44) that "Charles's empire resembled a modern multinational corporation more than a state. Although it was governed in accordance with an overarching legal principle, the imperial public law (*ius publicum*), it had no common legal system and no single administrative structure. It did not even have a single language."
33. Maltby, *The Rise and Fall of the Spanish Empire*, pp. 33–42.
34. Elliott, *Imperial Spain*, pp. 168–169.
35. It is estimated that between 23,000 and 27,000 kilograms of gold was brought to Spain by 1525. After the Aztec Empire was conquered, gold exports increased dramatically. By the 1550s, around 4,200 kilograms were flowing into Spain every year. Carla Rahn Phillips, "The Growth and Composition of Trade in the Iberian Empires, 1450–1750," James Tracy (ed.), *The Rise of Merchant Empires: Long-Distance Trade in the Early Modern World, 1350–1750* (Cambridge, 1990), p. 83.
36. Davis, *The Rise of the Atlantic Economies*, pp. 40–56.
37. Phillips, "The Growth and Composition of Trade in the Iberian Empires," p. 84. The silver mined in the Americas in the sixteenth century made up 74% of the world's total silver production. Ward Barrett, "World Bullion Flows, 1450–1800," Tracy (ed.), *The Rise of Merchant Empires*, p. 225.
38. The silver amalgamation process was introduced to Mexican mines in 1556 and to mines at Potosí in 1573. The *mit'a* was a mandatory labor system in which a certain number of workers were drafted from Indian villages.
39. Timothy H. Parsons, *The Rule of Empires: Those Who Built Them, Those Who Endured Them, and Why They Always Fail* (New York, 2010), p. 137.
40. Gyeong-cheol Ju, *Daehanghae Sidae*, pp. 242–243, 255–257.
41. John Lynch, *Spain 1516–1598: From Nation State to World Empire* (Oxford, 1981), chap. 4.
42. Davis, *The Rise of the Atlantic Economies*; Elliott, *Empires of the Atlantic World.*
43. M. Drelichman and H. Voth, "Institutions and the Resource Curse in Early Modern Spain," Elhanan Helpman (ed.), *Institutions and Economic Performance* (Cambridge, Mass., 2008).
44. James D. Tracy, *Emperor Charles V, Impresario of War: Campaign Strategy, International Finance and Domestic Politics* (Cambridge, 2002).
45. As the *servicio* came to represent an increasing portion of the crown's revenue, a greater burden fell on the common people (and not the aristocrats and *hidalgos* who were exempt from taxes) and the wealthier commoners worked even harder to gain tax-exempt status. According to Elliott, 13% of the Spanish people enjoyed the privilege of tax exemption. This reflected the high percentage of Spaniards who belonged to the lower and higher nobility, a distinctive characteristic of the country. In England and France around the same time, the nobility did not exceed 5% of the population. For more on tax exemption, see Elliott, *Imperial Spain*, pp. 203–204.
46. Giovanni Muto, "The Spanish System: Centre and Periphery," Richard Bonney (ed.), *Economic Systems and State Finance* (Oxford, 1995), pp. 241–242. Revenue increased from 1 million ducats in 1522 to 4 million ducats in 1556, when Philip II came to the throne. It continued to increase afterward, reaching 10 million ducats in 1598 (around the coronation of Philip III), 18 million ducats in 1654, and 30 million ducats in 1674.

47. Tracy, *Emperor Charles V*, p. 102, table 5.2. Most of the rapidly increasing revenue from Naples was spent in Italy.
48. Tracy, *Emperor Charles V*, pp. 100, 104.
49. By region, 36% came from Germany, 34% from Genoa, 10% from Antwerp, and 17% from Spain, but only 7% of loans came purely from Spaniards. Two German families—the Fuggers and the Welsers—provided 34.5% of the loans. Five other banking families in Genoa and Antwerp became Charles V's financial backers. Tracy, *Emperor Charles V*, pp. 100–101.
50. Maltby, *The Rise and Fall of the Spanish Empire*, p. 47.
51. Maltby, *The Rise and Fall of the Spanish Empire*, p. 48.
52. Elliott, *Imperial Spain*, pp. 255-258; Maltby, *The Rise and Fall of the Spanish Empire*, p. 101. Braudel and other scholars argue that Philip's decision to move the capital to Madrid and to manage the empire from Castile ultimately divorced the empire's economic center from its political center. This distorted the resource distribution inside the empire and weakened the empire, they say. But Parker disagrees, arguing that Philip's decision is understandable given Castile's fiscal revenue, its powerful infantry units, and its large number of ships. Parker also says that the Netherlands was not Philip's highest priority for policy making. For more on this, see Fernando González de León and Geoffrey Parker, "The Grand Strategy of Philip II and the Revolt of the Netherlands," Graham Darby (ed.), *The Origins and Development of the Dutch Revolt* (London, 2001), pp. 111–112; Fernand Braudel, *The Mediterranean and the Mediterranean World in the Age of Philip II* (New York, 1973), vol. 2, p. 950.
53. The reason that Philip II stood up to all these enemies is that, just like his predecessor, he viewed the empire in terms of the medieval code of honor. He was concerned that the loss of any part of the empire would tarnish not only his personal reputation but also the empire's prestige and cause other regions to defect in turn. For more on this, see González de León and Parker, "The Grand Strategy of Philip II," pp. 109–111.
54. To counter Philip II's policies, around 400 members of the nobility and religious leaders drew up the Compromise of 1565 and presented Margaret of Parma with a petition to the same effect in 1566. Margaret accepted their petition, but this did not assuage the Protestants' concerns, which culminated in 1566 in a mass campaign to destroy religious images. Philip seized this as an excuse to dispatch the Duke of Alba to the Netherlands, who set up a special tribunal called the Council of Troubles and set about systematically eliminating those suspected of heresy. As a result, around 9,000 people were put on trial between 1567 and 1572, of whom more than 1,000 were executed.
55. Geoffrey Parker, *The Army of Flanders and the Spanish Road, 1567–1659*, 2nd ed. (Cambridge, 2004), pp. 115–116; Parker, *The Dutch Revolt*, revised ed. (London, 1985), chaps. 1–3.
56. The Holy League had mobilized 203 galleys and 50,000 soldiers for the battle, while the Ottoman Empire's forces consisted of 208 galleys and 88,000 troops. The Ottomans' losses in the battle were enormous: 15 galleys were destroyed and 190 taken, while 30,000 men were killed and 8,000 were taken prisoner. Kamen, *Empire*, pp. 183–184.
57. In the early sixteenth century, Portugal's Asian merchants controlled one-third of the global spice trade. It is worth noting Elliott's argument that Spain's annexation of Portugal helped it strengthen its naval forces. Elliott, *Imperial Spain*, p. 276: "It [the annexation of Portugal] had given Spain a great accession of naval strength, making the combined Spanish and Portuguese merchant fleets the largest in the world: 250,000–300,000 tons, against the 232,000 tons of the Netherlands and the 42,000 of England."
58. The interest the crown owed on its debts rose from 320 million *maravedí* in 1554 to 550 million *maravedí* in 1560. Meanwhile, the crown's regular income in 1559 was just 530 million *maravedí*. Accordingly, the Spanish government had to default on its debt once again in 1560. Juan Gelabert, "Castile 1504–1808," Bonney (ed.), *The Rise of the Fiscal State*, p. 209.
59. For a brief introduction to the fiscal burden of the wars during Philip II's reign, see Geoffrey Parker, "War and Economic Change: The Economic Costs of the Dutch Revolt," *Spain and the Netherlands 1559–1659: Ten Studies* (London, 1979), pp. 178–203 (the figures quoted

here appear on p. 187). According to Parker, the Army of Flanders received around 8,000 Castilian reinforcements each year during the Dutch War for Independence, and about 30,000 Castilian troops were mobilized between 1631 and 1639. In addition, a tremendous amount of money was transferred from Castile for military expenses. Between 1556 and 1624, at least 218 million ducats were transferred to the Netherlands from Castile, while the monarchs received just 121 million ducats in revenue from precious metals shipped from the New World during the same period (p. 188). Castile's public debt in 1557, when Philip came to the throne, was 36 million ducats, but by his death in 1598 it had increased to 85 million ducats (p. 188).

60. While the crown's regular income had increased to 1.6 billion *maravedí* by 1584, interest payments still amounted to 1.2 billion *maravedí*. Gelabert, "Castile 1504–1808," p. 212.
61. Gelabert, "Castile 1504–1808," p. 213.
62. Gelabert, "Castile 1504–1808," p. 214; Elliott, *Imperial Spain*, p. 286.
63. Of course, the troubles at Medina del Campo cannot be completely explained by the fiscal crisis. Alberto Marcos Martín, "Medina del Campo 1500–1800: An Historical Account of Its Decline," I. A. A. Thompson and Bartolomé Yun Casalilla (eds.), *The Castilian Crisis of the Seventeenth Century* (Cambridge, 1994).
64. Gelabert, "Castile 1504–1808," pp. 215–223.
65. For recent research on the seventeenth century crisis, see the following: "AHR Forum: The General Crisis of the Seventeenth Century Revisited," *American Historical Review* 113 (October 2008), pp. 1029–1099; Jan de Vries, "The Economic Crisis of the Seventeenth Century after Fifty Years," *Journal of Interdisciplinary History* 40 (Autumn 2009), pp. 151–194.
66. Thompson and Casalilla, *The Castilian Crisis*, p. 61. The population of 20 cities in Castile increased by 84% between 1530 and 1594, and the population of farming villages is estimated to have continued to increase until 1580.
67. Thompson and Casalilla, *The Castilian Crisis*, p. 46; Kamen, *Spain 1469–1714*, p. 223.
68. Thompson and Casalilla, *The Castilian Crisis*, pp. 27–28.
69. Thompson and Casalilla, *The Castilian Crisis*, pp. 15–17; Elliott, *Imperial Spain*, p. 315.
70. Thompson and Casalilla, *The Castilian Crisis*, p. 82.
71. For more on the polarization of rural areas, see Thompson and Casalilla, *The Castilian Crisis*, pp. 82–94, and Dennis O. Flynn, "Fiscal Crisis and the Decline of Spain (Castile)," *Journal of Economic History* 42 (March 1982), pp. 144–145. For estimates of demand for wool, see Thompson and Casalilla, *The Castilian Crisis*, pp. 101–113.
72. Thompson and Casalilla, *The Castilian Crisis*, p. 121, table 6.1.
73. Thompson and Casalilla, *The Castilian Crisis*, pp. 118–119.
74. Ibid.; Elliott, *Empires of the Atlantic World*, pp. 226–229.
75. Parsons, *The Rule of Empires*, p. 119.

Chapter 3
The Netherlands: The First Commercial State

The independence of the Dutch Republic heralded the arrival of commercial society in a world that was dominated by agriculture. It was a truly revolutionary moment that marked the demise of agricultural society, which was characterized by decelerating economic growth, and the advent of commercial society, the first economic society with accelerating economic growth. To be sure, there had been agricultural societies in which commerce thrived and great wealth was amassed, as we saw with Spain in the last chapter. But the wealth of agricultural societies did not lead to capital accumulation in the modern sense and was instead squandered on capturing territory, acquiring political power, and pursuing higher social status.

But in the Netherlands, the world's first commercial society, the wealth that was acquired through domestic and foreign trade was accumulated as capital and then reinvested to facilitate accelerating economic growth. Even more surprisingly, the first capitalist hegemonic state and the first modern economy formed in the face of obstacles such as unproductive soil, inadequate natural resources, and a relatively small population [1].

In this chapter, we will be examining the reasons why the first commercial society emerged not from traditional powers such as Spain or France but from a minor state in the Low Countries, as well as the historical significance of its emergence. Another intriguing aspect of what happened in the Netherlands is that its hegemony lasted for so short a period. If the Netherlands was able to gain independence from Spain, the greatest power of its age, and build the world's first system of expansive reinvestment, why was it unable to maintain its commercial advantage for long? Answering this question will serve not only to elucidate the historical significance of commercial society in the Netherlands but also to identify the historical limitations of the system of expansive reinvestment in commercial society.

T.-Y. Kim and D. Kim, *The Secrets of Hegemony*,
DOI 10.1007/978-981-10-4416-8_3

Historical Background of the Netherlands

In order to understand the Dutch Republic's economic success, we must first take a brief look at the history of the Netherlands before the Republic's establishment and especially the social, economic, and political changes that occurred after the Middle Ages. The Netherlands is perhaps best-known for two things: first, that a significant portion of the coastal regions in the heart of the country is below sea level, and second, that the bulk of agricultural production consists not of cereals but of tulips and other cash crops. "It is a very small country taken up on the seaward side with barren sand-dunes, subject both from this quarter, and from the rivers and canals with which it is intersected to frequent flooding, and fit only for the grazing which is the country's sole wealth," one French diplomat observed during the reign of Louis XIV in 1699. As this suggests, the Dutch people's efforts to overcome their unfavorable environmental conditions were an important factor in setting their economic course [2].

Since the poor soil in the Netherlands was not suited for cereal farming and because the country was quite distant from the origin of the classic manorial system, the feudal system never became deeply rooted there during the Middle Ages [3]. According to Jacques le Goff, this meant that the system that was "essentially the appropriation by the seigneurial class [. . .] of all the surplus agricultural production achieved by the peasant masses" did not hold sway over the Netherlands [4]. Thus, the development of agricultural society in the Netherlands during the Middle Ages diverged from Europe's typical feudal societies.

It is often said of feudal society that there were no incentives to improve productivity because the feudal lords used extra-economic coercion to appropriate most of the peasants' surplus. But it is actually very likely that this characterization confuses cause and effect. Since agricultural production tends to diminish when there is virtually no opportunity to improve production through technological advances, peasants were more likely to do the least amount of work required to survive than to work hard for gradually decreasing yields. But the lord of the manor had to collect the peasants' surplus for several reasons (including to maintain his own power), which gave him a reason for encouraging the peasants to produce a surplus. This enabled production to increase to a certain extent in some areas where the feudal lords were powerful.

Since the feudal system failed to take root in the Netherlands, the "colonization" that took place throughout Europe in the late Middle Ages proceeded in a distinctive manner there. On a fundamental level, this colonization was an attempt to relieve population pressure on the land by clearing new land (and for Spain, by conquering it). Through the end of the eleventh century, Dutch peasants who were relatively free from the control of feudal lords led the way in clearing and settling the land. Of course, some large reclamation projects were led by people like Floris V, Count of Holland, and the Bishop of Utrecht, but even here free peasants played an important role.

Since the reclaimed areas were prone to flooding, it was crucial to erect and maintain dikes, and this work was put in the hands of autonomous peasant communities. The peasants also had a major role in draining the reclaimed land. When the peat swamps were cultivated, for example, farming compacted the peat and caused the land to settle. To prevent this, the peasants organized on their own to build and maintain drainage facilities. Thus, the peasants of the Netherlands gained a measure of autonomy by contributing to reclamation projects and managing reclaimed land [5].

Despite various efforts by the peasants, Dutch agricultural output could not keep up with population growth in the late Middle Ages. Neither the existing land nor the reclaimed land was suitable for growing grain, and the cost of maintaining the land continued to increase. Because of this, cash crops and stock raising, which demanded less labor, gradually came to make up a greater share of agriculture. The result was that, by the beginning of the fourteenth century, Dutch peasants had already begun to leave the countryside and move to the cities.

Of course, this was made possible by the feudal system's weak presence in the Netherlands. Since the Dutch feudal lords had little or no control over the peasants, it was easy for the peasants to move. In addition, there was a proclivity toward individualism that had developed in the previous period of colonization. In other words, the peasants' experience clearing and settling the land was the result not of their feudal lords' extra-economic coercion but rather of their own spontaneous efforts as individuals. Such peasant migration caused urbanization to begin earlier in the Netherlands than elsewhere in Europe, and a large number of commercial cities formed there in the fourteenth century [6].

Urbanization in the Netherlands followed a different pattern from other regions. As a general rule, urbanization in Europe was a process whereby cities developed from the commercial footholds that were established as overseas trade recovered during the late Middle Ages and from the administrative or economic centers built in new territory according to the needs of the state. The standard pattern of urbanization was for the centers of trade and administration established in this manner to preside over a hierarchy that included the smaller towns and rural regions that surrounded them.

But in the Netherlands, instead of such a hierarchical structure forming around specific cities, cities of various sizes appeared independently and simultaneously in different regions. The urbanization that began in the Netherlands in the fourteenth century accelerated in the sixteenth century. At that time, commerce, shipping, and fishing were developing rapidly in the Netherlands, while trade in agricultural products quickly expanded as livestock raising, dairy farming, and cash crops grew in prominence. This was made possible by the development of a transportation network that linked several cities through inland waterways and sea routes. So by 1600, more than 30% of the one million people in the Netherlands at the time (and 45% in the case of Holland) lived in cities of more than 2500 people [7].

This early urbanization resulted in several changes that favored economic development. It is generally accepted that urbanization in the late Middle Ages contributed greatly to the formation and spread of the modern concept of property rights. Urbanization's cultural impact was not limited, of course, to inculcating the concept of property rights. Urbanization in the Netherlands and other parts of the Low Countries was also closely linked to the spread of Christian humanism to Northern Europe after Renaissance humanism flourished in the Italian city-states.

This is illustrated by the fact that Erasmus, a leading proponent of Christian humanism, was born in the Low Countries and that his network of intellectuals was established in the cities of the region. Christian humanism, which denounced the corruption and abuses of the Catholic clergy, thrived in the Low Countries, which helps explain why people there responded with such enthusiasm to the Protestant Reformation. Given the high literacy rate and the early development of the publishing industry in the cities of the Low Countries, the books of Martin Luther gained a wide readership, while new Protestant doctrines such as Calvinism could quickly become disseminated [8].

The theory that the spread of Reformation ideas (and Calvinism in particular) played a decisive role in the development of capitalism was famously articulated by Max Weber. Weber's idea that Calvinists' sense of vocation and their concept of double predestination led them to pioneer capitalism seems to have few adherents today. But in the Netherlands, at least, the historical significance of the Reformation cannot be easily ignored.

Calvinist doctrine and organizations not only provided the Dutch with a crucial motivation for their political defiance of the Spanish Empire, but they also served to tie together the seven provinces that fought in the Dutch War for Independence. The Calvinist doctrine of vocation allowed the Dutch to justify virtues such as self-discipline and moderation while affirming the importance of the rational calculation of profits and losses, something that Dutch merchants and manufacturers already did on a daily basis. As such, this doctrine likely contributed to the economic development of the Dutch Republic, though it is difficult to demonstrate a causal relationship [9]. Religion helped in more practical ways as well. The property confiscated from the Catholic monasteries early in the revolt was distributed among the cities and the countryside, where it was invested in charitable projects and in educational and training programs [10].

While urbanization in the Netherlands began with changes in the agricultural sector, it was able to continue because of developments in commerce and industry. One especially remarkable change in this regard was the success that the Dutch achieved before the War for Independence in bulk shipping on the Baltic Sea. The states along the Baltic Sea had long been primary producers of cereals and of the raw materials of shipbuilding (boards, lumber, masts, pitch, and tar), and since the end of the Middle Ages the Baltic had been the main arena of activity for the merchants of Holland and Zeeland and of the Hanseatic League. By the early sixteenth century, it was largely Dutch merchants who were loading the cheap and abundant grain and raw materials of the Baltic and shipping them to the Low Countries for redistribution. Toll records show that 70% of the ships that plied the Baltic Sea between 1497 and 1503 were Dutch and that 78% of the Dutch ships were from Holland [11].

The Dutch merchants' success in the Baltic trade can be attributed to the size of their fleets, the efficiency of their ships (which lowered the cost of shipping), and the technological advantage on which this depended. The reason so many ships were available when Dutch merchants were making inroads in bulk shipping on the Baltic was because of the rapid growth of the fishing industry around this time. The herring fishery (called the Great Fishery) grew with particular speed after a ship called the herring buss was brought into service in the mid-fifteenth century.

The herring buss, much longer than it was wide, was durable enough to stay at sea for extended periods of time (between five and eight weeks). It could support a crew of 18–30 fishermen, which meant that herring could be prepared and preserved as soon as they were caught. The buss was the mainstay of Dutch fleets in the herring fishery, which recorded an annual yearly catch of 20,000 *last* (around 10,000 tons) in the 1640s, worth around three million guilders. Still other records show that 1500 ships took part in the herring fishery in the first half of the seventeenth century, employing about 12,000 fishermen [12].

But the value of the herring fishery went beyond the herring catch and the industry's direct effect on employment. The process of catching, processing, and exporting herring also promoted the development of trade and various other related industries. The herring fishery was most active between the months of May or June and September, while a brisk trade based on herring was conducted for the rest of the year. Dutch merchants exported herring to the Baltic Sea region and imported grain that they then re-exported to Western Europe and the Iberian Peninsula in return for unrefined salt and various manufactured goods. The Dutch refining industry (the businesses that extracted the salt needed to process herring) underwent major development during this time, and the raw materials needed for salt refining were procured from the coast of the Netherlands, Portugal, and France. Trade with Portugal in particular had a major effect on the development of Dutch trade even after the Netherlands gained its independence.

The growth of the fishing industry and trade brought about the development of the shipbuilding industry. Trade in the northern part of the Low Countries was boosted in the fifteenth century by the availability of cheap labor and the conversion of herring busses into merchant ships and in the late sixteenth century by the appearance of the full-rigged ship. Full-rigged ships were well-suited for transporting large quantities of grain and raw materials from the Baltic Sea. The fluyt, developed in 1595, was a ship with a firm hull and protruding sides that could carry a large cargo while being sailed by a small crew. This made it possible to ship huge amounts of goods while minimizing toll payments. Backed by the increase in trade volume and technological advances, shipyards in the Netherlands produced between 400 and 500 ships each year between 1625 and 1700 and provided jobs for around 10,000 workers. This was equivalent to 5% of the adult male population working in manufacturing in Holland at the time. Shipbuilding was the largest industry in the Netherlands [13].

The development of the shipbuilding industry drove the development of related industries. In addition to ropes, various navigational tools, candles, and the printing of nautical charts, the lumber industry grew along with the shipbuilding industry.

A great amount of lumber went into building ships: the construction of a single warship in the seventeenth century required around 2000 oak trees, representing a century of growth in 50 acres of forest. Thus, securing a steady supply of so much lumber was essential for the Netherlands to maintain its advantage in shipbuilding and in maritime trade. The Netherlands was able to do so because it dominated trade with Norway and other coastal states on the Baltic Sea [14].

Through the mid-sixteenth century, the Netherlands had achieved great success in bulk shipping on the Baltic Sea through its development of the herring fishery and related industries, including salt refining, shipbuilding, and lumber. But even these successes did not equal the economic brilliance of the Southern Netherlands. The economic center of the Low Countries at the time was Antwerp, which enjoyed a monopoly on the spice trade in the Spanish Empire. In Antwerp and the surrounding area, the textile industry (a major part of the trade in luxury goods in Europe) reached a high degree of development. Antwerp was at the center of a luxury goods trading network that included the Iberian Peninsula, Italy, and Northern and Western Europe, while Amsterdam and other cities in the northern part of the Low Countries functioned as outports that supplied grain, wood, and various other raw materials to Antwerp's trade network. Consequently, there was a tremendous disparity between Amsterdam and Antwerp. This is illustrated by the fact that the value of products exported from Amsterdam between 1543 and 1545 only accounted for 4% of the total value of exports from the Low Countries, while Antwerp represented 80% of the value [15].

For the northern provinces of the Low Countries to upgrade their economy under these conditions, they needed to apply the technical and commercial expertise they had acquired in the Baltic trade to help them enter the European market for high value-added luxury goods. This also meant that the northern provinces would have to develop manufacturing as Antwerp had done with the textile trade, which was one of the linchpins of the luxury goods trade. In other words, the economic destiny of the northern provinces would depend upon the extent to which they could overtake Antwerp, which enjoyed a position of privilege within the Spanish Empire. It is in this sense that the Dutch revolt against the authority of the Spanish Empire was a decisive turning point.

The Dutch War for Independence: The Golden Age Begins

During the Eighty Years' War, which lasted from 1568 to 1648, the Dutch created the first territorial state in European history in which commercial interests played a central role. During their long struggle, the Dutch people's primary objective was to set up an economic system that was free from the Spanish Empire. When the Spanish onslaught was particularly relentless at the end of the 1580s, the Dutch were briefly forced to ask for protection from King Henry III of France and Queen Elizabeth of England. That suggests how desperate they were to escape from the shadow of the Spanish Empire [16]. Dutch persistence ultimately guaranteed the merchants' political position and social status and resulted in a new economic system in which the wealth that the merchants accumulated was reinvested not for the acquisition of territory or the pursuit of power but rather for the accumulation of more wealth. That is to say, the Netherlands was the birthplace of the first commercial society with expansive reinvestment and accelerating economic growth.

Even though the Dutch Republic that was forged in the War for Independence had the structural weakness of being a loose confederation of seven provinces, the Dutch in that confederation were able to maintain and operate a close-knit network of commerce, manufacturing, and agriculture. This was possible because they shared a common interest: the accelerating growth of their commercial economy. The result was the creation of a new society in which politics was decentralized but the economy was highly integrated. Furthermore, the wealth accumulated through commerce was used to increase military power, not only through taxation but also in the form of government bonds that circulated on the financial market. Thanks to this, the Dutch Republic was able to open up new markets outside of Europe while maintaining its independence not only from the Spanish Empire but also from rising European powers such as England and France. This became the driving force for further development in the system of expansive reinvestment. In this sense, the Dutch Republic was the first modern state to experience accelerating growth deriving from the virtuous cycle of war and the economy.

The Revolt

There is no simple explanation for why a few northern provinces of the Low Countries defied the Spanish Empire—the most powerful empire of its time—in an attempt to gain their independence. But in terms of the establishment and development of commercial society, the most important factor for the revolt must naturally be found in the merchant class's shifting attitude toward the Spanish Empire. As can be seen from the developmental history of the Low Countries, the Spanish Empire provided a number of benefits. The city of Antwerp in particular was able to maintain its superior position in the trade in luxury goods and in the international financial industry because it was part of the Spanish Empire, while other cities were able to profit from trade that was protected by the imperial army.

The problem, however, was the gradually increasing tax burden. The costs of maintaining the empire and expanding the emperor's authority had increased faster than the benefits that the empire provided. In the Low Countries, the tax burden began to rapidly increase in the early sixteenth century, and by the mid-sixteenth century, there were attempts to levy taxes using different methods than before. In 1557, the Spanish Empire's fiscal crisis reached its peak, and it finally had to suspend payments to creditors. The inevitable result was a complete overhaul of tax policy. Accordingly, the cost of being imperial subjects was a heavy burden for the Dutch commercial class.

Until the 1540s, when Charles V was still on the throne, there were no major changes to the Spanish Empire's fiscal policy in the Low Countries. Just as before, fiscal demand was covered by loans backed by land that belonged to the crown and by a subsidy, called *beden*, that was decided in negotiations between the governor and provincial representatives. This subsidy was particularly important, since it accounted for three-fourth of fiscal income. Once the subsidy was determined, it was collected in the following manner: the total amount was divided between the various provinces, including Flanders, and the parliaments of each province allotted the amount that each city should pay.

But as state debt drastically increased amid the continuing wars, there were increasing calls for more taxes to be collected from the Low Countries. This led in 1542 to the imposition of a 10% tax called the "tenth penny" on real estate and profits that individuals made on loans, along with a consumption tax levied on beer, wine, and wool fabric [17]. But these taxes were still not nearly enough to cover the Spanish Empire's sharply increasing fiscal expenditures. After military spending rose because of the Hapsburg-Valois War that broke out in 1551, Philip II was forced to suspend payments to creditors again in 1557. As we discussed in chapter two, Philip II had to deal with enormous debts accrued by his predecessors, and he sought ways to reduce the money that Spain was transferring to the Low Countries while increasing the taxes it collected from them. This culminated in tax code reform that included a uniform 10% tax on all commercial transactions [18].

While the rulers of the Spanish Empire no doubt thought that tax reform was inevitable if they were to escape from the impending fiscal crisis, the provinces of the Low Countries saw these measures as being extremely dangerous. The Duke of Alba, who was in charge of the tax reform, expected that it would bring in more than 13 million florins (around 6.5 million ducats) in yearly revenue. Considering that Charles V had collected 730,000 ducats in taxes from the Low Countries in the 1540s, this was truly an immense sum of money [19]. There were also complaints about the manner of tax collection. The new taxes were taken up by tax collectors under the direct control of the imperial governor, which was seen as an infringement on the provinces' autonomy in regard to fiscal matters.

The provincial parliaments sought a compromise with the Duke of Alba and were prepared to pay the special subsidies (though not the one-time tax on capital) in the traditional manner. But in 1571, the Duke of Alba declared that he would implement the new taxation policies regardless of what the provincial parliaments decided. In the spring of 1572, he took the drastic step of deploying soldiers to the shops of merchants and shopkeepers in Brussels who refused to pay the taxes, but the merchants and shopkeepers remained defiant. Several of the provincial parliaments, including that of Flanders, dispatched envoys to Spain to protest the Duke of Alba's misdeeds [20].

What had begun as a political and religious backlash to the introduction of the Inquisition, the persecution of Protestants, and the attack on the privileges of the local nobility spread around the country because of Philip II's tax reform and the Duke of Alba's draconian measures. Merchants are always hesitant to defy the political authorities because of their concerns about the economic ramifications of political change, but the tax reform made even the most prudent merchants join the resistance.

Making matters even worse was the poor timing of the tax reform. During the 1560s, the Low Countries were enduring a severe economic recession. Trade in grain from the Baltic Sea had been interrupted by a war between Denmark and Sweden, while England's ban on trade had delivered a devastating blow to Flanders' textile industry. On top of that, there was a lean harvest and a famine in 1565 and 1566; a horrific flood in the northern coastal region claimed the lives of 25,000 people in 1570; and an outbreak of plague and bitter cold in 1571 and 1572 led to a shortfall in the grain supply and caused the price of goods to skyrocket [21]. The fact that the tax reform occurred during this economic recession was the catalyst that caused unrest to escalate into a full-scale revolt against the Spanish Empire.

Establishment of the Dutch Republic

The establishment of the Union of Utrecht by the seven northern provinces in 1579 turned the revolt into a war between the Dutch Republic and the Spanish Empire. For several decades after hostilities began in earnest in the late 1560s, Dutch troops faced an uphill struggle. In battles both small and great—including the Siege of Haarlem in 1572 and the Siege of Antwerp in 1585—they were unable to withstand the superior firepower of the Spanish troops and the fighting prowess of the *tercio*, the Spanish army's distinctive offensive square formation [22].

But in the late 1590s, the tide of battle finally started to turn. In 1597, a Dutch force of 15 infantry companies defeated Spanish regulars for the first time. And while the Dutch were defeated in the Siege of Ostend, which lasted from July 1611 to September 1614, it was a costly victory for the Spanish, who lost 55,000 soldiers during the siege. By thus overcoming their disadvantages in the first phase of the war, the seven provinces in the Union of Utrecht preserved their original territory and even managed to acquire some territory in the Southern Netherlands.

One factor that helped turn the war around was the military reforms instituted by Maurice of Nassau and his brothers during the late sixteenth and early seventeenth centuries [23]. The objective of the military reforms was to crush the Spanish *tercio*, which was composed of pikemen and musketeers, by applying overwhelming firepower from the latest firearms. The reforms were inspired by the flintlock musket, which was developed in the 1510s. Until that point, musketeers had served to support the pikemen or in close quarters combat. But Maurice and his brothers adopted three measures to make musketeers the primary fighting unit.

First was adopting the tactic of volley fire. The firearms of the time were inaccurate and took a long time to reload. To overcome those limitations and to concentrate firepower on the enemy, Maurice began arranging the musketeers in several lines. After the musketeers in the front line fired a volley, they would move to the back line to reload while the next line of musketeers continued to fire.

Second was deploying the troops in a linear formation that was wider than the deep square formations of the Spanish army. This enabled the Dutch troops to maximize their firepower while minimizing the losses they suffered when the enemy returned fire. But since troops in a linear formation lacked the psychological stability that resulted from being in a mass of other soldiers, this kind of formation was prone to collapsing under enemy fire. In order to offset this problem, Nassau and his brothers gave their soldiers intense training. These repeated drills improved soldiers' facility with their firearms, tightened discipline, and strengthened the bond between soldiers, which kept soldiers from fleeing the battle line [24].

Third was developing the officer corps. The greater emphasis on repeated drills and discipline made the quality of the officer corps more important. Maurice believed that an army's operations depended upon its unity as an organization and that the task of maintaining the army's organizational unity and efficiency fell to officers who were knowledgeable about their profession. At the time, the officer corps in most European armies was almost entirely composed of members of the nobility who adhered to the medieval code of chivalry. Most officers in the Dutch army, on the other hand, were professional soldiers. Rather than individual courage and honor, these officers were more concerned with fulfilling their role inside the organization of the army. The Dutch army was able to secure such loyalty from its officers because they were being paid their wages by the state, which was controlled by the States General, the Republic's legislature. The same was true of the enlisted men.

After these military reforms, the refurbished Dutch army put a higher priority on protecting commerce than on political goals such as territorial expansion. While the Netherlands was the first modern state to initiate the virtuous cycle of war and the economy, the size of its military was still limited by its fiscal ability [25]. And despite the military reforms, the Dutch ground forces did not fight many battles. This reflected Maurice's prudence as a commander: he strove to minimize unnecessary casualties in battle. His defensive strategy helped him to repel several ill-advised assaults by the Spanish, even as he avoided ordering foolish attacks himself. Maurice always bore in mind that the primary objective of the Dutch army was not crushing the Spanish army or expanding the Republic's territory but rather blocking the Spanish army's offensives so as to defend the Netherlands' commercial base.

The activity of the Dutch navy was also important for the Republic's security and its economic development. There are differing views among historians in regard to the Dutch navy. Scholars who downplay the role and ability of the Dutch navy point out that the Netherlands did not even have a permanent navy until 1652. The Dutch navy lacked administrative coordination and integration, and it did not even have enough warships to fight a naval war.

But it is important to remember that, despite these flaws, until 1648 the Dutch navy held its own against the Spanish navy—the world's strongest navy at the time—and was generally successful at securing trade routes and protecting the trade convoys that were crucial to its economy. Just as the Dutch army focused on defense instead of territorial expansion, the Dutch navy can be said to have focused on protecting Dutch trade. In this sense, then, the Dutch navy played a noteworthy role.

It seems clear that attempts to reform the Dutch navy did not have the dramatic success of the Dutch army reforms. As early as the 1580s, there was a push to combine the navy and the privateers that were operated by each province. But the interests of the various states proved irreconcilable, so separate admiralty colleges were set up in five different locations. Each of the admiralty colleges operated privateers, issued trading permits with enemy states, and had the authority to levy taxes. What was unusual about this arrangement is that the admiralty colleges levied taxes on overseas trade instead of collecting duties for protecting convoys as they long had done [26]. The Dutch navy was funded by tariffs, with which it maintained 30,000 tons of warships in the 1620s and between 40,000 and 45,000 tons of warships in the 1630s and 1640s.

The Dutch naval strategy was designed to meet economic needs by supporting the Dutch economy, which by 1600 had become the center of a global trade network. As such, the Dutch navy focused on protecting trade—and especially the routes and trade convoys of entrepôt trade—from the privateers and warships of enemy states.

At first, the Dutch navy concentrated on protecting the Republic's coast and its internal waterways and on preventing Spain from imposing a naval blockade. In the early seventeenth century, when Dutch merchants began to establish themselves in Asian trade and the Atlantic trade, the Dutch navy's role was to assist this overseas expansion. Not only the warships of the Dutch navy but also private merchant vessels were mobilized for this task [27]. When the truce ended and war resumed in 1621, the Spanish navy adopted a new strategy of directly attacking Dutch trade convoys and the vessels in the herring fishery. After this, the Dutch navy turned its attention to enforcing a naval blockade in the Flanders region, providing escorts for convoys, and sending ships on reconnaissance [28].

The Dutch navy made substantial progress toward achieving these goals. In the Battle of Nieuwpoort in 1600, the Republic's combined fleet crushed a contingent of the Spanish navy that had remained in Nieuwpoort after the Spanish fleet launched a surprise attack on the harbor of Dunkirk. At the Battle of Gibraltar in 1607, the Dutch attacked a Spanish fleet that was at anchor and sank around 50 ships. Around 4000 Spanish sailors and marines died in the battle. The hardest-fought naval engagement during the War for Independence was the Battle of the Downs, which took place in October 1635. In the battle, a Dutch fleet led by Maarten Tromp ambushed a Spanish fleet in the English Channel that was carrying reinforcements to Dunkirk. The Dutch sank 60 of the 75 Spanish ships and killed 15,200 Spanish sailors and marines. The Dutch suffered less than 1000 casualties during the engagement, reports tell us [29].

The Dutch military successes would not have been possible without fiscal backing. As we have previously mentioned, the decisive reason for the decline of the Spanish Empire was Spain's economic system. As an agricultural society, Spain could not cope with the burden of an expanding empire and the cost of waging war. Thus, the Dutch Republic's ability to handle the fiscal burden of military action during the War for Independence was just as important as its military reforms or strategic and tactical successes. This ability also demonstrates that the commercial society of the Netherlands had produced a fiscal regime that could effectively support the virtuous cycle of war and the economy.

Indeed, the Dutch Revolt and War for Independence demanded a tremendous amount of fiscal expenditures. During the late 1580s, the Dutch army cost an average of three million guilders a year, but by the early 1600s this had increased to nine million guilders. Even during the truce that began in 1609, the army cost seven million guilders a year. After hostilities resumed in 1621, expenditures on the army increased even faster. In the year 1621 alone, 14 million guilders were allocated to the army.

The reason that army spending increased so fast was the fortifications that were being built on a large scale along the Republic's borders. Compared to the army, the navy was relatively inexpensive. The share of the budget devoted to total military expenses (including naval expenditures) can be found in the 1641 budget. In that year, we find that Dutch military expenses accounted for 87% of the Republic's entire budget of 24 million guilders (excluding fiscal expenditures by the various provinces and regions). Just 9% of the budget was spent on administration, and only 4% was allocated to pay interest on government debt [30].

As military expenditures shot up, there was a concomitant increase in taxes. Taxes collected by the States General accounted for an extremely small portion of the Republic's total fiscal income (less than 1% in 1641); more than 80% of that income came from local taxes imposed by each province according to population and economic size. In the 1640s, the chief part of the tax burden was born by Holland, at 60% [31]. The bulk of Holland's fiscal income came from the consumption tax and land tax, with the consumption tax in particular representing two-thirds of this income. According to one estimate, the per capita consumption tax burden for residents of Holland increased from less than three guilders in 1584 to 10 guilders in the 1630s. Between the 1550s and the 1630s, Holland's fiscal revenue (including the consumption tax) increased by a factor of about thirty. Even accounting for the fact that the population doubled and the price of goods tripled over the same period, the per capita tax burden still rose around fourfold [32].

Despite its soaring tax receipts, the Dutch Republic was still forced to rely upon a variety of loans just as the Spanish Empire had. Its decentralized political structure notwithstanding, the Republic found it easy to take out loans, and at a lower interest rate than Spain. Parker relates how, during one emergency, the Netherlands was able to procure a huge loan of one million florins at 3% interest in just two days [33].

Naturally, this reflected investors' confidence about the Dutch Republic's future. But it took the Republic some time to earn their trust. When the fate of the Republic was uncertain during the 1570s, loans were not readily available, and the state's debt remained small. In 1574, the Republic only owed its creditors 1.4 million guilders. Even in 1600, when the Republic was in a considerably better position militarily, the government only owed five million guilders, and the interest rate was high, at 8%. But the Republic's debt began to balloon in the 1620s, and between

1621 and 1647 it took out 115 million guilders in loans. Intriguingly, though, the interest rate continued to fall even as debt rose astronomically. By the 1640s, the interest rate was down to 4% [34]. This offers a striking contrast with the agricultural society of Spain.

One factor that presumably made it affordable for the Netherlands to fund its wars was the long-term public bond system (called *renten*) that was already in operation in the 1550s. In 1515, the provincial legislatures officially acknowledged their responsibility to pay interest to the holders of public bonds. In the 1540s, Holland adopted a system that linked a particular tax to the interest paid on the long-term public bonds (which can be regarded as the centerpiece of the financial revolution). In the 1550s, the state adopted the practice of raising money through the bond market, replacing the mandatory public bond system.

But given the instability during the early stage of the Dutch revolt and struggle for independence, long-term government bonds were not warmly received by the market, and the tax burden greatly increased as a consequence. This prompted the use of short-term loans based on a kind of promissory note known as *obligaten* that were issued by tax collectors. Short-term loans were provided not only by the Dutch but also by foreign merchants. For example, the merchants of Ipswich (a town in northern England that had become the home of a group of refugees who had fled the Low Countries) invested 50,000 lb, while the Company of Merchant Adventurers of London, who used Antwerp as a base for their trade in wool cloth, invested 100,000 lb [35]. In other words, while it is true that the Netherlands used the financial revolution to effectively fund the war, the ultimate incentive for investors and tradespeople was the confidence that the accelerating growth of the Dutch economy meant that the Republic could be counted on to return a profit on their investments.

Growth During the War

The war with the Spanish Empire obviously tested the mettle of the Dutch Republic. But surprisingly, economic growth continued in the country throughout the long war, and early in the seventeenth century, the system of expansive reinvestment was perfected there for the first time in history. Around the time that the Spanish Empire went into decline, unable to cover the astronomical cost of the war or to boost decelerating growth, the Netherlands had put into place an institutional framework that could sustain the virtuous cycle of war and the economy.

As previously mentioned, the innovative measures that were introduced in the military and fiscal sectors were focused on protecting Dutch trade and motivating merchants and manufacturers to engage in economic activity. With the aid of these measures, the Dutch economy flourished for the duration of the war. The Dutch textile industry—including wool cloth and linen producers—had lagged behind England and the Southern Netherlands, but in the 1580s it began to pick up speed, and the growth trend in the shipbuilding, lumber, and brewing industries became noticeable as well.

There were also numerous changes in the area of trade. Until this time, Dutch merchants had mostly depended on bulk shipping in the Baltic Sea (which had little added value), but now they began to take an interest in the trade in luxury goods. This made them more aggressive in seeking market share in areas such as the Mediterranean, the Levant, East Asia, and the Atlantic that had previously been dominated by the merchants of Italy, Portugal, Spain, and England. The new vigor of Dutch commerce was exemplified by the Dutch East India Company (Vereenigde Oost-Indische Compagnie, or VOC), established early in the seventeenth century. The establishment of the VOC provided Dutch merchants with an opportunity to use the technology and experience they had acquired in bulk shipping and shipbuilding to take over the trade in luxury goods as well. It also signaled that the Netherlands' system of expansive reinvestment was in full operation.

As a great deal of research has already been devoted to how the Netherlands was able to grow during the war, we will not examine that in detail here. One observation that should be made, however, is that the war itself led to structural changes and economic growth in the Netherlands. To begin with, the fact that the Dutch Republic preserved its independence—using bold military reforms and fiscal innovations to compensate for its unfavorable position early in the war—made possible the country's economic advancement. But that was not the only benefit of the war. It also caused the downfall of Antwerp, which had been the economic hub of the Spanish Empire. That downfall gave the Netherlands the chance it needed to become the undisputed center of entrepôt trade as it simultaneously engaged in bulk shipping and the luxury trade, supported by its export-oriented manufacturing base.

Antwerp's economy collapsed after the Spanish Empire stopped paying its creditors in 1575 and after the city itself came under siege from 1584 to 1585. The city's collapse provided the Dutch manufacturing and commercial sectors with an abundant supply of fresh workers and capital. People from the Southern Netherlands had been migrating north since the rebellion broke out in the 1560s, but the speed and scale of this migration changed dramatically after Spanish troops captured Antwerp. Around 100,000 people reportedly fled the city at this time.

The skilled workmen and merchants among these refugees settled in the commercial and manufacturing centers of Holland and Zeeland. As large numbers of skilled workers moved to the Netherlands, the export-oriented manufacturing sector—which had performed poorly until the 1580s—entered a phase of remarkable growth. At the time, Leiden was the center of the wool cloth industry. Because of the influx of migrants, the population more than doubled in just 20 years (from about 12,000 in 1581 to 26,000 in 1600), and the city was reborn as the primary production center of the "new draperies" brought in by immigrants. In the 1570s, Haarlem had a population of around 14,000; by 1622, this had increased to 39,000. This was the result of the rapid growth of the linen industry following immigration by skilled bleachers from the Flanders area.

Amsterdam by itself absorbed around 30,000 of these immigrants, who made up one-third of the city's population in 1600. The category of migrants to take note of here are the merchants. According to Braudel, so many merchants immigrated from the Southern Netherlands that they accounted for one-third of the merchant community in Amsterdam between 1580 and 1630. These merchants not only brought their personal networks and their knowledge of the network of merchants that connected northern and southern Europe, as well as Europe and the world outside it, but they also supplied a great deal of commercial capital. They increased the amount of merchants' capital in Amsterdam by around 50% and played a particularly important role in raising capital for the Bank of Amsterdam and the VOC [36].

Of course, the Dutch Republic was not the inevitable destination of refugees from the Southern Netherlands. Indeed, a significant number of the prosperous merchants and skilled workers who left Antwerp headed to the Protestant regions of northwestern Germany, regions where the luxury trade and manufacturing had a longer history. But the majority of refugees from the Southern Netherlands (and most of those who went to northwestern Germany) ultimately ended up settling in the Dutch Republic.

There were various reasons for this. One reason was that the Dutch Republic's control of bulk shipping ensured a steady supply of foodstuffs. In addition, the sophisticated transportation network that connected the sea with inland waterways made it easy to acquire materials to build houses, and by the 1590s it was widely believed that the Republic would ultimately withstand the Spanish attacks. But the biggest reason of all was supportive policies adopted by the Republic. In order to attract these immigrants, Dutch cities competed with each other to provide a range of incentives. Those incentives included tax breaks, freedom from guild rules, a supply of child labor, loans, and guaranteed sales [37].

Therefore, the decline of Antwerp and mass immigration by merchants and manufacturers from that city enabled the manufacturing centers of the Netherlands to acquire the capital and technology they needed to produce high-end textiles (including new draperies, linens, and cotton cloth). They were also able to take advantage of the trade network that had been built by merchants from the Southern Netherlands. And when Philip II closed the ports of the Iberian Peninsula to foreign vessels with the hope of putting pressure on the Netherlands, this only made Dutch merchants turn their attention to the spice trade. Dutch merchants had already been weighing the idea of expanding into Russia and the Levant, and this spurred them to actively explore the possibility of opening up trade routes to Asia. Because of this, a convoy that was jointly funded by Amsterdam merchants embarked for Asia in 1595, and the VOC was launched in 1602.

These events show that the Dutch Republic in the 1590s was prepared to emerge as the hegemonic power in the global economy. The fledgling state had defended its independence against the Spanish Empire, which boasted the strongest military of its day. It also had an edge in bulk shipping, a competitive manufacturing industry, and a trade network for luxury goods, which were backed by the manufacturing sector, commercial base, and capital that had been accumulating since the fifteenth century.

But there was also a social transformation underway that suggested that the Netherlands would pursue economic hegemony even more aggressively in the future. The merchants who had been far from political power in traditional agricultural societies were now the political elite in the Netherlands. The merchant elite that emerged in the 1590s differed in a number of respects from the city office-holders from commercial and manufacturing families—known as regents—who had dominated political and economic matters in the Netherlands until then. The new merchant elite were much wealthier than the elite that had preceded them. They were interested in the trade in luxury goods, and they also wanted to monopolize markets to ensure success in the new competition over commerce. It was they who provided the initial capital needed to expand into Asia, and it was they who led the way in establishing the VOC, which would coordinate trade in the overseas colonies [38].

Perfection of the System of Expansive Reinvestment: The Dutch East India Company

The first country to take an interest in opening up a sea route to Asia and monopolizing the spice trade was Portugal. As we saw in chapter two, Portugal's expansion into Asia was quite different from Spain's conquest of the Americas. Two historical circumstances determined the nature of Portugal's maritime expansion. First, as scholars of world history have emphasized in recent years, the Asian economy already had an extensive yet dense international trade network that encompassed the Eurasian continent and the oceans around it even before the arrival of the Western powers. Second, this international trade network was supported by developed cities and surrounded by a number of powerful states and empires.

While Portugal had an advantage in regard to certain military technologies (such as the cannons on its ships) [39], this by itself was not enough to overpower the economic and political forces in the region. Therefore, Portugal was forced to find opportunities to participate in the highly developed Asian trade network. The strategy that Portugal adopted in pursuit of this aim was using force to capture a few nodes in the existing trade network, collecting tribute from merchant ships that passed by these nodes and from the rulers of the surrounding regions, and securing spice and other trade goods with the help of local merchants. This is how Portugal's expansion into Asia differed from Spain's conquest of the Americas, which required ruling a huge amount of territory.

But there was also one way in which Portugal's expansion into Asia and Spain's conquest of the New World were fundamentally alike. This was the fact that, despite Portugal's maritime expansion, it also failed to transcend the type of economic growth that is characteristic of agricultural society. Just as the Spanish conquistadors had sailed to the Americas in order to overcome the limitations of diminishing agricultural production and decelerating economic growth (goals that had also fueled the medieval Reconquista), the Portuguese also meant to seize territory and to appropriate labor surplus through extra-economic coercion. But conditions in Asia were very different from in the Americas, and the trade in spices and other luxury products fell into the hands of the merchants of Asia and of various European countries.

By contrast, Dutch expansion into Asia strictly obeyed the logic of commercial society. This does not mean, of course, that Dutch merchants never employed military force. Even before the VOC was established, Dutch merchant fleets had relied upon the state's military power. The VOC itself used force to overthrow the local governments in spice-producing areas, and they violently oppressed groups of European merchants.

What set the Dutch apart was the purpose of the extra-economic coercion they employed. In the 1590s, the new merchant elite of the Netherlands were more proactive than the elite they had replaced in securing the state's military and institutional support for their efforts to gain a monopolistic position in Asian trade. In other words, what was important to them was not territory and plunder but commerce and profit, and the support of the state was but a supplemental tool for achieving their commercial objectives.

It was in the 1590s that Dutch merchants began to take an interest in Asian trade, which was then controlled by Portugal and Spain. Until this time, spices had been imported by Portugal and exclusively traded in Antwerp. This meant that Dutch merchants had to buy the spices they needed at Antwerp and then resell them in the markets of northern Europe.

But in the 1580s, the merchants of northern Germany started competing with Dutch merchants in the spice trade in northern Europe. At the same time, demand for spices in Europe continued to increase, which caused prices to rise since the supply of spices available through Portugal was limited. Given the escalation of the war between the Netherlands and Spain and the collapse of the spice trading system centered on Antwerp, it was inevitable that competition in the European spice market would intensify. Under these circumstances, Dutch traders began to fear that if they did not become more competitive they might be driven out of the market for good. This is why the merchants sent their own fleets to Asia in the 1590s.

In the 1590s, Dutch merchants ventured into Asia through a number of early firms called *voor-compagnien* that were purely commercial syndicates that pooled capital to fund projects. The reason the merchants adopted this kind of business arrangement was because sailing to Asia was not practical for merchants to do on their own. These voyages took longer than intra-European commerce and carried greater risks.

What the *voor-compagnien* most needed to ensure their success, though, was support from the state. This is illustrated by Compagnie van Verre, the first group of Amsterdam merchants to embark upon trade with Asia. The group was founded with capital from major merchants and small stockholders, but it also received a number of privileges from the Dutch Republic. The state loaned it weapons, exempted it from customs duties, and legally guaranteed it any rights it might claim in Asia in the future [40].

While the voyage of the Compagnie van Verre was not a great success, it did motivate Dutch merchants to accelerate their efforts to trade with Asia. Through 1602, a total of 65 ships in 15 fleets made the journey to Asia. The *voor-compagnien* had poor returns, however. With so many companies competing for Asian trade, the price of trade goods rose in Asia and fell in Europe. In addition, as the Dutch Republic was still at war with Spain, Dutch ships were at a high risk of being attacked by Spanish and Portuguese privateers and merchant ships. So the managers of the *voor-compagnien* concluded that they needed to limit competition by combining the existing companies and securing more support from the state. This led to negotiations between the managers of the *voor-compagnien* and the States General that culminated in 1602 with the birth of the Dutch East India Company (VOC) [41].

The VOC had an unusual ownership and management structure that in a sense parallels that of the modern corporation. The VOC's initial capital was locked down for ten years, which broke with the tradition of paying back not only profits but the entire principal to investors at the end of each voyage and thus ensured that the VOC could remain in business. The VOC also adopted a system of limited liability, which lowered risk for investors.

There were also some respects in which the VOC was similar to the state-run enterprises of today. As long as VOC managers were faithful to their contractual obligations, stockholders were unable to take part in its management, rather like the relationship between the government and government bondholders. Just as bondholders can buy and sell their bonds but not participate in government policy-making, VOC stockholders could not participate in company management. Thus, the VOC can be said to have represented a mixture of the characteristics of corporations and state-run enterprises.

The VOC had raised a huge amount of capital—tenfold more than the English East India Company (EIC), which was established in 1601—and this gave it an advantage in terms of scale. In addition, the VOC was effectively able to combine support from the state with the acumen of its professional managers. As a result, the VOC played a key role in setting up the system of expansive reinvestment in the Netherlands. Furthermore, the capital that the VOC amassed also helped the Netherlands acquire economic hegemony on the basis of its accelerating economic growth.

The VOC represented the first successful combination of capital and state power, and its innovative nature is also exemplified by the manner in which it employed military force. As we have already mentioned, what the Netherlands and Portugal had in common was their reliance on military power to establish themselves in Asia. The difference between them was that Portugal regarded commerce as a way to plunder, which was its source of profit, whereas the Netherlands used military force in the pursuit of commercial profit. The VOC was able to exercise military force in East Asia because this was specified in its founding charter. Article 35 of the charter stated that the VOC could perform state functions—such as signing treaties, declaring war, building forts and trading posts, and augmenting its military forces—on behalf of the States General. This authorized the VOC to acquire and deploy an independent military force [42].

Relying upon its ability to raise a huge amount of capital and on its private army, the VOC began to monopolize the spice trade. Spices were the main product that the VOC traded. Pepper, for example, accounted for 56% of the VOC's total revenue between 1619 and 1621 and 50.3% of its total revenue between 1648 and 1650. When clove and nutmeg are included, spices accounted for between 70 and 75% of the VOC's total revenue during the first half of the seventeenth century. In order to control the production sites of these crucial trade items in Asia and to monopolize their supply in Europe, the VOC did not scruple to use force. The supply of pepper was impossible to regulate because it was produced in various places, but this was not true of the other spices.

An infamous example of the VOC's heavy-handed approach was the Amboyna Massacre, which occurred in 1623. According to an agreement between the English East India Company (EIC) and the Netherlands, the English had established a trading post on the island of Ambon, the primary site where clove was grown. But in an attempt to weaken English control of Ambon, the Dutch used a seditious plot as a pretext to execute 20 people, including English, Japanese, and Portuguese [43]. In this way, the English were cut out of the spice trade. In 1641, the Dutch also drove the Portuguese out of Malacca. This gave the Netherlands a clear advantage in the spice islands in the 1650s, and they were able to gain a monopoly over nutmeg on the Banda Islands and clove on Ambon and the Moluccas.

But acquiring a monopoly over the spice trade was not the only challenge that the VOC had to overcome in order to maintain its profits. Since there was virtually no demand for European products in the Asian market, the trade deficit increased along with the soaring imports of spices. To compensate for this, the VOC dived into regional trade in East Asia. The trading posts that the Dutch had built for the spice trade proved instrumental in intra-Asian trade as well. From the VOC's seizure of Ambon in 1605 until the mid-seventeenth century, the VOC set up trading posts in 20 or so locations and built a dense network connecting them. This made the VOC a force to be reckoned with in intra-Asian commerce (unlike the EIC, which largely focused on direct trade between Asia and England during this period). The Dutch made considerable profits by shipping cotton from southern India to Indonesia and Chinese silk from Taiwan to Japan and by trading Indonesian spices for Japanese silver and copper in Nagasaki.

The VOC's success not only provided the Netherlands with an opportunity to gain an edge in global trade but also laid the foundation for the financial revolution in the Netherlands. The appearance of transferrable VOC stock in the Amsterdam capital market made it possible for investors to seek speculative profit without sacrificing their liquidity, and the burgeoning stock market grew alongside the bond market, which joined it in 1609.

To be sure, the capital market had existed before the Dutch began trading in Asia. But as we have already observed, it cost more to trade in Asia than in Europe or on the Atlantic Ocean, requiring between two to four times more in initial capital.

Furthermore, it took a long time to sail to Asia, and such voyages represented a greater risk. One out of every five ships that departed for Asia during the period of the *voor-compagnien* never returned home, and even successful journeys took at least two years.

Since Asian trade entailed so much risk and required so much initial capital, the VOC took the form of a corporation and adopted limited liability. Because of these choices, the company was able to raise half of its initial capital of 6.4 million guilders by issuing stocks. The creation of the institutional framework needed for this stock to be freely traded stimulated rapid growth in the capital market and enabled the Netherlands to undergo a financial revolution before any other country in Europe [44].

The End of Acceleration

The first half of the seventeenth century was the golden age of the Dutch economy, with the VOC dominating the Asian spice trade and intra-Asian trade. After getting started in bulk shipping, the Netherlands first took over the luxury goods trade in Europe during its war for independence and then gained control of trade with Asia, which was the area with the highest added value. At the same time, the success of the financial revolution helped the Netherlands maintain its military strength as it rose to become a hegemonic power in the global economy.

But this golden age was short-lived. By the 1670s, economic growth in the Netherlands had already begun to slow. By 1715, the state's finances were in such trouble that it could no longer even pay the interest on its debts [45]. But this was just one of several signs of decline. In the 1670s, the population of the Netherlands stopped growing. Its population remained stable from the 1670s until 1815, but compared to the population growth in the emerging power of England, the population of the Netherlands underwent a relative decline. The population of the Netherlands as a percentage of England's population stood at 35% around 1715 but fell to 21% in 1815. The level of urbanization in the Netherlands had climbed to 45% in the 1670s before dropping to 37% in 1815, while the level of nominal wages and energy consumption stagnated after the 1670s. Consequently, the Netherlands' per capita gross national product did not increase between 1670 and the 1800s even as its population remained the same [46].

Why was the Netherlands unable to prolong its golden age? This is a question that has long occupied historians' attention, but what we will emphasize in this chapter is that during the mid- and late seventeenth century there were signs that the virtuous cycle of war and the economy in the Dutch Republic was in trouble. This resulted from a number of factors working in conjunction. For one, the Dutch economy was fundamentally dependent on commerce, and there are inherent limitations on the value that can be created in the system of expansive reinvestment in commercial society. On top of that, the Netherlands ceded its military advantage to England and other rivals during the mercantilist competition that intensified after the mid-seventeenth century. This was when the Netherlands began to deviate from the virtuous cycle of war and the economy that it had enjoyed during its war for independence.

The Dutch Republic's political system did not help it overcome this crisis. Its loose federal system had taken shape during the transitional period between the Middle Ages and the early modern period, and the various provinces were unable to look beyond their own interests either to propose or to execute innovative plans for overcoming the country's socio-economic crisis. Amid these circumstances, the Netherlands was plunged into war once again when it was invaded by France in 1672. The war dealt the Netherlands a blow from which it would not soon recover. It also spelled the end of the Dutch economic hegemony.

What exactly were the limitations that the Dutch system of expansive reinvestment ran into? There are three problems that can be identified. First, the main products of commercial society were created in the agricultural, mining, and craft sectors—all areas in which production tends to diminish. During the first part of the seventeenth century, for example, the Netherlands' most important commercial products were spices, but in the second half of the seventeenth century, this market was oversupplied. Spices no longer guaranteed the high added value they once had, and the Dutch could not find a comparable replacement product.

Second, the development of commercial society depended heavily upon the development of means of transportation, and here too the Netherlands ran into difficulties. Maritime transport was limited in terms of size and speed because of technical constraints on shipbuilding, while land transport developed very slowly until the invention of the railroad. Even when the Netherlands acquired trade routes, maintaining those routes required a huge amount of military spending. Given the technological level of the time, however, Dutch expertise in the areas of shipbuilding, navigation, and weapons manufacture could be easily imitated by its rivals.

This problem was linked to the third limitation that the Netherlands faced. Since the system of expansive reinvestment in commercial society did not generally rely upon innovation in the supply sector fueled by technological innovation, a technological advantage could not be long maintained in the age of commercial societies. The low level of technology, in other words, meant that technological advancements in a specific manufacturing sector could be easily copied or stolen by rivals.

These limitations combined to undermine the commercial advantage that had undergirded the economy of the Netherlands. First, trade on the Baltic Sea—so important that the Dutch called it the "mother trade"—began to falter and decline. It is important to note here that there was no appreciable change in the Dutch Republic's relative share of Baltic trade. Until at least the 1730s, the Dutch Republic still controlled 70% of the grain that was shipped from the Baltic to western Europe.

The change instead appears in the total scale of trade. In the first half of the seventeenth century, trade on the Baltic Sea was worth an average of 68,500 *last* a year; in the second half of the seventeenth century, this decreased to an average of

55,800 *last*. In the first half of the eighteenth century, the decline became even starker, with the volume of trade falling to a yearly average of 31,800 *last*. This phenomenon was caused by an overall decline in demand as European population growth slowed and by the rise of England and other new grain exporters [47].

An even greater threat to the Dutch economy, however, was a structural change in trade with Asia. The VOC had enjoyed an effective monopoly on the spice trade through the first half of the seventeenth century, while the EIC and other rivals of the Dutch had focused their energy on the textile trade. But now the spice trade was becoming less and less profitable, while the textile trade was rapidly gaining in relative importance. When the VOC was established, pepper was still a luxury item in Europe, but as competing commercial interests in Europe rushed into trade with Asia, the supply of pepper in Europe increased dramatically. This resulted in an oversupply of pepper, and by the 1680s, it was no longer a luxury item. Around the same time, importers of clove and other spices ran into another problem: overall spice consumption was contracting because of population decline. Clove consumption, for example, declined from between 450,000 and 500,000 lb in 1620 to between 400,000 and 425,000 lb in 1655 and to 300,000 lb in the 1740s.

Thus, while the Dutch spice trade was in decline, textiles came to represent a much greater share of trade. As we have already mentioned, spices accounted for about 70% of the VOC's total revenue in the first half of the seventeenth century. But in the second half of the seventeenth century, spices decreased as a percentage of total trade as cotton cloth and other textiles increased, and by the middle of the eighteenth century, the textile trade made up 40% of total revenue. Tea and coffee also became more important trading items.

The problem confronting the VOC was that it could not acquire a monopolistic position in these growing commercial sectors as it had in the spice trade. While spices were only cultivated in a handful of locations, textile production was widely distributed across various regions. Even worse, Asian producers, brokers, and states were deeply involved in the production and distribution of these products. The VOC failed to adapt to the changing commercial environment.

While the VOC's monopolistic position was being undermined, the EIC was growing at a brisk pace. The contrasting fortunes of the two companies are aptly illustrated by the tea trade. The Netherlands sought to achieve a monopoly in the tea trade with the same techniques it had used in the spice trade. That is, it attempted to apply the methods that had worked with tribes and petty states on the spice islands to China, then the largest empire in Asia. The Chinese government retaliated by barring the VOC from the tea trade.

In 1717—while these events were underway—the EIC began directly importing tea that was shipped to Guangdong by fleets of Chinese junks. This led to an extraordinary increase in the volume of tea imports. The VOC finally adopted the EIC's methods, but by then it had already lost control of the market. The Dutch failure in the tea trade had wider economic ramifications. Encouraged by its success, the EIC pioneered the new trading strategy of exchanging Indian cotton cloth for Chinese tea and opium, which brought incredible returns. Meanwhile, the VOC was gradually falling behind in this competition.

The difference between the strategies pursued by the Dutch and English East India Companies in their trade in Asia foreshadowed a subsequent shift in the balance of power between the Dutch Republic and England (later Great Britain). As economic growth stalled while the Dutch Republic struggled to find a new product with high added value, a showdown with its powerful rival England brought the Netherlands' limitations into full view. War between the two countries ultimately knocked the Netherlands out of the virtuous cycle of war and the economy.

War with England and Its Consequences

Between 1650 and 1690, the Netherlands fought three wars with England. On a fundamental level, England used these wars to challenge the Netherlands' economic hegemony [48]. The Dutch had been forced to fight a long war with Spain in order to create the new system of expansive reinvestment, and now they had to defend themselves against other challengers. The Dutch Republic had to fight against England, Spain, and France, and these wars eroded the Republic's economic advantage.

The Anglo-Dutch Wars began shortly after Oliver Cromwell came to power in England through the upheaval of the English Civil War. Cromwell believed that fulfilling the mission of the Protestant Reformation and defending England amid the intensifying mercantilist rivalry required that he expand the navy and strengthen commerce. This could only mean competing with the Netherlands.

Since the end of the sixteenth century, Dutch merchants had been making inroads in the Levant and other areas where England had traditionally held an advantage, and the Netherlands was also aggressively preventing the English from trading in Asia. England had no choice but to compete with the Netherlands if it wanted to ensure the safety of the realm and to lay the groundwork for economic growth. This led to the introduction of the Navigation Acts. The enforcement of these laws turned the rivalry between the two countries into a military confrontation. They fought two wars between 1652 and 1654 and between 1665 and 1667, and France's participation in the third war, which began in 1672, put the Netherlands' economic hegemony into jeopardy.

Neither the Netherlands or England emerged as the clear victor in the three wars. In the long term, what was more important than who won these long and costly wars was the severe harm they inflicted on both countries' navies. During the two years of the First Anglo-Dutch War, for example, the Netherlands lost around 1500 merchant vessels, while England's navy was so weakened that it could barely defend the English Channel [49]. In the Third Anglo-Dutch War, which was triggered by a clash in East Asia, the Netherlands had to contend not only with England (which had greatly strengthened its navy after the Second Anglo-Dutch War) but also with France. The French army seized 48 Dutch cities, Utrecht among them, and the Dutch resorted to the desperate measure of opening the dikes in Holland and Zeeland to halt the French advance. But despite these hardships, the Dutch fleet enjoyed considerable successes in its raids on English and French colonies in India and North America [50].

The Netherlands' failure to gain a military advantage in these three wars despite its overwhelming economic advantage can be attributed to several factors. The most important of these was the unique political structure of the Dutch Republic. The opposing interests of the Dutch provinces and the tense relations between the States General and the military leaders hindered the war effort. For example, the parliament of Holland (the richest province in the Republic) was controlled by regents from commercial families who supported the autonomy of the cities and provinces and pushed to decentralize power and prioritize trade, while the stadholders from the House of Orange who led the Dutch army favored a unified state. This debate could be traced back to the disagreement between the governor and the regents during the war for independence, and it continued during the Netherlands' wars with England. Since the two main political factions in the Dutch Republic were unable to set a consistent course for state policy, the state could hardly be expected to prosecute the war effectively.

The friction between the conflicting interests of the provinces also caused problems for the operations of the Dutch navy, which played a critical role in the Anglo-Dutch Wars. As we have already seen, the Republic's political system placed the navy under the control of each provincial parliament. The provinces reserved the right to allocate money for building Dutch warships, along with the authority to make appointments for them. In other words, the Dutch fleet was organized and operated as a combined fleet consisting of contingents from each province.

So when there was a clash between the provinces' interests, those clashes played out in the operations of the combined fleet and affected its strategy. This was illustrated by an incident that occurred during a naval battle in the Second Anglo-Dutch War. While the battle was raging, a squadron of the combined fleet left the line of battle after receiving a summons from its local government. This shows that the provincial fleets placed a higher priority on the interests of their own province than on the interests of the Dutch Republic as a whole.

Another problem facing the Dutch navy was a shift in its technological advantage. Since the Dutch navy typically operated in coastal waters, its ships tended to be rather small. Such ships could only carry between 80 and 90 cannons and also had trouble sailing against the wind. Adding more guns to maximize the ships' firepower made them top-heavy. This put them at a disadvantage, making them liable to capsize when they were hit by enemy fire and took on water. By way of contrast, the English navy already had three-decker ships with more than 100 guns, and by the 1660s it had acquired big warships that weighed more than 1000 tons. The Dutch navy countered by augmenting its warships' mobility, but this by itself was not enough to compensate for the massive firepower of the warships in the English and French navies.

These weaknesses of the Dutch Republic, which were related to its formation from a coalition of commercial cities, were laid bare by wars and other crises. Unlike other European states that were pushing for more centralization, the Dutch

Republic's weak central government was unable to control its cities and provinces. The central government struggled to raise the money needed to build up the navy, even with war right around the corner. The first ships in the Dutch navy were repurposed merchant ships rather than warships by design, a fact that suggests that the Dutch preoccupation with short-term profits distracted them from making long-term investments in the military. As a consequence, the state's limitations were on full display during the confrontation with England.

In fact, the Dutch Republic's economic hegemony began to be challenged as soon as it was recognized as an independent state in 1648. When Spain gave up trying to recover its lost territory and stopped vying for hegemony in Europe, it seemed as if peace had come to the Netherlands at last. But the Netherlands' commercial advantage gave its neighbors—England and France in particular—cause to oppose it and also provoked sporadic attacks in the Baltic Sea from Denmark and Sweden. Under these conditions, the Dutch Republic had no choice but to spend a significant portion of its resources on defending its borders and on protecting its overseas bases, territories, and trade network. This necessitated a series of tax increases that caused the real per capita tax burden in Holland to double between 1659 and 1713.

As fast as the tax burden rose, the Dutch provinces' debt increased even faster. Even the end of the three wars with England (and later France) did not bring relief from taxes and debts. As soon as William III, Prince of Orange, was crowned king of England during the Glorious Revolution, the Dutch Republic and England joined forces to fight in the Nine Years' War. By the end of that war, Holland was spending more each year on its loans than it received in ordinary taxes.

Such increases in the state debt seriously compromised the Dutch Republic's investment and production capacities. By 1659, the Republic was forced to spend a significant portion of the tax receipts earmarked for strengthening the army and the navy on paying interest. Accordingly, government debt had grown to 200% of the national income by 1713. These facts show that the Netherlands had deviated from the virtuous cycle of war and the economy. To be sure, the Netherlands was not the only state in which endless wars caused military expenditures to soar. What should be noted here, however, is that England, the Netherlands' rival, found a way to effectively fund large-scale wars in the form of the financial revolution (which began at the end of the seventeenth century) while the Netherlands failed to do so.

Historians attribute this difference to the unique origins of the fiscal systems of England (Great Britain after 1707) and the Netherlands. After the Restoration in 1660, England gradually reformed its fiscal system. For example, it created a system for assessing and collecting taxes (indirect and otherwise) that was more centralized and efficient than any other state and that could be consistently applied throughout the entire country. This led to the growth of a government bond market around the Bank of England. In the Netherlands, by contrast, the fiscal system was still the responsibility of the seven provinces. The state had preserved a system in which not only tax assessment and collection but also the distribution of tax revenues was independently decided by each province.

During the war for independence, the Dutch Republic's decentralized fiscal organization was sufficient for defending its territory and for protecting the economic activity of its citizens. But such a system could not cope with the mercantilist competition that was raging at the end of the seventeenth century. A system that allowed the provinces to collect taxes in a manner appropriate to their tax-bearing ability may have been effective for individuals. But the cost of war was increasing enormously, and that cost could only be covered by a coordinated and compulsory system of taxation managed by the central government.

The ultimate consequence of this was that the Dutch merchants could no longer make full use of their abilities. That is, they could no longer count on the protection of the state, unlike their English counterparts, who were able to rapidly expand their business and trade around the world with the powerful English navy at their back. As a consequence, hegemony in the global economy slipped from the Dutch grasp.

The Historical Limitations of the Dutch System of Expansive Reinvestment

The Netherlands built the first mature commercial society in history on the foundation of the system of expansive reinvestment. Despite this, the golden age of the Dutch Republic did not last for long. During the mid-seventeenth century, the countries of Europe had left behind the threat of religious conflict and civil war and were starting to concentrate on state formation. During a time of full-fledged mercantilist competition, the Netherlands could not effectively fend off the formidable challenge posed by states like England and France that had more territory, larger populations, and bigger armies.

Even so, the decline of the Netherlands differed from that of the agricultural empire of Spain. The merchants who had led the Netherlands into its golden age still had their advanced commercial network and their corporate foundation, and they still owned a great deal of capital. During the mid-seventeenth century, speculative mania passed over the Netherlands, and in the late seventeenth century, great quantities of Dutch capital were moved out of the Netherlands and into the financial markets of London. This tells us that the Dutch decline could not have been caused by the exhaustion of the nation's wealth. The same inference can be drawn from the fact that, despite the slump in the commercial and manufacturing sectors, the Dutch enjoyed the highest standard of wages in the world at least until the end of the eighteenth century [51].

As this shows, the problem for the wealthy merchants and manufacturers of the Netherlands was not a lack of capital or experience but rather uncertainty about the future. Just a few generations before, when the seven provinces of the Dutch Republic had fought the Spanish Empire, the world's most powerful state, they had waged war much more efficiently than Spain's agricultural empire. Spain had to make painful sacrifices in order to cover the ballooning cost of its military spending amid decelerating economic growth, but the Netherlands concentrated its energy on protecting commerce, which was the source of its national wealth. This helped the Netherlands to launch the virtuous cycle of war and the economy, which turned the war into a springboard for economic growth.

But by the mid-seventeenth century, the military situation had changed. England and France were fully aware that the outcome of the war was ultimately decided by the economic power of the state, and they therefore used every available means to protect their commerce and industry. England was building a fiscal-military state that would prove more efficient than the Netherlands' fiscal system. Under such circumstances, military defeat was tantamount to a loss of economic influence, and the Netherlands had no choice but to devote more of its resources to the war effort despite the fiscal burden that this involved. This made it gradually harder for the Netherlands to sustain the virtuous cycle of war and the economy that had helped it become a hegemonic state in the first place.

If the Netherlands' system of expansive reinvestment had retained the vitality it had enjoyed in the first half of the seventeenth century, the outcome would obviously have been different. But that would not have been easy either. As we have already seen, the secret to the success of the Netherlands' system of expansive reinvestment can be found in how it combined bulk shipping and the luxury goods trade to become a hub of the global entrepôt trade.

But mercantilist competition became more heated in the mid-seventeenth century, and this signaled the beginning of a zero-sum game in the areas of trade in which the Netherlands had held a definite advantage. The merchants of rival countries became more combative in taking advantage of their governments' military force to force Dutch merchants out of their monopolistic position and more proactive in seeking out new products and new markets. In addition, the merchants and governments of these rival states began to block Dutch merchants from accessing their domestic and colonial markets. England's Navigation Acts offer one example of how these states cut off Dutch merchants' access to their markets and began promoting domestic manufacturing products to replace the imports that had been supplied by Dutch merchants.

Meanwhile, the weaknesses and limitations of the Dutch economy's dependence upon the system of expansive reinvestment in commercial society started to become manifest. The Netherlands succeeded at bringing the global trading network under its temporary control, but it was negligent in supplying its own manufacturing products to that trade network. Of course, after the fall of Antwerp, there was brisk investment in a number of manufacturing sectors, including the high-end textile manufacturing, and this did help Dutch products gain prominence in the European luxury goods market. But relatively less investment went into developing and producing everyday products for the lower class and the "middling sort," who would emerge as gradually more important segments of the market. If the Dutch had invested robustly throughout the entire manufacturing sector (and not only in luxury goods) and had thus made Dutch manufacturing products more competitive than their rivals in terms of quality and price, the Netherlands might have been able to overcome the mercantilist regulations of various European countries and break into markets in Asia and the Atlantic.

These facts imply that the system of expansive reinvestment in the Netherlands failed to develop into the system of expansive reproduction based on innovation in the supply sector. This is the factor that deserves the greatest emphasis in explaining the Netherlands' decline, since it has implications for the fate of any commercial society that lacks an industrial base. To understand how this happened—how England, which challenged the Netherlands' commercial advantage, was able to transition from the system of expansive reinvestment to the system of expansive reproduction—we must look at the formation of England's commercial society and at its distinguishing characteristics.

References

1. Immanuel Wallerstein, *The Modern World System II: Mercantilism and the Consolidation of the European World Economy, 1600–1750* (New York, 1980); Jan de Vries and Ad van der Woude, *The First Modern Economy: Success, Failure, and Perseverance of the Dutch Economy, 1500–1815* (Cambridge, 1997). For the observation that the Netherlands was the first state to escape from the Malthusian Trap to achieve continuous economic growth, see the following: Douglass C. North and Robert Paul Thomas, *The Rise of the Western World: A New Economic History* (Cambridge, 1973), pp. 102–106, especially p. 105; Jan de Vries, "Dutch Economic Growth in Comparative-Historical Perspective, 1500–2000," *De Economist* 148:4 (2000). Around 1600, the Dutch Republic is estimated to have had a population of around 1.5 million. In contrast, 10 million people were living on the Iberian Peninsula and between 16 and 20 million people were living in France around the same time.
2. Quoted in Braudel, *Civilization & Capitalism 15th–18th Century, vol. 3: The Perspective of the World* (New York, 1984), p. 177.
3. De Vries and van der Woude, *The First Modern Economy*, p. 17.
4. Jacques le Goff, *Medieval Civilization 400–1500*, trans. Julia Barrow (Oxford, 1988), p. 226.
5. De Vries and van der Woude, *The First Modern Economy*, pp. 16–18.
6. De Vries and van der Woude, *The First Modern Economy*, p. 19.
7. De Vries and van der Woude, *The First Modern Economy*, pp. 59–62; Jan de Vries, *European Urbanization 1500–1800* (London, 1984).
8. Jonathan Israel, *The Dutch Republic: Its Rise, Greatness, and Fall 1477–1806*, paperback with corrections (Oxford, 1998), pp. 74–82, 102–104; Diarmaid MacCulloch, *Reformation: Europe's House Divided 1490–1700* (London, 2003).
9. In the mid-seventeenth century, the Dutch stumbled upon another kind of anxiety deriving from the disconnect between the emphasis on self-discipline and moderation on the one hand and the growth of a consumer lifestyle made possible by capitalistic development on the other. For more on this, see Simon Schama, *The Embarrassment of Riches: An Interpretation of Dutch Culture in the Golden Age* (London, 1987).
10. Jan de Vries, *The Dutch Rural Economy in the Golden Age, 1500–1700* (New Haven, 1974), pp. 210–211.
11. De Vries and van der Woude, *The First Modern Economy*, pp. 350–351.
12. De Vries and van der Woude, *The First Modern Economy*, pp. 244–246, 251, 267. In the early eighteenth century, the herring fishery began facing stiff competition from the fishing fleets of Scotland and Scandinavian countries. As a result, the herring catch at the end of the eighteenth century was down to one-quarter of its level in the 1640 s and its value was down

to one-third. The value of the herring fishery in 1775 is estimated to have been around one million guilders (around two million guilders if the cod and whaling catch are included). By way of showing what share of the Dutch agricultural sector this represented, De Vries and Van der Woude note that the manufacturing sector in early 1700 was worth two million guilders, while cheese bound for market was worth between 1.8 and 2 million guilders (p. 267). The next figures are found in Braudel, *Civilization & Capitalism vol. 3*, p. 189. According to estimates that Braudel cites, the fishing catch amounted to 300,000 tons, conflicting with the figures we quoted. According to these scholars, the 1630s can be seen as the glory days of the herring fishery. After the development of the fluyt, the buss became smaller and the size of the crew was reduced to 12 or 13, which suggests that between 6,000 and 7,000 fishermen were engaged in the trade.

13. De Vries and van der Woude, *The First Modern Economy*, p. 296.
14. The Netherlands' advantage in the shipbuilding industry was the result of a combination of factors. Among the factors cited by Parry are carpentry techniques for shipbuilding, the efficient use of material, labor-reducing machinery, standardized production on a large scale, material purchases on a large scale, and inexpensive transportation of material. In short, Parry argued, the Netherlands' technical advantage and its control of trade on the Baltic Sea were what enabled the Dutch shipbuilding industry to grow. J. H. Parry, *The Age of Reconnaissance: Discovery, Exploration, and Settlement, 1450–1650* (London, 1963), p. 211.
15. De Vries and van der Woude, *The First Modern Economy*, p. 360.
16. Israel, *The Dutch Republic*, pp. 208–210, 212–213, 218–230.
17. De Vries and van der Woude, *The First Modern Economy*, pp. 93–94. These taxes had significant consequences. The provinces had complete discretion over how exactly to raise money for the subsidy, and the approach they took was to issue bonds backed by the revenue from the consumption tax. Even after the Republic won its independence, this method continued to play a crucial role in helping it maintain its finances. James D. Tracy, *The Founding of the Dutch Republic: War, Finance, and Politics in Holland, 1572–1588* (Oxford, 2008), p. 75.
18. The taxes that were also introduced at this time were a 5% tax on real estate transactions and a 1% tax on all capital. While the tax on capital was an extraordinary one-time tax, the taxes on real estate and commercial transactions were permanent. Geoffrey Parker, *The Dutch Revolt*, revised ed. (London, 1985), p. 115.
19. See chapter two.
20. Parker, *The Dutch Revolt*, pp. 116–117.
21. Marjolein 't Hart, "The Dutch Revolt 1566–81: A National Revolution?," David Parker (ed.), *Revolutions and the Revolutionary Tradition in the West 1560–1991* (London, 2000), pp. 16–17.
22. The Siege of Haarlem lasted for about seven months, and the Siege of Antwerp continued for more than a year, from July 1584 until the following August. More than half of Antwerp's population of 100,000 had already fled before the Spanish army arrived. Even after the siege ended in 1585, the city never regained its previous economic glory.
23. Maurice studied at Leiden University under Justus Lipsius, a humanist who was well-versed in the history of war. During that time, Maurice took a great interest in finding a way of breaking the Spanish army's *tercio* square formations, which were threatening the survival of the Netherlands. Inspired by the military classics of ancient Rome, he came to the conclusion that the way to overpower the *tercio* was by increasing firepower. That led to the military reforms of the 1590s.
24. Frank Tallett, *War and Society in Early Modern Europe, 1495–1715* (London, 1992). pp. 24–25.
25. The Dutch army of the time was not small relative to its population. In 1588, there were about 20,000 soldiers in the Dutch army, and this increased to 62,000 by 1607. From the resumption of the war in the 1620s until 1648, the army was maintained at a level of 55,000 to 60,000 men. At the end of the sixteenth century, France had between 50,000 and 60,000 men in arms, and the number grew to 200,000 during the Thirty Years' War. But considering that the

Netherlands had a population between 1.5 and 1.8 million people while France had a population of 20 million, the relative size of the Dutch army is impressive. Jan Glete, *War and the State in Early Modern Europe* (London, 2002), pp. 155–157.

26. In addition to this, the admiralty colleges were in charge of building warships, recruiting marines, and regulating the shipping and fishing industries. Israel, *The Dutch Republic*, p. 295.
27. After the establishment of the Dutch East India Company and West India Company, the navy played a lesser role in protecting the trade convoys in Asia and the Atlantic. These companies started arming their trading ships.
28. Glete, *War and the State in Early Modern Europe*, pp. 162–171.
29. The Netherlands was also harmed by the Spanish navy. Particular damage was caused by Spanish privateers based in Flanders: between 1642 and 1644, they seized or sank a total of 354 ships, including three warships and three armed merchant vessels. Under repeated attacks by privateers, Dutch trade in the Baltic and the Mediterranean was severely damaged as well. Jonathan Israel, *The Dutch Primacy in World Trade, 1585–1740* (Oxford, 1989), p. 137.
30. De Vries and van der Woude, *The First Modern Economy*, p. 100; Marjolein 't Hart, "The United Provinces, 1579–1806," Richard Bonney (ed.), *The Rise of the Fiscal State in Europe c. 1200–1815* (Oxford, 1999), p. 312.
31. 't Hart, "The United Provinces, 1579–1806," pp. 317–319. As we explained previously, tariffs were collected and used by the admiralty colleges. Interestingly, tariffs only accounted for 12.2% of the Republic's fiscal revenue in 1641.
32. De Vries and van der Woude, *The First Modern Economy*, pp. 95, 103.
33. Geoffrey Parker, *Spain and the Netherlands 1559-1659: Ten Studies* (London, 1979), p. 102.
34. De Vries and van der Woude, *The First Modern Economy*, pp. 114–115; 't Hart, "The United Provinces, 1579–1806," p. 315.
35. Tracy, *The Founding of the Dutch Republic*, pp. 107–108.
36. Braudel, *Civilization & Capitalism vol. 3*, pp. 187–188; Patrick K. O'Brien et al. (eds.), *Urban Achievement in Early Modern Europe: Golden Ages in Antwerp, Amsterdam and London* (Cambridge, 2001), pp. 75–76. Of the 320 people who had accounts at the Bank of Amsterdam in 1620, half were immigrants. Of the 88 major stockholders in the VOC, 41 were from the Southern Netherlands, but the total amount of stock that they held was 25% greater than the total stock held by stockholders from the Dutch Republic.
37. Marjolein 't Hart, "Freedom and Restrictions, State and Economy in the Dutch Republic, 1570–1670," *Economic and Social History in the Netherlands*, 4 (1993).
38. Israel, *The Dutch Republic*, pp. 344–348.
39. Until that time, naval battles had generally consisted of ramming the enemy's ships or boarding them and fighting at close quarters on the deck. The Portuguese, however, built ships with broadside guns that allowed them to employ the new tactic of firing on the enemy's fleet from a distance. This new tactic was first unveiled at the Battle of Diu in 1510.
40. Gyeong-cheol Ju, "The Dutch East India Company and Trade in Asia: The First Stage of Globalization," *American Studies* 28 (American Studies Institute at Seoul National University, 2005), p. 6.
41. Niels Steensgaard, *The Asian Trade Revolution of the Seventeenth Century* (Chicago, 1972), p. 127.
42. In the early seventeenth century, the VOC's armed forces numbered around 3,000, but by 1750 they had increased to 17,000.
43. Giles Milton, *Nathaniel's Nutmeg* (London, 1999).
44. Oscar Gelderblom and Joost Jonker, "Completing a Financial Revolution: The Finance of the Dutch East India Trade and the Rise of the Amsterdam Capital Market, 1595–1612," *The Journal of Economic History* 64 (September 2004); Larry Neal, *The Rise of Financial Capitalism: International Capital Markets in the Age of Reason* (Cambridge, 1990), chap. 6.
45. M. Prak, *The Dutch Republic in the Seventeenth Century* (Cambridge, 2005), p. 263.
46. De Vries, "Dutch Economic Growth in Comparative-Historical Perspective, 1500–2000," *De Economist* 148:4 (2000), pp. 457–461.

47. De Vries and van der Woude, *The First Modern Economy*, pp. 416–417.
48. This is not of course the reductive claim that these wars can be explained solely in economic terms. As Steven Pincus has shown in his research, relations between England and the Netherlands were affected as much by division within Protestantism as by commercial competition. For more on this point, see Steven Pincus, *Protestantism and Patriotism: Ideologies and the Making of English Foreign Policy, 1650–1668* (Cambridge, 1996).
49. Israel, *The Dutch Republic*, pp. 713–725.
50. Israel, *The Dutch Republic*, pp. 766–855.
51. For the fad for speculation, see Schama, *The Embarrassment of Riches*; Mike Dash, *Tulipomania: The Story of the World's Most Coveted Flower & the Extraordinary Passions It Aroused* (New York, 2001). For the flow of capital, see Neal, *The Rise of Financial Capitalism*. For wage levels at the end of the eighteenth century, see Robert C. Allen, *The British Industrial Revolution in Global Perspective* (Cambridge, 2009), chap. 2.

Chapter 4
From Commercial Society to Industrial Society in Great Britain

Whereas the Netherlands built the first system of expansive reinvestment in the early modern period, England overcame the Netherlands' commercial advantage to set up an empire that spanned the globe. After weathering a political crisis in the mid-seventeenth century, England not only acquired the characteristics of a mature commercial society through heated commercial and military competition with the Netherlands and France but also succeeded at surmounting the limitations of commercial society and evolving into an industrial society through the simultaneous development of naval power and domestic manufacturing [1].

Great Britain was able to perfect commercial society because it had achieved the virtuous cycle of war and the economy, the most critical factor for attaining hegemony. During the fifty years from the late seventeenth century until the early eighteenth century, Britain implemented measures related to its fiscal and financial systems, its tax collection regime, and its military strategy that were necessary for it to become the world's strongest empire and trading nation. In addition, Britain not only maintained a system of expansive reinvestment based on intermediary trade as the Netherlands had but also successfully acquired the system of expansive reproduction and transformed into an industrial society. The system of expansive reproduction in industrial society represents the addition of innovation in the supply sector to the system of expansive reinvestment in commercial society, and Britain took the first step toward industrial society by supplying manufactured goods produced at home to the trade network its merchants had created around the world.

Since numerous studies detail what Britain accomplished in the eighteenth century, we will not elaborate those accomplishments here. In line with the original purpose of this book—which, as we have said, is to explain the types of economic development and the formation of hegemony—we will instead examine the structural characteristics of the virtuous cycle of war and the economy that was based on the system of expansive reinvestment that formed in Britain. This will help us better understand why Britain emerged victorious from the intense

T.-Y. Kim and D. Kim, *The Secrets of Hegemony*,
DOI 10.1007/978-981-10-4416-8_4

mercantilist competition in the early modern period and also why it was Britain that underwent the transition from the system of expansive reinvestment to the system of expansive reproduction.

Formation of Commercial Society

England's transformation into a commercial society occurred during the period of political turmoil between the Civil War (1642–1651) and the Glorious Revolution (1688). But before examining this period, we must first consider some of the historical developments in the medieval and early modern periods that helped commercial society become established in seventeenth-century England.

Two historical developments in particular are worth noting. First was the fact that, since commercial agriculture had developed in England early on, the nobility and gentry had become accustomed to appropriating economic surplus through the market rather than through extra-economic coercion [2]. A development that was particularly important in this process was the growth of the gentry. As many noble houses collapsed during the Hundred Years' War and the War of the Roses, the position of the gentry became relatively more important. The gentry started taking an interest in commercial agriculture in the late fifteenth century—playing a leading role in the enclosure movement—and when the property of Catholic churches and monasteries was seized as part of King Henry VIII's religious reforms, the gentry bought up this land at cut-rate prices.

The gentry as a group were defined not by their bloodlines (as the nobility were) but rather by the amount of land they owned and the income they earned from renting out that land. Because of England's unique system of primogeniture—in which the eldest son received the entire inheritance—the gentry were closely connected (by blood and otherwise) with merchants, bureaucrats, and skilled professionals. As the gentry emerged as a major social force in England, property became the most important factor in determining one's social standing, and market-oriented agriculture became established as the means of increasing one's property.

The second important historical development was the early growth of the wool industry in England. By the thirteenth century, wool exports were already such an important industry in England that the monarch signed an agreement with wool producers and merchants about collecting taxes [3]. The wool industry developed even more rapidly during the Tudor period.

Early on, as Thomas More lamented in *Utopia*, the amount of pastureland had greatly increased during the first phase of enclosure. A considerable number of the peasants who were driven from the land by enclosure were absorbed into rural industries like wool processing. This was an important development that set the English economy down a different path from Spain's. In Spain, the development of the sheep raising industry led to the decline of cereal cultivation and the manufacturing industry. This did not occur in England because of the simultaneous development of commercial agriculture and rural industry.

Instead of relying solely on wool exports, England's woolen cloth traders also supplied the raw materials for rural manufacturing while controlling production as well. Considering the importance of exports of wool and woolen cloth—which accounted for between 80 and 90% of England's trade—the merchants who controlled these exports became more influential as well. For example, London cloth merchants established the Company of Merchant Venturers quite early, in 1407, and were closely involved not only in the city politics of London but also in the crown's economic policy making [4].

While these two developments would have a major long-term impact on the direction of Britain's economic development, they did not immediately bring about a mature commercial society. Textile exports powered economic growth through the Tudor period, but they began to fall sharply in the 1550s because of inflation and the Dutch war for independence. This was accompanied by a rapid drop in real wages and a massive increase in the number of the poor, which plunged the English economy into a deep recession.

England's merchants and manufacturers made a variety of efforts to overcome this crisis. They introduced and began to produce "new draperies" and fustian (thick, sturdy cotton cloth), and they enthusiastically adopted coal to cut back on the cost of fuel. In the area of trade, they attempted to find new markets instead of just relying on the markets of northern Europe. English merchants began to trade in Africa, Russia, the Mediterranean, and the Atlantic [5]. These expansionary efforts by merchants instigated the 1588 confrontation between the English navy and the "invincible armada" of Spain, the most powerful state of the day.

England managed to defeat the Spanish Armada, albeit with much difficulty, but it could not afford to dedicate regular military forces to commercial expansion as the Spanish Empire or Dutch Republic were doing. In fact, the war greatly increased England's fiscal expenditures and prolonged its economic recession. Making matters worse, the country was plunged into political chaos when civil war broke out. The Netherlands of course had also been long engaged in a civil war of sorts, so England was hardly the only country that had to deal with political commotion. But the two countries' civil wars had different effects on their economies—and particularly on commerce.

This difference was related to the varying degrees of political influence wielded by merchants in England and the Netherlands. During the civil war, the merchants of the Dutch Republic actively participated in the policy making process in the States General and in the provincial parliaments, ensuring that their commercial interests were reflected in policy and strengthening commerce in the state as a whole. But the political elite in England, by contrast, were sharply divided over issues of religion and the constitutional order, which coincided with a conflict between the established merchant elite (represented by the Company of Merchant Venturers) and new groups of merchants to dissipate the state's power [6].

The effect that such differences had on the economy is well illustrated by the early history of the two countries' East India Companies. The English East India

Company (EIC) was established in 1600, shortly before the Dutch East India Company (VOC) was established in 1602. But the EIC could not hope to compete with the VOC either in terms of its initial capital or its method of operation. When the EIC launched, it had 10 times less starting capital than the VOC. In addition, the EIC had to return both the profit and principal at the end of each voyage, which kept it from maintaining continuity in its business operations.

A more important difference was that the EIC did not receive as much institutional support from the state as the VOC did. Just like a state-managed enterprise today, the VOC could rely on the state for various kinds of assistance needed for trade, such as weaponry. This stands in contrast with the EIC: far from receiving institutional support from the state, it had to dedicate a great deal of time and effort simply to protect its monopoly from unauthorized merchants. Backed by staunch support from the state, the VOC used its abundant capital and brutal force (such as in the Amboyna Massacre of 1623) to quickly conquer major trading bases. During the same period, the EIC had little to show for its efforts [7].

The English government and Parliament began to take a serious interest in commercial competition after the formation of the Rump Parliament and the execution of King Charles I in 1649. That was when England was finally able to deal with the economic damage and chaos of the Civil War. Having for the moment overcome the Royalists' opposition to regicide and repelled the threat posed by Scotland, Ireland, and the states of Continental Europe, Parliament immediately turned its attention to the issue of commerce. Meanwhile, the merchants who had been divided by the political tumult realized the need to use government and Parliament to protect and advance their own economic interests. This led to vigorous debate in the Rump Parliament about trade and a number of other issues related to the English economy [8].

One particularly important subject of debate was how to deal with the economic threat of the Netherlands. The Netherlands at the time not only held a monopoly on the highly profitable spice trade through the VOC but also controlled trade on the Baltic Sea through its system of inexpensive and efficient shipping. Furthermore, the Dutch had taken advantage of England's lax control of its colonies during the Civil War to engage in brisk trade with English colonies in the West Indies and in North America.

Even more mortifying for the English was the fact that the Dutch were busily engaged in a herring fishery not far from the coast of Britain. The Netherlands' trade in the Baltic Sea and its herring fishery were important not only because of the profit they earned but also for strategic reasons. As we discussed in Chap. 3, the Netherlands converted its fishing and trading ships into warships when it went to war, and the Baltic Sea was a main production site for materials needed by the navy. England could no longer allow itself to be excluded from an economically and strategically important trade network or—what was worse—to be forced out of trade with its own colonies.

Thus, England undertook a series of measures aimed at blockading the Dutch and protecting the commercial activities of English merchants. In October 1650, Parliament passed a bill banning foreigners from trading with England's American colonies unless authorized by Parliament or by the Council of State. While this act was ostensibly a punitive measure against colonies like Barbados and Virginia that supported the Royalist cause during the Civil War, it actually targeted trade between the colonies and the Netherlands. In the same month, Parliament passed another bill in which it promised to guarantee the safety of all merchant ships by providing them with naval escorts and arranged to cover the cost of the escorts with customs duties.

Then in October 1651 Parliament passed the famous Navigation Act, which contained two main provisions. First, it stated that products imported into England or English colonies had to be carried on English ships or ships of the country of origin. Second, it stated that non-English ships carrying products of foreign origin had to be from the country of origin or from the port where they were first loaded. These regulations were designed to prevent the use of Netherlands' cheap and efficient shipping and to harm the intermediary trade of a country that had become the warehouse of the world's merchants [9].

By passing the Navigation Act, the English state acknowledged that it had been remiss in protecting commercial interests and expressed its commitment to aggressively protect those interests in the future. This made friction between England and the Netherlands inevitable. Indeed, England was not the only country that was concerned about the rise of the Netherlands. After the end of the Thirty Years' War (1618–1648), the major powers of Europe began to focus on state formation, and it was widely believed that national power ultimately derived from a powerful military and on the economic—and in particular commercial—power propping up that military. In other words, this was the dawn of the period of mercantilism [10].

A number of scholars, including Charles Kindleberger, have argued that wars mark critical turning points in the shift from one hegemonic power to another and that the Anglo-Dutch Wars were just such a turning point [11]. During the three wars, England competed with the Netherlands in trade in the Atlantic colonies and in Africa, and England also succeeded at strengthening its navy, which would come to play a crucial role in its hegemony [12]. Expressed another way, it was during these three wars that the system of expansive reinvestment based on the virtuous cycle of war and the economy began to manifest itself in England.

The Anglo-Dutch Wars consisted of three separate wars that occurred over a period of two decades and fundamentally represented a struggle for commercial profit [13]. The First Anglo-Dutch War (1652–1654) ended with the signing of the Treaty of Westminster in April 1654, which forced the Netherlands to acquiesce to England's Navigation Act. The Second Anglo-Dutch War (1665–1667) was the hardest fought of the three wars. After the first war, the Dutch had been active in trade with Spain, in the Levant, and in Asia, while the English had distinguished itself in trade with the West Indies and in West Africa. While the Dutch held the upper hand in the first stage of this war, they could not maintain their advantage, and the war concluded with the Treaty of Breda in 1667. This treaty gave England control over the eastern seaboard of North America, including the Dutch colony of New Amsterdam (which later became New York City). In the Third Anglo-Dutch

War (1672–1674), the Netherlands had to simultaneously fight France on land and England at sea. In order to focus on the conflict with France (which posed a direct threat to its territory), the Dutch Republic had no choice but to reach terms with England in 1674 with the second Treaty of Westminster.

During these three wars, neither England nor the Netherlands was able to achieve a clear victory. Despite this, the wars made clear that the Netherlands could not maintain its hegemony in the gradually intensifying mercantilist competition for much longer. During the same period, England succeeded at strengthening its military while challenging the Dutch hegemony over trade. Importantly, England augmented its navy and began treating standardized ships of the line as its primary naval instrument (instead of repurposing merchant ships as warships). England's ships of the line became the basis of a convoy system that wiped out piracy and protected merchant vessels, along with other economic benefits such as lowering the cost of shipping and reducing insurance premiums [14].

Around the time that England's rivalry with the Netherlands was pushing the two states toward war, England was starting to take more interest in Asian trade and in its Atlantic colonies. We have already noted that the EIC lagged behind the VOC for about half a century after its establishment. But this situation began to change when Cromwell revised the EIC's ownership and management structure. The biggest change involved how profits and the principal were handled. Previously, the EIC had distributed profits and returned the principal to investors after every voyage and then raised more capital, but under the new system it only distributed the profits while holding on to the previously invested capital. This enabled the EIC to maintain the continuity of its business. The EIC also increased military spending to protect its ships.

When the EIC was given a new charter in 1657, it began to resemble a modern corporation, and its modernization process was completed with the adoption of a system of limited liability in 1665, after the death of Cromwell. Since these measures coincided with structural changes that were occurring in Asian trade in the mid-seventeenth century, they enabled the EIC to grow rapidly. It was around that time that the spice trade began to become less profitable and demand for cotton cloth and other new products began to rise. The EIC had always been at a disadvantage in the spice trade, and its new ownership and management structure helped it make inroads in the cotton cloth market [15].

Cromwell's interest in the EIC derived from his subscription to the belief that trade was no longer an individual issue but was rather directly linked to the interests of the nation as a whole. This interest was also evident in the military expedition called "Western Design." Soon after the end of the First Anglo-Dutch War, Cromwell dispatched a fleet to the West Indies to attack the Spanish-controlled island of Hispaniola. While Cromwell did not succeed in conquering the Spanish West Indies, he did incorporate the island of Jamaica into the English Empire and opened the door for England to become the greatest beneficiary of the sugar revolution. Cromwell also greatly contributed to England's commercial expansion by seizing the port of Dunkirk, which was the key to the Flanders region controlled by the Spanish Empire.

Thus, the virtuous cycle of war and the economy gradually began to take effect in England while Cromwell was in power. As one historian has said, "he was ahead of his times." It is significant that Cromwell—though devoutly religious himself—was more concerned that his son "mind and understand Business, read a little History, study the Mathematics and Cosmography" rather than being raised for service in the church. Cromwell believed that England's future depended upon its commercial success [16].

Establishment of the System of Expansive Reinvestment

The Financial Revolution

England's system of expansive reinvestment, which had slowly began taking shape under the Commonwealth, faced another crisis during the reign of King James II. In the half century that culminated in the Civil War, the English economy had been stagnant, held back by the Dutch commercial advantage; during the Restoration, however, developments in the English economy were rapidly bringing commercial society to fruition. Though agriculture still accounted for an overwhelming share of the economy, the country was swiftly urbanizing, while rural industry, urban industry, and (most importantly) domestic and foreign trade were growing rapidly. This commercial and industrial development was made possible by advancements in transportation and communication. By the late seventeenth century, construction had already begun on toll roads and canals, and a mail service had been launched that connected all parts of England.

But even amid such positive developments, the English could not afford to be complacent about the future. While England and the Netherlands were in conflict, the new European power of France was enjoying remarkable growth. Louis XIV, the French king at the time, was a devout Catholic who was fixated on building an absolutist monarchy. As his power continued to grow, the English worried whether they could really preserve their economic vitality and their religious freedom. These worries grew when England's new Catholic king, James II, revealed his desire to turn England into an absolute monarchy in the style of France. This provoked a sharp debate about the changing balance of power between states and about the future of England.

The ultimate result of this debate, of course, was the Glorious Revolution. This revolution was long regarded as a political incident in which opposition to James' attempts to strengthen the monarchy led to the establishment of a constitutional monarchy that would guarantee civil liberties. More recently, though, the revolution's religious aspect has received more attention. In this view, the revolution was the result of the combined effort of English and Dutch people who were committed to rescuing the Protestant world from Louis XIV's ambition of building a Catholic universal monarchy [17]. What we will focus on here is not the various interpretations about the origins of the revolution but rather the revolution's connection with the development of commercial society. To do so, we must first understand how civil liberties and constitutional monarchy were linked to the English people's economic activity and why the English were so afraid of the threat of a Catholic universal monarchy.

The Glorious Revolution resulted from fears about the Catholic universal monarchy and from suspicions that James shared not only Louis's religious convictions but also his political philosophy of absolutism. The Catholic universal monarchy to which Louis aspired represented a type of internationalism under which the entire world would be subjected to French rule, centered on the Catholic Church and the monarchy. To be sure, the universal monarchy had also been a threat when Charles V and Philip II ruled the Spanish Empire, but France posed a much more credible threat. Even at its zenith, the Spanish Empire had looked weak, being unable on a number of occasions to even maintain payments to its creditors. But France was gradually growing stronger thanks to its powerful military, huge territory, large population and aggressive mercantilism.

The English viewed the French threat in the light of new ideas about economics and the international order that were circulating at the time. Once the Westphalian system of states was set up following the Thirty Years' War, the nation-state became the basic unit of European politics. Furthermore, the idea spread that the sovereignty of each state had to be respected in order to prevent religious wars and other catastrophes. Since the nation-state was also the basic economic unit in competition between states, states could hardly afford to tolerate infringements of their sovereignty, since these threatened the state's very survival. These arguments were particularly persuasive in England, which had become a united nation during a difficult and tumultuous period that spanned the Civil War, the Commonwealth, and the Restoration and which would brook nothing that threatened that unity [18].

But even as fears of France became widespread, James implemented policies that only aggravated those fears. In place of the Commonwealth that Cromwell had established, James sought to set up a centralized absolute monarchy in the manner of France. Only this method, he believed, would stabilize the English political system—preventing it from being swayed by public opinion as the Dutch Republic was—and help England maintain and improve its position in the new international order. To this end, James sometimes tried to impose his religion on all his subjects (by force, if need be) and to supervise and regulate their economic activity according to the needs of the crown.

But James's ideas conflicted with new theories about economic freedom and the role of the state. By the mid-seventeenth century, the idea that trade was the foundation of the English economy had already become the prevailing view, and there was a growing tendency to criticize monopolistic companies that relied upon concessions from the crown and to advocate the freedom of commercial activity. This tendency reflected the dominance of a new way of thinking: namely, that increasing the national wealth required devoting more labor to manufacturing and that stimulating productive labor required allowing the free exchange of the fruits of labor. This way of thinking implied that the state ought to encourage productive labor and to adopt the policy of expanding trade by eliminating outmoded laws and customs that interfered with free economic activity [19].

The Glorious Revolution was a major first step toward making these views a reality. It did more than just enshrine basic civil liberties and property rights in the Bill of Rights [20]. In a way, an even more important result was limiting the monarch's power while giving Parliament (and the House of Commons in particular) control over the budget and taxation and enabling it to pass legislation that would affect the overall national economy. It was also this revolution that established the principle that Parliament must meet and be dissolved regularly, regardless of the wishes of the monarch. The result was that a new Parliament was formed every three years (later, every seven years).

In addition, sessions of Parliament gradually became longer, and the House of Commons began to have more work to do. This accustomed the English to resolving various problems through the legislature. Merchants and manufacturers in particular began to lobby Parliament to protect and advance their economic interests [21]. By putting the House of Commons in control of the budget and taxation and motivating merchants and manufacturers to use the House of Commons to protect their economic interests, the revolution helped keep the political system stable in subsequent years.

Immediately after the Glorious Revolution, the Nine Years' War began, pitting England against France. From this time until 1815, England (soon to be Great Britain) fought a total of six wars with France. During this period—often called the Second Hundred Years' War—the cost of war increased astronomically. With every unfavorable shift in the fortunes of war and with the end of every war, Britons worried whether the state would go bankrupt [22].

Despite these concerns, the British state remained strong. Even amid these wars, Britain's domestic and foreign trade grew rapidly, and the Industrial Revolution began in the manufacturing sector. In other words, the eighteenth century was a time when Britain not only perfected its system of expansive reinvestment (driven by the virtuous cycle of war and the economy) but also transitioned to the system of expansive reproduction. The economic influence that this brought to Britain transformed it into an undisputed hegemonic power.

During the early modern period, all the major powers devoted themselves to the search for effective ways to fund their hugely expensive wars (without cannibalizing their fiscal and economic base). As we have previously discussed, one of the reasons that the Dutch Republic was able to gain its independence from the Spanish Empire and become a hegemonic power was that the Dutch Republic could fund its wars much more effectively than the Spanish Empire.

Particularly important was the Dutch Republic's introduction of a system of long-term government bonds that depended on the market's confidence in the Republic's government. Under this system, the government issued public bonds (just as a corporation might raise its initial capital from investors) and used the proceeds to cover the cost of the war. Later, the government took advantage of the economic opportunities afforded by the war to gradually pay back bondholders.

Thanks to this institutional innovation, the Netherlands was able to effectively wage war while reducing the burden of fiscal expenditures. The British learned important lessons from the Dutch experience. They adopted several Dutch innovations, including long-term government bonds, to successfully bring about the financial revolution, and they went one step further by developing a tax collection system to support those government bonds, resulting in a fiscal-military state.

The primary breakthrough of the financial revolution involved the government raising a large amount of money and either paying back the interest and principal over a long period of time or only paying interest without paying back the principal at all. This eliminated the need for the government to take out short-term loans [23]. Early on, the Netherlands had developed a system in which it paid interest in the form of an annuity to people who bought government bonds instead of paying back the principal, and England adopted this system soon after the Glorious Revolution.

The English government also devised a way to raise money by selling lottery tickets. The tickets were issued in small amounts, and several prizes were offered to increase the number of winners. The lottery winners were paid their prize money in installments over the course of several years. In the Million Lottery of 1694, everyone who bought a lottery ticket was guaranteed to receive one pound in prize money each year for 16 years.

England also found ways to raise money from corporations. It was in fact a standard government practice to give corporations special privileges in exchange for loans, but the English system was unusual in several respects. Not only was the government able to raise a great deal more money, but the corporations saw their stock being traded briskly on the market. The organization that did the most to establish this system was the Bank of England.

The Bank of England was established as part of a deal between the English government and merchants for the purpose of raising funds for the Nine Years' War. On the condition that they would loan the government 1.2 million pounds, merchants set up a corporation through which they were entitled to provide the market with various financial services. The Bank of England could profit from the fees it charged for services such as discounting bills of exchange, making private loans, and issuing bank notes, and it received 8% interest and a yearly handling fee for the 1.2 million pounds (raised by issuing bank stock) that it loaned the government. As a guarantee that this interest would be paid, Parliament earmarked the revenue from excise tax on certain products and from customs duties to interest payments to the Bank of England. Stockholders in the Bank of England received dividends and when necessary could sell their stock on the stock market to recover the principal of their investment and any profit that had accrued. After the government's deal with the Bank of England, a number of other corporations—including the EIC, the South Sea Company, and the Royal African Company—also loaned the government the funds it needed in a similar manner.

In this way, the government was able to fund its wars while minimizing the burden of paying back the principal. Since this money was raised through corporations, there were a number of incidental benefits, such as stimulating the stock market and developing a variety of financial services. This helped lessen the danger of crowding-out, that is, when investment in the private sector contracts because capital is concentrated in the public sector. Furthermore, the Bank of England and other major investors satisfied the government's need not only for long-term loans but also for short-term funding that was needed to eliminate imbalance in the liquidity flow.

Thus, the British government relied upon a series of innovative measures introduced during the generation after the Glorious Revolution in its continuing efforts during the eighteenth century to convert short-term debt into long-term debt and to replace the long-term and permanent government bonds it had already issued with new bonds with low interest rates [24]. The fact that the Spanish Empire and France paid high interest rates (from 8 to 10%) on money they had borrowed for their wars shows just how remarkable England's success was in this area [25].

But why was it in Britain that the financial revolution came to fruition? In order for perpetual bonds and other financial instruments to succeed, the most crucial factor was confidence in the market. To earn this confidence, the British government and Parliament first had to make a clean break with the practice (exemplified by the Spanish Empire and by the British government in 1672) of defaulting on sovereign debt when fiscal pressure became too severe. Britain had to convince investors that it would definitely pay the interest on government debt and that stockholders and bondholders could recover the principal on their investment whenever they wanted.

The methods by which creditors could recover their principal were closely linked to the development of the financial market. As we discussed earlier, the establishment of the Bank of England shows that the system of government debt was taking shape just as the London financial market was developing. Each time the government took out a long-term loan, Parliament guaranteed that the interest on that loan would be covered by revenue from a specific tax, which convinced creditors that the government would pay the interest on its debt [26].

It was one thing for Parliament to enact laws linking interest on government debt with specific taxes, and another to actually collect the income stipulated by law. But tax collection was another area in which eighteenth-century Britain did exceedingly well. Tax receipts soared in the century after 1715, increasing tenfold in terms of nominal prices and fourfold in terms of real prices, taking inflation into account (see Fig. 4.1). Converting tax receipts into the per capita tax burden, we find that the British paid twice as many taxes as the French in the mid-eighteenth century and three times as many taxes at the end of that century [27]. From this, we can infer that the British tax collecting authorities became more efficient during the eighteenth century.

Britain is frequently regarded as an epitome of small government—but the fact that a government is small does not necessarily mean its rule is weak. In Britain after the Glorious Revolution, the power of the government agencies in charge of handling fiscal affairs and tax collection increased immensely. Previously, the center of government had been the Privy Council, but the Privy Council's role shrank while the Treasury gained influence. Under the supervision of the Treasury, committees were set up to handle customs duties and excise taxes—the Board of

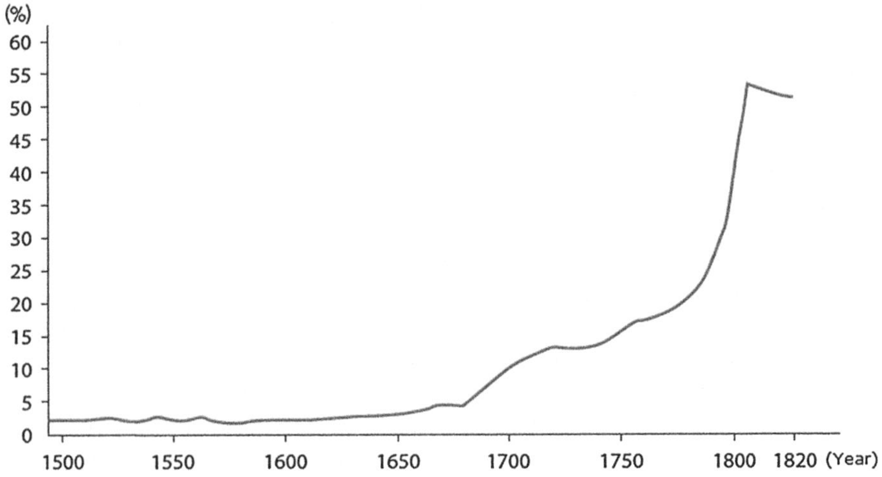

Fig. 4.1 Total taxation (1490–1820). *Source* Patrick O'Brien, "The Nature and Historical Evolution of an Exceptional Fiscal State and Its Possible Significance for the Precocious Commercialization and Industrialization of the British Economy from Cromwell to Nelson," *Economic History Review* 64:2 (2011), p. 428

Customs and Board of Excise, respectively—and there was a large increase in the number of officials who were sent out to levy taxes [28]. This set Britain apart from France, which still relied on a system of contractors for tax collection, and it helped the British government stay relatively free of the corruption that was always a liability when contractors were hired to collect taxes.

In addition to creating taxation infrastructure, another change was that indirect taxes accounted for a rapidly increasing portion of tax receipts (see Fig. 4.2) [29]. The bulk of tax receipts came from excise taxes and customs duties. These are both indirect taxes, which are not as perceptible as direct taxes, or taxes that are directly imposed on income or property. Since excise taxes and duties are collected from producers, importers, and exporters, they are not as noticeable to most consumers, which reduces the likelihood of resistance to taxation.

These excise taxes and duties had a major impact not only on fiscal revenue but also on the structure of industry and trade. As is clearly illustrated by Sir Robert Walpole's tariff reforms of 1722, duties were abolished for raw materials and manufactured goods that could boost imports or help with import substitution, while high tariffs were imposed on imported good that competed with domestic products. In this manner, the British government was able to promote growth in specific areas of industry and trade.

Since excise taxes and customs duties were not unilaterally imposed on all products, merchants and manufacturers were able to participate actively in the process of proposing, enacting, and repealing specific taxes by means of the Board of Customs, the Board of Excise, the Treasury, and the House of Commons [30].

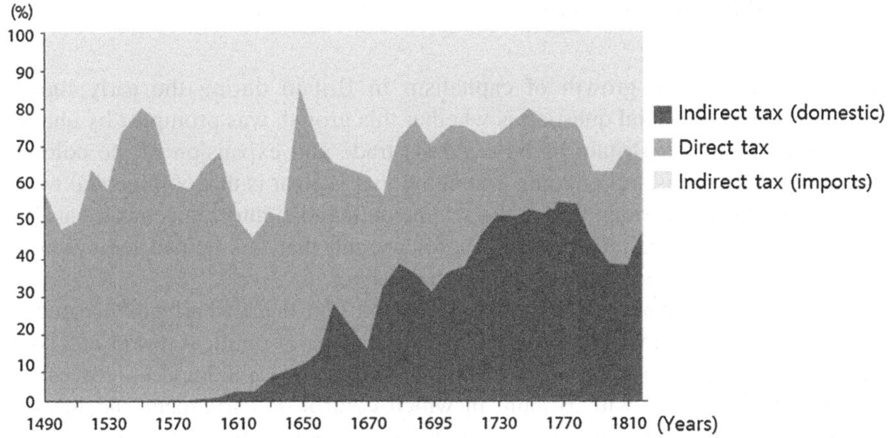

Fig. 4.2 Direct and indirect tax levied by the Central Government (9-year average). *Source* Patrick O'Brien, "The Nature and Historical Evolution of an Exceptional Fiscal State and Its Possible Significance for the Precocious Commercialization and Industrialization of the British Economy from Cromwell to Nelson," *Economic History Review* 64:2 (2011), p. 429

This meant that resistance to a specific tax would not erode confidence in the taxation system itself.

The fiscal revolution that occurred after the Glorious Revolution made it possible for the British government and Parliament to take out massive loans. Government debt increased from around 1 million pounds in 1688 to 15 million pounds about a decade later, and then to 78 million pounds in 1750 and 244 million pounds in 1790. This rapid increase in government debt was due to the cost of wars fought to secure naval supremacy, trade routes, and market dominance. Government debt was a mechanism that could be used to equally redistribute budget expenditures, which fluctuated greatly between peacetime and wartime, and to gradually repay the debt accrued during war with regular tax revenues. If these budget expenditures had been incurred in wars aimed at expanding territory or increasing royal authority with no consideration of economic interests, Britain would have gone into decline prematurely as the Spanish Empire did. But Britain used profitable wars (which is to say wars that facilitated the virtuous cycle of war and the economy) to solidify its political and economic hegemony during the commercial age.

Of course, the British were able to endure the huge government debt and the highest tax burden in Europe at the time because Britain's commercial economy was growing at an accelerated rate. Therefore, explaining Britain's attainment of hegemony in the eighteenth century in terms of the virtuous cycle of war and the economy requires us to take a comprehensive look at the condition of the British economy.

The Development of Commerce

When discussing the growth of capitalism in Britain during the early modern period, one controversial question is whether this growth was prompted by changes that were internal to Britain or by overseas trade and expansion of the colonies. Though this debate is still ongoing, one thing that is clear is that commercial wealth was accumulated in Britain during the seventeenth and eighteenth centuries at a rate that could be fairly described as revolutionary and that this helped the system of expansive reinvestment become firmly established.

As we have previously observed, one reason that the Netherlands became the first commercial state was that merchants' acquisition of political power and social status enabled them to accumulate economic surplus as capital and to reinvest that capital. This contrasts with Britain, in which control of Parliament and the government remained with social forces whose power derived from the land—namely, the aristocracy and the gentry. Importantly, however, productive investment had already become routine even for these groups, as the pursuit of profit became the fundamental objective of economic activity. It was on this basis that Britain's commerce thrived, enabling the system of expansive reinvestment to reach maturity and later facilitating the transition to the system of expansive reproduction.

Many scholars emphasize, of course, that the capital that was accumulated through commerce did not account for a large portion of Britain's total capital and in many cases was not even converted into industrial capital. Even in 1760, for example, when British commercial activity was fully developed, capital in the agricultural sector accounted for 74% of total capital, while commerce and manufacturing together only represented 7% of capital [31].

It is not the percentage of capital in the commercial sector that can explain Britain's economic growth, however, but rather the speed of commercial growth. This is because (as we have repeatedly emphasized) the accelerating growth of commerce increases demand throughout the entire society, which in turn leads to a rapid increase in agricultural and industrial production. It would be imprudent to disregard the fact that commercial development hastened the development of economic infrastructure. During the seventeenth and eighteenth centuries, institutions such as banks, clearing houses, insurance companies, stock exchanges, and the postal system were becoming more ingrained in Britons' economic lives, and the services provided by these institutions contributed to the development not only of commerce but also of agriculture and industry. Nor should we ignore the fact that the experience, knowledge, and human capital accumulated in commerce were transferred to other industrial sectors [32].

In eighteenth-century Britain, not only was there substantial growth (both quantitative and qualitative) in domestic trade, but this growth was closely linked to overseas trade. A crucial role in this growth was played by merchants—that is, people engaged in overseas trade, per the original definition. At this time, British merchants had an advantage in a global commercial network that linked not only the countries of Europe but also Asia, Africa, and the Americas. Thus, the raw materials and consumer goods that were produced in various parts of the world were conveyed to other parts by British merchants, while the raw materials and consumer goods that were imported by British merchants stimulated domestic trade and manufacturing in Britain. Furthermore, it was through this network of merchants that the manufactured goods of Britain began to be exported not only to Europe but to the global market, laying the groundwork for industrialization [33].

Before we look at how overseas trade changed, let us review once more the factors that aided the development of domestic trade. First, it is necessary to recall the overwhelming importance of the market in the agricultural sector. Market-oriented agricultural production began in the late Middle Ages, but there was even more development during the seventeenth and eighteenth centuries as urbanization accelerated and the domestic market expanded.

One part of this was the definite establishment of regional specialization in agriculture. Britain's breadbasket, for example, was in eastern and southern England; ranchers in the Scottish Highlands and Wales raised cattle and sheep for the meat market; and several counties in western England with ample pastureland specialized in cattle rearing and dairy. Though climate and soil quality no doubt played a role in this, regional specialization was essentially made possible by the existence of a national market through which agricultural products could freely circulate, crossing the boundaries between different regions. Therefore, the development of regional specialization serves as evidence that a national market in the full sense of the world (a market without internal tariffs or tolls) had already formed in Britain before the Industrial Revolution [34].

Since Great Britain is an island, it is unsurprising that a shipping network linking the ports along the coast developed relatively early. Furthermore, the conditions were favorable for the development of a national market by connecting the rivers leading to those ports with markets in the interior. But no matter how favorable the natural conditions, ports, rivers, and markets cannot be connected without human effort. Thus, it is necessary to remember that in the early seventeenth century the English were already working to improve the transportation network by fixing waterways, installing floodgates, and laying canals. Turnpikes and primitive railways also appeared around the same period. Such investment in British transportation infrastructure expanded even more in the eighteenth century, ushering in the transportation revolution. Accordingly, eighteenth-century Britain had a more compact national market than any other country [35].

England also witnessed the development of industries that had freed themselves early on from the medieval guild system. One such industry was woolen cloth manufacturing. As we have previously mentioned, the wool and woolen cloth industries had flourished under the protection of the crown since the Middle Ages. Around the time that England was transitioning into a commercial society, the putting-out system (in which traders distributed raw materials and tools to rural craftspeople working from their homes) was extended to woolen cloth manufacturing. The putting-out system took advantage of the cheap labor in farming villages; another advantage was that it could respond with greater flexibility to changes in consumer preferences and other market conditions without being hampered by the rules of the craft guilds. The expansion of the putting-out system turned woolen cloth production into a major rural industry: in the second half of the seventeenth century and through the eighteenth century, consumption of wool increased by 13% each decade [36].

The development of agriculture on the one hand and commerce and manufacturing on the other led to a rise in English incomes. Wages steadily increased between the mid-seventeenth century and the mid-eighteenth century until, by the beginning of the Industrial Revolution in the late eighteenth century, the wages of English workers were higher than anywhere else in the world [37].

A development that was even more closely linked to commercial growth was a substantial increase in the purchasing power of the "middling sort," as the nascent middle class was called. As can be seen from recent studies about the consumer revolution in the eighteenth century, this was a time of unprecedented growth in the kinds of products consumed by the middle class and in the amount that they consumed. This growth was spurred by factors including the progress of urbanization, the expansion of domestic and international commerce, the decline of the fairs, the development of retail outlets, and the growth of the market for newspapers and other periodicals.

The middle class began consuming products that had hitherto only been consumed by the nobility and other members of the privileged class, which in turn stimulated demand for consumption in the lower class. This led not only to more development in the domestic market but also to what has been called the "industrious revolution"—the phenomenon whereby workers were willing to endure harder work for longer hours in order to increase the income they needed to buy new consumer goods—which created consumer demand that motivated even more productive activity [38].

The growth of domestic commerce and manufacturing and the increasing vitality of consumer activity owed a great deal to overseas trade, which grew more rapidly in the eighteenth century than ever before. Indeed, overseas trade was so brisk in the eighteenth century that imports and exports grew by 132% between 1699 to 1701 and 1772 to 1774, even as the population of England only grew by 33%.

The volume of imports and exports increased faster than the population partly because of the rise in domestic consumers' purchasing power, but a more basic reason was the thriving business in re-exporting imported goods. According to estimates by Deane and Cole that have long been widely accepted, imports increased by 523% between 1700 and 1800; exports by 568%; and re-exports by 906%. Furthermore, between 1700 and 1770, re-exports accounted for between 30 and 37% of England's export volume and between 50 and 68% of Scotland's export volume.

Re-exportation was able to increase in this manner, of course, because of Britain's ability to import sugar, tea, tobacco, and coffee from its colonies. The growth of overseas trade also led to a boom in export-oriented manufacturing. Consequently, during the first half of the eighteenth century, domestic industry only grew by 7%, while the export industry posted a growth rate of 70%. Between 1750 and 1770, domestic industry achieved the same level of growth, while the export industry grew by no less than 80% [39].

Notwithstanding some skepticism about the importance of overseas trade in the eighteenth century, such figures indicate that overseas trade was directly connected to the growth not only of domestic commerce but also of the manufacturing industry. As Eric Hobsbawm put it, "If a spark was needed, [foreign demand] is where it came from." [40] This is what distinguishes British overseas trade in the eighteenth century from Dutch commercial activity in the seventeenth century. Re-export trade was the driving force behind the Netherlands' rise as a hegemonic power in the seventeenth century. As we have already seen, Dutch hegemony was based on its system of entrepôt trade, in combination with the trade in spices and other luxury goods and with bulk shipping, an area in which it had held an advantage since before its war for independence.

But eighteenth-century Britain took over a global trade network that joined commerce not only with Asia (where the Netherlands had held a monopoly) but also on the Atlantic and inside Europe. By using this network to export domestic manufactured goods, Britain also managed to develop industry at home. That is to say, eighteenth-century Britain had built an engine that would power its transition from its highly developed system of expansive reinvestment to the system of expansive reproduction.

Trade between Britain and the non-European world played an important role in the growth of Britain's overseas trade in the eighteenth century. As estimates of re-exports show, trade between Britain and Europe (and exports in particular) were able to grow because of increasing imports from the non-European world. Trends in export trade indicate that 82% of the goods manufactured for export in Britain in 1701 went to the European market; in 1772–1773, this rate fell to 40%. In terms of import trade, 74% of imported products had been manufactured in Europe in 1713–1717, but this dropped to 33% in 1803–1807. In terms of the total value of foreign trade, trade with Europe as a percentage of the total decreased by the same rate—from 74 to 33%—between 1713 and 1803 [41]. To understand the growth in Britain's overseas trade in the eighteenth century, therefore, we need to look at changes that took place in trade with the non-European market—that is, with Asia, Africa, and the Americas.

The most important player in Britain's trade with Asia was the EIC. As we have previously mentioned, the EIC was gradually able to gain the advantage over the VOC, its Dutch rival, as demand fell for spices and rose for cotton cloth, tea, and coffee in the second half of the seventeenth century. Importation of tea began in earnest in the 1710s. At the beginning of the eighteenth century, tea only made up 1% of the EIC's total imports, but tea's share of imports rose to 10% in 1720, 20% in 1747, and more than 40% in 1760. In terms of the volume and value of tea, 8.8 million pounds (worth 610,000 lb sterling) was imported between 1721 and 1730 and 37 million pounds (worth 1.69 million pounds sterling) between 1751 and 1760. In terms of total volume, imports increased more than fourfold [42].

These figures, however, do not accurately reflect the total volume and value of the tea that was actually imported to Britain at this time. There was an astonishing growth in the demand for tea not only in Britain but also in the colonies, and there was also a strong incentive to sidestep the EIC when importing tea, since it was possible to receive refunds on duties when re-exporting imported tea. This led to a flourishing trade in contraband tea, which prompted the EIC to ask for lower duties on tea, for the abolition of tariff refunds, and for stricter enforcement of regulations. But since the price of legally imported tea was still more expensive than contraband tea, it was impossible to eradicate smuggling, either in Britain or in the American colonies [43].

The stature of tea as an import good was surpassed, however, by textiles, and especially cotton cloth. While the EIC's imports of cotton cloth were significant in and of themselves, their greatest legacy was the demand for cotton cloth that they created in the British market, since this demand led to the growth of the domestic cotton cloth industry. Put another way, imports of cotton cloth were initially part of the regular trade in luxury goods, but they ultimately contributed to the development of the British economy by promoting the development of domestic industry.

In the seventeenth century, cotton cloth was still a new product. Fustian (a weave of cotton and linen) had been produced and imported by way of Venice since the fifteenth century, but there were no products made purely of cotton. When the EIC began importing Indian calico in the late seventeenth century, consumers responded with such enthusiasm that people started talking about the "calico craze." Indian cotton goods were light, excellent at absorbing moisture, highly durable, and—most importantly—could be dyed in various colors. On top of that, they were much cheaper than linen. When the calico craze began, woolen cloth manufacturers (who had long dominated the British textile industry) lobbied Parliament to ban the import and sale of calico in 1700 and 1720. But cotton cloth (and in particular high-end products) continued to be brought into Britain, which spurred efforts to produce cheap cotton goods in the country.

Another development that occurred as Britain was completing its system of expansive reinvestment and transitioning to the system of expansive reproduction was the growth of trade on the Atlantic. When the English started to take an interest in America in the early seventeenth century, their goal (like the Spanish) was acquiring precious metals and other luxury goods. But as the experience of the Virginia Company shows, the Spanish were already in control of the production sites of precious minerals in the New World, and the areas where the English settled—North America and the West Indies—had no products for the taking. In fact, conflict with the natives and local diseases claimed the lives of most of the first settlers in the British colonies, leaving just a few survivors, who relied on shipments of food and supplies from home.

Amid these desperate circumstances, the destiny of the colonies in North America and the West Indies was transformed by the fishing industry and by the cultivation of new crops such as sugar and tobacco. With the discovery of the economic potential of plantation crops such as sugar and tobacco, money began to flow back into the colonies from English traders and landowners who had turned away from the colonies in disappointment because of the series of initial failures. In the second half of the seventeenth century, trade with the colonies increased remarkably [44]. By 1699–1701, sugar and tobacco ranked first and third in terms of total value among imports from the non-European world (with calico ranking second).

The development of plantation agriculture was a true innovation. It not only opened up new trade routes but also caused the migration of millions of people from Britain and Africa to North America and the West Indies. Furthermore, the rapid movement of capital and credit paved the way for the growth of a new group of traders, landowners, and manufacturers in Britain and its colonies. Initially, plantation agriculture was limited to tobacco and sugar, but in the eighteenth century this expanded to rice, indigo, and coffee.

The New England Colonies and Middle Colonies in North America could not specialize in plantation corps, but they did see growth in industries such as fishing, grain farming, mining, and manufacturing. And as the economy grew, the population grew with it. In the West Indies, the unfavorable climate meant that population growth largely depended upon the importation of black slaves; in the North American colonies, the number of white settlers grew rapidly with immigration and natural population increase. Thus, populations that had been just 55,000 (in North America) and 59,000 (in the West Indies) in 1650 and 1651 had increased to 2,280,000 and 480,000, respectively, by 1770 and 1771 [45].

The growth of Britain's Atlantic colonies contributed to the growth of Britain's economy in a number of ways. The colonies supplied various raw materials (such as iron and naval stores) for which Britain relied on imports as well as new products like sugar, and they enabled the accumulation of commercial experience and the development of the maritime shipping industry [46]. Consequently, the traders who did business with the colonies and the numerous plantation owners who returned to Britain from the West Indies amassed a vast amount of personal wealth and gained more social and political influence.

Furthermore, the goods imported from the colonies enriched the British consumer lifestyle. The colonial imports served as business opportunities for manufacturers, who could process them for sale in the British and European markets or could make various other products that were needed for their consumption. These opportunities were reflected in the sugar refining, tobacco pipe manufacturing, and ceramics industries that appeared in Bristol and London.

The Atlantic colonies were also an excellent market for British manufactured goods. In contrast with India and Africa, the Atlantic colonies had been settled by British and European immigrants and their descendants, who wanted to maintain the customs and lifestyle of their home countries. Since the Navigation Acts banned the colonies from developing the kind of industry that could rival British manufacturers, the colonists had no choice but to import goods from home if they wanted to enjoy a European way of life.

Even without such mercantilist regulations, though, the outcome would have been largely the same. At least until the Seven Years' War (1756–63), the Navigation Acts were not strictly enforced, and regulations that could have posed a serious threat to the colonists' economic interests were periodically mitigated through negotiations with Parliament and the government [47]. As it happened, the

Table 4.1 Exports of British products

	1699–1701	1722–1724	1752–1754	1772–1774
Woolen cloth products				
Continental Europe	2745	2592	3279	2630
Ireland and channel Islands	26	19	47	219
America and Africa	185	303	374	1148
India and Asia	89	72	230	189
Other products				
Continental Europe	456	367	647	987
Ireland and channel Islands	60	40	168	280
America and Africa	290	376	1197	2533
India and Asia	22	15	408	501

(unit: 1000 pounds)
Source Ralph Davis, "English Foreign Trade, 1700–1774," *Economic History Review*, 2nd ser., 15 (1962), p. 291

colonists preferred to import goods from England and focus on agriculture and the fishing industry instead of trying their hand at manufacturing, where they were highly uncompetitive [48]. Thus, by the middle of the eighteenth century, the colonies had emerged as the most important market for the British manufacturing industry (with the exception of woolen cloth), as seen in Table 4.1.

The first thing to notice in Table 4.1 is how the woolen cloth industry, which was the center of Britain's manufacturing sector, compensated for a relative slump in the European market with growth in the Atlantic market. But what is especially noteworthy in regard to Britain's long-term economic development (especially compared to the Netherlands) is the correlation between the development of manufacturing industries other than woolen cloth and the expansion of non-European markets.

In absolute terms, of course, the woolen cloth industry remained the largest of Britain's export industries. But when we look at the value of exports between 1699 to 1701 and 1772 to 1774, the woolen cloth industry accounted for a rapidly decreasing percentage of total manufacturing (falling from 78 to 49%), while other manufacturing industries came to account for a much greater share. In this way, America and Africa's share of overall manufacturing increased from 12 to 43% during the same period.

What is just as interesting as these quantitative changes is the incredible variety of the categories of products exported to the American colonies. In the 1770s, for example, newspapers in New York carried advertisements for as many as 9000 kinds of manufactured goods. Even granting that not all these products were of British manufacture, this still indicates the diversity of the manufactured goods that were exported from Britain [49]. Such diversity shows that the eighteenth-century British manufacturing sector was expanding beyond its traditional focus on the woolen cloth industry and that the colonial market played a major role in this. In other words, trade with the colonies not only contributed to the completion of the system of expansive reinvestment but also made possible the transition to the system of expansive reproduction.

A substantial amount of the labor needed for the colonial economy's rapid growth was provided by African slaves. When the colonies were first settled, English colonial businessmen attempted to use the labor force from home. This was partly because of the idea that the colonies should absorb surplus labor from England (along with groups that had been politically and religiously divisive), but it was mostly because the American Indians could not be used as labor. This led to the adoption of the system of indentured servitude. Under this system, brokers provided the cost of passage to the colonies for those who wanted to move there (that is, the indentured servants). The brokers were then compensated by colonial plantation owners who could use the indentured servants' labor for a set period of time (typically four, five, or seven years).

But the system of indentured servitude was not a lasting solution to the labor supply. For one thing, indentured servants became legally independent after their period of servitude was over. For another, these servants were still white settlers, and as such they sought to exert their rights through the local courts, limiting landowners' ability to exploit them. A more fundamental problem was that the number of people who wanted to move to the colonies was gradually falling. This was tied to a substantial rise in demand for labor in Britain as the growth of its population slowed in the second half of the seventeenth century [50].

It was around this time that the institution of slavery came to be regarded as an alternative. Granting some regional differences, slavery almost entirely replaced indentured servitude in the early eighteenth century, reflecting a huge boom in the slave trade. Through the slave trade—which was begun by Portuguese traders in the mid-fifteenth century—about 12 million Africans were transported to various parts of the Americas through 1880. English merchants may have entered the slave trade later than those of other countries, but once they were in the business, they expanded their operations with fearsome energy. From 1662 until 1807, when the slave trade was abolished, English merchants supplied around 3.3 million slaves to the Southern Colonies of North America and the West Indies. In the early days of the trade (from 1662 to 1670), there were only about 6700 slaves a year, but by the 1760s, the yearly total had increased to 42,000.

The slave trade was not particularly profitable compared to other trading activities. According to one study, the average rate of return for slave traders was 7.6% in Bristol between 1770 and 1792 and between 8 and 10% in Liverpool during the second half of the eighteenth century. These rates are not that high, considering that merchants who were doing business in the Levant during the same period thought that 10% was an adequate rate of return. Nevertheless, the slave trade attracted an enormous amount of investment since it was an important economic link between the Atlantic colonies and Britain. Bristol merchants, for example, invested between 50,000 and 60,000 lb in the trade per year in 1710 and 1711, 150,000 lb a year in the 1730s, and an average of 280,000 a year between 1788 and 1792, while Liverpool merchants invested 200,000 lb a year in the 1750s and as much as one million pounds around 1800 [51].

The question of how slavery and the slave trade contributed to the development of the British economy has long been a vexed one. The traditional hypothesis—that the profit earned from slavery and the slave trade was converted directly into the capital that was needed for the Industrial Revolution and that consequently Britain achieved its economic growth in the modern era through the sweat and blood of Africans—is no longer very convincing. Yet it is undeniable that Africa and the Atlantic colonies contributed to Britain's economic growth in a number of ways [52]. To be sure, the volume of products exported to Africa accounted for less than 1% of Britain's overseas trade in the eighteenth century, but these exports played a decisive role in maintaining the triangular trade pattern on the Atlantic Ocean.

The main products that Britain exported to Africa at the time were textiles. Interestingly, the 1750s saw a change in the primary site of production of these textile exports. Prior to this, textiles had been imported by the EIC and then re-exported to Africa. After the 1750s, though, a larger share of these exports came from cotton cloth that was produced in England, and in Lancashire in particular. Thus, as we have already mentioned several times, England's trade on the Atlantic promoted the development not only of commerce but also of manufacturing [53].

Nevertheless, it is undeniable that the wealth that was accumulated through the slave trade with the Atlantic colonies contributed to the growth of the British economy. There are no precise estimates of how much wealth Britain accumulated through the slave trade. Nevertheless, an observation by mid-eighteenth century economic commentator Malachy Postlethwayt that Britain earned 1.68 million pounds in profits from the slave trade in 1750 implies that a substantial amount of wealth was accumulated through the trade.

More detailed estimates are available, on the other hand, for the amount of wealth that was accumulated in the colonies that depended on the institution of slavery. The most striking of these estimates concern the West Indies. According to one estimate, the assets of white settlers in Jamaica in 1774 amounted to as much as 28 million pounds, while there were around 51 million pounds in total assets throughout the entire British West Indies. In other words, the average white settler had assets that were worth more than 1000 lb. This was more than ten times the average assets of white settlers in the Southern Colonies of North America. Given that North American colonists at this time had the highest per capita income in the world, these figures suggest just how rich the white settlers in the West Indies were.

The plantation owners in Jamaica and other islands in the West Indies also transferred the fortunes they made in the colonies back home to Britain. Because of the climate and for various social reasons, these planters preferred to return home from the colonies as soon as they made their fortunes instead of settling in the colonies. In Jamaica in 1775, for example, 40% of planters were either absentee owners or minors; after the abolition of the slave trade, that percentage rose above 80%. It seems certain that the direct transfers of wealth that these rich individuals made in the form of land and bonds, the cost of managing their plantations, and the fees charged by the British merchants who brought them consumer goods contributed to Britain's economic growth. According to one estimate that hints at the scale of this contribution, demand in the West Indies accounted for 35% of the increase in Britain's total exports between 1748 and 1776 and for 12% of the increase in Britain's industrial output in the quarter century before the American Revolutionary War [54].

Thus, British traders expanded rapidly into Asia and the Atlantic in the eighteenth century and exceeded Dutch commercial activity at its peak in terms of the volume of transactions and the variety of products. As we have already mentioned several times, the British system of expansive reinvestment that was perfected in this fashion also included the manufacturing sector (which was not the case in the Netherlands). The British built a commercial network that linked all the continents on the globe, and through that network they were able to export mass quantities of their own manufactured goods. As the system of expansive reinvestment grew in size, Britain's manufacturing output grew along with it, while rapid technological innovation occurred in the manufacturing sector. While the Netherlands had only been able to build a system of expansive reinvestment that depended upon intermediary trade, Britain was able to make the transition from the system of expansive reinvestment to the system of expansive reproduction.

Another fundamental reason why Britain and the Netherlands had different developmental experiences was Britain's success at protecting and promoting its economic interests through numerous wars in the eighteenth century. In a certain sense, Britain's complete reorganization of its political system after the Glorious Revolution, its wholehearted adoption of the financial revolution, and the lively commercial activity of its individual merchants and companies were all fundamentally possible because Britain defended its territory and protected its subjects' commercial interests from the formidable challenges posed by its rivals during these wars.

In other words, Britain was able to succeed because its military investments had built a powerful navy and because it had a financial system that could effectively mobilize military power [55]. Of course, having a financial system that was effective at funding war was no guarantee of victory in wars or mercantilist competition. Therefore, the British success in the eighteenth century must also be explained by the military and diplomatic efforts of the British government to sustain an organic relationship between the financial system and economic activity and also to effectively protect its territory and guarantee its subjects' safety.

The Fiscal-Military State

As we have already mentioned, Britain and France were rivals for hegemony over the entire world from the Glorious Revolution in 1688 until the end of the Napoleonic Wars in 1815. We do not intend to address the causes or outcomes of the various wars that were fought as part of this rivalry, since our focus is on examining how Britain perfected the system of expansive reinvestment in the eighteenth century and under what conditions it transitioned to the system of expansive reproduction. Toward this end, it will suffice us to examine what was characteristic of Britain's military in the Second Hundred Years' War with France and how Britain's military and diplomatic strategy was tied to the development of its commerce and manufacturing sectors.

No discussion of the development of British military power would be complete without mentioning the British navy. There were of course instances when the army determined the outcome of war, as with the Duke of Marlborough in the War of the Spanish Succession and the Duke of Wellington in the Napoleonic Wars. But the British army tried to avoid participating directly in wars in Continental Europe as much as possible, and it did not receive the ample investment that the navy did. The English experience in the Civil War was of course a major influence here. As the history of eighteenth-century political thought reveals, the fear that a powerful army might be a tool of tyranny and a threat to civil liberties survived in the "Country" ideology of the Radical Whigs and the Country Tories.

The navy, in contrast, was welcomed since it did not pose a direct threat to civil liberties and since it was the most important means of protecting Britons' religious and commercial liberties from the forces of absolutism. In addition, the British believed themselves to be a commercial people who pursued the free and peaceful exchange of goods, labor, and information, unlike the Spanish and French, whose absolutist monarchs were obsessed with expanding their territory. Therefore, the British regarded the navy as a precious bulwark for their commercial liberties [56].

To be sure, this does not mean that eighteenth-century Britain exclusively pursued the blue-water policy—that is, the policy of using naval power to expand its influence outside Europe and particularly in its colonies in order to protect and promote its commercial interests while remaining aloof from military action in Continental Europe and its complicated politics. Given the British monarchs' own interests and France's position on the Continent, Britain could hardly ignore Continental affairs, and it had to intervene in Continental politics if only to protect its interests in the colonies.

Britain's challenge was to find a way to appease domestic opposition to excessive military intervention on the Continent while also transcending the dichotomy between Europe and empire in order to effectively protect the diverse interests of the British government and people. These goals could not be achieved by clinging dogmatically to any one policy. For this reason, Britain exhibited a greater flexibility and pragmatism in its foreign and military policy in the eighteenth century than any other country [57].

Britain owed the success of its military and foreign policy to its ability to protect its colonies and commercial interests and to maintain the balance of power while limiting its military activity on the Continent. Britain was able to achieve these results through the effective use of two strategies. Britain's first strategy was to use the alliance system to check the power of the most threatening state on the Continent. To achieve this goal, Britain was even willing to make a temporary alliance with France. Britain's second strategy was moving aggressively in pursuit of commercial hegemony both inside and outside of its colonies, backed by the power of its navy and, to a lesser extent, its army. At the same time, of course,

Britain had to check the strength of France and its other major rivals on the Continent.

When Britain could not help intervening militarily in Europe, it did so by sending the smallest possible expeditionary force, and always as part of a coalition army. Britain was able to lead an alliance while limiting its own military participation in this way because it had an efficient fiscal system at its disposal for hiring mercenaries and providing its allies with economic assistance. At the beginning of the Seven Years' War, for example, the British government provided King Frederick II of Prussia with 675,000 lb a year. William Pitt the Elder, the statesman who led Britain and its allies to victory in this war, later remarked that "America was conquered in Germany." The implication of Pitt's remark is that, as a maritime power, Britain needed allies in Europe to be able to maintain its empire and to profit from commerce.

Needless to say, it cost a great deal of money for Britain to force France and other rivals to pour their energy into Continental wars. But this proved to be an effective way of preventing France from investing directly in its navy, which minimized the likelihood of France threatening Britain's colonies, its trade routes, and Great Britain itself. Despite its considerable fiscal expenditures, Britain was able to take advantage of a virtuous cycle: Investing in the navy helped Britain protect its commercial activity, and this in turn enabled Britain to effectively raise money to cover its military costs.

This is the paradigmatic way in which the state developed through the virtuous cycle of war and the economy in commercial society. Whereas the goal of war in agricultural society was waging war directly and seizing territory from a vanquished enemy, the goal of war in commercial society was economic profit. Thus, commercial states had no problem with giving aid to third countries to fight their proxy wars. During the Seven Years' War, for example, Britain's commercial and manufacturing sectors grew substantially even as its merchants were preyed upon by privateers. This tells us that a virtuous economic cycle fueled by an effective fiscal system and military strategy had taken hold in Britain—in other words, the system of expansive reinvestment [58].

To be sure, all this development was the product of special advantages that were unique to Britain. Since the Glorious Revolution, Parliament had served to facilitate communication between the British government and people. This meant that policies were decided not through compulsion but through consent, which created harmony between the interest of the government and the economic activity of profit-seeking individuals. In this regard, Britain presents a striking contrast with Russia and France, two countries that had a larger population and more land than Britain at the time but failed to effectively marshal their national resources despite their economic potential.

The fundamental reason for such differences was that the French and Russian economies were based on agriculture, while Britain's economy was based on commerce. Since agricultural production tends to diminish, peasants were unmotivated to increase production. Forcing the peasants to pay taxes did boost production, but this effect was bound to diminish as well. Even when such states increased their territory through military victories, there were virtually no benefits for the peasants who had to shoulder the cost of war. Therefore, national power could not be efficiently mobilized through compulsory and oppressive means as Russia and France tried to do.

In commerce, by way of contrast, added value tends to increase, which gives merchants an intrinsic motivation to seek out greater profit. War disrupted commercial networks, of course, but merchants considered funding war to be a profitable investment since victory in war expanded commercial influence and guaranteed greater profits in the fierce mercantilist competition. Accordingly, the British government was able to win over the merchants through Parliament and to efficiently concentrate and mobilize the nation's resources with the merchants' cooperation and consent. This was the force that enabled the commercial state of Britain to surpass huge agricultural empires to attain the status of hegemonic state.

From Commercial Society to Industrial Society

Britain's victory in the Seven Years' War seemed to solidify its hegemonic status. France appeared to have been permanently banished from North America and India, where it had been threatening Britain. On an economic level, France's sugar colonies in the West Indies—the most important source of imports in its overseas trade—had been annexed by the British empire. But the joy of victory proved short-lived. Just a decade later, Britain went to war with its own colonies. Britain had adopted reform measures in an attempt to tackle government debt, which had ballooned during the Seven Years' War, and to strengthen its strategic advantage in the colonies. Those reforms incited a backlash from the North American colonies.

The unexpected result was that Britain, which had the most powerful navy of the age and immense financial resources, lost its colonies. A combination of various factors was at work here, including the British government's miscalculation of the colonists' resolve to gain their independence, its failure to effectively adapt to the new style of guerilla warfare that raged across the vast territory of the North America colonies, and the logistical difficulty of providing military supplies and soldiers to battlefields that were 3000 miles away. But the biggest factor of all was that Britain had to wage war simultaneously against several powerful countries without the assistance of its allies [59].

The defeat of the British army at Yorktown in 1781 inevitably led to the independence of the American colonies. The British at the time were concerned that they were in decline just as the Spanish Empire or the Dutch Republic had been in centuries past. As we have already seen, North America had already become Britain's most important trading partner and the main market for its manufactured goods by the mid-eighteenth century. Thus, it was only natural that the British would wonder whether they could maintain the commercial advantage they had enjoyed since the end of the Seven Years' War after losing colonies of such importance. But paradoxically, the American colonies' independence only contributed to Britain's economic development. After independence, trade between Britain and the United States increased at an even faster rate. Between 1781 and 1792, exports grew by a staggering 141% and continued to grow thereafter. Thus, the United States remained the most important market for Britain's manufactured goods [60].

How could this have been possible? The answer, of course, is to be found in the Industrial Revolution. The Industrial Revolution got fully underway in Britain during the generation after the American Revolutionary War, and major British industries such as textiles and iron acquired a large share of the American market. At this point, we must mention once again the difference between Britain and the Netherlands. As we have already seen, the Netherlands went into rapid decline as it fought wars against England and France in the mid-seventeenth century. This stands in contrast with Britain, whose economic growth did not slow but only accelerated even after Britain lost its North American colonies, which were an important market and a source of raw materials. Both of these two states built advanced commercial societies, but one of them forfeited its commercial vitality after military defeat, while the other succeeded at transitioning from a commercial society to an industrial society.

Such different outcomes can be explained as follows. First, the relationship between the Netherlands and England in the mid-seventeenth century was fundamentally different from the economic relationship between Britain and the United States in the late eighteenth century. The Netherlands and England were both commercial states, and their relationship was fraught with rivalry. The United States, however, was not a commercial state like Britain but an agricultural state, which allowed the two states to enjoy a complementary relationship or even a partnership. During the mercantilist competition that triggered the Navigation Acts and three wars, the Netherlands yielded its advantage in the Atlantic trade to England. In trade with Asia, the Netherlands failed to come up with a new product that could substitute for pepper. But by opening up a market for tea and cotton cloth, England gained an opportunity to seize commercial hegemony. Therefore, the relationship between these two states was a typical example of a zero-sum game in which wealth could not be shared.

In contrast, Britain was forced to acknowledge the independence of its erstwhile American colonies, but this only meant that it had lost political control over the colonies. It did not infringe on Britain's naval supremacy or trading rights, which were of more importance to a commercial empire. The American economy was specialized for raw materials and agricultural products, and it needed Britain's manufactured goods. Americans had so long been accustomed to these goods that they had no choice but to further expand trade with Britain even in the aftermath of the Revolutionary War. In other words, the relationship between the producers in the British economy and the consumers in the American economy constituted a positive-sum game, in which their interests coincided.

The Netherlands and Britain also differed in regard to their governments' economic capacity to weather a crisis. If the Netherlands had emerged victorious from its competition with England and if it had effectively repelled the French invasion, its decline would probably have been delayed. But the Netherlands failed to overcome this crisis, while Britain regarded the crisis as an opportunity. This points to internal differences between the Netherlands and Britain—more specifically, differences in their systems of expansive reinvestment.

Britain transformed its system of expansive reinvestment into a system of expansive reproduction, but the Netherlands failed to do so. The Dutch failure cannot be simply or briefly explained, but it is possible to enumerate several important factors. As we have mentioned previously, the most important factor was that the Dutch depended on entrepôt trade and thus did not develop a domestic manufacturing base. A number of factors played a role in this as well. First, it is worth noting that not only did urbanization occur earlier in the Netherlands than in any other country, but the craft guilds in its cities were very influential. This made it difficult to adopt technological innovations and to develop rural manufacturing that could have lowered the production cost or to develop new industries that would have been free of the guilds' regulations. Another factor was the high wages in the Netherlands, which made the prices of Dutch manufactured goods less competitive on the international market after the mid-seventeenth century. Britain, on the other hand, was able to offset its relatively high wages through technological innovations based on cheap energy. But the Netherlands did not have access to such advantages.

The Netherlands and Britain were also different in respect to the scale of their markets. Even in the eighteenth century, the Netherlands remained the richest country in Europe in terms of per capita income. But fundamentally, the Netherlands was a small country with a small population. Around 1700, the Netherlands had a population of just 1.9 million, while Britain had more than 5 million people. Population growth in the Netherlands remained stagnant throughout the eighteenth century, but Britain's population began to increase rapidly in the mid-eighteenth century.

Another thing to consider when discussing market size is the colonies. Dutch influence in the American continent faded after the 1650s, and the VOC became less competitive in the second half of the seventeenth century amid changes in the structure of trade and growing local resistance to the VOC's monopoly. But England at the end of the seventeenth century was able not only to increase the EIC's influence in India but also to secure raw materials and commercial products in North America and the West Indies, not to mention a rapidly growing market.

Since the colonial market could be controlled with relative ease, it was a life-saver for British manufacturers. As we have observed before, the colonies had already become the most important market for exports of British manufactured goods by the mid-eighteenth century. The American colonists were accustomed to Britain products and to the credit and services that British merchants provided. When the Revolutionary War was winding down, the colonists turned their back on France and the French merchants who had generously supported them during the war and returned to Britain's manufacturers and merchants. This is yet another reminder of the importance of the colonial market.

The Dutch defeat in competition over the Atlantic colonies suggests that the Dutch Republic's political failure was another factor that contributed to its economic decline. During the Republic's war with the Spanish Empire, the seven provinces of which it was composed employed government bonds and various other financial instruments to effectively fund the war, and these measures helped them successfully defend their territory. But as is suggested by the admiralty colleges that were set up in various provinces because of their competing interests, the Netherlands failed to acquire a powerful navy. Since the Dutch States General was unable to reconcile the interests of the various provinces, it was also unable to effectively counter the threat of France, which had a strong central government, or to compete with England, which had developed a small but effective central government and a legislature that could balance the interests of the country as a whole.

Britain was a commercial society like the Netherlands, and the integral connection between Parliament, the government, and the financial market in the private sector allowed it to cover the state's ever-increasing military expenditures with long-term bonds and tax receipts. But since the various Dutch provinces still managed their own fiscal affairs into the eighteenth century, the Netherlands was eventually no longer even sure of protecting its territory from foreign invasion [61]. Therefore, the Dutch Republic collapsed as soon as it was invaded by the French Revolutionary Army in 1795.

From the mid-seventeenth century (when mercantilist competition began to intensify) until the early nineteenth century, there were several conditions that had to be met before any one state could acquire economic hegemony over both Europe and the whole world. Britain aspired to be a commercial society as the Netherlands did, but it differed from the Netherlands in that it developed its manufacturing industry at the same time that it was commercializing. It also created an institutional framework through which British government policy could reflect the British people's commercial interests. In this way, Britain was able to acquire the fiscal foundation and the military strength to protect and advance its own interests from the commercial challenges and the military and diplomatic threats of rival states.

As is illustrated by the Netherlands, which became a republic before Britain did, a political system that guarantees property rights and other civil liberties does not necessarily lead to continuous economic development. Perhaps an even more important condition for economic growth is building a state that is powerful enough to protect its territory and property so that it can guarantee civil liberties. It was in this respect that Britain achieved greater success than any other state [62]. In other words, a strong state built a strong economy, and a strong economy was the condition for a strong state.

Another crucial factor in Britain's hegemony was that the British were able to keep expanding their commercial advantage on their industrial base. In that sense, Britain's Industrial Revolution, which began in the mid-eighteenth century, was the decisive moment when commercial society with its system of expansive reinvestment gave way to industrial society with its system of expansive reproduction. In the next chapter, we will examine how Britain transitioned from commercial society to industrial society and how this transition affected the way in which Britain exercised its hegemony.

References

1. It would of course be anachronistic to use the term "Great Britain" to refer to England and Scotland before they were combined in the Act of Union of 1707. Therefore, we use the term "England" to refer to events prior to 1707 and "Great Britain" (or "Britain") for events subsequent to that date.
2. Maurice Dobb, *Studies in the Development of Capitalism* (London, 1947); T. H. Aston and C. H. E. Philpin (eds.), *The Brenner Debate: Agrarian Class Structure and Economic Development in Pre-industrial Europe* (Cambridge, 1985).
3. Douglass C. North, *Understanding the Process of Economic Change* (Princeton, 2005), p. 143. What we are emphasizing here is that the share of the English crown's fiscal income that came from feudal support gradually decreased, while the share that came from taxes on trade and manufacturing increased. The bulk of this came from the tax on wool exports. For more on this, see Eileen Power, *The Wool Trade in English Medieval History* (New York, 1941).
4. E. M. Carus-Wilson, *Medieval Merchant Venturers* (London, 1954), pp. 143–182; Robert Brenner, *Merchants and Revolution: Commercial Change, Political Conflict, and London's Overseas Traders*, 1550–1653 (London, 2003), pp. 6, 52.
5. Kenneth R. Andrews, *Trade, Plunder and Settlement: Maritime Enterprise and the Genesis of the British Empire, 1480–1630* (Cambridge, 1984).
6. For more about the split in the merchant class and the relationship between civil war and revolution, see Brenner, *Merchants and Revolution.*
7. P. J. Marshall, "The English in Asia," Nicholas Canny (ed.), *The Oxford History of the British Empire, Vol. 1: The Origins of Empire* (Oxford, 1998).
8. Brenner, *Merchants and Revolution.*
9. Lawrence Harper, *The English Navigation Laws: A Seventeenth-Century Experiment in Social Engineering* (New York, 1939).
10. Ronald Findlay and Kevin H. O'Rourke, *Power and Plenty: Trade, War and the World Economy in the Second Millennium* (Princeton, 2007). chap. 5.
11. Charles Kindleberger, *Gyeongje Gangdaeguk Heungmangsa 1500–1990* [World Economic Primacy: 1500–1990], trans. Gyeong-cheol Ju (Kachi, 2004) pp. 81, 202, 205–211; Paul Kennedy, *The Rise and Fall of the Great Powers: Economic Change and Military Conflict from 1500 to 2000* (New York, 1987).
12. N. A. M. Rodger, *The Command of the Ocean: A Naval History of Britain, 1649–1815* (London, 2004), chaps. 1–3.
13. Charles H. Wilson, *Profit and Power* (London, 1957), pp. 56–59; J. E. Farnell, "The Navigation Act of 1651, the First Dutch War, and the London Merchant Community," *Economic History Review*, 2nd ser., 16:3 (1963–1964), pp. 439–454; Brenner, *Merchants and Revolution*; Jonathan Israel, *The Dutch Primacy in World Trade, 1585–1740* (Oxford, 1989), pp. 269–279. For a criticism of this economic analysis, see Pincus, *Protestantism and Patriotism: Ideologies and the Making of English Foreign Policy, 1650–1668.* In his criticism of research that emphasizes the economic origins of war, Steve Pincus focuses on the influence of ideologies like Protestantism and Republicanism. But Pincus's position does not appear to present any major problems for our argument about war, since (as Israel's study examines in detail) the Netherlands and England did compete fiercely in trade in the Levant, the Mediterranean, Asia, and the Atlantic during the half century before the war. In addition to this, Charles Wilson notes that there was a severe economic recession in the early 1650s. As Robert Brenner emphasizes, it is undeniable that the new groups of London merchants, and in particular the unlicensed merchants engaged in trade with the colonies, criticized the monopoly of the authorized companies while at the same time attempting to undermine the influence of Dutch merchants in the Atlantic colonies. Even more important than these considerations, however, is the growing realization in England during this period that merchants as a whole and commercial interests were an important matter for the state to

address and that they had to be protected by the navy. Indeed, Pincus focuses on the fact that, as the English vigorously debated the struggle against the Spanish Empire under the Hapsburgs, the Dutch Empire, and the French monarchy (which could be called "universal monarchies") in coffeehouses and taverns, they acquired a conceptual understanding of the national interest. Pincus links this development to the emergence of nationalism. The argument we are making is that commercial interests were at the heart of the concept of "national interest." To be sure, the relationship between England's commercial interests and nationalism is a topic that requires further study and debate.

14. Rodger, *The Command of the Ocean.*
15. Philip Lawson, *The East India Company: A History* (London, 1993).
16. George Louis Beer, "Cromwell's Policy in Its Economic Aspects II," *Political Science Quarterly* 17 (1902), pp. 46, 66.
17. The Whig interpretation is so well-known that it scarcely seems necessary to cite any particular sources. For a recent interpretation that emphasizes the religious aspect—and in particular the international coalition of Protestants—see Tony Claydon, *William III and the Godly Revolution* (Cambridge, 1996); Tony Claydon, *Europe and the Making of England 1660–1760* (Cambridge, 2007).
18. Steve Pincus, *1688: The First Modern Revolution* (New Haven, 2009).
19. Pincus, *1688: The First Modern Revolution.*
20. For the best-known results, see Douglass C. North and Barry Weingast, "Constitutions and Commitment: The Evolution of Institutions Governing Public Choice in Seventeenth-Century England," *Journal of Economic History* 49:4 (1989).
21. Paul Langford, "Property and 'Virtual Representation' in Eighteenth-Century England," *The Historical Journal* 31 (March 1988); Joanna Innes, "Parliament and the Shaping of Eighteenth-Century Social Policy," *Transactions of the Royal Historical Society*, 5th ser., 40 (1990); Paul Langford, *Public Life and the Propertied Englishman 1689–1798* (Oxford, 1990); Julian Hoppit, "Patterns of Parliamentary Legislation, 1660–1800," *The Historical Journal* 39 (March 1996); Julian Hoppit (ed.), *Parliaments, Nations and Identities in Britain and Ireland, 1660–1850* (Manchester, 2003). After the Glorious Revolution, the Parliament of England met each year, and its sessions also became longer. For more on this point, see Hoppit (ed.), *Parliaments, Nations and Identities*, p. 5.
22. In regard to the rate of increase of military expenditures, wars before 1688 typically did not cost more than 2 million pounds, but the War of the Spanish Succession cost 7 million pounds a year while the American Revolutionary War cost 20 million pounds a year. Brewer, *Sinews of Power*, p. 30.
23. P. G. M. Dickson, *The Financial Revolution in England: A Study in the Development of Public Credit 1688–1756* (1967; London, 1993); Bruce G. Carruthers, *City of Capital: Politics and Markets in the English Financial Revolution* (Princeton, 1996), chap. 3.
24. As a result, Britain converted its existing liabilities in 1752 into Consolidated Annuities (Consols), or bonds with an interest rate of 3.5%. In 1757, Consols were issued at a lower interest rate of 3%. Consolidated 3% Annuities were very popular with overseas investors, and with Dutch investors in particular. Niall Ferguson, *The Ascent of Money: A Financial History of the World* (London, 2008), p. 76.
25. Larry Neal, *The Rise of Financial Capitalism: International Capital Markets in the Age of Reason* (Cambridge, 1990), chap. 1.
26. The fact that a significant number of the Whig elites who dominated British politics in the first half of the eighteenth century held government bonds or stocks in the Bank of England also helped increase confidence in the market. Significantly, both the interest rate on government bonds and the dividend rate on Bank of England stock fell while the Whigs were in power. D. Stasavage, "Partisan Politics and Public Debt: The Importance of the 'Whig Supremacy' for Britain's Financial Revolution," *European Review of Economic History* 11:1 (April 2007).
27. Peter Mathias and Patrick K. O'Brien, "Taxation in Great Britain and France, 1715–1810," *Journal of European Economic History* 5 (1976); Patrick K. O'Brien, "Political Economy of British Taxation, 1660–1815," *Economic History Review*, 2nd ser., 41:1 (1988).

28. According to Brewer, the staff in the tax collection agencies increased threefold between 1690 and 1783, while the workers specifically assigned to collecting excise taxes increased more than fourfold (from 1,150 in 1690 to 5,000 in 1783). John Brewer, *The Sinews of Power: War, Money, and the English State, 1688–1783* (London, 1989), p. 66, table 3.2.
29. Mathias and O'Brien, "Taxation in Great Britain and France, 1715–1810"; O'Brien, "Political Economy of British Taxation, 1660–1815."
30. Daeryoon Kim, "In Search of 'Affectionate Regard': American Merchant Lobbies and the State during the Atlantic Imperial Crisis," *Parliamentary History* 30 (June 2011).
31. C. H. Feinstein, "Capital Accumulation and the Industrial Revolution," R. Floud and D. McCloskey (eds.), *The Economic History of Britain Since 1700, Vol. 1* (Cambridge, 1981), p. 129, table 7.1.
32. Jacob M. Price, "What Did Merchants Do? Reflections of British Overseas Trade, 1660–1790," *Journal of Economic History* 49:2 (1989).
33. For the work and role of merchants, see Richard Grassby, *The Business Community of Seventeenth-Century England* (Cambridge, 1995); David Hancock, *Citizens of the World: London Merchants and the Integration of the British Atlantic Community, 1735–1785* (Cambridge, 1995); Perry Gauci, *Emporium of the World: The Merchant of London 1660–1800* (London, 2007).
34. Keith Wrightson, *Earthly Necessities: Economic Lives in Early Modern Britain* (New Haven, 2000), pp. 226–248. For agricultural specialization, see in particular pp. 232–235. For agriculture and urbanization in the eighteenth century, see E. A. Wrigley, "British Population during the 'Long' Eighteenth Century," Roderick Floud and Paul Johnson (eds.), *The Cambridge Economic History of Modern Britain, Vol. I: Industrialisation, 1700–1860* (Cambridge, 2004); Robert C. Allen, "Agriculture during the Industrial Revolution, 1700-1850."
35. Wrightson, *Earthly Necessities*, pp. 245–248; Simon Ville, "Transport," Floud and Johnson (eds.), *The Cambridge Economic History of Modern Britain.*
36. Yeong-seok Lee, *Gongjangui Yeoksa: Geundae Yeongguk Sahoewa Saengsan, Eoneo, Jeongchi* [History of the Factory: Production, Language, and Politics and Modern British Society] (Blue History, 2012), pp. 22–51; Charles H. Wilson, *England's Apprenticeship 1603–1763* (London, 1965), pp. 185–205, 288–312.
37. Robert C. Allen, *The British Industrial Revolution in Global Perspective* (Cambridge, 2009), pp. 33–34.
38. Neil McKendrick, John Brewer and J. H. Plumb, *The Birth of a Consumer Society: The Commercialization of Eighteenth-Century England* (Cambridge, 1982); John Brewer and Roy Porter (eds.), *Consumption and the World of Goods in the 17th and 18th Centuries* (London and New York, 1993); Maxine Berg, *Luxury and Pleasure in Eighteenth-Century Britain* (Oxford, 2005); Jan de Vries, *The Industrious Revolution: Consumer Behavior and the Household Economy, 1650 to the Present* (Cambridge, 2008).
39. Ralph Davis, "English Foreign Trade, 1700–1774," *Economic History Review*, 2nd ser., 15 (December 1962); Phyllis Deane and W. A. Cole, *British Economic Growth 1688–1959*, 2nd ed. (Cambridge, 1969), pp. 41–50; Price, "What Did Merchants Do?" pp. 271, 276; according to another estimate, 85% of the tobacco and 94% of the coffee imported in the 1770s were re-exported to Continental Europe. Niall Ferguson, *Empire* (London, 2003), p. 16.
40. Crafts estimates, for example, that exports as a share of Britain's national product increased from 8.4% to 14.6% between 1700 and 1760. N. F. R. Crafts, *British Economic Growth during the Industrial Revolution* (Oxford, 1985), p. 131. E. J. Hobsbawm, *Industry and Empire: The Making of Modern English Society, 1750 to the Present Day* (New York, 1968), p. 32.
41. Crafts, *British Economic Growth*, p. 131.
42. K. N. Chaudhuri, *The Trading World of Asia and the English East India Company 1660–1760* (Cambridge, 1978), p. 388.
43. Hoh-Cheung and Lorna H. Mui, "Smuggling and the British Tea Trade before 1784," *American Historical Review* 74:1 (October 1968). In an attempt to resolve this problem in the

North American colonies, Parliament reduced duties with the Tea Act of 1773, which was the direct cause of the infamous Boston Tea Party. Inside Britain, duties on tea were lowered in 1784, which resolved the problem of smuggling, at least to a certain degree.

44. Edmund S. Morgan, *American Slavery, American Freedom: The Ordeal of Colonial Virginia* (New York, 1975); Richard S. Dunn, *Sugar and Slaves: The Rise of the Planter Class in the English West Indies, 1624–1713* (Chapel Hill, NC, 1972).
45. Patrick O'Brien, "Inseparable Connections: Trade, Economy, Fiscal State, and the Expansion of Empire, 1688–1815," P. J. Marshall (ed.), *The Oxford History of the British Empire, Vol. 2: The Eighteenth Century* (Oxford, 1998), p. 100.
46. Nancy F. Koehn, *The Power of Commerce: Economy and Governance in the First British Empire* (Ithaca, 1994).
47. James A. Henretta, *"Salutary Neglect": Colonial Administration under the Duke of Newcastle* (Princeton, 1972); Alison G. Olson, *Making the Empire Work: London and American Interest Groups 1690–1790* (Cambridge, Mass., 1992).
48. John J. McCusker and Russell R. Menard, *The Economy of British America 1607–1789* (Chapel Hill, NC, 1985).
49. Berg, *Luxury and Pleasure*, pp. 287–288; T. H. Breen, "'Baubles of Britain': The American and Consumer Revolutions of the Eighteenth Century," *Past and Present* 119 (1988), p. 80.
50. An immense amount of research has been done on the slave trade and on slavery as an institution. For this book, we have generally relied on Kenneth Morgan, *Slavery and the British Empire: From Africa to America* (New York, 2007), which deftly summarizes previous research, while also referring to other studies when necessary. For the decline of the system of indentured servitude, see pp. 18–21 and 29–30.
51. Morgan, *Slavery and the British Empire*, pp. 67–68, 79, 81. One of the most notorious aspects of the slave trade was the Middle Passage. The fatality rate for Africans during the journey across the Atlantic, which took from four to six weeks, is estimated to have been about 20% in the first half of the eighteenth century and less than 10% during the second half of the eighteenth century. See p. 74 of the same book.
52. We are referring, of course, to the hypothesis of Eric Williams. *Capitalism and Slavery* (Chapel Hill, NC, 1944); Barbara L. Solow, "Caribbean Slavery and British Growth: The Eric Williams Hypothesis," *Journal of Development Economics* 17 (1985).
53. Morgan, *Slavery and the British Empire*, pp. 67–68.
54. Morgan, *Slavery and the British Empire*, pp. 36, 46–50, 83.
55. This is the point that receives the most emphasis in Patrick K. O'Brien's research. Patrick K. O'Brien, "Fiscal and Financial Preconditions for the Rise of British Naval Hegemony 1485–1815," LSE EH Working Paper 91/05 (November 2005); O'Brien, "Fiscal Exceptionalism: Great Britain and its European Rivals from Civil War to Triumph at Trafalgar and Waterloo," LSE EH Working Paper 65/01 (October 2001).
56. Linda Colley, *Britons: Forging the Nation, 1707–1837* (New Haven, 1992); Kathleen Wilson, *The Sense of the People: Politics, Culture and Imperialism in England, 1715–1785* (Cambridge, 1995); Nicholas Rogers, *Crowds, Culture, and Politics in Georgian Britain* (Oxford, 1998). The navy was also of economic importance. The total tonnage of ships that belonged to the navy increased from 100,000 tons in 1685 to about 325,000 tons in 1760, and demand also increased for the cannons that were needed to arm the warships. This not only resulted in the growth of the shipbuilding industry (the naval shipyard was the largest workplace in eighteenth-century Britain) but also contributed to the development of the steel refining industry.
57. Daniel Baugh, "Great Britain's 'Blue-Water' Policy, 1689–1815," *International History Review* 10:1 (February 1988); Jeremy Black, *A System of Ambition? British Foreign Policy 1660–1793* (London, 1991); Brendan Simms, *Three Victories and a Defeat: The Rise and Fall of the First British Empire* (London, 2007).
58. For the events of the Seven Years' War and their significance, see Fred Anderson, *Crucible of War: The Seven Years' War and the Fate of Empire in British North America, 1754–1766* (London, 2000).

59. Simms, *Three Victories and a Defeat*; P. J. Marshall, *The Making and Unmaking of the Empires: Britain, India, and America, c. 1750–1783* (Oxford, 2005).
60. François Crouzet, "Toward an Export Economy: British Exports during the Industrial Revolution," *Explorations in Economic History* 17 (1980), pp. 54–57.
61. Marjolein 't Hart, "Mobilising Resources for War: The Dutch and British Financial Revolutions Compared," Second Low Countries Conference, April 20–21 (Antwerp, 2006), pp. 14–15.
62. Patrick K. O'Brien, "Mercantilism and Imperialism in the Rise and Decline of the Dutch and British Economies, 1585–1815," *De Economist* 148:4 (2000).

Chapter 5
The Maturity and Decline of British Industrial Society

In 1851, the Great Exhibition—the first world's fair in history—was held at Hyde Park in London. The fair made it manifestly clear that Britain was the "workshop of the world." On display were 100,000 items submitted by no fewer than 14,000 companies, with support provided by around 300 regional committees that had been organized voluntarily. By throwing open its doors to the countries of the world with the fair, Britain hoped to show that this new era it was leading was characterized by harmony and cooperation and based on free trade [1].

Britain's industrial prestige at the time was sufficient to support such confidence. Its cotton textile industry, which had powered the Industrial Revolution, consumed between 2 and 3 million tons of raw cotton in the 1840s; its yearly coal production reached 49 million tons in 1850; and steam engines, which were the driving force of industrialization, were supplying 1.29 million horsepower of energy every year. Backed by this vigorous industrial activity, the per capita GDP of Britain (which had a population of 21 million in 1850) was 64% higher than Germany's and 30% higher than the United States' [2].

To be sure, it was the Industrial Revolution that brought Britain such overwhelming economic power. We mentioned in Chap. 4 that Britain at the end of the eighteenth century had begun the transition from the system of expansive reinvestment in commercial society to the system of expansive reproduction in industrial society. A manufacturing industry developed in Britain (though not in the Netherlands) that could supply the products needed for trade in the Atlantic and produce goods to replace the high-quality manufactured goods being imported from Asia, thus spurring technological innovation. This was what we meant when we defined the Industrial Revolution as the evolution of the system of expansive reinvestment into the system of expansive reproduction based on technological innovation in the supply sector and the exploitation of new sources of energy.

Previously, we also explained that economic growth continued to accelerate under the system of expansive reproduction because of two characteristics. The first of these characteristics concerns the aspect of demand. Whereas growth under the system of expansive reinvestment occurs when demand increases as capital

T.-Y. Kim and D. Kim, *The Secrets of Hegemony*,
DOI 10.1007/978-981-10-4416-8_5

accumulates and wages rise, growth accelerates even further under the system of expansive reproduction through a cycle in which accumulated capital enables the development of new products, creating further demand. The second characteristic has to do with the aspect of supply. Growth under the system of expansive reinvestment is based on agricultural and manual production, while growth under the system of expansive reproduction is based on the factory system, which draws its energy from fossil fuels and relies on technological innovation.

Therefore, in order to understand Britain's economic hegemony in the mid-nineteenth century, we will need to consider how the Industrial Revolution occurred and how the system of expansive reproduction became established in Britain. Of course, a great deal of research has already been published about the Industrial Revolution. Rather than referring to each of these numerous studies, our focus here will be on identifying the factors that enabled the Industrial Revolution to occur in Britain from the perspective of the transition to the system of expansive reproduction. In this way, we will be able to systematically explain the beginning of the Industrial Revolution, the efforts by later industrializing states to catch up with Britain in the second half of the nineteenth century, and Britain's relative decline in subsequent years.

What is particularly important to pay attention to here is the role of the state. Previous studies have only dealt with this issue in a cursory manner by drawing attention to the state's indirect role in the establishment of property rights and Parliament's influence on the creation of a free market. But the role of the state needs a more thorough assessment than this. Just as the system of expansive reinvestment that led to the Industrial Revolution was brought into being through a state policy of protectionism, the Industrial Revolution itself was able to occur because of technological innovation and the development of the manufacturing sector under the influence of a state policy of selective protectionism. This helps us understand not only the Industrial Revolution in Britain but also the process of development in states that industrialized later such as Germany and Japan. Perhaps it was no coincidence that these late industrializing states took an interest in state-led industrial policies.

Elements of the Industrial Revolution

The most crucial prerequisite for the Industrial Revolution was the maturity of the system of expansive reinvestment. If not for the virtuous cycle of the system of expansive reinvestment (in which economic surplus is accumulated as capital and invested in commerce, which in turn promotes the growth of the entire economy), there would have been little chance of innovation occurring in the production and supply sector. But the establishment of the system of expansive reinvestment did not necessarily mean that there would be a transition to the system of expansive reproduction, since innovation in the supply sector does not always occur under the system of expansive reinvestment.

As we have already seen, the Netherlands provides an effective illustration of this point. The Dutch Republic was unable to maintain its economic advantage in the mid-seventeenth century because its deviation from the virtuous cycle of war and the economy meant that it could no longer protect or expand its markets, and because the commercial system based on entrepôt trade did not lead to the development of the domestic manufacturing industry. In other words, the establishment of the system of expansive reinvestment was a necessary condition for the Industrial Revolution, but not a sufficient condition. Therefore, if we are to explain Britain's Industrial Revolution, we need to first determine what aspect of Britain's system of expansive reinvestment contributed to the Industrial Revolution.

As we have repeated on multiple occasions, the heart of the system of expansive reinvestment was the development of commerce. What should be noted here is that eighteenth-century British commerce was more advanced than other European countries and that it was closely connected to domestic manufacturing. One example can be found in the cotton textile industry that triggered the Industrial Revolution. The cotton textile industry began to develop in earnest in the second half of the eighteenth century; by the early nineteenth century, it had become Britain's most important industry, in terms of both its production value and the share it represented of total exports. Between 1784 to 1786 and 1814 to 1816, the value of cotton textile exports increased more than 20-fold. This made up more than half of the increase in Britain's overseas exports during the same period. The added value that was created in the cotton textile industry greatly increased as well. In 1770, cotton textile production was the smallest sector of the textile manufacturing industry, at 2.6%; by 1831, its share had grown to 22.4%, a full 10% higher than the former key sector of woolen textiles [3].

The rapid growth of the cotton textile industry was the product of growth in overseas trade that was spurring technological innovation. Cotton textiles were first introduced to British consumers through the commercial activity of the East India Company (EIC). Customers were enthusiastic about the product, which resulted in a flood of foreign-made cotton textiles into Britain. The protectionist trade measures that were adopted in response caused British manufacturers to become interested in the domestic production of cotton textiles. Their success in this business area can ultimately be explained by their ability to take advantage of trade on the Atlantic (which had grown rapidly during the eighteenth century) to gain a steady supply of raw cotton from North America and their ability to secure markets in America and Africa in which to sell their finished products. These are crucial links in the chain of the development of the Britain cotton textiles industry [4].

The growth of the system of expansive reinvestment resulted not only in the development of specific sectors of the manufacturing industry but also in an increase in domestic demand. As the system of expansive reinvestment matured, the British people's level of income increased overall, and as urbanization accelerated, exchange in the markets became established as part of people's everyday lives.

London in particular was the center of commerce, finance, and manufacturing, and it became a huge metropolis that was home to one-quarter of England's population. In London at this time, not only the middle class but also the poor took for granted the practice of purchasing their daily necessities in the markets.

The innovations in the distribution sector that began in this way—including permanent markets, retail outlets, and regular publications—quickly spread into the countryside, backed by developments in transportation and communication. This made it possible for domestic demand to grow even faster. As we mentioned in Chap. 4, such changes brought about the consumer revolution in eighteenth-century Britain [5]. The most important developments resulting from the consumer revolution were the frequently changing consumer trends in cotton cloth and other textiles and the fact that these changing trends became a major topic of interest in Britain society. British consumers had long been accustomed to woolen cloth—which was heavy, coarse, and drab—and they were exhilarated by the appearance of linens, silks, and cotton goods in a wide range of colors. This initiated a virtuous cycle in which existing demand for textiles led to technical innovations in the supply sector and in which the products created with these new technologies created new demand [6].

The increase in demand obviously whetted manufacturers' spirit of enterprise. But even more important is the fact that the conditions were already in place for manufacturers to move into new business areas. This observation is also closely linked to the development of the system of expansive reinvestment. The growth of commerce undermined Britain's system of medieval craft guilds and produced the commodity and finance markets, which made it easier to raise capital. There are not many examples of capital accumulated in the commercial and financial sectors being directly converted to industrial capital (though there were merchants and financiers who directly invested in industrial sectors such as iron and mining that required a great deal of initial capital). But in the early phase of the Industrial Revolution, when working capital was far more important than fixed capital, it was easy for manufacturers to enter a business with the credit provided by merchants and wholesalers, the assistance their friends and relatives provided, and their own savings and retained earnings [7]. Furthermore, manufacturers did not even need to have technical knowledge. They could become successful simply by identifying the promising technical skills of other people and combining them with their own business acumen, as in the case of James Watt and his business partner Matthew Boulton [8].

The fact that British businesspeople and engineers were able to raise capital in a variety of ways that were suitable to the nature of their business and also able to easily enter a unified market made it possible for them to focus on improving existing products and on producing and releasing new ones. As is shown by the history of the steam engine, important inventions during the Industrial Revolution came to fruition through the continuing effort of numerous people who were attempting to improve the economic and technical efficiency of existing inventions.

This new technology did not even need to be developed by the British. Returning to the example of the steam engine, the British did not hesitate to import and perfect technology that had been developed overseas. This was because the system of expansive reproduction added economic value to technology and offered the possibility of achieving even greater profit through improving upon that technology. The original technology for Thomas Newcomen's 1712 steam engine had been developed in France by Denis Papin in 1691. The Leblanc process for soda ash production, the chlorination dyeing process, and the sheet glass manufacturing process were all technologies that originated in various parts of France and were commercialized in Britain [9].

Technological innovation was linked to the level of wages. Rising wages spurred technological innovation in the two areas of supply and demand: they created an incentive for the development of labor-saving technology, and they increased consumers' purchasing power, allowing them to buy more new products. According to one estimate that compares the wages of construction workers in major world cities including London from the Middle Ages until the nineteenth century, the wage gap between London and other cities began to appear in the early sixteenth century. By 1775, the wages of workers in London were 300% higher than workers in Vienna and 25% higher than workers in Amsterdam. As British workers' wages rose, efforts were made to reduce the labor cost.

Rising wages also made it possible for workers to buy preference goods and even luxury goods on top of their daily necessities (like food, fuel, and clothing), which increased demand not only for import products but also for products of domestic manufacture. Furthermore, workers became more interested in education and in training, which raised the educational level of society as a whole. This expanded the intellectual foundation needed to sustain technological innovation [10].

In short, the development of the system of expansive reinvestment expanded domestic and foreign markets, increased the amount of capital, raised the level of wages, and brought about the consumer revolution, provoking technological innovation in the manufacturing sector. But running the new machines (which relied on steam engines and other new sources of power) also required a huge amount of fuel. In addition, accelerating urbanization—particularly the rapid growth of London's population—was accompanied by a major increase in household demand for fuel. Thus, as long as the fuel problem remained unresolved, the Industrial Revolution could not progress either.

The solution to this issue came in the form of coal. Britain's production of coal began to rapidly increase in the seventeenth century. Yearly coal production reached between 2.5 and 3 million tons in 1700 and between 10 and 13 million tons in 1800. As coal production increased, the forested areas that had been reserved for cutting wood (the traditional source of fuel) became available for agricultural or industrial purposes. Thus, coal served as a dynamo that slashed the cost of fuel, spurred urbanization, and cranked up production. It also paved the way for widely distributing machines that could provide a degree of power that far exceeded what human or animals had once provided. This made it possible to move from traditional production methods, which depended entirely on the amount of the factors of production, to modern economic growth, which depends on production efficiency [11].

Whereas Britain's abundant coal reserves were a natural boon, the political turmoil from the French Revolution to the Napoleonic Wars proved to be a historical windfall that unexpectedly assisted Britain's Industrial Revolution. As we have already mentioned, Britain was able to establish the system of expansive reinvestment because the government achieved the virtuous cycle of war and the economy by actively protecting commercial activity, opening and defending foreign markets, and keeping its territory safe. While the French Revolution and the Napoleonic Wars far surpassed previous wars in terms of scale and cost, one common thread running through all these wars was that Britain's victory was ensured by the fiscal system that had developed under the system of expansive reinvestment [12].

There were two senses in which the French Revolution and the Napoleonic Wars contributed to Britain's Industrial Revolution. First, they increased Britain's control over the American market. France decided to put fiscal pressure on Britain through the Continental System, while Britain attempted to trap France on the Continent through a naval blockade. As a result, not only France but also other European belligerents suffered a major reduction in trade with the United States. This inflicted a serious blow on manufacturers in Continental Europe that had depended on the American market while energizing British manufacturers [13].

Second, the French Revolution and the Napoleonic Wars further increased the flow of Continental capital into Britain. An enormous amount of foreign capital—Dutch capital in particular—flowed into the British financial market in the mid-eighteenth century. As extreme instability settled over the Continent during the French Revolution and the Napoleonic Wars, Britain became a haven for capital. Napoleon's strict Continental System was partly successful in preventing British capital from reaching its European rivals, but the system could not prevent Continental capital from entering Britain. The capital that reached Britain during these years was invested in the government bond market, where it helped Britain win its wars and also contributed to the expansion of industries such as iron mills and infrastructure such as canals, ports, and turnpikes [14].

The state's role in the development of Britain's system of expansive reproduction was not limited to providing security, protecting assets, and producing war-related economic profit. As we have already mentioned, after the Glorious Revolution the British government and Parliament continued to take an interest in alleviating the economic difficulties of merchants and manufacturers and in mediating their conflicting interests. To be sure, the British government and Parliament did not actively propose industrial policies or economic development plans during the process of industrialization in the manner of states that industrialized later. For this reason, historical and theoretical interpretations of the Industrial Revolution have paid scant attention to the role of the state. But a more detailed examination of the actual historical records shows that the British government and Parliament both took an interest in economic issues in various ways and played a role in promoting economic development [15].

The first issue to consider is the effect that mercantilist protectionism had on industrial development. As is widely known, the British government and Parliament consistently adopted policies in support of the manufacturing sector. This tradition of protectionism can be traced back as far as King Henry VII's efforts to promote England's wool manufacturing industry by recruiting skilled workers from the Low Countries and selecting an area to specialize in woolen textile production and the high tariffs that he used to regulate exports of wool [16]. The Wool Act at the end of the seventeenth century—which stymied the growth of the manufacturing industry in the colonies by banning overseas exports of woolen cloth manufactured there—was also intended to protect the domestic manufacturing industry [17].

This tradition of protectionism continued in the eighteenth century. Sir Robert Walpole's customs reform of 1722 was designed to encourage exports of domestically manufactured products and to suppress imports of finished products. By lowering tariffs on imports of raw materials and by paying refunds and bounties on exports of products manufactured in Britain, these reforms made British exports more competitive [18]. Aside from the considerable economic benefits of these measures, it is also important that merchants and manufacturers were directly involved in the process of introducing, repealing, and revising particular tariffs. As is shown by the numerous periodicals and pamphlets from this period that dealt with economic policies, even ordinary citizens participated in these debates. Thus, the Navigation Acts and various other protectionist measures were constantly debated, negotiated, and adjusted according to economic conditions, the state's fiscal situation, and commercial and manufacturing interests [19].

The British government and Parliament also took an interest in encouraging technological innovation. The Industrial Revolution was not the product of a handful of technological breakthroughs; rather, it was the outcome of continuing technological innovations and improvements which were commercialized and spread throughout society. As such, a culture that produces and spreads helpful information, along with institutions that facilitate this, were essential for the Industrial Revolution, and these can be seen as having contributed decisively to the formation of the system of expansive reproduction.

Of particular note is Britain's patent system. While the patent system was created in 1624, it was not widely used until the mid-eighteenth century. By the time the Industrial Revolution was in full swing, the number of patent applications began to increase dramatically. Inventors and technicians were making money by patenting their inventions, which led many to believe that the effort put into inventions would pay economic dividends. Of course, there were many technological innovations during the Industrial Revolution that were not patented. There were also some who believed that patents were actually obstructing technological progress. Even so, it can hardly be denied that the patent system disseminated interest in innovation by giving individual inventors exclusive rights to their inventions for a certain period of time. Another method that the British government and Parliament used to promote technological innovation was paying a bounty to specific inventors [20].

Furthermore, the British government and Parliament devoted attention to blocking the outflow of technology. As British manufactured goods gained prestige around the world, there were increasing efforts in other countries to adopt British technology. The explosion in the activity of industrial spies at the time was part of these efforts. The British Parliament responded by enacting a series of laws that strictly regulated the emigration of skilled workers and even made it illegal to help such workers emigrate. Skilled workers who were caught violating these laws were subject to fines and imprisonment and forfeited their citizenship. In wartime, they could even be convicted of treason.

Machinery was also subject to regulation. The main area of concern was exports of textile machinery to the United States. In 1783 and 1799, manufacturers in Manchester and Birmingham lobbied for bans to be placed on machinery exports. According to one anecdote, these bans were so strict that the businessman who established the Waltham-Lowell system for textile manufacturing in the city of Boston in the early nineteenth century had no choice but to commit the designs of the latest machinery to memory.

These measures were not very effective, however. The restrictions on emigration failed to get meaningful results because of administrative constraints and the relative ease of emigration at that time, and they were repealed in 1824. The regulations on exporting machinery were not strictly enforced either, since they conflicted with the interests of machinery manufacturers and were thought to contradict the doctrine of free trade. But because of the unyielding demands of the textile lobby, the ban on machinery exports was not lifted until 1843 [21].

Thus, the system of expansive reinvestment was a precondition for industrialization, but by itself it did not guarantee that industrialization would occur. This raised the question of why only Britain was able to make the transition from the system of expansive reinvestment to the system of expansive reproduction. Therefore, we briefly looked at how Britain's system of expansive reinvestment was connected to the Industrial Revolution. We learned that Britain's system of expansive reinvestment played a role in expanding domestic and foreign markets, increasing the amount of capital, raising wages, and providing an incentive for entrepreneurship and technological innovation. We furthermore observed how Britain's abundant reserves of coal and the economic opportunity that it exploited during the wars at the end of the eighteenth century also aided in the transition to the system of expansive reproduction.

Additionally, we emphasized the role that the state played under the system of expansive reinvestment, a subject that has not received adequate scholarly attention. It was the British government and Parliament that acquired and protected markets in the sharp rivalry with other powers. If not for their deliberate choices and policy initiatives, the system of expansive reinvestment could never have reached maturity. Furthermore, the British government and Parliament adopted proto-industrial policies that protected and built up the domestic manufacturing industry and promoted technological innovation under Britain's system of expansive reinvestment, which depended not only on commerce but also on the domestic manufacturing industry. If not for such industrial policies, Britain's abundant coal reserves and its wars would have been meaningless. That is to say, if the British government had not promoted the development of mines and worked to build the transportation network needed for the distribution of coal, that coal would have remained a hunk of ore in the ground and would never have become Britain's invaluable "black diamond." If the British government had not marshaled its strength and led the nation to victory in the French Revolution and the Napoleonic Wars, it could not have taken advantage of the opportunity those wars afforded. Therefore, the role of the state in Britain's Industrial Revolution demands our consideration.

Britain's Golden Age as an Industrial Empire (1840–1870)

- Free Trade

The end of the Napoleonic Wars signified that Britain had bested France in their long struggle to become the hegemonic power. It also showed that Britain was transforming from the world's dominant commercial power to the "workshop of the world." While Britain's rivals in Continental Europe were concentrating their energy on weathering the storms of revolution, Britain's trade and industry were continuing to grow. Britain's economic vitality was truly remarkable, as is illustrated by the fact that most of the uniforms worn by Napoleon's soldiers had been imported from Britain.

During the century after the Napoleonic Wars, Britain attempted to use the technological and economic advantages it had secured through the Industrial Revolution to replace the mercantilist system with free trade. This meant that Britain was now confident that its commerce and industry, which had flourished under the protection of the state, were fully capable of maintaining their advantage even amid pure competition. Consequently, Britain adopted the policy of persuading European countries to accept the principles of free trade and of compelling the relatively weaker countries of the non-European world to open their doors to trade. This demonstrates that Britain's ruling elite were convinced that they could achieve the virtuous cycles of the system of expansive reinvestment and the system of expansive reproduction even while reducing the fiscal burden needed to rule the colonies, as they had done during the age of mercantilism.

The doctrine of free trade, of course, had already been elucidated in the latter part of the eighteenth century. During the Seven Years War, for example, Josiah Tucker argued that it was irrational to wage war for commercial reasons and that the nation's wealth consisted not of the gold and silver brought in through trade but rather from the people's productive labor. As a consequence, Tucker said, developing domestic industry and domestic markets to stimulate the people's productive activity was more important than opening up markets overseas, and Britain's trade advantage ultimately derived from the quality of its products and from those products' competitive prices [22].

Just like Tucker, Adam Smith also criticized mercantilist assumptions about the origins of the wealth of nations as well as the merchants and government officials who accepted those assumptions. According to Smith, merchants had colluded with government officials to protect their monopolies while sacrificing domestic producers and customers in the process. These merchants insisted that even war could be condoned for the sake of commercial profit, as if their interests were the same as the national interest. Such behavior created hostility between states and between nations.

These merchants' dedication to their monopolies also worsened relationships between Britain and its colonies, Smith explained. Britain had adopted a series of measures that repressed the economic liberties of its colonists in order to protect merchants' interests, and the resulting grievances built up until the American colonies declared their independence. Commerce was supposed to stimulate cooperation and the free exchange of people and goods, but commercial interests had effectively turned it into a source of conflict. For such reasons, Smith argued, the only way to restore commerce to its original role was to repeal the arbitrary policies of mercantilism and to refrain from provoking unnecessary conflict with the colonies. In the end, this would also contribute to world peace and the advancement of the human race, he believed [23].

While the outline of free trade doctrine had already been delineated by the end of the eighteenth century, it was not immediately reflected in government policy. Despite the theoretical soundness and philosophical profundity of *The Wealth of Nations*, its arguments could not be implemented until a number of factors had been taken into account, including commercial and manufacturing interests, international competition, and the state of military power [24]. Even after all those factors had been considered, accepting the doctrine of free trade ultimately required that Britain's commercial and manufacturing sectors be capable of remaining competitive despite the protective policies of Britain's rivals. It was only then that policy makers and commercial and manufacturing interests felt confident that free trade was in Britain's interest and were willing to put Smith's ideas about free trade into practice.

From this perspective, it is hardly coincidental that cotton textile manufacturers took the lead in advocating the system of free trade. In the late eighteenth century, they had already started calling for the liberalization of imports of raw materials and foodstuffs and of exports of British cotton goods [25]. Their argument was that implementing a free trade regime would cause the cost of production to fall and overseas consumption to rise accordingly.

This argument clearly represented a prediction about a new international division of labor. In a nutshell, this prediction was that the countries that produced raw materials and foodstuffs would freely export them to Britain and then use the income from those exports to purchase British industrial goods. As a result of this, the international division of labor would mature and the scale of trade would expand [26]. What Britain's manufacturers ultimately expected was that they would be the greatest beneficiaries of this international division of labor. As trade grew in scale, they believed, producers in countries that exported raw materials and agricultural products would remain dependent on British industrial products even as they continued to cultivate agricultural products with diminishing yields. Britain's manufacturers almost seem to have been aware that, since industrial growth accelerates and agricultural growth decelerates, Britain would gradually consolidate its economic advantage over agricultural states.

Free trade in theory, however, turned out to be quite different from free trade in practice. Instead of behaving according to the theory of the political economists, the groups that called for free trade strictly pursued their own agendas. For example, the cotton textile manufacturers who most strongly supported free trade called for the liberalization of exports of cotton products and imports of raw materials, but they wanted strong regulation on exports of cotton textile machines and on the emigration of skilled workers. Since the British government and Parliament were also concerned about the outflow of technology and workers, as we have already mentioned, they kept those regulations in place for as long as possible.

But the manufacturers of textile machinery found themselves in a different position. Domestic cotton textile manufacturers may have been their most important clients, but that did not mean that the machinery manufacturers welcomed a ban on exports of machinery. With improved productivity driving a rapid increase in production in the machine industry, there was not enough domestic demand to absorb all of these companies' manufacturing capacity. During every recession, therefore, there were calls to liberalize machinery exports.

An even greater obstacle than the conflicting interests of the industrial lobbies was the opposition of the landed class. Despite the rapid growth of commerce and manufacturing, British politics in the early nineteenth century was still controlled by large landowners. During the eighteenth century, the aristocrats and the gentry had supported the development of commerce and manufacturing because this development (along with the increasing population and urbanization) ultimately coincided with their own economic interests. As demand for land and agricultural products increased, landowners' rent and assets rose accordingly. With tax receipts collected from commercial and industrial activity making up the majority of fiscal income, the land tax decreased relative to other taxes [27]. But free trade was a different story altogether. Allowing cheap grain from overseas to flow freely into Britain was diametrically opposed to landowners' interests, and therefore they attempted to keep the Corn Laws in place.

Despite the adamant opposition of the landowners, the Corn Laws were repealed in 1846. This was the result of a combination of factors. The theories of political economists such as Jeremy Bentham, James Mill, and David Ricardo and an emphasis in public discourse about the moral and theological legitimacy of free trade contributed to the abolition of the Corn Laws [28]. But just as Smith's arguments were not immediately accepted despite their theoretical soundness, the arguments in favor of abolishing the Corn Laws were not persuasive until the economic conditions had changed. Indeed, the abolition of the Corn Laws was the product of overall political and economic changes that made it impossible for British politicians to keep protecting agriculture.

The most fundamental of these changes took place in the industrial sector. While there was virtually no change in the total number of English farmers between 1600 and 1800, their share of the total population fell from 55% in 1700 to 40% in 1820 and then to less than 25% in 1851. Meanwhile, the share of Britons working in manufacturing and mining increased to around 30% in 1801 and then to 40% in 1841. This shift in the population's vocational distribution occurred at the same time as urbanization. The percentage of the population that lived in cities of 5000 or more increased from 21% in 1750 to 28% in 1800 and then to 45% in 1850 [29].

One thing that was made clear by such structural shifts was that British agriculture could no longer support the growing population. To be sure, agricultural productivity and output had started to increase during the agricultural revolution of the seventeenth century, but the rate of increase of production began to slow around 1750. In addition, rapid population growth pushed down per capita production and consumption. If grain imports had been discontinued, the drop in per capita production would have been even more severe.

As a result, the price of grain increased. Until the third quarter of the eighteenth century, the price of grain had increased only sporadically, but subsequent to that the increase was rapid: grain prices rose two- to threefold during the French Revolution and the Napoleonic Wars [30]. When the price of grain continued to climb, critics began to argue that the Corn Laws were harming manufacturers and workers by inflating the price of grain, even though duties on wheat had already been abolished in 1815. Joseph Hume, for example, an advocate of free trade, proposed completely liberalizing grain imports in 1829. Observing that the "greater part of the world" was "dependent upon us for manufactures," he argued that the only way to increase exports of such goods was permitting free exchange between British manufactured goods and foreign grain [31].

These shifts in the population distribution and the increase in the price of grain brought on a political crisis. As the price of grain began to soar at the end of the eighteenth century, land prices and rent rose along with it. From 1796 until 1815, part of landowners' income was transferred to the state in the form of income tax, but the income tax was abolished in 1816. This meant that the government had to rely on excise taxes and tariffs as it had done previously in order to repay the debt accrued during the French Revolution and the Napoleonic Wars. This naturally triggered a sharp backlash from landowners. The land tax that landowners had to pay in addition to indirect taxes was low, being based on property appraisals from 1694. With the abolition of the income tax, landowners' tax burden had decreased even further.

Meanwhile, the fiscal burden on manufacturers and workers had gotten even heavier. This led to renewed calls for reform of the political system, which was in the grip of the landed class. Arguments for such reform had started to appear in the late eighteenth century. There was a widespread belief that as long as the landowners had control of Parliament, measures such as the Corn Laws that protected landowners' interests would remain in place, and the sacrifices of manufacturers and workers would continue. The outcry over what was known as "Old Corruption" quieted to some extent after the electoral overhaul accomplished through the Reform Act of 1832. But since the Reform Act failed to provide workers with any benefits, it gave a boost to the labor movement. With radicals who wanted complete free trade joining the offensive, landowners could no longer keep the Corn Laws on the books [32].

Consequently, the Corn Laws were repealed in 1846, and the Navigation Acts—which had symbolized the mercantilist system—were abolished two years later. As this shows, it took quite a long time for free trade to become the foundation of British economic policy. This was partially because of the time needed for the arguments for free trade to spread and for policy makers to be persuaded of their merits. But another implication is that it took a long time for the British economy to grow enough to be able to handle free trade.

Thus, despite the arguments of theorists who frequently claim that free trade is the ideal system for economic growth, the introduction of free trade was not a prerequisite for economic growth, even in Britain. Free trade was not a spear that Britain wielded so that it could become an industrial state; it was rather a shield that Britain held up to reinforce its own technological and economic advantage after it had already become an industrial empire.

Furthermore, the absolute laissez-faire system that was proposed by radicals like Richard Cobden during the reforms of the 1840s was not implemented either. As is shown by a recent study that concludes that the average rate of tariffs in Britain in the first half of the nineteenth century was higher than in France, free trade was implemented selectively, to the extent that it coincided with Britain's economic interests [33].

- Free Trade Imperialism

The adoption of free trade also had an effect on Britain's approach to empire. As we have already mentioned, Tucker and Smith raised questions about the economic value of empire and alleged that restrictions on the colonies hindered mankind's material advancement and its moral improvement. But regardless of this moral criticism, Smith observed that no state in history had ever given up its colonies of its own accord.

After being forced to surrender its American colonies, Britain tightened its formal control of India. This situation gradually lent weight to the idea that a new justification was necessary for colonial rule. The advocates of free trade in particular argued that Britain's colonial subjects were not yet ready to rule themselves and that Britain first needed to civilize them by teaching them the doctrine of liberty and the British institutions that backed this up. According to this "civilizing" agenda, free trade with Britain would allow colonized peoples to experience for themselves the value of hard work and to learn how to become financially independent, ultimately helping them cultivate a capacity for self-government.

The free trade imperialism that thus emerged is distinct from the colonial policy during the Age of Mercantilism and from the New Imperialism that appeared in the 1870s. Even so, imperialism's fundamental policies or objectives had not changed in any major way. On an economic level, Britain's imperialism was only fundamentally important as a means of maintaining the virtuous cycle of the system of expansive reproduction. As the countries of Europe began to turn their attention to domestic problems and to industrialization after the end of the Napoleonic Wars, colonies took on even greater importance as a source of raw materials and as a market for manufactured goods. Under these conditions, free trade was naturally understood to be a method of effectively exploiting the colonies. Therefore, the argument of the free trade advocates that a peaceful world order could be established through commerce was belied by the British empire's rapid expansion during the period of free trade.

If anything had changed, it was not the purpose of imperialism but rather the manner of expansion and of rule. The primary method of expansion had been formal rule of territory and political control, but this was replaced by market penetration through trade. According to a classic study by John Gallagher and Ronald Robinson, the British government devoted its energy to extracting various concessions, including opening ports, so that British merchants and manufacturers could freely trade there. Once it had achieved these goals, however, it reduced its political interference in these colonies to the minimum necessary.

The most widely used method at the time were free trade agreements. Radical supporters of free trade such as Cobden were opposed to expanding free trade through bilateral agreements on the grounds that these could reflect the interests of particular groups. Instead, these radicals called for the unconditional opening of the markets, but their agenda was practically unacceptable [34]. Since Britain's rivals believed that free trade would ultimately work strictly in Britain's favor, they were not inclined to follow Britain's example. The markets of the non-European world proved very difficult for the British to enter, and they could not begin trading in those markets without the protection of the states in question.

As a result, Britain began to establish a series of free trade agreements. Britain signed treaties with Persia in 1836 and 1857, with the Ottoman Turks in 1836 and 1861, and with Japan in 1858. It brought free trade to India in 1813 and also reached a free trade agreement with China in 1833. The key provision of these treaties, of course, was the most-favored nation clause [35]. Thanks to this clause, Britain was able to enjoy the benefits resulting from the expansion of free trade while keeping diplomatic effort to a minimum. This made free trade an efficient way of mobilizing specific regions to contribute to Britain's system of expansive reproduction for the minimum cost [36].

A widely used method of rule involved changing the political and social systems of client states so as to maintain Britain's economic advantage without relying on military and administrative resources. In South America, for example, trade increased after Britain forced the ports in the region to open early in the nineteenth century. The locals who profited from trade with Britain became the political elite in the region and used their influence to ensure that trade would continue. For such a method of rule to be effective, of course, the local elite of the client states needed to profit from their relationship with Britain, and they also needed to have enough power to suppress groups that were opposed to British influence. When local commercial interests were strong enough to challenge British merchants, Britain brought to bear the power of the state, including its military resources [37].

Therefore, free trade imperialism does not mean that Britain completely abandoned formal rule and relied solely on trade, or that it was able to impose its will on client states through its commercial advantage alone. Rather, it means that the British people in the mid-nineteenth century optimistically believed that they could sufficiently profit from their colonies through free trade alone even without ruling them formally and that the subjects of their client states would also benefit from trade with Britain.

This optimistic belief was grounded in the British people's confidence in their technological advantage. During the mid-nineteenth century, they prided themselves on this point, even referring to themselves as "the titans of technology." [38] Doubtless, not only the technological achievements in the cotton textile industry (the driving force behind the Industrial Revolution) but also technological innovations in iron mills and the machine industry and advances in the transportation and communication sectors that led to canals, turnpikes, and railroads laid the technological foundation for Britain's imperial expansion.

The steamships, telegraph lines, and railroads that started to spread in the middle of the nineteenth century were all the products of the technological expertise and knowledge accumulated during the First Industrial Revolution, and they supported Britain's commerce and shipping and increased the efficiency of its colonial rule. According to J. R. Seeley, a noted historian from the end of the nineteenth century, the steam engine and the telegraph had turned the British Empire into a living and moving creature: "Science has given to the political organism a new circulation, which is steam, and a new nervous system, which is electricity." [39]

As the history of the Opium Wars indicates, steam-powered ships greatly expanded the scope of British commerce, since they could steam up rivers into the interior as sailing ships had been unable to do. The railroad helped integrate markets in the non-European world by linking harbors to cities and towns in the interior. The telegraph was closely related to the development of railroad networks, as it was necessary for coordinating the schedules of numerous trains operated by various railroad companies and for preventing accidents. Once underwater cables were laid in the 1860s, enabling intercontinental communication, the telegraph also began to play a political and military role. Previously, imperial administrators had had to rely on the post, which took from as short as a few weeks to as long as a few months. But now that it only took a few hours to deliver news from Britain to the colonies, a completely new method of imperial rule became possible [40].

British merchants and manufacturers realized sooner than anyone else how helpful the new technologies and inventions would be for managing the colonies and for doing business in them. This point is best illustrated by India. Cotton textile exports to India began increasing rapidly at the beginning of the nineteenth century, but they were hampered by the poor condition of the roads. Cotton textile exporters in Manchester began lodging complaints about the road conditions with the Indian colonial government in 1834 and asked it to build railroads in the 1840s.

These requests became policy when the EIC was dissolved and the British government increased its direct control over India following the Indian Rebellion of 1857. It was at this point that railroad work began in earnest. In 1860, there were only 1000 miles in the entire Indian railroad network, but by the early 1870s, this had expanded into a 5000-mile transcontinental system linking the cities of Bombay, Delhi, Calcutta, and Madras. The construction of the railroad in India displayed Britain's technological prowess to the entire world and further developed the division of labor in which Indian cash crops were exchanged for British industrial goods. The colonial government was also able to take advantage of the railroads and the telegraph network to increase the efficiency of troop movements and the transmission of information.

The construction of the Indian railroads gave the British a new area in which to invest. British capital that had been accumulated during the economic boom in the mid-nineteenth century was poured into the Indian railroad, which guaranteed a stable interest rate of 5%. To be sure, British overseas investment was not limited to the colonies. Around the same time, there was also a huge investment boom in railroads in the United States, and an immense amount of British capital flowed into that country as well [41]. British investments in the United States began to increase even further in the 1860s, and between 1865 and 1914, the American market accounted for almost 35% of all British overseas investments. Overseas investment grew swiftly after the 1850s. In 1850, around 6.8% of Britain's total wealth was invested overseas; by 1870, this had increased to 14.4%; and just before World War I, it had climbed all the way to 35.2% [42].

Nineteenth-century Britain was able to exercise hegemony in the global economy because of the success of the Industrial Revolution. Espousing free trade, Britain not only boosted trade with India and the rest of its existing colonies but also managed to bring new regions into its sphere of influence without even conquering their territory or ruling them formally. This allowed Britain to acquire a more stable and less expensive source of the raw materials it needed for industrial activity and to export a corresponding amount of its manufactured goods. In order to maintain this virtuous cycle in its system of expansive reproduction, Britain invested briskly in basic infrastructure projects such as railroads and telegraph lines.

Britain's relationships with its empire and with the world during the period of free trade appeared to be ideally suited for operating its system of expansive reproduction. But Britain could not sustain its advantage. Flaws in the British economy manifested one after another in the great depression that started in 1873, and Britain's industrial advantage faced a tough challenge from the United States and Germany. In the next section, we will examine the economic problems that dogged Britain after it made its splendid transition from commercial empire to industrial empire.

Britain's Relative Decline During the Industrial Age

The great depression began with a stock market crash in Vienna, Austria, in 1873, and continued intermittently for the next two decades. Over this period, the price of goods continued to fall. This was fundamentally caused by an oversupply resulting from greater productivity. In addition, the development of heavy industries created a tendency for the ratio of fixed capital to working capital to increase and the rate of profit to decrease.

Consequently, corporations not only in Britain but also in the United States and Europe had to deal with the issue of continually falling profit. There was a general need during the great depression to control supply to keep prices from falling and to stabilize the price of goods, and this need expressed itself in attempts to gain a monopoly over the market. Viewed in this context, the New Imperialism of the second half of the nineteenth century was ultimately one of the methods used to respond to this crisis, and it can be concluded that competition between states and between corporations became even more intense during this period.

The great depression was even harsher on British companies, with prices dropping more severely in Britain than other countries. Assuming a wholesale price index of 100 for 1871 to 1875, wholesale prices fell to 92 between 1876 and 1880, 83.5 between 1881 and 1885, 70.6 between 1886 and 1890, and 68.3 between 1891 and 1895. Since prices were falling faster than the cost of production, British companies were keenly aware of their falling profits [43].

In the mid-nineteenth century, Britain's economy began to grow more slowly than the United States and Germany, which were in the middle of rapid industrialization. Economic growth slowed even further during the great depression, making the situation look even worse. In absolute terms, Britain's per capita GDP in the 1890s was higher than ever before, but the rate of increase fell from 2.4% in 1870 to 1.4% in 1913. Assuming that the most important yardstick for assessing the soundness of the system of expansive reproduction is the improvement of productivity based on technological innovation, Britain's economic conditions in this period look even more severe. The rate of growth of total factor productivity increased from 0.4% in 1820 to 0.75% in 1870 before dropping to 0.45% in 1913 [44].

Even after the great depression ended, this situation remained largely the same. Britain posted a GDP growth rate of 2.1% between 1890 and 1900, 1.5% between 1900 and 1907, and 1.6% between 1907 and 1913. This contrasts with Germany, which experienced 3.5, 2.7, and 3.3% growth during the same periods. Growth in the United States was even faster, and its GDP increased by 3.9, 5.23, and 2.8% during these periods.

When industrial production (the most important category of production in terms of the system of expansive reproduction) is examined separately, it becomes clear how quickly Germany and the United States were catching up with Britain. Assuming that each country's industrial output in the 1870s was 100, Britain's industrial output only grew to 199 in 1900 and to 249 in 1913. Germany's output increased to 321 and 526 and the United States' output to 401 and 730 during the same period [45].

During Germany's initial phase of industrialization in the 1840s, it mostly imitated British technology and products. German manufacturers at the time tried to pass off their shoddy knockoffs as British products, which provoked so many complaints from British manufacturers that it gave rise to the system of labeling a product's country of origin. During the 1850s, the German government adopted protective trade policies that helped German manufacturers start to produce domestic versions of various products—including machines and steam locomotives—that had until that point been imported from Britain. Heavy industry also underwent full-fledged development with the blessing of the state. By the 1870s, Germany had developed technology and products in the areas of steel, chemicals, and electricity that were more advanced than Britain's [46].

While industrialization in the United States also began with mimicking British technology and products, the conditions of industrialization there were different from in Germany. The United States had the advantages of a vast domestic market and abundant natural resources, but it suffered from a chronic shortage of labor and capital. The United States solved its labor shortage by bringing in a huge number of immigrants from Britain and other European countries. It also made innovations in resource- and capital-intensive technology that could put its abundant natural resources and the huge amounts of overseas capital to use in production. After the American Civil War, for example, work on building railroad lines began around the country, and the pace of industrialization increased noticeably as federal government policies became more friendly to big business. During the great depression, corporations emerged that achieved economies of scale and scope by reorganizing their corporate structure, developing innovative approaches to management, and introducing new marketing techniques that took advantage of the railroads and the telegraph network. Aided by these developments, the United States became a powerhouse in new industrial sectors such as steel, chemicals, electricity, electronics, and automobiles, posing a threat to Britain's hegemony [47].

While industrialization in both the United States and Germany proceeded under a system of protective trade, there were some differences between the two, in particular between their market-centered and state-centered approaches. However, they were similar in the sense that they both depended upon inventions and scientific and technological development and also carried out the Second Industrial Revolution, which was characterized by achieving economies of scale and scope through large-scale facility investment.

During the same period, Britain was falling behind in technological innovation as it remained dependent on industries developed during the First Industrial Revolution. This fact is borne out by export trade figures. During the period between 1865 and 1874, immediately before the great depression, British exports were posting 4.5% of growth each year. But exports only grew by 3.3% during the first phase of the great depression from 1874 to 1883 and by 1.3% from 1890 to 1901. Even so, Britain's absolute share of the global industrial goods market barely decreased. In 1880, Britain accounted for 41.4% of global trade in industrial goods, which meant that it retained its lead over Germany (19.3%) and the United States (2.8%). As late as 1890, similar conditions were in place, with Britain controlling a 40.7% share of industrial trade, compared to Germany at 20.1% and the United States at just 4.6%.

But the problem was not the amount of exports but the types of products being exported. Britain's export trade was still dominated by textiles, iron, machinery, and coal. The United States and Germany, on the other hand, were exporting the products of the Second Industrial Revolution, including oil, processed foods, electric and electronic goods, steel, and non-ferrous metals. This is also confirmed by one economic historian's analysis of a list of British manufacturing exports. New industrial sectors only accounted for 17.7% of Britain's manufacturing exports in 1899, as opposed to 62.9% for traditional industrial sectors with shrinking markets. In short, the problem facing Britain was that it had been slow to develop new industries, and in particular ones that were capital-intensive [48].

In order to explain this problem, the first thing to note is that Britain's overseas investment expanded rapidly while its domestic investment remained sluggish. Looking at the savings rate, which indicates how much capital was available for investment, Britain maintained a savings rate between 11 and 15% between 1871 and 1913, which was about the same as Germany and France. But domestic investment stood at just 7% of GDP, which was about 5% behind the United States and Germany. In addition to this, Britain's overseas investment was rapidly increasing. Between 1865 and 1872, Britain's overseas capital investment was close to 5% of GDP, while income from overseas capital investment accounted for 5% of GDP in the early 1870s. There were between 1 and 1.2 billion pounds of capital exports in 1875, but this increased to 4 billion pounds just before World War I.

Consequently, overseas assets, which had represented just 6.8% of the national wealth in 1850, rose to 35.2% by 1913 [49]. Even before Britain's relative decline became evident in World War I, the London capital market was only supplying 5 million pounds, which represented 10% of the investment capital in the domestic manufacturing sector. This was just 3% of the total amount of capital invested overseas at the same period [50].

But even if Britain had regulated overseas capital investment, it cannot be said for certain that the Second Industrial Revolution would have succeeded in Britain. Even if the capital invested overseas had instead been invested in Britain, this by itself would not have guaranteed improved productivity and the development of new industrial sectors. Quantitative growth of the economy resulting from capital investment cannot greatly increase marginal productivity unless it is accompanied by qualitative growth of the economy based on technological advancement [51]. Before attributing Britain's poor performance in the Second Industrial Revolution to excessive overseas capital investment, therefore, we must first prove that the failure of Britain's manufacturing firms to develop new technology resulted from a severe shortage of capital. But Britain in the late nineteenth century did not face the chronic capital shortage that plagued the United States and Germany.

Next, we must consider whether any effort was made (either by the state or by companies in the private sector) to develop new technologies or industrial sectors. If such efforts had been made, capital would have been invested there. But looking at an industrial map of Britain at the time, we can see that the industrial location and regional distribution remained largely the same as before and that there were few large corporations that achieved economies of scale and scope. Therefore, Britain's financial institutions did not take an interest in new systems like investment banks and universal banks as their German and American counterparts did. Perhaps it would be more accurate to say that they did not need to do so. In other words, there was no reason for capital in the British private sector *not* to congregate in overseas investments that guaranteed a higher or more stable income than new and uncertain technologies.

Therefore, Britain's relative decline should not be wholly blamed on overseas capital investment or on problems with the financial system. To explain this decline, we need to understand how various systems and practices that came into being amid the free competition of the First Industrial Revolution ended up hampering technological innovation and new capital investment [52].

Since this is a sizeable topic, we will focus on just a few of the salient points before continuing. First is the influence exerted by the size of the market. This point is especially clear when Britain is compared with the United States. Britain's total area was smaller than the area of the three American states of New York, Pennsylvania, and Ohio, while its population density was much higher. Because of these geographic and demographic differences, the optimal size of British companies was smaller than American companies. The small size of Britain's domestic market and growth potential meant that British companies at the end of the nineteenth century were under less pressure than American companies in the areas of production and distribution.

For this reason, no major changes occurred in the management methods of Britain's corporations either. As Alfred Chandler Jr, observed when he used the term "personal capitalism" to describe how Britain's industrial capitalism was dominated by family companies, Britain's companies still depended on family management. As a result, they did not actively invest in hiring professional managers and creating an organizational hierarchy, and it was naturally difficult for them to separate ownership from management. It was easier, of course, for family-run companies to enter new areas of business and to reinvest their accumulated earnings, which made them well-suited for the First Industrial Revolution, when the fixed capital ratio was relatively low. But such companies were poorly suited for the Second Industrial Revolution, which involved more complicated technology and a much larger optimal unit of production [53].

It would have been possible to compensate for the small size of the market by expanding into overseas markets, as is shown by the example of Germany in the late nineteenth century. Germany became aware of the limitations of its small domestic market early on and focused its attention on exports. By the end of the nineteenth century, Germany had a competitive presence in markets around the world (except for the United States).

And in fact, the export market had also made a significant contribution to Britain's success in the First Industrial Revolution. In that case, why was Britain unable to prevail over Germany in the overseas market in the late nineteenth century? The answer lies in the fact that Britain already had a convenient market: namely, its empire. Since Germany was a latecomer to the scramble for colonies, it could not count on the protection and advantages conferred by imperial power. Thus, the only way that it could gain access to overseas markets was through the competitiveness of its products. British companies, on the other hand, had access to the monopolistic market of the British empire, which represented the largest share of the world still under colonial control. So at a time of intensifying competition,

British companies were gradually becoming less competitive in the global market, as Britain sold the products from the First Industrial Revolution and contented itself with trade inside the empire [54].

In the end, it may have been unrealistic to expect a long-term vision or creative thinking from Britain's industrialists, considering that they had little motivation to change their corporate structure or management methods and that they had an easy way to avoid competition in the global market. But a more serious problem was that Britain's industrialists failed to exploit the industrial potential of new technologies even in areas where Britain already had the technological advantage and surrendered the lead in those areas to companies in Britain's rivals.

The steel industry provides one of the best examples of this. Until the mid-nineteenth century, when British industry was at its prime, Britain was the world's top producer of iron. But as the iron industry was reorganized around steel, Britain's steel producers were soon surpassed by those of the United States and Germany. The Bessemer process, which was one of the most important innovations in steel production, was developed in Britain, but it was American companies such as the Carnegie Steel Company that recognized this process's importance and maximized its potential through large-scale facility investment. Then there was the telegraph, which appeared in the mid-nineteenth century. This too was first developed in Britain, but it was German companies such as Siemens that brought the telegraph to technical perfection and reaped the most profits from laying the European and intercontinental telegraph networks [55].

A more serious problem in the long run was the fact that scientific and technical education were being neglected at a time when the relationship between technology and industry were becoming even more important. The story is often told how the First Industrial Revolution was led by amateur inventors and by craftsmen and skilled workers in the workshops. This tradition had deep roots in British companies, and they did not bother to conduct systematic research into technology or management techniques. Nor was it common for those companies to hire formally educated scientists or professional technicians.

In this sense, it can be said that Britain at the turn of the twentieth century lacked the conditions under which the Second Industrial Revolution could have naturally occurred. For Britain to have maintained its lead over the United States and Germany, therefore, the British government would have had to subsidize new industrial sectors and actively promote technological innovation as the German government did. If the government had adopted such policies, the massive amount of capital that was in British hands could have been pumped into technological innovation, which might have launched the Second Industrial Revolution.

Even if the British government had not adopted aggressive industrial policies, it could have gotten some results simply by encouraging domestic investment. If the capital invested overseas had been converted to domestic capital, one study estimates, the capital input per capita would have increased, making Britain's GDP prior to World War I about 38.8% higher than it actually was. According to another estimate, if Britain's investment rate had remained comparable to Germany's, per capita investment in 1911 would have been about 25% higher [56]. Thus, if the

British government and Parliament had regulated overseas capital investment, adopted a policy of protecting the domestic market, and subsidized new industries, the competitiveness of British industry would certainly not have declined. But far from implementing industrial policies, the British government and Parliament adhered to the system of free trade. In other words, the relative decline of British industry was the result of the state failing to do its job.

The primary cause of these developments can be found in the economic base and political tendencies of Britain's political elites. Even into the First Industrial Revolution, the economic base of Britain's political elite was land. But as the agricultural sector contracted after the Corn Laws were repealed and the system of free trade was expanded, real estate holdings gradually became less important and financial assets more so. The London financial market, which had developed during the frequent wars of the eighteenth century, kept growing until the Napoleonic Wars as the number of government bonds increased. When Britain became the center of global commerce during the era of free trade in the nineteenth century, there was a surge in demand for the various services provided by the London financial market. This was also when overseas investment began to soar.

Around this time, a group of people appeared who received most of their income from stocks and bonds issued by various governments and companies. The members of this group sought to profit from the capitalist market economy without participating in productive activity. Their wealth allowed them to enjoy a life of leisure as the landed aristocrats had done before them and to control powerful offices in various areas, including Parliament, the government, and the church. These new capitalists—dubbed by historians as "gentleman capitalists"—set the course of British capitalism in the late nineteenth century [57].

These gentleman capitalists thought it was beneath a gentleman's dignity to make money through direct involvement in production, and they took no interest in the state of the British manufacturing sector. The curriculum at the prestigious public schools that they typically attended paid little heed to industrial or technical matters. Despite educational reforms that took place at the Rugby School and other public schools in the mid-nineteenth century, they neglected not only the applied sciences but even the natural sciences. Considering that it was in these public schools that the future rulers of the British Empire were supposed to be trained in the virtues and talents they would need in their careers, it would have been foolish to expect them to provide practical education in areas such as industrial technology [58].

Once these gentleman capitalists (whose education was unrelated to industry or technology and who made a living from interest on investments or from work in the financial industry) become established as the ruling elite, their values and attitude spread through society as a whole. Even industrialists sought to retire from industry and to adopt the lifestyle of a gentleman once they had achieved some degree of success. As a result, the spirit of enterprise that had been exhibited by countless manufacturers, skilled workers, technicians, and inventors during the First Industrial Revolution gradually faded. Enterprise was replaced by the pursuit of the security brought by regular dividends from investments and by the fantasy of striking it rich through short-term trading.

As long as these gentleman capitalists were in charge, their apathy to the manufacturing sector meant that the British government was unlikely to adopt the kind of proactive policies that could have compensated for the relative decline of British industry. To the contrary, these people supported polices that coincided with their own economic interests. Thus, the gentleman capitalists played a part in derailing the system of expansive reproduction that had remained in effect through the mid-nineteenth century.

When Britain's industrialists were faced with rapidly growing companies in Britain's rivals and their governments' protectionist policies, they asked the British government and Parliament to reconsider the free trade system, but their requests were rejected. Since financial income was the primary source of income for the gentleman capitalists, they were unwilling to abandon the free movement of goods and capital, while the British government and Parliament were likewise reluctant to give up the surplus in trade on services brought by foreign capital investment. In the end, the free trade regime was left in place, and Britain's manufacturing firms were left at a disadvantage against thriving competitors in states with protective trade policies. This made manufacturing companies more eager to move into the British colonial market, where they could maintain a relatively monopolistic position inside the imperial system, than into the developed countries where Britain was losing its competitive edge. The cost of maintaining the empire increased accordingly.

In order for the colonial market to substitute for the markets of the developed world, Britain would have had to change the way it ran the empire. In fact, there were efforts in Britain starting in the 1890s to combine the empire into a single market and to prevent Britain's rivals from making economic inroads in the colonial market. The main point of controversy in these efforts (which were known as "constructive imperialism") was the tariff agreements with the colonies. Since Britain's main rivals were using high tariffs to protect their markets, the British government took the same approach with the empire.

This led to a movement to reform tariffs. The tariff reforms of 1903 emphasized preferential tariffs on imperial trade between Britain and its colonies. The colonies were to give preferential treatment to imports from British manufacturers, while Britain was to give preferential treatment to agricultural products from the colonies. This reinforced the position of manufacturers in Britain and of food and raw material producers in the colonies.

What this reform shows us is that Britain's economic status had declined so severely that the international division of labor between Britain and the colonies—which had formed naturally when Britain was the world's top manufacturing state during the mid-nineteenth century—could no longer be sustained without government support. But this effort also ended in failure. The British people's commitment to free trade was still too deeply rooted for them to accept tariff reforms, and the economic ties between Britain and its colonies had also grown slack under the system of free trade. An even bigger factor was resistance from the city financiers. When Joseph Chamberlain pushed for tariff reforms, the city bankers came out in opposition to his plans [59].

The British government's failure to adopt pro-industry policies was also evident in the bimetallism debate at the end of the nineteenth century. As we have previously observed, one of the characteristics of the great depression was the steady drop in the price of consumer goods. Bimetallism was proposed as a way to correct this. Adhering to the gold standard, proponents of bimetallism warned, would limit Britain's ability to increase the amount of currency in circulation. In contrast, making silver a key currency alongside gold would give Britain more flexibility in adjusting the money supply. Bimetallism was also attractive to manufacturers. They believed it would be easier for consumers in states whose key currency was silver (which was undervalued compared to gold at the time) to purchase large amounts of British products if they were denominated in silver currency. Thus, the proposal was welcomed by the industrialists of Lancashire, who depended upon markets in regions like India that had adopted the silver standard.

The gentleman capitalists, however, were strongly opposed to bimetallism. One reason was that profits in the insurance industry (one of their main areas of business) fundamentally depended on the instability of producers. Another was that they had greatly benefited from the fall in prices and from the relative rise in the price of gold. Since they held bonds that could be converted to gold, an increase in the price of gold translated directly into more income. Thus, at the turn of the twentieth century, the interests of the industrial sector and the financial sector were sharply at odds. Since the power over policy decisions was in the hands of the gentleman capitalists (whose interests were aligned with the financial sector), policies that could have improved the position of the industrial sector were unlikely to succeed [60].

State Policy and Industrial Society

The tariff reform campaign and the bimetallism controversy ended without any significant results, implying that Britain's hegemony was fading. In the meantime, the United States and Germany were quickly catching up with Britain, the former through powerful protective measures and the latter through state-led industrial policies. Britain was too intoxicated on its early economic development to pay heed to policies that could have promoted technological innovation or made its manufacturing sector more competitive.

Britain clung to its system of free trade, as if free competition would forever guarantee the glory of the British Empire. During that time, the capital that had been accumulated between the Industrial Revolution and the period of free trade imperialism was invested not in the domestic manufacturing sector but in the overseas market. While the massive surplus in trade on services profited numerous investors, including the city financiers, it did little to prevent the decline of Britain's industrial empire.

Britain dedicated all of its energy to fighting the two world wars that followed, but it eventually found itself no longer able to maintain its status as a hegemonic power. After World War I, Britain surrendered the position of the world's number one creditor to the United States. During World War II, it barely managed to survive with the aid of American weapons and loans. Britain's vaunted overseas assets had mostly vanished, and it no longer even had the strength to maintain its empire.

Earlier, we observed that previous studies of the origin of the Industrial Revolution either have concluded that it occurred despite the British state's mercantilist policies or have limited their attention to the significance of the Parliamentary system and the establishment of property rights. In regard to this, we have argued in this book that the Industrial Revolution represented the transition from the system of expansive reinvestment to the system of expansive reproduction and that appropriate government intervention was necessary to launch a virtuous cycle in the system of expansive reproduction.

The implication of this argument is that Britain's Industrial Revolution could not have happened if the British government and Parliament had not used protectionism and proto-industrial policies to actively support the domestic manufacturing sector during the period of intense commercial competition with European rivals in the seventeenth and eighteenth centuries. It was only when Britain's manufacturing sector eclipsed those of its neighbors during the early and mid-nineteenth century that the British government and Parliament introduced the free trade system to support a division of labor between Britain and the outside world. This enabled Britain to maintain the virtuous cycle in the system of expansive reproduction at the minimum cost, at least for a time.

But this virtuous cycle could not be sustained since the British government and Parliament were unable to implement the policies required to maintain Britain's industrial advantage. While modern corporations in the United States and Germany were pouring their energy into the Second Industrial Revolution, Britain's manufacturing firms were content to remain in conventional industrial sectors or relied on the markets of the empire, where they could avoid fierce competition.

The financial sector and the working class, who were the beneficiaries of the free movement of goods and capital, were opposed to abolishing the system of free trade. The working class, which had gained the franchise during the age of popular democracy, was itself a formidable presence, but it was the city financial sector that propped up the system of free trade. As long as the gentleman capitalists, who earned their wealth from financial assets and who held traditional values, influenced the British government's policy decisions, the government and Parliament could not offer a constructive alternative that could have reversed the decline of British industry.

This government's failure endangered the virtuous cycle of war and the economy that was essential for Britain maintaining its hegemony. As we have already mentioned, the driving force that enabled Britain to build a system of expansive reinvestment based on globe-spanning commercial interests despite ferocious mercantilist competition was its powerful navy. Even during the nineteenth century, when Britain advocated "splendid isolation" according to the doctrine of free trade, it maintained the "two-power standard," which meant keeping its navy stronger than the navies of its two most powerful rivals. In this manner, Britain was able to minimize conflict with the powers of Continental Europe until the outbreak of World War I and to protect and expand Britain's commercial interests and empire in the non-European world at a relatively low cost.

But the situation changed dramatically when a newly unified and industrialized Germany began building up its military. Assisted by advanced railroad and telegraph networks and equipped with new firearms, the German army demonstrated its might by crushing first the Austrian army and then the French army. When Germany moved to expand its naval power, Britain responded by launching a naval arms race, which required a massive fiscal outlay. This meant that Britain had to emerge from its long isolation and start looking for allies.

Amid this new competition, Britain did not live up to its status as a hegemonic state and failed to secure an overwhelming advantage. The new phenomenon of total war—which was hinted at toward the end of the nineteenth century but not fully unveiled until World War I—was the product of the development of technology and heavy industry, or in other words of the Second Industrial Revolution. As such, Britain found it hard to compete with Germany or the United States in terms of military might. The consequences were devastating. As the history of World War I shows, Britain achieved victory in the first total war by mobilizing all of the state's resources, but doing so basically required it to surrender its hegemonic position to the United States. During Britain's rise to hegemonic status, war had been the force driving its economic growth. The only things that World War I brought Britain, however, were the destruction of property and weaker competitiveness in the market. The virtuous cycle of war and the economy was no longer functioning.

This situation was made even worse by World War II. During the first part of the war, Britain was forced to fight alone against the awesome strength of the Axis Powers, and eventually it was no longer able to resist without the assistance of the United States. That was how the age of Britain passed, making way for the age of the United States. That was when the United States, which had once been a British colony, took over Britain's position as hegemonic state.

References

1. Martin Daunton, *Wealth and Welfare: An Economic and Social History of Britain 1851–1951* (Oxford, 2007), pp. 6–7; J. A. Auerbach, *The Great Exhibition of 1851: A Nation on Display* (New Haven, 1999).
2. It is instructive to compare the figures above with France and Germany. In raw cotton consumption, France and Germany recorded just 610,000 and 410,000 tons, respectively; in coal production, just 4.4 million and 6.7 million tons; and in motive power produced by steam engines, just 370,000 and 260,000 horsepower. Joel Mokyr, *The Enlightened Economy: An Economic History of Britain 1700–1850* (New Haven, 2009), p. 476.

3. François Crouzet, "Toward an Export Economy: British Exports during the Industrial Revolution," *Explorations in Economic History*, 17 (1980), pp. 64–65; N. F. R. Crafts, *British Economic Growth during the Industrial Revolution* (Oxford, 1985), p. 22.
4. It is difficult to know for certain what percentage of cotton textile exports went to the African market. In the majority of estimates, America and Africa are treated as a single category. But in the case of gingham exports during the mid- and late eighteenth century, it is clear that the West Africa market accounted for a larger share than North America and the plantations in the West Indies. On the other hand, when we look at the export volume of wrought iron and nails between 1750 and 1770, 34% went to North America and 29% to the West Indies, compared to 4% for West Africa, and this trend continued with no major changes in the period from 1775 to 1800. For more on this point, see Joseph E. Inikori, *Africans and the Industrial Revolution in England: A Study in International Trade and Economic Development* (Cambridge, 2002), pp. 437, 457.
5. What is noteworthy here is that domestic demand was more than twice as great as overseas demand during the eighteenth century. D. E. C. Eversley, "The Home Market and Economic Growth in England 1750–1780," E. L. Jones and G. E. Mingay (eds.), *Land, Labour and Population in the Industrial Revolution* (London, 1967), p. 227. On the importance of London, see E. A. Wrigley, *People, Cities and Wealth: The Transformation of Traditional Society* (Oxford, 1989), chap. 6. For the consumer revolution, see Neil McKendrick, John Brewer and J. H. Plumb, *The Birth of a Consumer Society: The Commercialization of Eighteenth Century England* (Cambridge, 1982).
6. John Styles, "Product Innovation in Early Modern London," *Past and Present* 168 (2000).
7. According to Deane's estimates, the investment rate in the first half of the eighteenth century was 5% of the national income, increasing to 6% in the second half of the eighteenth century and to 10% by the 1850s. Crafts estimates that the investment rate increased more gradually than Deane: 4% in 1700, 6% in 1760, 7% in 1780, 7.9% in 1801, and 11.7% in 1831. Despite the differences between these two estimates, what is important is that they both show the investment rate increasing continuously. This results from the fact that, as we mentioned earlier, a large amount of fixed capital was not necessary in most industrial sectors in the early period of the Industrial Revolution. Phyllis Deane, "Capital Formation in Britain before the Railway Age," François Crouzet (ed.), *Capital Formation in the Industrial Revolution* (London, 1972), pp. 117–118; Crafts, *British Economic Growth*, p. 73. For examples of commercial capital being converted to industrial capital, see Stanley D. Chapman, "Fixed Capital Formation in the British Cotton Industry, 1770–1815," *Economic History Review*, 2nd ser., 33:2 (1970), p. 249; Stanley D. Chapman, *Merchant Enterprise in Britain: From the Industrial Revolution to World War I* (Cambridge, 1992), pp. 37–39, 57–74.
8. Joel Mokyr, "Entrepreneurship and the Industrial Revolution in Britain," Mokyr et al., *The Invention of Enterprise: Entrepreneurship from Ancient Mesopotamia to Modern Times* (Princeton, 2010), p. 185.
9. Robert C. Allen, *The British Industrial Revolution in Global Perspective* (Cambridge, 2009); Joel Mokyr, *The Enlightened Economy*; Gavin Weightman, *The Industrial Revolutionaries* (New York, 2007); Peter M. Jones, *Industrial Enlightenment: Science, Technology and Culture in Birmingham and the West Midlands 1760–1820* (Manchester, 2008).
10. Allen, *The British Industrial Revolution*, pp. 34 (estimates), 135–144; Phyllis Deane, *The First Industrial Revolution* (Cambridge, 1965), pp. 154–155.
11. E. A. Wrigley, *Continuity, Chance & Change: The Character of the Industrial Revolution in England* (Cambridge, 1988), chap. 3; Kenneth Pomeranz, *The Great Divergence: China, Europe and the Making of the Modern World* (Princeton, 2000).
12. Even though Britain's fiscal system was the most efficient of its time, even it was severely strained by the French Revolution and the Napoleonic Wars. This becomes evident in the pattern of tax receipts. During the eighteenth century, tax receipts generally represented between 8% and 10% of the national income, but during the war, this increased to between 12% and 23%. Thus, between 1802 and 1812, the per capita tax burden on the British was

nearly three times that of the French. Martin Daunton, *State and Market in Victorian Britain: War, Welfare and Capitalism* (London, 2008), pp. 42, 56–57.

13. François Crouzet, "Wars, Blockade and Economic Change in Europe, 1792–1815," *Journal of Economic History* 24:4 (1964), pp. 567–588.
14. In 1760, for example, about 40% of stock in the Bank of England, the EIC, and the South Sea Company was held by the Dutch. J. F. Wright, "The Contribution of Overseas Savings to the Funded National Debt of Great Britain, 1750–1815," *Economic History Review*, 2nd ser., 50 (1997), pp. 657–674; Larry Neal, "A Tale of Two Revolutions: International Capital Flows 1789–1819," *Bulletin of Economic Research* 43:1 (1991).
15. Daunton, *State and Market*, pp. 2–3; Martin Daunton, *Progress and Poverty: An Economic and Social History of Britain 1700–1850* (Oxford, 1995); Perry Gauci, "Introduction," Gauci (ed.), *Regulating the British Economy 1660–1850* (Aldershot, 2011).
16. Thanks to these efforts, Britain's wool industry and wool textile industry developed simultaneously, something that did not happen in Spain or the Netherlands. In the long run, this can be regarded as the starting point for Britain's transformation from an agricultural state to a commercial and industrial state. D. C. Coleman, *The Economy of England 1450–1750* (Oxford, 1977), pp. 52–53, 80–81.
17. These measures, which were enacted at the request of the British woolen textile manufacturers' lobby, were mostly aimed at Irish woolen textile manufacturers. Louis M. Cullen, *An Economic History of Ireland Since 1660* (London, 1972), p. 34.
18. C. H. Wilson, *England's Apprenticeship, 1603–1763* (London, 1971), pp. 267–269.
19. P. K. O'Brien, T. Griffiths and P. Hunt, "Political Components of the Industrial Revolution: Parliament and the English Cotton Textile Industry, 1660–1774," *Economic History Review*, 2nd ser., 44 (1991), pp. 395–423; David Ormrod, *The Rise of Commercial Empires: England and the Netherlands in the Age of Mercantilism, 1650–1770* (Cambridge, 2003), pp. 49–51; William Ashworth, "The Intersection of the Industry and the State in Eighteenth-Century Britain," in Lissa Roberts, Simon Schaffer, and Peter Dear (eds.), *The Mindful Hand: Inquiry and Invention from the Late Renaissance to Early Industrialisation* (Amsterdam, 2007), pp. 349–378; Julian Hoppit, "Bounties, the Economy and the State in Britain, 1689–1800," Gauci (ed.), *Regulating the British Economy*, pp. 139–160.
20. According to MacLeod, the number of patent applications started to increase in the 1760s, and the full-fledged use of the patent system began in the 1780s and 1790s. Christine MacLeod, *Inventing the Industrial Revolution: The English Patent System, 1660–1800* (Cambridge, 1988), pp. 146, 150.
21. David J. Jeremy, "Damming the Flood: British Government Efforts to Check the Outflow of Technicians and Machinery, 1780–1841," *Business History Review* 51 (1977), pp. 1–34.
22. Seven of Tucker's major pamphlets are included in R. L. Schuyler (ed.), *Josiah Tucker: A Selection from His Economic and Political Writings* (New York, 1931).
23. Adam Smith, *An Inquiry into the Nature and Causes of the Wealth of Nations*, R. H. Campbell and A. S. Skinner (eds.), 2 vols. (Oxford, 1976); Istvan Hont, *Jealousy of Trade: International Competition and the Nation-State in Historical Perspective* (Cambridge, Mass., 2005); Nicholas Phillipson, *Adam Smith: An Enlightened Life* (New Haven, 2010).
24. It was not until the 1820s that the doctrine of free trade actually began to gain support. For this topic, see Kenneth Morgan, "Mercantilism and the British Empire, 1688–1815"; Anthony Howe, "Restoring Free Trade: The British Experience, 1776–1873," Donald Winch and Patrick K. O'Brien (eds.), *The Political Economy of British Historical Experience, 1688–1914* (Oxford, 2002).
25. Bernard Semmel, *The Rise of Free Trade Imperialism: Classical Political Economy the Empire of Free Trade and Imperialism 1750–1850* (Cambridge, 1970), p. 135.
26. P. J. Cain and A. G Hopkins, "The Political Economy of British Expansion Overseas, 1750–1914," *The Economic History Review*, 2nd ser., 33:4 (1980); Martin Lynn, "British Policy, Trade, and Informal Empire in the Mid-Nineteenth Century," Andrew Porter (ed.), *The Oxford History of the British Empire, Vol. 3: The Nineteenth Century* (Oxford, 1999).

27. Joel Mokyr and John V. C. Nye, "Distributional Coalitions, the Industrial Revolution, and the Origins of Economic Growth in Britain," *Southern Economic Journal* 74 (2007); Daron Acemoglu and James A. Robinson, "Political Losers as a Barrier to Economic Development," *American Economic Review* 90 (2000), pp. 126–130.
28. It ought to be noted, however, that political economists held a wide variety of views about free trade. The development of free trade was the product of politics, not of simple intellectual developments. Boyd Hilton, *The Age of Atonement: The Influence of Evangelicalism on Social and Economic Thought, 1785–1865* (Oxford, 1986); Donald Winch, *Riches and Poverty: An Intellectual History of Political Economy in Britain, 1750–1834* (Cambridge, 1996), pp. 1–31.
29. Wrigley, "British Population during the 'Long' Eighteenth Century," Floud and Johnson (eds.), *The Cambridge Economic History of Modern Britain Vol. I: Industrialisation, 1700–1870*, pp. 88–91.
30. Allen, *The British Industrial Revolution*, pp. 99, 115.
31. Quotation found in Semmel, *The Rise of Free Trade Imperialism*, p. 147.
32. Philip Harling, *The Waning of "Old Corruption": The Politics of Economical Reform in Britain, 1779–1846* (Oxford, 1996).
33. John Vincent Nye, "The Myth of Free-Trade Britain and Fortress France: Tariffs and Trade in the Nineteenth Century," *Journal of Economic History* 51 (1991).
34. Anthony Howe, *Free Trade and Liberal England 1846–1946* (Oxford, 1997), pp. 70–110.
35. Semmel, *The Rise of Free Trade Imperialism*; John Darwin, *The Empire Project: The Rise and Fall of the British World-System 1830–1970* (Cambridge, 2009), p. 39.
36. John Gallagher and Ronald Robinson, "The Imperialism of Free Trade," *Economic History Review*, 2nd ser., 6 (1953).
37. Darwin, *The Empire Project*, pp. 614–642.
38. Robert Kubicek, "British Expansion, Empire, and Technological Change," Porter (ed.), *The Oxford History of the British Empire Vol. III: The Nineteenth Century*, p. 248.
39. J. R. Seeley, *The Expansion of England: Two Courses of Lectures* (London, 1883), p. 72; Daniel Headrick, *The Tools of Empire: Technology and European Imperialism in the Nineteenth Century* (New York, 1981).
40. Niall Ferguson, *Empire* (London, 2003), pp. 168–169.
41. For the most vivid description of the speculation boom that was triggered by the American railroad project, see Anthony Trollope, *The Way We Live Now* (London, 1875).
42. Daunton, *Wealth and Welfare*, p. 245; Michael Edelstein, "Foreign Investment, Accumulation and Empire, 1860–1914," Roderick C. Floud and Paul Johnson (eds.), *The Cambridge Economic History of Modern Britain, Vol. 2 Economic Maturity, 1860–1939* (Cambridge, 2004), p. 205.
43. S. B. Saul, *The Myth of the Great Depression, 1873–1896* (London, 1969), p. 31.
44. N. F. R. Crafts, "Long-run Growth," Floud and Johnson (eds.), *The Cambridge Economic History of Modern Britain*, p. 13; see estimates in Daunton, *Wealth and Welfare*, pp. 170, 175. According to Daunton's estimates, GDP grew by 2.2% each year between 1856 and 1873 but fell by 1.8% between 1873 and 1913, while total factor productivity fell from 0.6% between 1856 and 1873 to 0% between 1873 and 1913.
45. Roderick C. Floud, "Britain 1860–1914: A Survey," Floud and D. N. McCloskey (eds.), *The Economic History of Britain since 1700: Vol. 2 1860–1939* (Cambridge, 1981), p. 8.
46. Jeffrey Fear, "German Capitalism," Thomas McCraw (ed.), *Creating Modern Capitalism: How Entrepreneurs, Companies, and Countries Triumphed in Three Industrial Revolutions* (Cambridge, Mass., 1995).
47. Nathan Rosenberg, *Technology and American Economic Growth* (New York, 1972), pp. 59–86; Alfred D. Chandler, Jr., *The Visible Hand: The Managerial Revolution in American Business* (Cambridge, Mass., 1977).

48. Daunton, *Wealth and Welfare*, pp. 220–222; Alfred D. Chandler Jr., *Scale and Scope: The Dynamics of Industrial Capitalism*, paperback ed. (Cambridge, Mass., 1994), p. 250; C. Knick Harley, "Trade, 1870–1939: From Globalisation to Fragmentation," Floud and Johnson (eds.), *The Cambridge Economic History of Modern Britain*, p. 171.
49. Sidney Pollard, "Capital Exports, 1870–1914: Harmful or Beneficial?" *Economic History Review*, 2nd ser. 38 (1985), p. 490; Daunton, *Wealth and Welfare*, p. 245.
50. Pollard, "Capital Exports, 1870–1914: Harmful or Beneficial?" pp. 500–502; Lance E. Davis and Robert J. Cull, "International Capital Movements, Domestic Capital Markets, and American Economic Growth, 1820–1914," S. L. Engerman and R. E. Gallman (eds.), *The Cambridge Economic History of the United States Vol. II: The Long Nineteenth Century* (Cambridge, 2000), p. 735.
51. Donald N. McCloskey, "Did Victorian Britain Fail?" *Economic History Review*, 2nd ser., 23 (1970).
52. Bernard Elbaum and William Lazonick, "An Institutional Perspective on British Decline," Elbaum and Lazonick (eds.), *The Decline of the British Economy* (Oxford, 1986), pp. 1–17.
53. Chandler, *Scale and Scope*, pp. 249–250, 268–294.
54. In regard to our discussion, a particularly noteworthy point is that the international market supported traditional industries including the cotton textile industry. For example, the international market accounted for 34.7% of cotton textile exports in 1879, but this increased to 51.7% by 1913. Daunton, *Wealth and Welfare*, p. 222; Cain and Hopkins observe that the empire's share of Britain's exports continued to increase at the end of the nineteenth century while exports to other manufacturing states fell, but they also note that exports increased not only in the imperial market but also in states that manufactured primary commodities. P. J. Cain and A. G. Hopkins, *British Imperialism: Innovation and Expansion 1688–1914* (London, 1993), pp. 167–169.
55. McCloskey, "Did Victorian Britain Fail?" p. 57.
56. Pollard, "Capital Exports," pp. 502–503; N. F. R. Crafts, "Victorian Britain Did Fail," *Economic History Review*, 2nd ser., 32 (1979), p. 537.
57. P. J. Cain and A. G. Hopkins, "Gentlemanly Capitalism and British Expansion Overseas, I: The Old Colonial System, 1688–1850," *Economic History Review*, 2nd ser., 39 (1986); P. J. Cain and A. G. Hopkins, "Gentlemanly Capitalism and British Expansion Overseas, II: The New Imperialism, 1850–1945," *Economic History Review*, 2nd ser., 40 (1987); Cain and Hopkins, *British Imperialism: Innovation and Expansion 1668–1914*.
58. In addition to Cain and Hopkins, see Martin Wiener, *English Culture and the Decline of the Industrial Spirit, 1850–1980* (Harmondsworth, 1981). For a criticism of Wiener's argument, see W. D. Rubinstein, *Capitalism, Culture, and Decline in Britain 1750–1990* (London, 1993); F. M. L. Thompson, *Gentrification and the Enterprise Culture: Britain 1780–1980* (Oxford, 2001).
59. Howe, "Restoring Free Trade, 1776–1873," in Donald Winch and O'Brien (eds.), *The Political Economy of British Historical Experience*, p. 209.
60. E. H. H. Green, "Rentiers versus Producers? The Political Economy of the Bimetallic Controversy c. 1880–1898," *English Historical Review* 103 (1988), pp. 588–612.

Chapter 6
The Formation of Industrial Society in the United States

The United States today is the most powerful superpower in history. Neither classical Rome nor ancient China—not even the Spanish and British Empires we have examined in this book—were able to exert the economic, military, and political influence that the United States has over the past century. The same is true of its institutional, ideological, and cultural influence. Whereas the hegemonic powers of the past have only held sway in one part of the world, American influence is global in its reach. It is in this sense that the United States can be described as the first global empire in history [1].

The hegemonic power of the past that came closest to the United States of today was Great Britain. At the end of the nineteenth century, Britain formally ruled one-fourth of the earth's territory and one-third of its people, and it controlled 20% of global industrial output and 40% of global trade in manufactured goods. While these figures are truly impressive, the American figures are even more so. Even today (when American influence over the global economy has waned considerably), the United States accounts for 30% of the world's industrial output with just 6% of its landmass and 5% of its population [2].

American influence today derives from the overwhelming power of its economy. No matter how you view it, the United States' economic development is remarkable. In the 1860s, the United States was an agricultural state, with the majority of Americans living in rural areas. Urbanization had brought one-quarter of Britain's population into its cities by 1750, but the United States did not reach a similar level until 1870. In the mid-nineteenth century, the United States was 17 years behind Britain in the cotton textile industry (the key industry in the Industrial Revolution) and 27 years behind Britain in pig iron production. But that was when American industrialization began to take off, and before long the United States was on Britain's heels. As a result, the United States surpassed Britain in pig iron production in 1890 and in cotton textile production in 1910. By the beginning of World War I, the United States had become an industrial state that accounted for more than 30% of the world's industrial production [3].

T.-Y. Kim and D. Kim, *The Secrets of Hegemony*,
DOI 10.1007/978-981-10-4416-8_6

The United States' economic development has been considered either exceptional or inevitable given several beneficial conditions that only the United States enjoyed. The first of these was its territory and natural resources. The American colonies possessed extensive fertile soil and abundant resources, and these resources became even more abundant as American territory continued to expand after independence. Mention is also made of the fact that the United States was free from the social and political obstacles that had delayed the modernization and industrialization of Europe since the Middle Ages. In short, as the argument goes, Americans did not have to deal with feudalism. Since the United States did not have various political, social, and cultural restrictions on individual liberties, meritocratic competition was able to dominate American society from the outset, which also enabled entrepreneurship to take root early on. This also led to the early establishment of liberalism grounded in personal freedom, the sanctity of private property, and the rule of law [4].

Indeed, the belief that the United States was fundamentally different from the old world of Europe and that it had the potential for unlimited economic development goes back all the way to the colonial period. As early as the Seven Years' War, in the mid-eighteenth century, Benjamin Franklin predicted that the center of the British Empire would move across the Atlantic Ocean to the American colonies. Franklin had in mind American's vast land and abundant resources, its growing population that doubled each generation, and the colonists' vigorous and enterprising spirit. This does not mean, however, that we ought to accept at face value the argument that the United States' economic development was its "manifest destiny." While vast territory and abundant resources are clearly an advantageous condition for economic development, they do not guarantee its occurrence. This point is made clear by the histories of China, Russia, and India, all of which have territory that is similar in size to the United States. As the phrase "the resource curse" suggests, abundant resources can sometimes even hinder economic development.

Nor is there a simple relationship between American liberalism and economic development. The claim that no other ideology than liberalism could have thrived in the United States seems unlikely given Americans' attachment to social hierarchy during the colonial period and the tradition of republicanism in which the welfare of the whole community was valued above the interests of the individual [5]. Furthermore, as Britain's experience illustrates, economic liberalism was not the driving force behind industrialization and economic development but rather their product. This also prevents us from concluding that the United States' economic development was the natural consequence of economic liberalism.

The United States' economic development should be understood not in terms of characteristics that were unique to the United States but rather in terms of the general type into which its economic development falls. We have already observed that since early modern times global economic hegemony has shifted from agricultural empires to commercial empires and then again from commercial empires to industrial empires, and that these shifts can be explained in terms of the characteristics of the economic systems inherent to each of those economic societies.

Historically speaking, the United States exhibited the characteristics of an agricultural empire, with its extensive territory and abundant natural resources, and there were even some who thought that the United States was destined to be an agricultural empire. Given that these characteristics persisted into the end of the nineteenth century, the United States did look like a unique country that combined the advantages of agricultural, commercial, and industrial empires.

But we must not forget that the economic engine of the United States during the twentieth century was ultimately powered by the system of expansive reproduction that was formed during the Second Industrial Revolution. While American agriculture and commerce were both vibrant during this same period, they both owed their vibrancy to the technological innovation and the market expansion that were produced by the system of expansive reproduction. It is for this reason that we think it is appropriate to understand the United States' economic development not as an exceptional case but rather as one example (admittedly a rather extreme example) of a general type of economic development. This approach will allow us both to fairly assess the historical development of the United States' economy and also to contribute to our knowledge of general types of economic development.

Just as we divided our analysis of Britain into two chapters, the first on the completion of Britain's commercial society and the second on the development and decline of its industrial society, it is also reasonable to divide our analysis of the United States into two chapters representing different periods. In this chapter, therefore, we intend to examine the establishment and development of the United States' system of expansive reinvestment.

Until the colonies declared their independence in 1776, America did not have a national economy in the modern sense of the word. The Thirteen Colonies were part of the British Empire's system of expansive reinvestment, and each colony's economic growth was determined by its function within the British Empire's economic system. Thus, independence meant that the United States, as a new sovereign state, was untethered from the regulations imposed by and the protection provided by the British Empire's system of expansive reinvestment. For several subsequent generations, Americans had to chart their course amid opposing visions about the future of the United States' economy. But this was also a period of rapid development of the United States' system of expansive reinvestment, and a new conflict with Britain prompted efforts to transition to a system of expansive reproduction through the development of the manufacturing sector.

This caused the beginning of the United States' industrialization but also exacerbated conflict between the agricultural South and the commercial and industrial North. This was a conflict between the South's agricultural society, which focused on growing cash crops for the global market and sought to support this business through continual territorial expansion and free trade, and the North's industrial society, which called for the country's independent commercial and industrial development and advocated protectionism.

This conflict culminated in the American Civil War, which left the United States with the major challenge of social unification. Ultimately, though, the war also served as an opportunity for the territory that the United States had acquired for several generations under the vision of an agricultural empire to be used to develop the system of expansive reproduction. Industry and capital in the North were able to take full advantage of the cheap agricultural products and raw materials from the sweeping farmland of the South and the Midwest and the markets for manufactured goods that they provided.

Consequently, the United States' system of expansive reproduction was based on a domestic market that was much larger than that of Britain (which had previously undergone similar development) and was thus able to develop much more quickly. In this chapter, we will examine the period leading up to the American Civil War, which can be called the starting point of these changes. In Chap. 7, we will review how the United States' system of expansive reproduction developed and matured after the Civil War.

The American Economy During the Colonial Period

The British colonization of North America began at Jamestown, at Chesapeake Bay, where 105 settlers landed in April 1607. Large numbers of English immigrants headed to the colonies with the hope of striking it rich by finding precious metals and spices as the Spanish and Portuguese had done, but life in the colonies turned out to be much more challenging than expected. Just nine months after Jamestown was founded, only 38 of the original settlers were still alive. The Virginia Company of London, which was in charge of the colony at the time, pumped 50,000 lb of capital into it through 1616 and sent over more than 1700 settlers, but the settlers found it difficult to keep the colony in operation, never mind making a fortune.

Nevertheless, the English people's excitement over the colonies did not subside. Despite the dismal tidings from Virginia, English settlers landed at various points along the Atlantic coast of North America. During this time, the purpose of the colonies changed as well: they were now intended to be places where colonists could establish themselves and farm the land [6]. Though there were numerous difficulties—including the high mortality rate and the shortage of invested capital and labor—the settlement of the colonies began to accelerate in the mid-seventeenth century. By the eve of the American Revolution, the original settlement of 105 colonists had become a huge area consisting of 13 separate colonies and 2.35 million people.

The colonies grew at a remarkable rate. As Franklin once observed, the population of the colonies doubled with each generation [7]. The population of the colonies grew by an average of 2.8% each year between 1650 and 1770, which meant that the population of the colonies multiplied an astounding 25 times during those 120 years. (Meanwhile, the population of Britain was increasing by an average of 0.2% a year.) During the same period, the colonies' GNP increased about 90-fold [8]. To be sure, this economic growth resulted from territorial expansion and population growth, since technological innovation was slow in colonial society and agriculture accounted for an overwhelming share of economic activity. Development in the full sense of the word—that is, development that is based on changes in productive technology, organization, and structure—was limited to a few areas, including shipbuilding and shipping. Even so, the colonies experienced economic growth at a speed and on a scale that was astonishing and indeed unprecedented.

Prior to independence, the colonies could not be regarded as a single economic system or unified market. The colonies built settlements and expanded in line with immigration trends and pioneering by the existing colonists, but such actions occurred spontaneously since the British government and Parliament rarely meddled in the colonies' economic development. In fact, the British government was worried about the possibility of their unification. Once unified, it was feared, the colonies could become a threat to Britain's authority.

One area in which the British government did take an interest was ensuring that the colonies were all contributing to Britain's economic development under the Navigation Acts. This reflected the longstanding British view of the colonies. It was assumed in Britain that the colonies should serve as a source of the raw materials and agricultural products that Britain needed (and particularly those products that Britain had to import). It was also thought that the colonies should support themselves without Britain's financial assistance. This meant that each of the colonies had to find a product that Britain needed, and if that was impossible, they had to find some way to cover the cost of buying goods from Britain.

The Southern Colonies in particular met British expectations. These colonies supplied the cash crops that Britain had to import and bought large quantities of manufactured goods from Britain. It was in Virginia where plantation farming began in the Southern Colonies. In the initial phase of settlement, Virginia colonists imported almost all their everyday products from Britain. This situation changed, however, when tobacco seeds were brought in from the West Indies in 1612. Tobacco cultivation was well-suited to Virginia's hot, damp climate, and the colonists were also able to take advantage of the farming and drying techniques of the local native population. Virginia began exporting tobacco in 1616, and over time the volume of exports rapidly increased. While there is no estimate of the total amount of tobacco produced in Virginia, Britain's customs records indicate that the export volume of tobacco from the Chesapeake area (including Virginia) amounted to 400,000 lb a year in 1630, 30 million pounds a year in 1700, and 100 million pounds a year in the 1760s [9].

For tobacco farming to succeed, a solution had to be found for the inadequate labor supply (a problem that faced not only Virginia but all the colonies). To attract immigrants, the Virginia Company implemented the headright system, which provided families of settlers with 50 acres of land per person. The planters who took advantage of this system to open a tobacco plantation needed more labor, which was supplied by the indentured servitude system. Under this system, which was adopted in 1620, planters could pay the passage for immigrants who could not afford it in exchange for receiving the right to those immigrants' labor for a set period of time [10]. The ratio of white indentured servants to black slaves remained four to one until the 1690s, when the supply of indentured servants began to decline because of competition between the colonies over indentured servants, the falling prices of African slaves, and changing labor conditions resulting from the decreasing population in Britain. In the early 1690s, African slaves rapidly replaced white workers, and the ratio of white indentured servants to black slaves reversed, becoming one to four [11].

The development process in South Carolina was similar to in Virginia. At first, the colonists of South Carolina had profited from supplying foodstuffs and wood to Barbados in the West Indies, but during the slump in the sugar plantations in the late seventeenth century, the colonists turned their attention to the fur trade and to cultivating various cash crops [12]. Their breakthrough came with rice farming, which began in the 1690s. Rice farming was extremely labor intensive, and it was fully dependent on the labor of African slaves. African slaves not only provided labor but also imparted rice farming techniques from Africa. As a result, the annual volume of rice exports from South Carolina had increased to 20 million pounds by 1730. Between 1705 and 1729, South Carolina also received generous subsidies to grow and export a number of crops that were needed to produce materials for the navy. South Carolina planters also cultivated indigo, a dye that was needed by Britain's textile manufacturers [13].

The process of development in New England was quite different from that of the Southern Colonies. After Virginia was established, the New England Colonies were settled by Puritans who left England in search of religious freedom. They wanted to set up the same family economic system based on independent farmers that they had practiced in England. Thus, immigrants tended to consist of families, and the gender ratio in the early period of immigration was six men to four women (in Virginia, this was four men to one woman). Given New England's cold weather and barren soil, it was not well suited for cash crops like tobacco or rice. But the settlers nevertheless attempted to maintain their way of life from home, and they imported various products from England.

This inevitably created an imbalance in imports and exports. During the initial phase of settlement, the New England colonists tried exporting furs, fish, and lumber to England, but they enjoyed little success because of the severe competition and the high cost of shipping. There were also attempts at local production of the various manufactured goods that were being imported from Britain, but these attempts were hindered by a shortage of labor and capital and, more importantly, by the apathy of the New England colonists, who wanted to be independent farmers. As one colonist wrote in the mid-seventeenth century, the New England farmers "deem it better for their profit to put away their [cattle] and corn for [clothing than] to set upon making of cloth." [14]

Consequently, the only way for the New England colonists to compensate for their chronic trade deficit was through trade and shipping. Just as in the Netherlands, the fishing industry turned out to be the starting point. Taking advantage of the chaos during the English Civil War, the New England colonists made inroads in the cod fishery that had previously been dominated by English fishermen, and they used this as the foundation for trade with the West Indies. Merchants in Boston in the 1640s and in Salem and Newport in the 1660s began to export fish, poultry, and lumber from New England, to re-export manufactured goods from England, and to re-export sugar from the West Indies. This also led to the development of the shipbuilding industry, which took advantage of New England's abundant supply of lumber.

As a result, trade and shipbuilding were the driving force behind economic development in New England in the seventeenth and eighteenth centuries. For example, the annual tonnage of ships leaving Boston Harbor for overseas ports increased from 20,927 tons in 1714 to 1717 to 42,506 tons in 1772, while the output of Massachusetts shipbuilders grew by 150% between 1697 to 1704 and 1769 to 1771 [15].

Thus, the process of development was quite different in the Southern Colonies, whose economy was based on plantation agriculture, and in the New England Colonies, whose economy was based on trade and shipbuilding. But in both regions, trade was a critical factor in economic growth. A similar phenomenon can be observed in the Middle Colonies. In the colonies of Pennsylvania and New York, for example, the economy was oriented on a system of independent farmers who relied on the labor of family members. In the mid-eighteenth century, however, demand for grain from Europe began to climb sharply as a result of population growth and poor harvests, causing these colonies' grain production to rapidly increase. Since direct trade in grain was permitted even under the Navigation Acts, merchants in the cities of Pennsylvania and New York processed wheat grown in the surrounding rural areas and exported this to southern Europe and other areas. This led to the growth of commerce and shipping and also to the development of the manufacturing industry, since wheat had to pass through an elaborate process of milling and packing before it could be exported [16].

Trade, therefore, was a crucial factor in the economic growth of the colonies. Furthermore, the colonists were able to expand their commercial activity thanks to the British Empire's advanced system of expansive reinvestment. In other words, the colonists were able to enjoy economic development because they got a free ride, so to speak, on this system of expansive reinvestment.

Under the protection of the Navigation Acts, the Southern Colonies had access to the credit and commercial services provided by British merchants and to a cheap supply of high-quality manufactured goods. The Middle Colonies profited from the grain trade, which was exempt from the restrictions of the Navigation Acts. While the New England Colonies were not able to provide the raw materials or cash crops that the British market demanded, they could make money through trade with the West Indies. Effectively, the Navigation Acts constrained the colonists' economic freedom to a certain extent by placing regulations on manufacturing and on the imports and exports of specific products, but they also provided the colonists with the protection of Britain's military and with its vast market [17].

These circumstances are clearly reflected in estimates of the trade balance between 1768 and 1772. When trade in goods is taken separately, the American colonists had a deficit of about 1.5 million pounds a year in their trade with Britain. But when the service balance and transfer balance are added to the equation, the picture looks a little different. In New England cities like Boston and in the area around Philadelphia and New York, the shipping industry was being developed by the burgeoning class of local traders. As a result, the American colonists posted a surplus of 720,000 lb in the service balance through shipping fees and other services.

The status of the transfer balance is even more intriguing. While the colonists only paid 40,000 lb to Britain in taxes, they got back a total of 440,000 lb in transfers (consisting of 400,000 lb in military expenditures and 40,000 lb in salaries for public officials). If both the service balance and the transfer balance are included, therefore, the current account for the American colonists just before independence was very nearly balanced [18]. This clearly shows how much the British Empire contributed to the economy of the American colonies. The British Empire provided the colonists not only with a market but also with credit, commercial services, cheap manufactured goods and military protection.

From the American Revolution to the Constitutional Convention

If the advantages provided by the British Empire exceeded the cost of being part of that empire, one could well ask what made the colonists challenge the empire's authority. It is generally known that the Seven Years' War gave rise to important changes in the relationship between the American colonies and Britain. As we saw in chap. 5, it was during this war that the mercantilist competition between Britain and France reached a climax. The military clash between the two countries began on the border between the American colonies and French-controlled Canada and spread to the West Indies, India, and Europe.

Victory in the Seven Years' War clinched Britain's advantage over France, but it had major ramifications for the American colonists as well. The victory drove out the French forces who had periodically harassed the colonists by forming alliances with Indian tribes on their borders. It also broke the power of the Spanish, who had been threatening the colonies from the south. The colonies now appeared to be safe from external threats.

But the Seven Years' War also brought a major change in Britain's attitude toward the American colonies. The British government and Parliament had long held a position that Edmund Burke described as "salutary neglect." The American colonies were supporting themselves without any help from Britain, supplying the raw materials and goods that Britain needed, and apparently serving as a faithful consumer of Britain's products. Therefore, British politicians had regarded the American colonies as little more than a way to consolidate their own power base by exercising their authority to appoint colonial governors.

After the Seven Years' War began, however, there was increasing support for the argument that the colonies should no longer be "neglected." A conflict that had begun in North America between the American colonists, French colonists, and

Indian tribes had escalated into a full-blown war between the powers of Europe, and the ensuing military action had forced Britain to make large-scale fiscal expenditures. After this, the British government and some members of Parliament contended that the situation in the colonies demanded Britain's close attention [19].

Indeed, the Seven Years' War demanded more fiscal expenditures than any preceding war. To pay for the war, the British government and Parliament raised the excise tax and the land tax and issued more debt to cover the remaining cost. As a result, state debt ballooned by 70% during the war, with Britain's total debt reaching 126 million pounds. The fiscal situation in the colonies, however, was completely different. The colonists' tax burden was minor compared to that of people living in Britain, and the colonial governments were compensated for most of the contributions they made to the British government during the war. Furthermore, the British soldiers and sailors stationed in the colonies had to procure their own supplies in the field, which led to a major boom in the colonial economy. The colonists even managed to profit significantly from supplying materials to French soldiers and colonists [20].

When these circumstances became known in Britain, both policy makers and the general public began to pay more attention to what was happening in the empire. It was clear that the American colonies were important not only for the British economy but also for Britain's strategic interests. The urgent challenge, therefore, was both to restore stability to the colonies in North America and the West Indies as cheaply as possible and to find a way to improve Britain's fiscal situation, which had deteriorated during the Seven Years' War.

Policy makers devised a number of solutions. First, they attempted to forestall the possibility of a military conflict in the colonies in order to avoid large-scale fiscal expenditures. This attempt led to the Proclamation of 1763 and the Quebec Act of 1774. The proclamation made it illegal for the colonists to settle beyond the Appalachian Mountains. It had two objectives: to minimize the likelihood of armed conflict with the Indian tribes that indiscriminate settlement could provoke and to restrict the colonists' range of settlement to the Atlantic coast, thus forcing them to remain dependent on British commerce. The Quebec Act was also designed to prevent the American colonies from expanding westward, which it sought to accomplish by placing the vast amount of territory to the west under the control of the Quebec government.

British policy makers also took an interest in trade. As we saw in chap. 5, excise taxes and customs duties accounted for an overwhelming majority of Britain's fiscal income during the eighteenth century. In order for Britain to service the debt it had incurred during the Seven Years' War, it needed to increase its fiscal income. It was not feasible to raise taxes receipts inside Britain, however, since the excise tax had already been raised as high as possible. This was made clear by several uprisings that occurred in the west of England after an excise tax was placed on cider after the war.

The solution proposed at this time was to increase the revenue from duties collected in the colonies. Toward this end, Parliament passed the Sugar Act of 1764 (officially known as the American Revenue Act), which regulated trade between the

New England Colonies and foreign colonies in the West Indies and forced the merchants of New England to concentrate on trade with the British West Indies. To achieve these goals, Parliament set up admiralty courts in the American colonies. The Townshend Acts of 1767 and the Tea Act of 1773 were also intended to increase customs revenue from the colonies. The Townshend Acts placed several items not formerly affected by the Navigation Acts within the scope of its regulations, while the Tea Act reduced tariffs on tea imported by the East India Company in an attempt to reduce consumption of contraband tea [21].

There was a fierce backlash from the American colonists. As soon as the Proclamation of 1763 took effect, the colonists protested that the British government was trying to prevent the Thirteen Colonies from growing. Since the French had been driven out of Canada, they argued, North America ought to be opened up to the colonists. They downplayed the friction with the Indian tribes as being a minor side effect of the process of "civilization." They also argued that the colonies in their current state could no longer support the rapidly growing population.

Furthermore, the American colonists said, the regulations on trade were unreasonable. Being able to trade directly with foreign colonies and European countries not only profited the colonists themselves but also the people of Britain, they argued. The New England colonists in particular had no agricultural products or raw materials to supply the British market, so the only way they could afford to import British manufactured goods was by making money through commerce with other countries. If this cycle was interrupted by unreasonable British regulations, the colonists warned, they would have no choice but to make for themselves the products they had hitherto imported from Britain. These attitudes were reflected in the non-importation and non-consumption campaigns to boycott British products in 1765, 1767, and 1774 [22].

The trade restrictions were not the only things that the colonists were unhappy about, however. They believed that these regulations were part of a scheme by certain groups—namely, the court party and the moneyed interests—to keep the colonies from developing and to suppress the colonists' liberties. From this perspective, the Proclamation of 1763 was a clear infringement not only on the freedom of movement but also on the natural right to use human labor to cultivate virgin soil and convert it into wealth.

The colonists' liberties were being suppressed in other ways as well. The Currency Act of 1764 prevented the colonists from issuing paper money or from using paper money to pay their taxes or pay back debts to British merchants. The colonists were concerned that these regulations were not only forcing them to make sacrifices for the benefit of British merchants but also threatening their former freedom to manage their own economic affairs. These concerns about the threat to freedom were further inflamed during the debate over the Stamp Act. Under the slogan "no taxation without representation," the colonists expressly denied that Parliament had the authority to tax them. Such taxation, they argued, robbed them of the basic rights to which they were entitled as British subjects [23]. With the colonists demanding their rights as British subjects and the British government and Parliament insisting on the principle of Parliamentary sovereignty, the dispute rapidly escalated. The punitive measures that Parliament adopted in response to the Boston Tea Party in 1773 ended up provoking armed conflict that soon led to all-out war.

When the war began, few expected that the Americans would be victorious. The mighty Royal Navy blockaded the Atlantic seaboard and could launch an assault on the main colonial ports at any time. The British army was full of officers with ample military experience and well-trained soldiers. This powerful army was backed by the British government's fiscal system, which was extremely efficient by the standards of its day.

The colonies, on the other hand, did not have the manpower or the organization to wage a full-out war. They had virtually no navy, and their army consisted of inexperienced militias and a handful of officers. The colonies also lacked any institutions that could compete with the British fiscal system. Furthermore, the relationship between the individual colonies was unclear. Since the Thirteen Colonies had all developed separately through bilateral relationships with Britain, it was hardly obvious that they could endure a war with Britain—the superpower of the age—let alone form a unified state [24].

There were a number of reasons why the colonies emerged victorious despite such unfavorable circumstances. First, the colonists avoided decisive battles with the British regulars and made effective use of guerilla tactics. Another important factor was the leadership of George Washington, who managed to unify soldiers who only had a vague identity as Americans. Britain's diplomatic isolation also contributed to the colonial victory. In contrast with previous wars, Britain was unable to find an ally in Europe, while the colonies received military and financial aid from France, Spain, and the Netherlands. Immediately after Britain's defeat at the Battles of Saratoga in 1777, France entered the war, which turned the revolution into an international conflict.

From that point forward, Britain had to shift its focus from fighting the colonists to defending its strategic and economic interests in Europe, the West Indies, and India. In the meantime, the colonies could concentrate on driving the British army off the continent with financial aid from countries like France [25]. In a certain sense, the most fundamental reason for the colonists' victory may have been that they wanted independence more than the British wanted to keep the colonies. The colonists' resolute pursuit of independence was likely grounded in the optimistic belief that, regardless of their conflicting economic interests, independence would bring them the opportunity to improve their economic conditions.

This is reminiscent of the Dutch struggle against the agricultural empire of Spain, which demanded endless sacrifices from its client states as it tried to transcend the limits of agricultural society, including decelerating growth. There were major differences between the two, of course. At the time of the American Revolution, the American colonists did not have an advanced system of expansive reinvestment as the Dutch did, and their adversary, the British Empire, was not an agricultural empire but rather a commercial empire in the process of becoming an industrial one. In the end, however, both the Dutch and the American colonists were afraid that, unless they gained their independence, the fiscal burden demanded by the empire might hinder any further economic development.

But military successes provided no solution to the colonists' fiscal crisis. There were several reasons for this crisis, but the fundamental one was that the Continental Congress (composed of representatives from the Thirteen Colonies) was unable to create an effective fiscal system. While the Second Continental Congress debated a proposal to use tariffs to fund the war effort, this proposal was not accepted.

The only alternative was for each state to voluntarily pay the cost of the war in installments as they had done during the colonial period, but as of 1777 not a single state had paid its share of the cost. In the end, the only way the colonists could find to pay for the war was by printing paper money. Between 1775 and 1779, they printed 225 million continental dollars. From the moment it came off the press, this fiat money began to decline in value. Through the end of 1777, the states used continental dollars to cover 90% of the cost of the war, but as circulation increased, the value of the continental dollars fell to about 20% of face value.

After that, the situation grew even worse. The fortunes of the war became cloudy as Britain concentrated its attack on the Southern Colonies. As a result, there was a huge increase in the number of continental dollars being printed, which led once more to inflation and a severe decline in the value of the continental dollars. The market was convulsed even further because each state was issuing its own paper money and Britain was placing a great deal of counterfeit currency into circulation. In order to overcome this crisis, a few of the states explored wage and price controls, while the Continental Congress ultimately took the drastic step of requisitioning supplies [26].

Another major problem was the severe economic chaos during the war. The force that had driven the rapid expansion of the Thirteen Colonies during the colonial period was Britain's system of expansive reinvestment, but once the war began, the colonies were cut off from the British market. In April 1776, they responded by throwing open their markets to the entire world. This led to more trade with France and European colonies in the West Indies, but it was not enough to offset the economic shock of Britain blocking access to its markets. After 1778, Britain's naval blockade of the Atlantic coast relaxed slightly as Britain shifted its strategic focus to the West Indies. But as the war became international, it only aggravated the crisis facing American trade with Europe and the West Indies. With exports already in grave decline, the inflation caused by the inflated money supply made the colonists' economic situation even worse [27].

Even after independence, the American economy was slow to recover. According to one recent estimate, by 1790 the per capita GNP had fallen from 804 $ to 437 $ (based on constant 1980 prices). According to another estimate of per capita wealth, the level of Americans' wealth in 1805 was 14% lower than in 1774 [28]. During the war, household production had flourished for a time because of rising prices, contracting trade, and increasing demand for military supplies, leading to a significant increase in the production of gunpowder, textiles, and iron.

But when imports of British products resumed shortly after the war, the modest capacity that had formed in the manufacturing sector atrophied once more.

Trade conditions worsened as well. When the war was nearing its conclusion, the Americans expected that they would be able to resume trade with Britain and the British West Indies, but the British government banned trade between the United States and the British West Indies in July 1783. Spain and France's resumption of mercantilist protectionism made matters worse as well. American traders sought a remedy in the Chinese and Indian markets, but it was not sufficient. American trade would not recover to prewar levels until the late 1780s [29].

The fiscal situation was not improving either. The Articles of Confederation, which were adopted in 1777, made clear that sovereignty belonged to each state and limited the authority of the central government to managing foreign policy, waging war, and resolving interstate disputes. Since the right of taxation was also reserved for the states, the central government's fiscal affairs depended on population-based contributions from each state. Since the Articles of Confederation did not even mention the authority to regulate the economy, the central government had no influence whatsoever on interstate commerce or overseas trade. As its fiscal affairs continued to deteriorate, the central government made a number of efforts to acquire sources of revenue, such as proposing a 5% tariff on all imports in 1781. But none of these efforts bore fruit, and the central government had to continue relying on overseas loans [30].

The central government's weakness had a negative impact not only on fiscal conditions but also on the United States' trading relations with Europe. The American economy was based on agriculture and trade, just as it had been before the war. Therefore, it would not be wrong to say that postwar reconstruction and economic growth depended on the commercial relationships that the newly independent country could establish with the powers of Europe.

The United States' relationship with Britain was of particular importance. American merchants vehemently opposed the British government's unilateral decision to exclude them from its West Indies market, but to no avail. The American government wanted to sign a commercial treaty with Britain, but the British government maintained that no negotiations could take place until a number of issues were resolved—specifically, until Americans repaid their debts to British merchants and until loyalists were compensated for the property that had been confiscated from them during the war. For the same reasons, the British government refused to remove its troops from border areas, as it had promised to do in the Treaty of Paris of 1783.

As the European powers saw it, all these problems originated from the fact that the decisions of the United States' central government were not binding on the state governments. Even if a European state made a commercial pact with the central government, it was unclear whether the individual states would faithfully implement that pact. In fact, several states, including Virginia, bypassed the central government to negotiate directly with Spain in an attempt to secure trading rights [31].

Under these circumstances, there was a critical need to clearly define the role of the central government as well as the relationship of the central government to each of the states. Otherwise, each state would freely pursue its economic interests at the expense of the other states, and it would be impossible to defend the United States' national interest amid ruthless international competition. These were the prevailing concerns when the Constitutional Convention was held in Philadelphia in the summer of 1787. The convention had originally been convened to debate whether to add sections related to taxation and to trade regulations to the Articles of Confederation. But these were not issues that could be resolved by amending the Articles of Confederation; they instead demanded a fundamental overhaul of the United States' entire political system.

During the Constitutional Convention, James Madison and Alexander Hamilton offered the most feasible solutions to these problems. Madison believed that the majorities that controlled each state's legislatures were infringing on the interests and liberties of the minorities because they placed their own interests above the interests of the republic (and nation) as a whole. Therefore, Madison said, it was critical for checks and balances to be established between the federal government and the states and between the executive branch, legislative branch, and judicial branch within the federal government to prevent the interests of any one faction from dominating the whole.

Hamilton's perspective was different from Madison's. He emphasized that the young country's very survival was still at stake as the nations of Europe jockeyed for position on the international stage. Since not only Britain but nearly all the European powers still aspired to expand their colonies, any conflict that occurred inside the United States because of the states' opposing interests could entice these powers to intervene. In order for the United States to survive such a perilous situation, Hamilton said, it needed to build an army and economy strong enough to compete with the European powers. For this reason, he argued that the United States should have a powerful federal government that could exercise authority over economic and fiscal matters, including the right of taxation [32].

Madison's ideas about the relationship of the federal government to the states were repeatedly revised during a series of debates. The discussion of fiscal and trade issues, on the other hand, proceeded more smoothly, which indicates just how bad things had gotten during the American War of Independence and the postwar period. In the Constitution that the convention finally adopted, the new federal government was authorized to levy duties and taxes, tariffs and other barriers interfering with interstate commerce were abolished, and new states were allowed to enter the union with the same rights as the original states. The Bill of Rights, which was adopted after the Constitution, was designed to protect the individual's right of property and other customary rights against the tyranny of the mob.

Thus, the Constitution created an institutional framework for unifying the states into a single market, which paved the way for regional specialization and division of labor inside the country. By affirming the inviolability of private property, the Constitution promoted vigorous corporate activity [33]. The structure of checks and balances between the federal government and the states that emerged through a series of debates over the Constitution in the end created conditions under which each state could craft its own policies aimed at economic development. Since the Constitution guaranteed the free movement of products and labor between the states, each state could employ a number of policies, including the right of taxation, to either promote or restrict immigration and commerce (within a limited range) in the ways best-suited to it. This encouraged competition between the states and contributed to the supply of various public goods [34].

From the System of Expansive Reinvestment to the System of Expansive Reproduction

After the Constitution was ratified, the administration of President George Washington and the first Congress focused their attention on tackling the fiscal and economic problems that had been accruing since the American War of Independence. Even before Alexander Hamilton took office as the first Secretary of the Treasury, Congress passed the Tariff Act [35]. Subsequently, Hamilton prepared a series of reports at the request of Congress—the *Report on Public Credit*, the *Report on a National Bank*, and the *Report on Manufactures*—in which he laid out a plan for the United States' fiscal system and economic development. He then proceeded to put this plan into action.

Since the United States had the inherent advantages of vast territory and abundant resources and since most Americans wanted economic success, Hamilton firmly believed that the United States would ultimately become an economic power that rivaled Britain. But this could not happen without human effort. The United States' first order of business was to become strong enough to survive as an independent and sovereign state. In order to do so, Hamilton believed, the United States needed a powerful and unified government capable of waging war, just like Britain. To become a war-making state in the manner of Britain, the United States would need the support of a sound fiscal system and national economy. These were the goals described by Hamilton's reports, which also detailed specific policies for achieving those goals [36].

In his *Report on Public Credit*, Hamilton proposed two measures for dealing with the government debt of 79.1 million dollars (nearly 40% of the United States' GDP in 1790). The first measure was to convert the federal government's debt into long-term bonds backed by revenue from tariffs and revenue from selling land owned by the government. The objective of this measure, the report said, was to make clear that the state meant to deal with its debts and to stimulate the bond market. The second measure was for the federal government to take over each of the state's debts and to pay them back with long-term bonds.

A variety of bonds that had been issued during the war were circulating in the market at prices that were much lower than face value. Hamilton's plan meant that a small number of people who had bought up large numbers of bonds on the market for cut-rate prices would reap huge profits while those who had already sold their bonds would suffer major losses. The federal government's plan to assume several states' debts also seemed unfair to the states that had already settled most of their debts.

Despite such objections, Hamilton moved forward with the measures. His first reason for doing so was that respecting the outcomes of market transactions (no matter how cheaply the government bonds had been bought for) was the only way to ultimately create a vibrant bond market. His second reason was that he wanted to concentrate capital in the hands of a few people. If a small number of the economic elite could exert a major influence over the bond market, their interests would be tied to the fate of the union, an outcome that Hamilton believed would strengthen the federal government. In addition to this, he believed that such an elite would become a social force that would lead the development of trade and manufacturing as they had in Britain.

Hamilton's belief that economic development was only possible when capital was concentrated with a minority of elites is also evident in the *Report on a National Bank.* Since an early point in the colonial period, the American economy had continually struggled with a shortage of capital and currency. This was clearly demonstrated by the furor over the Currency Act, which increased tensions between Britain and the colonies in the 1760s, and by Shays' Rebellion in the late 1780s, which was caused in part by the shortage of currency in circulation.

It was urgent, therefore, to supply enough currency and credit to stimulate economic activity while also preventing states and individuals from issuing too much currency. Hamilton believed that the solution was to establish a national bank —the Bank of the United States—that would be similar to the Bank of England. The Anti-Federalists and Republicans like Thomas Jefferson objected that such a bank would only benefit the moneyed interests, as the Bank of England did. Such a bank, they said, would ultimately lead to political decay.

But Hamilton responded that allowing a small number of people to exercise control over the Bank of the United States (which was supposed to manage tax receipts and handle government bonds and short-term loans) would actually be beneficial to the country in the future. Hamilton's argument was that concentrating capital in the hands of the few was the only way for capital to accumulate, and that the accumulation of capital was necessary for the commercial and industrial development that would guarantee the country's survival.

Indeed, Hamilton's plan was not only designed to overcome short-term fiscal and economic problems. He envisioned the United States transitioning from an agricultural society into a commercial society and then evolving into an industrial society, just as Britain was doing at the time. In the words of a New England Federalist in 1789, "an agricultural nation which exports its raw materials, and imports its manufactures" could be neither "opulent" nor "powerful." [37] Hamilton's commitment to this point is evident in his *Report on Manufactures*, in which, he argued that the federal government ought to use industrial policy to protect infant industries. His argument was reinforced by the fact that the United

State was hampered by its lack of experience with manufacturing and that Britain's own industrial development had been assisted by government policy.

Hamilton's specific proposals included protective tariffs, subsidies, tax exemptions for imports of raw materials, and a variety of incentives, but he placed particular emphasis on the role of subsidies. While tariffs can serve as an effective instrument of industrial policy, they can also cause rival states to impose retaliatory tariffs. Such tariffs would have taken a heavy toll on American exports, which were essential to the United States' fiscal and economic stability. It would take a long time for commerce and industry to catch up to agriculture in the American economy, and until that time a balance had to be maintained between exporting primary commodities and promoting the development of manufacturing [38].

Hamilton's sweeping development strategy faced strident criticism. The Anti-Federalists who had opposed the ratification of the Constitution and the Republicans who sought to limit the role of the federal government were concerned that Hamilton's policies would concentrate economic power in the hands of a small minority and ultimately cause the United States to degenerate into an aristocracy or monarchy like Britain.

But despite these concerns, Hamilton's strategy helped the fledgling state greatly improve its fiscal condition and weather its economic crisis. Once a solution had been found to the problem of government debt, which had threatened the United States' very survival, it became easier to secure capital not only from within the United States but also from overseas. In fact, this led to excessive speculation that brought on a financial crisis in 1791, but Hamilton quickly dealt with the crisis by having the Treasury Department buy up large amounts of government bonds. As capital flowed into the market, trade (the driving force of the American economy) began to revive, and business activity bounced back as well [39].

The French Revolution and the subsequent French Revolutionary Wars contributed significantly to the American economic recovery in the 1790s. While trade by various European countries was disrupted during these sharply contested wars, Americans took advantage of the occasion to make immense profits. France, Spain, and Britain had closed their markets to the United States for some time after the American War of Independence, but now all of them sought to secure a supply of foodstuffs and raw materials from the United States.

Even greater profits were made as European merchants came to rely upon the services of American merchants and commercial fleets as they sought to avoid privateers and the maritime and continental blockades. This made possible rapid growth in the American economy. According to a classic study by Douglass C. North, the United States exhibited the traditional features of export-led growth between 1793 and 1807. Exports accounted for between 10 and 15% of GNP, and imports grew even faster than exports. The resulting trade deficit was offset by the added value from shipping and trade services and by European capital that was invested in the United States to avoid Europe's political instability [40].

The wartime boom, however, did not last forever. The United States banned imports in 1806 with the Non-Importation Act and then all trade the following year with the Embargo Act, inflicting a severe blow on trade and shipping. The situation was made even worse by the war with Britain that began in 1812. The import ban and the trade embargo were triggered by conflict with Britain over the trading rights of neutral states. Britain's stance on the issue of trade with neutral states was based on rules it had written in 1756, which stated that trade that was forbidden in peacetime was also forbidden in wartime. Applying this principle meant that trade between British colonies and France, which was illegal according to the Navigation Acts, was also illegal during a war.

To get around these regulations, American merchants adopted the strategy of first shipping products from the British West Indies to the United States and then re-exporting them to France. But as the Napoleonic Wars intensified in the summer of 1805, Britain introduced the new doctrine of the "continuous voyage" and began to seize American vessels that were involved in such re-exporting. American ships fell under an even greater risk of being seized in 1806 when Napoleon declared the commercial activities of the ships of neutral states to be illegal as part of his Continental System [41].

These were the circumstances under which the Jefferson administration reacted to pressure from Britain by banning imports in 1806 while engaging in ineffective negotiations. When France began seizing American ships as well in 1807, the Jefferson administration declared an embargo on trade. The results were horrendous. In the year that the trade embargo took effect, shipping revenue from Massachusetts merchant fleets (which accounted for 40% of merchant ship tonnage in the United States) fell by 15 million dollars, an amount that was equivalent to the federal government's fiscal income in 1806. In 1808, the United States' total exports decreased by 80% while imports fell by 60% [42].

The Jefferson administration's decision to take the extreme measure of a trade embargo despite the staggering losses that were expected was largely the product of Jefferson's Republican convictions. In contrast with Hamilton, Jefferson's main goal was creating the Republican ideal in the United States [43]. According to Jefferson, the only way a republic could be preserved was for its citizens to actively participate in politics, for them to put the welfare of the nation as a whole before their own interests and for them to practice "public virtue," as he called it, by resisting the abuse of power. For the citizenry to obtain the public virtue that Jefferson valued so highly, however, it was essential for each of them to own enough property to be able to support themselves without relying on the wealth and power of other people. The United States was indeed better suited for such a system than any other country in history. As an agricultural society with weak trade and industry, the United States offered fewer opportunities for the pursuit of luxury and personal gain and less temptation for corruption and bribes among the powerful.

It was from this perspective that Jefferson and the other Republicans welcomed the growth of trade in the 1790s, though for different reasons than Hamilton. While Hamilton expected that the growth of trade would bring about the accumulation of commercial capital and lead to industrial development, Jefferson believed that the growth of trade (even if not inherently desirable) could be a force to suppress the growth of manufacturing and to support the expansion of agriculture [44]. Since Americans had grown accustomed to consuming manufactured goods, American agricultural products would have to be freely traded with European manufactured goods if the United States was to continue focusing on agriculture. Therefore, Jefferson supported free trade and believed that it was necessary to take bold action if the monarchies of Europe clung to their outdated mercantilist policies and refused to adopt free trade.

Another reason that Jefferson could not overlook Britain's infringement of the United States' right to neutrality was the deeply rooted anti-British sentiment felt by him and the other Republicans. In their view, Britain was treating the United States as an inferior country, as if it were still a colony. The Royal Navy's seizure of American vessels not only violated the commercial freedom to which Americans were undeniably entitled, but it also reflected Britain's arrogant assumption that it could determine the United States' neutrality.

Jefferson thought that tolerating this arrogance would be tantamount to admitting that the United States was still inferior to Britain. Therefore, bold action was necessary, if only to guarantee that American independence would be respected. In March 1807, William Duane, editor of the *Aurora* magazine and a supporter of the Republicans, asked his readers, "Will you abandon your rights? Will you abandon your independence? Are you willing to become colonies of Great Britain?" It seems clear how Jefferson would have responded [45].

The trade embargo was abolished on March 4th, 1809, the day that James Madison was inaugurated as president, but the conflict with Britain continued. The Royal Navy was still attacking American merchant vessels and impressing American sailors for service. Americans' hostility to Britain was intensified by friction on the two countries' borders. After Jefferson took power, the federal government had taken a considerable interest in territorial expansion. Expanding territory was essential not only to increase the number of independent yeoman farmers but also to prevent the Federalists from returning to power and to ensure the future of the Republican Party [46]. The population of the New England region had already reached the saturation point, while yeoman farming could not take root in the old Southern states, which were already dominated by large plantation owners. Consequently, there was a tremendous desire for new land, just as there had been before the American War of Independence.

While the Federalists sought to regulate western expansion (which was a thorny political issue because of its connection with the expansion of the slave system) in order to maintain social order and political stability, Jefferson and the Republicans had another idea. Jefferson had criticized the Federalists' expansionary fiscal policy and promised not to pass down debt to his descendants. And yet it was also Jefferson who spent the huge sum of 15 million dollars on the Louisiana Purchase in 1803, which shows that the Republicans thought territorial expansion was necessary to preserve a republican form of government [47].

None of the politicians of the time were more knowledgeable about the classics than Jefferson, and his study of the agricultural empire of classical Rome had shown him that the only way to overcome the constraints of agricultural society (namely, the deceleration of economic growth) was through territorial expansion. So while Jefferson wanted the United States to continue expanding in the manner of an agricultural empire, he thought that newly acquired territory should be turned into separate self-governing states in order to prevent the socio-economic inequality and political uncertainty that had led to the downfall of the Roman Republic.

While the Jeffersonian Republicans were at the zenith of their influence, settlements on the borders were asking for protection from local Indian tribes and from the British who were covertly supporting them. The apparent solution seemed to lie in Canada, which was under British control, and in Florida, which was under Spanish control. There was a growing push in Congress to invade Canada, backed by the assumption that Britain was too preoccupied with the Napoleonic Wars to pay attention to matters in North America. There was also increasing public support for going to war with Britain and putting pressure on Spain (which was allied with Britain) to sell Florida to the United States. As the South and West clamored for war, Madison found himself without any alternatives for resolving the conflict with Britain, having already exhausted the options of trade embargo and diplomacy. At last, he gave the Senate a detailed account of the United States' grievances with Britain and asked the Senate to choose a course of action. The Senate voted for war, and Madison made the declaration.

This marked the beginning of the War of 1812, also called the second American war of independence. Since the United States was completely unprepared for war, the outcome was predictably abysmal. A traditional tenet of republicanism was that standing armies of professional soldiers should not be maintained since they were tools that tyrants could use to oppress civil liberties. True to form, the United States was barely able to muster 6700 troops, and it was not until the end of 1812 that it managed to put together a regular army. Congress authorized an expansion of the army, but there were hardly any volunteers. Meanwhile, the state militias could not be effectively mobilized either since they refused to operate outside their borders [48]. Consequently, the American invasion of Canada ended in failure, and British troops that landed in the South briefly occupied and torched the American capital of Washington. The American navy was also helpless to prevent the Royal Navy from imposing a formidable blockade of the Atlantic coast. In the end, the Madison administration had no choice but to end the war by signing the Treaty of Ghent in December 1814 [49].

The economic consequences of the war were severe. When the trade embargo took effect in 1807, exports had reached 100 million dollars, but they shrunk to 27 million dollars in 1813 and to 7 million dollars in 1814. Imports exceeded 130 million dollars in 1807 but were down to 13 million dollars in 1814. As a result, the federal government's fiscal income—which largely depended upon duties on imported goods—inevitably shrank as well. Fiscal revenue amounted to 13 million dollars in 1811 but declined to 6 million dollars in 1814 [50].

Nevertheless, the economic consequences of the trade embargo and the War of 1812 were not entirely negative. This period marked the beginning of a structural transformation of the American economy. Americans had long depended upon British manufactured goods, and when the supply of these goods was cut off, it created a powerful incentive to produce these goods inside the United States. Another contributing factor was the fact that merchants who had lost business opportunities and investments with the suspension of trade began to pour their capital into the manufacturing sector. In this sense, the period from the enactment of the trade embargo until the War of 1812 can be regarded as a watershed moment in the history of the United States' economic development. It was the first step in the transition from the system of expansive reinvestment, which had depended on agricultural production and trade, to the system of expansive reproduction, which was based on technological innovation in the manufacturing sector.

In fact, the history of manufacturing in the United States goes back to before the American War of Independence. As political strife with Britain intensified after the Seven Years' War, the colonists tried to put pressure on Britain's merchants and manufacturers through the non-importation and non-consumption campaigns. Between 1767 and 1769 and after 1774, there was a movement for the colonies to meet their own demand for manufactured goods, and craft production was actively encouraged.

During the first phase of the American War of Independence, there was also a campaign for the United States to achieve economic independence by developing its domestic manufacturing sector. Thus, there was a great deal of both craft production and self-sufficient household production throughout the colonies, though the area that showed the most interest in fostering the manufacturing sector was New England, which had not depended on producing and exporting specific cash crops [51]. During the American War of Independence, military demand helped the gunpowder, shoemaking, cotton textile, iron, and steel industries to thrive, while the paper and pottery industries also prospered more than they had before [52].

This interest in manufacturing surged from the 1760s until the United States gained its independence, but it subsided after British products began to flow back into the American market. Until the Constitution came into effect, the United States' central government and the state governments had to focus on the issues of fiscal revenue, debt, and trade, and even afterward they could not afford to pay attention to the manufacturing sector [53]. Of course, the federal government became even less inclined to promote manufacturing after the Republicans took power in 1800. Despite these circumstances, efforts continued in New England to foster the manufacturing sector.

Scholars had long believed that manufacturing spread the earliest and the most widely in New England because agriculture there had stagnated unlike the Middle States and the South. The region was struck by an agricultural crisis in the 1790s, and farmers suffered from an excessive tax burden and a shortage of currency, as Shays' Rebellion showed. This caused workers to migrate from the farming sector to the shoemaking and cotton textile industries. The cotton textile industry benefited in particular from the cheap labor of women and children.

Recent studies, however, have cast doubt on this interpretation. According to one estimate, the number of farm workers in New England continued to increase until the 1840s, and the agricultural workforce did not begin to shrink in earnest until the 1860s. In contrast to the general view, these studies claim that New England agriculture actually prospered and that the manufacturing sector could not have developed without the demand of farm workers [54].

Even so, it should be noted that New England's agricultural sector was still oriented on a subsistence economy, in contrast with the large-scale commercial agricultural sector of the South. Just as with the yeoman farmers of Britain before the Industrial Revolution, the yeoman farmers of New England were gradually absorbed into the industrial sector. The plantation economy of the South had an agricultural foundation that could sustain the economic system of agricultural society, but agricultural society in New England gradually began to serve the secondary role of meeting the needs of the industrial sector during the transition from the system of expansive reinvestment to the system of expansive reproduction.

Craftsmen and small-scale manufacturers used capital amassed in the farming sector and the non-farming sector (consisting of retailers and professional workers) to produce and supply various items that were needed in farming areas, including boxes, building materials, furniture, and carriages. An even bigger change was the gradual emergence in the 1790s of manufacturers who marketed their products to all of New England and to the even larger market outside of New England. Shoemaking and cotton textile manufacturing were the industries that underwent the most development. In the shoemaking industry, Massachusetts firms divided labor among smaller workshops and used wholesalers in the Boston area to supply products not only to New England but also to the Middle States and the South.

But it was the cotton textile industry that played the biggest role in the development of the American manufacturing sector, just as in Britain. The American cotton textile industry began in the New England countryside in the 1790s. The industry needed substantial capital and technical expertise as well as nearby markets, and the bountiful farming districts of New England provided not only a workforce but also capital and markets. Furthermore, the city merchants also contributed to the development of the cotton textile industry by providing capital and distribution networks.

Textile production in the American colonies had long depended upon manual labor by women in the countryside. Extracting the thread from raw cotton and producing textiles was a slow process that required long hours of work [55]. That is also why it was not until the 1730s—when first a spinning machine and then a weaving machine were invented—that the British cotton textile industry really began to develop. Just as British manufacturers were eager to develop and implement new technology during the first phase of the Industrial Revolution, so the American textile industry also began with the introduction of technology. Since the British government had banned the export of machinery in order to prevent the outflow of technology, acquiring new technology was not easy. But this situation began to change when Derbyshire-born Samuel Slater arrived in the United States in 1789 with detailed knowledge of the machinery he had operated in Britain. At the request of Moses Brown, a merchant from Rhode Island, Slater built a spinning machine and established America's first cotton mill in December 1790. Slater's cotton mills soon spread throughout New England [56].

Just as in Britain, the spread of spinning machines created demand for innovations in weaving. Once again, the solution involved bringing over technology from Britain. Francis Cabot Lowell, a Massachusetts merchant, had been struggling because of the Embargo Act and the Non-Intercourse Act and the French and British navy's seizure of merchant vessels, and he had been watching for new business opportunities. While visiting cotton mills in the British county of Lancashire, Lowell mastered the requisite technology, and he devised a plan to set up cotton mills in the United States with the help of a machinist by the name of Paul Moody.

Lowell set up a mill in Waltham, Massachusetts, in 1813, at a time when the terms of trade had been harmed by the war. Instead of simply replicating the mills he had seen in Britain, Lowell built his mill according to an innovative design, which cost the huge sum of 300,000 $. The mill was the first to integrate the spinning and weaving processes, and it ran on water power, an apt choice given Massachusetts' abundant water resources. Slater and Lowell's mills soon inspired imitations throughout New England and beyond. There were 15 cotton mills in the United States prior to 1808, but this number increased to 87 by the end of 1809. By 1814, 243 cotton mills were in operation in 15 states [57].

The end of the War of 1812 put American cotton textile producers in a serious bind. Once trade with Britain resumed, British merchants and manufacturers who had suffered major losses because of the interruption of trade during the war years began to flood the American market with high-quality British goods for low prices. This was worrying news indeed for American manufacturers (and especially cotton textile producers), whose business had flourished between 1807 and 1814. Since American cotton textile manufacturers had just started to industrialize, they were completely unable to compete with the superior technology and productivity of Britain's cotton textile industry.

With the resumption of trade in 1815, no fewer than 71 million yards of British cotton textiles crowded into the American market, causing the price of cotton textiles to plummet. The price of imports fell 20% in 1815 and 15% more the following year, while the price of American cotton textiles only decreased 9%. Under such circumstances, the only way for American cotton textiles to survive was to receive government protection. For this reason, Lowell and other cotton textile producers asked the government to institute protective tariffs against British products [58].

Fortunately for the cotton textile producers, there was a growing sense even among the Republicans who controlled the federal government and Congress at that time that the American manufacturing industry needed to be protected [59]. Unlike traditional Republicans like Jefferson, a number of new leaders in the party believed that the United States could not rely solely on agriculture and trade if it was to become independent from the economic influence of Britain and other powerful countries. The National Republicans, as they had come to be called, thought it was necessary to promote domestic trade and the manufacturing industry to facilitate balanced economic development and in so doing to acquire the economic might that could compensate for the military weakness the United States had exhibited in 1812. National Republicans like Henry Clay of Kentucky and John Calhoun of South Carolina (who would later lead the Southern separatists) believed that such projects were ultimately the responsibility of the federal government. This shows the extent to which they sympathized with the cotton textile manufacturers' request for protective tariffs.

But even given agreement about the need for protective tariffs, determining the rate of those tariffs was a different matter. Hamilton had argued much earlier in the *Report on Manufactures* that subsidies were a more effective policy than protective tariffs, and indeed tariffs on British cotton textiles had the potential to provoke another conflict with Britain. Even within the United States, it was not easy to reach an agreement to increase tariffs. The traditional Republicans continued to support free trade, while the Southern planters, who depended on exports to the British market, protested that protective tariffs would ultimately force them to sacrifice for the benefit of Northern manufacturers. Along with the Southern planters, New England merchants also supported free trade with Britain. As a consequence, protective tariffs required a cautious approach that could placate different interest groups.

The National Republicans came up with an ingenious solution. The Tariff of 1816 placed a 25% tariff on textiles and a 20% tariff on other products. The 25% tariff on textile products was secretly designed to protect American cotton textile producers while avoiding a trade dispute with Britain. Since American textile manufacturers focused on cheap products and British manufacturers exported premium products, British cotton textiles could still be competitive in the American market even with a 25% tariff. Cheaper imports, however, were subject to what was effectively a higher tariff rate because of the "minimum principle," which meant that imported textiles were never assessed at less than 25 cents per yard regardless of their actual price. As a result, imports of British goods continued, but cheap cotton textiles from India could not compete with cheap American cotton textiles [60].

It was around this time that tariffs began to be accepted in the United States as an instrument not only of fiscal policy but also of industrial policy. As the debate about the Tariff of 1816 illustrates, however, the issue of tariffs was always a controversial one because of the conflicting interests of different regions and industrial sectors. When numerous small-scale manufacturers in cities such as Philadelphia, New York, and Baltimore demanded higher tariffs after the Panic of 1819, for example, Congress debated a bill that would have levied tariffs ranging from 20 to 100% depending on the product, but the bill ultimately failed because of the opposition of Southern lawmakers.

With increasing calls for protectionism coming mostly from the Northeast, tariffs were raised substantially in 1824. Massachusetts legislators came out in opposition of the higher tariffs, however, on the grounds that the duties on imported wool would make textiles more expensive to produce. This led protectionists to submit legislation in 1827 (called the Woollens Bill) that would have simultaneously raised tariffs not only on wool but also on imported woolen textiles. The plantation owners of South Carolina (who had steadfastly opposed protectionist measures) vehemently opposed the bill, and it was narrowly defeated, with the deciding vote cast by Vice President John Calhoun, who was himself from South Carolina.

When events took this turn, Northern protectionists held meetings in various places in support of protective trade that culminated in a national rally in Harrisburg, Pennsylvania, in the summer of 1827. As support for protectionism grew in the months before the presidential election, allies of Andrew Jackson and opponents of President John Quincy Adams and Henry Clay proposed a huge increase on duties for various raw materials, including wool, iron, hemp, and molasses. This was part of a scheme concocted by Martin Van Buren that was designed to whip up support in Pennsylvania, New York, Kentucky, and the Ohio Valley.

After the bill was debated in the Senate, duties were raised not only on raw materials but also on manufactured goods. The South denounced the legislation, which they called the "Tariff of Abominations." In the years to come, the tariffs would be revised again and again. Tariffs on wool were reduced in 1832, the tariff rates were adjusted in 1833, and the rates were even raised in 1842. Thus, tariffs became a topic of fierce debate because of their connection with the economic interests of various regions and the feuds between political factions [61].

Even as the tariffs were being debated, the cotton textile industry could count on government protection. According to one classic study, the effective tariff rate on cotton textiles reached 71% in the period from 1830 to 1832. Even though tariff rates were decreased by the Compromise Tariff of 1833, the price of American cotton textiles fell even faster, which meant that the effective tariff rate actually rose to 82%. Therefore, some scholars contend that American cotton textile producers were fully capable of being competitive even without protective tariffs by 1816 (when protective tariffs were being introduced) at the earliest and by 1824 at the latest, and that as a consequence it was unreasonable to maintain the protective tariffs afterward. But since British products still had an overwhelming advantage over American products in the area of premium cotton textiles even after 1824, other scholars argue that British premium textiles would have sold for even less than lower-quality American textiles if not for the tariffs. In the end, tariffs gave the American cotton textile industry the time it needed to achieve enough growth to compete with the British cotton textile industry [62].

As we have already mentioned, the politicians who supported protecting the manufacturing industry differed from the Republicans of Jefferson's time in their belief that a strong economy could not be built through territorial expansion alone. While the new Republican Party agreed that territorial expansion was necessary for the development of the United States, they thought that agriculture, commerce, and manufacturing could not develop in unison unless new states that joined the union were integrated into a single market with the old states. If balanced development did not take place, they believed, the American economy would always be at the mercy of global price fluctuations and geopolitical changes.

These beliefs were inherent in the American System that Clay proposed during the debates about the Tariff of 1824. His system consisted of four main elements. The first element was imposing duties to secure fiscal soundness and to promote the manufacturing industry. The second was expanding finances by selling public land rather than levying the consumption tax and land tax (introduced during the War of

1812), since these caused domestic economic activity to contract. The third was protecting the central bank in order to keep the federal government fiscally sound and to secure monetary stability by eliminating the uncertainty caused by the excessive currency issued by state and local banks. The fourth and last element was expanding public works projects (which Americans then called “internal improvements,” borrowing an eighteenth-century British term), which were to be funded by tariffs and by the sale of public land [63].

Along with protecting manufacturing, another issue that Clay considered important was expanding the transportation and communication networks. The territory of the United States had expanded rapidly since Jefferson’s second term in office, and this expansion continued after 1815. From the time the United States became independent until 1819, it gained control of all the eastern and central part of the North American continent south of Canada, from the Atlantic Ocean to the Great Plains. Jefferson’s purchase of the Louisiana Territory in 1803 doubled the territory of the United States, and Spain ceded Florida and its surrounding colonies to the United States in 1819. The country that had initially been composed of 13 states had expanded to 22, starting with Vermont in 1791 and reaching Alabama by 1819.

After the War of 1812, migration beyond the Appalachian Mountains proceeded rapidly. As the National Republicans had hoped, the sale of public land began to accelerate. Just 500,000 acres of public land were sold in 1813, but the amount increased to 4 million acres in 1818 [64]. In order to integrate the growing country and also to stimulate the economic activity of settlers that had moved to new territory, it was essential to expand the transportation and communication networks that connected these markets.

In fact, there had been calls to improve the transportation network since the 1790s. During the economic boom taking place at the time, an effort was made to build roads that would connect the big cities along the Atlantic coast with the farming areas in the interior. Just as in Britain in the mid-eighteenth century, this effort manifested itself in the building of turnpikes. The construction of these toll roads was spearheaded not by the federal or state governments but by small businesses with less than 100,000 $ in capital. As these companies built an increasing number of short roads (often less than 20 miles in length), different areas were slowly linked together. Between the 1790s and 1830s, 11,000 miles of turnpikes were built in this manner, and 30 million dollars were invested in these projects.

The turnpikes were not very profitable, however, and they did little to reduce the cost of shipping. Neither did they lead to any major technological innovations (aside from making the surface of the road a little smoother), and investors made few profits because so many people were unwilling to pay the toll. Since the tolls were expensive as well, ranging between 12 and 17 cents per ton-mile, turnpikes were not financially feasible for long-distance transportation of freight [65].

Thus, a different shipping method was needed for cheap and bulky agricultural products and raw materials, and this method proved to be the canal. Canals were much more expensive and technically demanding to build than turnpikes. During the 1790s, a number of companies began small-scale canal construction projects, but they had trouble securing funds and had little to show for their efforts.

Nevertheless, interest in canals remained strong, particularly in the state of New York. The construction of the Pittsburgh Pike (linking Philadelphia to Pittsburgh) and the National Road (linking Baltimore to the Ohio Valley) around this time led to so much growth in Philadelphia and Baltimore that New York felt threatened. Confronted with stiff competition, the people of New York undertook a canal project in 1792 that was supposed to connect the Hudson River and Lake Ontario. 400,000 $ was sunk into the project, but the canal remained incomplete, and no more capital could be raised from the private sector. The lesson learned from this failure was that large-scale infrastructure projects like canals need government support.

The question was what organization should support such projects, and how it should fund them. Not only the Federalists but also the Republicans agreed on the need to build roads and canals. Even Jefferson, who believed that the American economy should be grounded in a combination of agricultural production and free trade, had expected that the federal government could invest its fiscal revenue in building roads and canals once it had settled its debt. In the *Report on Roads, Canals, Harbors, and Rivers* in 1808, Albert Gallatin, who was Treasury Secretary during the Jefferson administration, even proposed investing 25 million dollars from the federal budget in transportation building projects.

This plan was not put into effect, however, because Jefferson and the other Republican leaders were not sure whether Congress had the authority to carry out public works projects. During the debate with the Federalists in the 1790s, the Republicans had argued that the federal government could not exercise any powers that were not specifically mentioned in the Constitution. According to this logic, since canals and other public works projects did not appear in the Constitution, the government could not build them without amending the Constitution [66]. This logic doomed not only Gallatin's plan but also the Bonus Bill, which attempted to use the profits from the Second Bank of the United States (chartered in 1816) to build a transportation network [67].

Given the uncertainty of receiving federal aid, state governments eventually took on the canal construction projects themselves. The state that moved first was New York, which had shown an interest in canal building since the 1790s. With the backing of Governor DeWitt Clinton, the state began construction on the Erie Canal in 1817 and completed the project in 1825. The canal was a mammoth project in which more than 7 million dollars was invested. Three-fourths of the capital came from the market, and the rest was provided by the state government. Despite early concerns about profitability, the Erie Canal proved a great success. The canal had already generated 1 million dollars of revenue before construction was complete, and between 1826 and 1835, it was returning 8% of profit each year.

The success of the Erie Canal spawned rivals. In 1826, Philadelphia began work on the 395-mile Main Line Canal, which cost 12 million dollars, while the Chesapeake and Ohio Canal was built around the same time in the South. But these two canals were not nearly as profitable as the Erie Canal. The profit margin at the

Main Land Canal was not even one-fourth that of the Erie Canal because challenging terrain drove up the cost of construction, and the situation was not any better at the Chesapeake and Ohio Canal. However, the profits of these canals do not tell the full story of their economic benefits. After the construction of the canals, shipping costs fell dramatically. Shipping freight on the canal only cost 2 or 3 cents per ton-mile, compared to between 10 and 20 cents on a toll road. This led to a corresponding increase in freight transport.

The turnpikes and canals promoted the integration of the domestic market by linking farming areas in the interior with the cities of the east, in which trade and manufacturing were growing rapidly. But market integration was facilitated most of all by the railroad. Railroads could link other markets to areas where the terrain prevented canals from being built, and they connected the vast area west of the Appalachians with the commercial and industrial areas of the Northeast.

As soon as the commercial viability of the railroad was confirmed in Britain in the 1830s, railroads began to be laid in the United States. A total of 4509 km of railroads were added to the national railroad network in the 1840s, 14,434 km in the 1850s, and 49,002 km during the American Civil War. About two-thirds of these lines were laid in the North, indicating the correlation between the construction of the railroads and the growth of manufacturing. Until the 1820s, farmers accounted for 58% of the total workforce in Massachusetts, but this fell to 40% in the 1840s and even more sharply to 15% over the next 10 years. The California Gold Rush (triggered by the discovery of gold in California in 1848) coincided with the construction of the railroads, showing that the development of the transportation network had a major influence on industrialization and migration.

Until the Civil War, of course, railroads were still being used to transport passengers more than to move freight, and it was not until the postbellum period that the railroads began to contribute significantly to market integration. Even so, the potential of the railroad had been demonstrated, and as westward expansion picked up speed, demand increased for a transcontinental railroad [68].

The American Civil War: The Path to the System of Expansive Reproduction

We have already seen that an agricultural economy was firmly established in the South when the United States gained its independence and that this economy was subordinated to Britain's systems of expansive reinvestment and expansive reproduction. In the North, however, commercial and manufacturing interests had been steadily growing since colonial times on the fringes of Britain's system of expansive reinvestment.

From independence until the mid-nineteenth century, the divergent interests of the North and South provoked a dispute over the future of the American economy. Southerners believed that their economy was directly tied to the country's expansion as an agricultural empire and to the preservation and extension of the system of slavery on which agricultural production depended, and they were willing to secede from the union and even to fight a war to defend it.

But for the Northern manufacturers and merchants who sought to establish and develop the system of expansive reproduction, preserving the union was a matter of great importance. If the South were to secede from the union, the Southern economy (which already depended heavily upon the British market) would tilt even further toward Britain and might even be readmitted into the British Empire. In such an event, not even the North's safety could be assured. On an economic level, closer integration between the North and South was important for Northern manufacturers who supported the Industrial Revolution. In order to overtake Britain's industrial economy given its technological lead, these manufacturers needed a steady supply of raw materials and agricultural products from the farming areas in the United States, and they needed to secure a market for industrial products in those farming areas through tariffs and various other measures of protective trade.

Because the economic interests of the North and South were so incompatible, the tensions and disputes between the two regions were not resolved despite a series of compromises that began in the early nineteenth century and continued for several generations. In the end, it was this difficulty that drove the North and South to resolve their differences through the drastic measure of civil war.

Trade and shipping in the North had been growing since before independence, and they developed even faster after the fiscal and economic crises during the American War of Independence and the postwar period were resolved with the adoption of the Constitution in 1787, which made possible the economic prosperity of the 1790s. The end result was the establishment of the system of expansive reinvestment in the United States. In order for that system to develop into the system of expansive reproduction (as had happened in Britain, but not the Netherlands), the United States needed a powerful military and technological innovation in the supply sector. That was why the Federalists (who were in power in the 1790s) followed the lead of Alexander Hamilton by seeking to create a fiscal-military state modeled after Britain and to develop a manufacturing sector supported by federal policies. But these efforts were interrupted by the ascendancy of the Republicans, who emphasized the power of the states rather than the power of the federal government and who sought a republican system of government that depended more on yeoman farmers than on commerce and manufacturing.

But the Federalists' vision had not disappeared completely. Between the Embargo Act of 1809 and the War of 1812, the Republican Party's principles faced a formidable challenge. The Republicans had believed that the future of the American economy lay in a combination of agriculture and free trade, but this vision collided with Britain's overwhelming military and economic might. This lent support to the argument that true American economic independence required the development of the manufacturing sector and the growth of the domestic market. There was a widespread belief that the United States' economic development ultimately depended upon fostering domestic manufacturing and linking it to the rapidly expanding domestic market. Since the United States had become a commercial and industrial power after Britain, it could not immediately compete with British merchants and manufacturers in the global market. Such ideas found expression in the use of protective tariffs to shelter the manufacturing sector and in public works projects in the transportation sector that joined capital from the private sector with government support.

As can be seen in the dispute between the industrial North and the agricultural South that was provoked by the tariff debate, the United States' economic development caused severe regional rivalry. Developing the manufacturing sector and integrating the domestic market represented the Northern vision, and Southerners were doubtful as to whether this development was actually in their interests.

By the 1850s, the interests of the North and South had become nearly impossible to reconcile. The industrialization that had begun in the War of 1812 had been confined to the North, and especially in New England. The pace of industrialization accelerated in the 1840s, prompting specialization and the division of labor. Since the United States had abundant land and natural resources but a shortage of skilled workers, American manufacturers enthusiastically adopted machinery. They also simplified designs so they could supply cheap and uniform industrial goods to consumers in the country's rural areas and cities, since the gap between rich and poor was less pronounced in the United States than in Europe. In addition, American manufacturers began exploring a new system based on standardized production technology and interchangeable parts. This new production system, which came to be called the American system of manufacturing, emerged in the musket industry, which had been receiving government support. It improved overall productivity and enabled the American manufacturing sector to overtake Britain in that area [69].

The manufactured goods that were produced by the North's swiftly developing industrial sector were generally consumed in the North. The reason that construction projects on turnpikes, canals, and railroads moved forward much more quickly in the North than in the South was that much greater profits could be made in the North by effectively integrating the urban centers of industry with the farming areas in the interior. As grain cultivation that did not rely on slave labor spread quickly in the West, farming and manufacturing became even more interconnected. Because of this, Northern industry before the Civil War was able to grow rapidly even without depending heavily on overseas markets or the Southern market [70]. With the Northern economy thriving to such an extent, the immigrants flowing in from overseas became concentrated in the North, not the South, which caused the population gap between the North and South to gradually increase [71].

This does not mean that the Southern economy was stagnating, however. Industrialization was also occurring in the South, though not as fast as in the North. Per capita figures from just before the Civil War show that the South ranked second worldwide in railroad construction, sixth in cotton textile production, and eighth in pig iron production. And while the South lagged behind the Northeast in per capita income, Southerners were the fourth wealthiest people in the world [72].

The heart of the Southern economy, of course, was plantation agriculture based on slave labor. Catalyzed by the invention of the cotton gin (a machine for removing the seeds from raw cotton) in 1793 and the development of the Industrial Revolution in Britain, Southern cotton plantations grew at an astonishing rate. Cotton output on these plantations increased a thousandfold between 1790 and 1860. During the period of 1820–1860, cotton production grew by 1050% while the slave population only grew by 150%, showing that there was a major boost in the productivity of slave labor as well.

Cotton exports played an important role not only in the South but in the American economy as a whole. After the 1820s, cotton accounted for more than half of American exports. In 1860, cotton exports were worth 192 billion dollars, or more than four times the federal government's fiscal income. Indeed, Britain counted on the American South to supply between 70 and 80% of the raw materials for its cotton textile industry [73]. Viewed in this light, Southerners' claim that "cotton is king" does not sound so preposterous. It is also important to consider the 4 million Southern slaves producing cotton, tobacco, and other cash crops. The economic value of these slaves is estimated to have been about 3 billion dollars [74].

Since the North and South had not only developed in different directions but also both remained prosperous just before the war, their dispute about the federal government's economic policy and the future of the American economy inevitably grew even more intense. Back in the 1830s, when international demand for American cotton had declined, there were widespread concerns that cotton plantation agriculture, based as it was on expensive slave labor, was in decline, just as tobacco had been before it. It was also widely thought that Northern industries like cotton textiles and steel were growing under the protection of tariffs while the South was left to shoulder the higher costs that resulted from these tariffs. This situation lent strength to the position that the South should undertake a program of industrialization as the North had. Investment in railroads and other infrastructure increased, and business gatherings and the print media were used to promote investment in the manufacturing sector [75].

But when the terms of trade shifted in favor of the South in the 1840s and especially after global demand for cotton soared in the 1850s, the attitude of Southerners changed as well. They became increasingly confident that they could remain prosperous while avoiding the problems facing the North, including the social conflict resulting from rapid industrialization and the public health and environmental problems caused by excessive urbanization. As Senator James Henry Hammond observed, cotton had made the Southern economy the center of the global economy: "No, you dare not make war on cotton. No power on earth dares to make war upon it. Cotton is king. Until lately the Bank of England was king; but she tried to put her screws as usual, the fall before last, upon the cotton crop, and was utterly vanquished. The last power has been conquered. Who can doubt, that has looked at recent events, that cotton is supreme?" [76]

To summarize the preceding argument, the South's economic prosperity in the 1850s shows that the South managed to take advantage of Britain and the United States' advanced systems of expansive reinvestment and expansive reproduction while preserving the system of production in its own agricultural society. This made it possible for the South to develop in a way that further reinforced the old social order that had preceded commercialization and industrialization. As Northerners struggled with the chaos of class conflict, Southerners had some reason to take pride in the fact that they had preserved an organic community in which social authority based on the master-slave relationship was identical to political authority. In short, the South's agricultural economy had brought the Southern elite adequate economic power even without any radical social change [77].

The Northern economy was the antithesis of the Southern economy. The ideal future of the United States as Northerners conceived it was a society based on free labor and property. In such a society, all people were free laborers who owned the product of their labor and who could improve their social position through their effort. Southerners argued that industrialization had made the plight of Northern workers even worse than that of the Southern slaves, who lived under the paternalistic care of the planters, but the Northern elite did not see this as being a problem. Even if workers had a hard lot at present, the elites argued, they could easily escape their lot through effort and ability. Since the Northern elite valued free labor and social mobility, they thought there were inevitable and fundamental constraints on the development of Southern society. They pointed to the fact that wealth was concentrated in the hands of a few plantation owners and that slave labor could never coexist with free labor and social mobility. Without the powerful incentive of gaining exclusive ownership over the product of one's labor, there was little chance that productivity would improve or that labor would shift to new industrial sectors. Thus, the South could not escape from an agricultural economy in which production was bound to diminish [78].

The North and South's divergent economic interests and visions ultimately collided over the issue of the expansion of slavery [79]. At the time of the American War of Independence and the framing of the Constitution, America's political leaders already recognized that slavery was an issue that could not be resolved in the short term because of the sharply conflicting interests of the North and South. The compromise that those leaders reached (the Northwest Ordinance of 1787) was to prevent slavery from expanding to new areas and to allow it to naturally expire in the areas where it was then practiced. That seemed like a viable plan during the 1780s, when there was a slump in exports of tobacco and other cash crops that depended on slave labor.

But the introduction of cotton to new territories in the 1790s dispelled the notion that slavery would disappear on its own and demonstrated the urgency of preventing slavery from spreading. Introducing slavery to new territories would upset the political balance between the slave states and the free states and change the course of the federal government's economic policy. This issue was temporarily settled by the Missouri Compromise, which maintained a political balance between North and South by admitting the slave state of Missouri and the free state of Maine into the union and banned slavery above the parallel 36° 30′N. Until 1850, this balance was maintained, with 15 slave states and 15 free states.

But this balance was upset when the United States acquired California, Utah, and New Mexico through the Mexican War in 1848, raising the question of whether slavery would be allowed there. The debate over the spread of slavery led to the replacement of the Missouri Compromise with the Kansas–Nebraska Act in 1854 and the establishment of the principle of popular sovereignty, which meant that the citizens of states that were to be newly admitted to the union would be allowed to decide for themselves whether to allow slavery. The Supreme Court's ruling in the Dred Scott decision in 1857 that Congress did not have the power to ban slavery in new territories tilted the balance even further in favor of the slave states.

With the federal government no longer recognized as having the authority to stop the spread of slavery, Northerners felt a growing sense of panic. The abolitionists grew more strident in their calls for the end of slavery. They argued that preserving the union was meaningless so long as slavery endured. Even the numerous Northern political leaders who did not sympathize with this argument were deeply concerned that the North could not realize its potential for economic development if it was surrounded by slave states.

Indeed, the Northern elite tried to protect the domestic manufacturing industry from competition with Britain, to build a vast domestic market by expanding agriculture (through yeoman farmers) in the new territories, and to integrate this market by improving the transportation and communication networks, but their plans were frustrated again and again by Southern opposition. Because of the South's long opposition to protective tariffs, debate over the Tariff of 1857 led to an awkward compromise that failed to adequately protect the interests of the North and particularly of Pennsylvanian manufacturers. The Homestead Act of 1860 would have given pioneers 160 acres of land for no cost to expand the system of yeoman farming based on the idea of free labor, but this was vetoed by President James Buchanan under pressure from the South. The Pacific Railroad bill of 1860 would have given federal aid to a transcontinental railroad construction project aimed at linking the East and West Coast, but the bill was blocked by Southern legislators.

With these and other measures aimed at economic development scuttled by Southern opposition, an increasing number of Northerners concluded that they could not accomplish anything until the issue of Southern slavery had been resolved. This drove more Southerners to contemplate seceding from the union as a means of defending their interests from Northern abolitionists. With tensions running high, the presidential election of 1860 was won by Abraham Lincoln of the Republican Party, which spoke for Northern interests and ideology. This inflamed the conflict between the two sides and led ultimately to the American Civil War [80].

References

1. Youngsoo Bae, *Miguk Yeoeronui Daeaneul Chajaseo* [In Search of Alternatives to American Exceptionalism], (Ilchokak, 2011), chap. 12.
2. Niall Ferguson, *Colossus: The Rise and Fall of the American Empire* (New York, 2004), pp. 15, 18.

3. Robert Fogel, *Without Consent or Contract: The Rise and Fall of American Slavery* (New York, 1991), p. 102; Martin Daunton, *Wealth and Welfare: An Economic and Social History of Britain 1851–1951* (Oxford, 2007), p. 167.
4. Youngsoo Bae, *Miguk Yeoeronui Daeaneul Chajaseo* [In Search of Alternatives to American Exceptionalism], chap. 1.
5. Bernard Bailyn, *The Ideological Origins of the American Revolution*, enlarged ed. (Cambridge, Mass., 1992).
6. Karen Ordahl Kupperman, *The Jamestown Project* (Cambridge, Mass., 2007); Peter C. Mancall, *Hakluyt's Promise: An Elizabethan's Obsession for an English America* (New Haven, 2007).
7. Benjamin Franklin, *Observations Concerning the Increase of Mankind, Peopling of Countries, etc.* (Boston, 1751).
8. For population estimates, see David W. Galenson, "The Settlement and Growth of the Colonies: Population, Labor, and Economic Development," Stanley E. Engerman and Robert E. Gallman (eds.), *The Cambridge Economic History of the United States Vol. I: The Colonial Era* (Cambridge, 1996), p. 169; John J. McCusker and Russell R. Menard, *The Economy of British America 1607–1789* (Chapel Hill, NC, 1985), pp. 211–235; GNP increased from 22 million dollars in 1650 to 1.89 billion dollars in 1774 (based on constant 1980 prices). McCusker and Menard, *The Economy of British America*, pp. 53–57.
9. McCusker and Menard, *The Economy of British America*, p. 121, figure 6.1.
10. The Virginia Company initially adopted a system of renting laborers to planters on contracts that were renewable on a yearly basis, but it soon abandoned this because planters were overworking their laborers.
11. Stuart Bruchey, *Enterprise: The Dynamic Economy of a Free People* (Cambridge, Mass., 1991), p. 36.
12. By the second half of the seventeenth century, Barbados (where sugar plantations first began) had a population density of 250 people per square mile. This drove white workers to leave Barbados after their contracts ended in search of other settlements, inflicting a blow on the food and lumber sectors that had depended on their labor. This demand was what the colonists of the West Indies and North America had in mind when they settled in South Carolina.
13. McCusker and Menard, *The Economy of British America*, pp. 170–181.
14. Edward Johnson, *Johnson's Wonder-Working Providence, 1628–1651*, ed. J. Franklin Jameson (New York, 1910), p. 211; quoted in McCusker and Menard, *The Economy of British America*, p. 97.
15. McCusker and Menard, *The Economy of British America*, pp. 91–111, 318–321; Daniel Vickers, "The Northern Colonies: Economy and Society, 1600–1775," Engerman and Gallman, *The Cambridge Economic History of the United States Vol. I*, p. 232.
16. McCusker and Menard, *The Economy of British America*, pp. 189–208.
17. John J. McCusker, "British Mercantilist Policies and the American Colonies," Engerman and Gallman (eds.), *The Cambridge Economic History of the United States Vol. I*, pp. 337–362.
18. McCusker and Menard, *The Economy of British America*, pp. 80–86, especially Table 4.1 on p. 81.
19. For the Seven Years' War, see Fred Anderson, *Crucible of War: The Seven Years' War and the Fate of Empire in British North America, 1754–1766*. (New York, 2001).
20. During the Seven Years' War, Britons were paying 26 shillings in annual taxes per capita, while the American colonists were paying just 1 shilling. John Steele Gordon, *An Empire of Wealth: The Epic History of American Economic Power* (New York, 2004), p. 54; for trade between the colonies and the enemy, see Thomas M. Truxes, *Defying Empire: Trading with the Enemy in Colonial New York* (New Haven, 2008); William Pitt, who led Britain during the war, is widely thought to have advocated the colonists' rights, but he denounced the colonists' violations of the Navigation Acts. For more on this point, see Anderson, *Crucible of War*, pp. 520, 578–579.
21. For a description of the shift in Britain's policy toward its North American colonies in the 1760s, see Nancy F. Koehn, *The Power of Commerce: Economy and Governance in the First*

British Empire (Ithaca, 1994); Daeryoon Kim, "'Daepyo Eopsi Gwase Eopda' reul Neomeo: Jeguk Gyeongjee Gwanhan Nonjaeng, 1763–1783" [Beyond "No Taxation Without Representation": The Debate about the Imperial Economy, 1763–1783], *Korean Journal of British Studies* 19 (2008), 29–60.

22. For the non-importation and non-consumption campaigns, see T. H. Breen, *The Marketplace of Revolution: How Consumer Politics Shaped American Independence* (New York, 2004).
23. For the Currency Act, see Joseph A. Ernst, "The Currency Act Repeal Movement: A Study in Imperial Politics and Revolutionary Crisis," *William and Mary Quarterly*, 3rd ser., 25 (1968); for the views of the colonists about the Currency Act, the Stamp Act, and the alleged British plot to suppress their freedoms, see Bailyn, *The Ideological Origins of the American Revolution*, chap. 4.
24. Gordon S. Wood, *The American Revolution: A History* (London, 2002), pp. 74–75.
25. Wood, *The American Revolution*, pp. 72–86; Brendan Simms, *Three Victories and a Defeat: The Rise and Fall of the First British Empire* (New York, 2008), pp. 579–661.
26. For the colonies' financial situation during the war, see Ben Baack, "Forging a Nation State: The Continental Congress and the Financing of the War of American Independence," *Economic History Review*, new ser., 54 (2001), pp. 639–656.
27. McCusker and Menard, *The Economy of British America*, pp. 361–362. The severe trade imbalance resulting from decreasing exports was mitigated by foreign loans and the activity of privateers. Privateers seized 12,000 commercial ships whose cargo was worth 18 million pounds (ibid., pp. 362–363). The United States also received 10 million pounds of overseas loans and aid between 1777 and 1783, and the military expenditures of the British and French armies also helped redress the deficit.
28. McCusker and Menard, *The Economy of British America*, pp. 374–375. Given the rapid economic recovery that began in the early 1790s, the situation in the United States immediately after independence must have been even worse.
29. The toll on the South was particularly severe. American exports from 1791 to 1792 were still just 75% of the level from 1768 to 1772, but exports in the Middle States and New England had already returned to or surpassed prewar levels. As a consequence, the South's share of exports fell from 64% in 1770 to 48% in 1790, while its share of wealth fell from 46% in 1774 to 32% in 1789. David R. Meyer, *The Roots of American Industrialization* (Baltimore, 2003), pp. 15–16.
30. Between 1784 and 1789, the United States received 2.3 million dollars in loans from the Netherlands but only 1.9 million dollars in contributions from the various states, which illustrates the fiscal predicament of the central government. Richard Sylla, "Experimental Federalism: The Economics of American Government, 1789–1914," Stanley E. Engerman and Robert E. Gallman (eds.), *The Cambridge Economic History of the United States Vol. II: The Long Nineteenth Century* (Cambridge, 2000), p. 487.
31. Wood, *The American Revolution*, pp. 142–144; Cathy Matson, "The Revolution, the Constitution, and the New Nation," Engerman and Gallman (eds.), *The Cambridge Economic History of the United States Vol. I*, pp. 372–382.
32. Max M. Edling, *A Revolution in Favor of Government: Origins of the U.S. Constitution and the Making of the American State* (Oxford, 2003).
33. Sonia Mittal, Jack N. Rakove and Barry R. Weingast, "The Constitutional Choices of 1787 and Their Consequences," Douglas A. Irwin and Richard Sylla (eds.), *Founding Choices: American Economic Policy in the 1790s* (Chicago, 2011), pp. 39–41.
34. Mittal, Rakove and Weingast, "The Constitutional Choices of 1787 and Their Consequences," pp. 42–46.
35. Douglas A. Irwin, "Revenue or Reciprocity? Founding Feuds over Early U.S. Trade Policy," Irwin and Sylla (eds.), *Founding Choices*, pp. 99–100. During the 1790s, tariffs were a crucial part of the federal government's fiscal income. In 1792, for example, tariffs accounted for 3.4 million dollars of the federal government's total fiscal income of 3.7 million dollars. After Hamilton was appointed Secretary of the Treasury, the revenue that was collected by customs houses at major ports directly managed by the federal government increased by 600%

between 1792 and 1795, and the federal government's fiscal income (largely consisting of tariffs) also increased by 26% each year between 1790 and 1795. In regard to these points, see p. 101 in the same article as well as p. 73 in the following article, which appears in the same book: Sylla, "Financial Foundations: Public Credit, the National Bank, and Securities Markets."

36. The following discussion of Hamilton's reports is indebted to Gordon S. Wood, *Empire of Liberty: A History of the Early Republic, 1789–1815* (Oxford, 2009), pp. 95–103, and Stanley Elkins and Eric McKitrick, *The Age of Federalism: The Early American Republic, 1788–1800* (Oxford, 1993), pp. 114–131.
37. Requoted from Wood, *Empire of Liberty*, p. 100. The argument is that agricultural states cannot become powerful because economic growth decelerates and eventually stagnates.
38. The goal of the *Report on Manufactures* was to support the growth of new industries. Hamilton was not interested in supporting existing industries that were already competing directly with foreign countries, and so the report did not consider providing assistance to craftsmen or household manufacturers. Wood, *Empire of Liberty*, p. 102.
39. Sylla, "Financial Foundations: Public Credit, the National Bank, and Securities Markets," p. 85. Evidence for the boost in business activity can be found in the fact that more than 200 laws related to establishing corporations were passed in the 1790s. This is twice the number of laws that were passed in the 1780s; Pauline Maier, "The Revolutionary Origins of the American Corporation," *William and Mary Quarterly*, 3rd. ser., 50 (1993), p. 54.
40. For the trade deficit and exports as a share of GNP, see Robert E. Lipsey, "U.S. Foreign Trade and the Balance of Payments, 1800–1913," Engerman and Gallman (eds.), *Cambridge Economic History of the United States Vol. II*, pp. 685, 691, Table 15.3; for the significance of exports and particularly re-exports for economic growth, see Douglass C. North, *The Economic Growth of the United States 1790–1860* (New York, 1966), pp. 24–26, 43–45. The value of American trade increased from 43 million dollars in 1790 to 246 million dollars in 1807, while the total value of re-export trade during the Napoleonic Wars was 490 million dollars. Wood, *Empire of Liberty*, p. 623; similar figures can be found in Charles Sellers, *The Market Revolution: Jacksonian America, 1815–1846* (Oxford, 1991), pp. 22–23.
41. Around 1,500 American vessels were seized between 1803 and 1812, 917 of them by Britain and 558 by France. Wood, *Empire of Liberty*, p. 646.
42. Wood, *Empire of Liberty*, p. 655; Irwin, "Revenue or Reciprocity?" pp. 115–116.
43. For the Jeffersonian Republicans, see Elkins and McKitrick, *The Age of Federalism*, pp. 195–208 and *passim;* for Jefferson's criticism of Hamilton and the emergence of the Republican Party, see Wood, *Empire of Liberty*, pp. 140–173.
44. Drew McCoy, *The Elusive Republic: Political Economy in Jeffersonian America* (New York, 1980), p. 186.
45. Quotation found in Wood, *Empire of Liberty*, p. 641.
46. Wood, *Empire of Liberty*, p. 357; McCoy, *Elusive Republic*, pp. 185–208.
47. In contrast with the huge amount of money spent on the Louisiana Purchase, the size of the federal government was greatly reduced under the Jefferson administration. Aside from Congress and officers in the military, there were just 153 employees in government ministries in Washington immediately after Jefferson took office; even in 1829, there were only 352. Sellers, *The Market Revolution*, pp. 36–37.
48. Wood, *Empire of Liberty*, p. 674. American privateers, on the other hands, were quite active. Between 1812 and 1813, they took no fewer than 500 vessels as prizes.
49. On the progress of the war, see Wood, *Empire of Liberty*, pp. 659–700. For Americans who wanted to incorporate Canada and Florida into the union and free themselves completely from the influence of Britain, the outcome of the War of 1812 was an obvious disappointment. They received some consolation, however, from the victory of American troops under Andrew Jackson in the Battle of New Orleans, which was the hardest-fought battle of the war. Thanks to this victory, which restored Americans' flagging pride, Jackson was transformed into an American hero, which would serve as the springboard to his later ascent to

leadership. For Jackson's victory, see Daniel Walker Howe, *What Hath God Wrought: The Transformation of America, 1815–1848* (Oxford, 2007), pp. 8–18.
50. Wood, *Empire of Liberty*, p. 689; Lipsey, "U.S. Foreign Trade and the Balance of Payments," p. 723.
51. See the sources quoted in note 15.
52. McCusker and Menard, *The Economy of British America*, p. 363.
53. As we have already mentioned, Hamilton's report was focused on the development not of existing industries but of new industries. While most of the tariffs that Hamilton proposed in the report were implemented, the rate of the tariffs was set low for fear of a clash with Britain over trade. Thus, the tariffs did not help protect infant industries in the short term. For more on this, see Douglas A. Irwin, "The Aftermath of Hamilton's 'Report on Manufacture,'" *Journal of Economic History* 64 (2004), pp. 800–821.
54. Meyer, *The Roots of American Industrialization*, pp. 15–54.
55. It took about 20 days of work for one adult woman to produce one pound of cotton yarn from raw cotton. The problem was that raw cotton was much trickier to handle than wool or linen. Gordon, *Empire of Wealth*, p. 88.
56. Wood, *Empire of Liberty*, p. 702; Meyer, *The Roots of American Industrialization*, pp. 96–111.
57. Bruchey, *Enterprise*, pp. 151–153; Meyer, *The Roots of American Industrialization*, pp. 113–119; Robert F. Dalzell, Jr., *Enterprising Elite: The Boston Associates and the World They Made* (Cambridge, Mass., 1987), pp. 26–44.
58. Imports from Britain were worth 85 million dollars in 1815 and increased to 151 million dollars the following year. Americans suspected that British merchants were dumping their products. Maurice G. Baxter, *Henry Clay and the American System* (Lexington, KY, 1995), p. 18.
59. Madison also apparently sympathized with this cause. During the first session of the 14th Congress (1815–1816), he asked Congress to find a way to support and promote the manufacturing industry that had arisen throughout the country during the European wars and had achieved an unprecedented degree of maturity. Baxter, *Henry Clay and the American System*, p. 19.
60. Sellers, *The Market Revolution*, p. 75; Peter Temin, "The Industrialization of New England, 1830–1880," Temin (ed.), *Engines of Enterprise: An Economic History of New England* (Cambridge, Mass., 2000), pp. 113–114; Jeremy Atack and Peter Passell, *A New Economic View of American History*, 2nd ed. (New York, 1994), p. 130. Under the protection of the tariff, the American cotton textile industry enjoyed rapid growth. In 1807, for example, there were about 8,000 spindles in operation at 15 to 20 companies, but in 1810, there were about 80,000 spindles at 87 companies. By 1831, this had increased to 1.25 million spindles. New England's cotton textile production increased from 4 million yards in 1817 to 323 million yards in 1840; Bruchey, *Enterprise*, p. 149.
61. Sellers, *The Market Revolution*, pp. 148–149, 272–273, 295–296, 316, 319–320, 330–331, 412; Howe, *What Hath God Wrought*, pp. 272–274, 407–408; Baxter, *Henry Clay*, pp. 21–33.
62. Paul A. David, "Learning by Doing and Tariff Protection: A Reconsideration of the Case of the Antebellum United States Cotton Textile Industry," *Journal of Economic History* 30 (1970). The disparity between the American and British cotton textile industries was caused not by a difference in fixed capital investment but rather by a difference in workmanship, which is hard to measure through factor input alone. This was a disparity that could only be overcome by enabling workers to accumulate experience in the field. Tariffs bought the American cotton textile industry enough time to do this. For more on this debate, see Atack and Passell, *A New Economic View of American History*, p. 130.
63. Baxter, *Henry Clay and the American System*, pp. 16–33.
64. Sellers, *The Market Revolution*, p. 132.
65. Albert Fishlow, "Internal Transportation in the Nineteenth and Early Twentieth Centuries," Engerman and Gallman (eds.), *The Cambridge Economic History of the United States Vol. II*, pp. 550–551.

66. In the debate about the establishment of the Bank of the United States, the Federalists and Republicans were divided in their interpretation of Article 1, Section 8, of the Constitution. The Federalists argued that this section—which gives Congress the power to make all laws that are "necessary and proper" for executing the powers listed in the Constitution—gave Congress broad discretion in all areas related to economic regulation and fiscal policy. The Republicans, on the other hand, argued that it was unconstitutional to exercise powers not mentioned in the Constitution, in accordance with the principle of strict construction.
67. Wood, *Empire of Liberty*, pp. 484–485; John Lauritz Larson, "'Bind the Republic Together': The National Union and the Struggle for a System of Internal Improvements," *Journal of American History* 74 (1987), pp. 363–387. As a consequence, while the federal government spent 60 million dollars on projects to improve the transportation network between 1790 and 1860, state and local governments spent 450 million dollars on such projects; John Joseph Wallis, "The Other Foundings: Federalism and the Constitutional Structure of American Government," Irwin and Sylla (eds.), *Founding Choices*, p. 183.
68. Atack and Passell, *A New Economic View of American History*, p. 178; Bruchey, *Enterprise*, pp. 268–270.
69. David A. Hounshell, *From the American System to Mass Production, 1800–1932: The Development of Manufacturing Technology in the United States* (Baltimore, 1984); for relative changes in the productivity of the United States, Britain, and Germany, see Stephen Broadberry, "How Did the United States and Germany Overtake Britain? A Sectoral Analysis of Comparative Productivity Levels, 1870–1990," *Journal of Economic History* 58 (1998), pp. 375–407. According to Broadberry, the productivity of the American manufacturing sector was 80% higher than that of the British manufacturing sector in the period from 1869 to 1871 (Table 1 on p. 378).
70. Meyer, *Roots of American Industrialization*, pp. 281–284.
71. Looking at how the share of the total American population in the two regions changed over time, 63% of Americans lived in the North and 37% in the South in 1840, while 65% lived in the North and 33% in the South in 1860. Robert E. Gallman, "Economic Growth and Structural Change in the Long Nineteenth Century," Engerman and Gallman (eds.), *The Cambridge Economic History of the United States Vol II*, p. 52, Table 1.15.
72. Fogel, *Without Consent or Contract*, p. 102.
73. Jonathan Hughes and Louis P. Cain, *American Economic History*, 6th ed. (New York, 2003), pp. 169, 170; North, *Economic Growth of the United States*, p. 233.
74. For a discussion of the phrase "cotton is king," see James McPherson, *Battle Cry of Freedom: The Civil War Era* (Oxford, 1988), pp. 100, 195–196; in 1860, the slaves were worth around 2.7 billion dollars, an amount that was equivalent to three times the capital invested in the entire American manufacturing industry. Freeing the slaves would have meant a 23% reduction in the per capita income of whites in the 11 states that produced cotton through slave labor. That is why Southerners could have seen abolitionism as a threat to their property rights. Roger L. Ransom and Richard Sutch, *One Kind of Freedom* (New York, 1977), Table 3; Atack and Passell, *A New Economic View of American History*, pp. 356–358.
75. McPherson, *Battle Cry of Freedom*, pp. 94–100.
76. Requoted from Fogel, *Without Consent or Contract*, p. 107.
77. McPherson, *Battle Cry of Freedom*, p. 100.
78. Eric Foner, *Free Soil, Free Labor, Free Men: The Ideology of the Republican Party Before the Civil War* (Oxford, 1970).
79. The following discussion draws upon McPherson, *Battle Cry of Freedom*, and David M. Potter, *The Impending Crisis: America Before the Civil War 1848–1861* (New York, 1976).
80. In addition to the sources cited in note 79, see Marc Egnal, "The Beards Were Right: Parties in the North, 1840–1860," *Civil War History* 47 (2001), pp. 30–56, and Richard F. Bensel, *Yankee Leviathan: The Origins of Central State Authority in America, 1859–1877* (New York, 1991).

Chapter 7
The Maturity of American Industrial Society

In Chap. 6, we examined how the American economy developed between the colonial period and the Civil War with a focus on the transition from the system of expansive reinvestment to the system of expansive reproduction. Given that there was more land than labor in the United States, it may have been inevitable for the American economy to specialize in agriculture both during the colonial period and for a long time afterward. But unlike the Spanish Empire before it, the American economy overcame the limitations of decelerating growth (resulting from the diminishing production that is characteristic of agricultural society) and successfully transitioned first to a system of expansive reinvestment and then to a system of expansive reproduction.

Two factors were the most important drivers behind this success. First, the American colonies served as a source of agricultural products and raw materials for Britain's advanced system of expansive reinvestment. This promoted the development of commercial interests in the colonies and enabled the system of expansive reinvestment to develop in the American economy at an early period. Second, even though American politics after independence was dominated by the Republican Party, which aimed to create a republic of yeoman farmers, support gradually increased for the view that American commerce and industry would have to be developed if the United States was to survive the challenges of the international system. This view, which was largely espoused by Northern commercial and industrial interests, helped to justify the policies of the federal government and of several state governments that were aimed at protecting industry and expanding social infrastructure.

Even in the mid-nineteenth century, of course, agriculture was a strong presence in the United States—especially the Southern planters who sought to profit from global free trade. Therefore, we can say that the United States of the time had the

T.-Y. Kim and D. Kim, *The Secrets of Hegemony*,
DOI 10.1007/978-981-10-4416-8_7

unique potential to become an agricultural empire, a commercial empire, and an industrial empire. Precisely for that reason, the direction of the American economy remained uncertain.

Southern planters who were adamantly opposed to giving up slavery proclaimed the superiority of agriculture and of free trade and were sharply opposed, both ideologically and politically, to the Northern values of free labor, protected trade, and the development of the domestic manufacturing industry. The conflict between the two regions meant that infrastructure expansion (including turnpikes, canals, and railroads) mostly occurred in the Northeast and the Midwest, which made the integration of the domestic market a distant prospect. It was amid such tensions that the American Civil War broke out.

The Civil War proved to be the decisive period in which the American system of expansive reproduction, which had been gradually taking shape since the early nineteenth century, at last transcended the ideological and political division between North and South and began to develop in earnest. By increasing the power of the federal government, the war laid the political foundation for a unified domestic market. The war also made possible the construction of national transportation and communication networks and the development of a mass production system in the manufacturing sector.

The modern corporation, which was created as part of this process, led the growth of productive capacity and productivity that was part of the Second Industrial Revolution. This helped the United States become the world's leader in industrial production on the eve of World War I. During the war and through the 1920s, the United States experienced another leap in productivity but soon plunged into the disaster known as the Great Depression. As the financial crisis spread around the world and effective demand plummeted, the United States' lead in industrial production actually caused the depression to last there longer than in any other country. It was not able to emerge from this depression until it fought yet another world war.

During two world wars and one depression, the American elite came to believe that the American system of expansive reproduction could not continue to develop unless the free market system was adopted throughout the world. This shift of attitudes led the United States to spearhead international systems of currency and trade epitomized by the Bretton Woods agreement and the General Agreement on Tariffs and Trade (GATT) and to lay the groundwork for the postwar economic boom by supporting the reconstruction of Europe and Japan. This resulted in the appearance of a new system that we will call the global system of expansive reproduction. With these facts in mind, this chapter will examine the American developmental path, which leads from the maturity of the American system of expansive reproduction in the mid-nineteenth century to the emergence of the global system of expansive reproduction in the mid-twentieth century.

The Economic Consequences of the American Civil War

The American Civil War caused horrendous property damage and loss of life in both North and South. The war dead numbered around 600,000, which amounted to 9% of the male population between the ages of 15 and 39. The economic value of the casualties amounted to at least 1.8 billion dollars. The cost of waging the war was enormous as well. Altogether, the North and South poured 6.7 billion dollars into the war, which was twice the total value of American exports between 1850 and 1860 and twice the national income in 1860 [1].

While the fiscal expenditures of the Union government in the North increased by a factor of 20 between 1860 and 1865 as it raised funds to cover the astronomical cost of the war, tax receipts only increased by a factor of five to nine. This caused the fiscal deficit to balloon. To fund the war, the Union government issued bonds with a low face value and urged a wide spectrum of the public to buy the bonds.

When regional banks (especially banks in New York) suspended specie payments, creating the risk of an economic contraction, the Union began printing large amounts of bills, called greenbacks, and established a central bank that prevented regional banks from issuing banknotes. Even so, the supply of currency more than doubled during the war. To prevent extreme inflation, the Union used taxation to increase the amount of wealth being transferred to the government, causing demand to drop in the private sector. This made it possible for the Union to avoid the worst of the inflationary crisis [2].

The Confederate government in the South was facing an even worse financial predicament. While the North was able to cover 20% of its wartime expenses through tax receipts, the South only managed to cover 12% of its expenses through taxes. The problem was the severe contraction in economic activity resulting from the Union navy's blockade of Southern ports and the battles constantly being fought in Confederate territory. Making matters worse, the Confederate government did not implement a strict monetary policy, which allowed an indiscriminate increase in the supply of currency and led to severe inflation. In the North, prices doubled or tripled, but in the South, they multiplied 92 times. Confronted with these difficulties, the Confederacy had no choice but to adopt economic regulations in the manner of a central government, despite its commitment to the autonomy of the state governments. The Confederate government confiscated Northerners' assets, explored price controls, and even set up its own manufacturers to provide supplies needed for the war [3].

The war ended with the South's defeat, of course, an outcome that was ultimately decided by the economic disparity between North and South. Southerners' greatest fear became a reality in 1863 with the Emancipation Proclamation, which freed the slaves without providing any kind of compensation to former slaveholders. The legal end of slavery in the United States came in 1864, as Congress passed a constitutional amendment granting suffrage to blacks.

The economic consequences of the Civil War have long been a vexed subject. The traditional view has emphasized that the war expanded the influence of

Northern industrial capital [4]. More recently, scholars have drawn attention to the absence of obvious differences in macroeconomic indicators such as GNP and industrial output before and after the war. According to these scholars, economic growth ebbed during the war, and even when the postwar recovery neared completion, economic growth did not obviously accelerate [5].

The United States' economic growth rate did in fact slow noticeably during the Civil War. The average yearly growth rate of GNP was between 1.51 and 1.87% from the 1830s until 1859, just before the war, but this fell to 0.46% between 1859 and 1869 [6]. Given the interruption of immigration and the loss of life caused by the war, it may have been inevitable that the growth rate would fall. Nor should we assume that there was a major increase in manufacturing production during the war. The production of individual firearms, to take one example, only accounted for 1% of iron production during the war [7]. It helps to recall that the Civil War was not a mechanized war waged with mass-produced munitions (as the world wars of the twentieth century would be), but rather the "last pre-industrial war," fought by soldiers bearing muskets and sabers.

However, the economic consequences of the Civil War cannot be inferred from quantitative indicators alone. Since long-term economic growth trends are determined by the characteristics of economic systems (a recurring theme in this book), the economic significance of the Civil War must also be evaluated by examining its influence on the characteristics of the American economic system. This is a point on which Charles Beard's classical interpretation merits further elaboration. One point to remember here is that American industrialization (concentrated in the Northeast and Midwest) proceeded at an even faster pace after the war and that the South was also integrated into the American economy, becoming part of the national market.

In the end, the most important legacy of the war was the preservation of the union, which ultimately made it possible for integration to begin from above, grounded in linguistic, religious, and cultural homogeneity. It was also significant that the federal government came under the control of the Republican Party, then based in the North, since the Republicans believed that the nation's future depended on developing the system of expansive reproduction. The Republicans continued to dominate the federal government until Woodrow Wilson became president just before World War I, and they were able to use their political power to create a favorable political environment for protectionism, improvements to the transportation and communication networks, and the emergence of modern corporations [8].

Bearing these facts in mind is important if we are to understand the path of the United States' economic development. Immediately after the Civil War, Britain maintained a firm grip on its position as the world's top producer of manufactured goods, and there seemed to be little chance of American industry triumphing over its competitors in the global market. This is what made it necessary to protect infant industries with tariffs and other trade barriers and to increase the speed of industrialization by expanding the domestic market instead of competing in the overseas market.

To be sure, the observation that a protectionist trade policy and innovations in transportation and communication laid the groundwork for the development of a system of expansive reproduction could just as easily be made about Britain. That said, one advantage that was unique to the United States was the vast domestic market created by national integration, a market that was much bigger than that of any other country. Focusing on this advantage can lead to facile conclusions about American exceptionalism. If the federal government had not adopted appropriate industrial policies that exploited those exceptional conditions, however, economic development could not have occurred. On this point at least, there is no fundamental difference between the successful establishment of the system of expansive reproduction in the United States and in Britain. This is why careful thinking is required to identify the specific developmental process in a general type, as well as the general type in a specific developmental process.

There can be no doubt of the economic effect of the protectionist policies and improvements of the transportation and communication networks that were consciously pursued by the American political elite. Agriculture continued to be the largest sector in the American economy even after the Civil War, but the manufacturing sector made up a rapidly increasing share of the economy. Between 1869 (when the United States finished rebuilding after the war) and 1899, industry's share of GNP grew from 24 to 33%, and the number of workers employed per place of business in the manufacturing sector had doubled by 1890.

The growth in the American domestic manufacturing sector brought changes to the composition of trade. In 1869, 14% of manufactured goods consumed in the United States were imported, but by 1909, this had fallen to 6%. In all areas of the manufacturing sector in which imports had accounted for at least 10% of consumption in 1869, the share of imports had decreased by more than half by 1909. The import substitution effect was even more noticeable in the iron and steel industries, in which the share of imports fell from 12 to 1.25% during the same period [9].

Development of the System of Mass Production

From the end of the American Civil War until World War I, American economic development was driven by growth in the manufacturing sector. While the growth of the American manufacturing sector during this period resulted from various factors, it is undeniable that the most important factor behind this growth was changes in the systems of production and distribution.

As we have previously mentioned, such changes also involved a qualitative aspect that cannot be assessed through quantitative indicators alone. The American economy underwent several crises around this time—most notably, the great depression of the late nineteenth century—that were characterized by continuously falling prices and profits (particularly in the agricultural sector). These crises spurred critical qualitative changes in the manufacturing and service sectors—including the combination of mass production and mass distribution, increased corporate investment in R&D, changes in corporate organization, and changes in control over the labor process. It was these changes that provided the impetus for growth and development.

The most important factor enabling these qualitative changes was the United States' immense size and the technological advances that integrated a sprawling nation into a single market. Since the time of Jefferson, the Republicans had the ambition of building an agricultural empire through territorial expansion. By converting this ambition into government policy, they managed to expand the United States to twice its size at independence. It was the construction of the railroad and telegraph networks that turned such a vast country into an integrated market.

In fact, the United States' railroad network was already the most advanced in the world even before the Civil War. There were 48,000 km of railroads in the country during the 1860s, which represented half the tracks that had been built in the entire world. But this does not even compare in scale or significance to the railroad boom that lasted from the end of the Civil War until the early 1890s. American railroads expanded rapidly during three concentrated bursts of construction: from 1868 to 1873, from 1879 to 1883, and from 1886 to 1892. The railroad network grew to 83,000 km in the 1870s, 149,000 km in the 1880s, 260,000 km in the 1890s, and 390,000 km in the 1900s [10].

The effect that railroad construction had on industrialization is well-known. In Britain, as we have already seen, the Industrial Revolution received an early impetus from ongoing projects to improve the canals, turnpikes, and waterways even before the railroads were built. But in the late industrializing countries that were emulating Britain, industrialization can be described, without hyperbole, as the story of railroad construction. Railroad construction was essential for market integration, which produced a domestic market capable of supporting a mechanized production system. Associated industries such as coal, iron, machinery, and electricity developed along with the railroad, reflecting the synergy that drove the growth of the entire manufacturing industry. Furthermore, railroad construction led to the development of the financial sector, including investment banks, which helped raise the funds necessary for construction [11].

In contrast with the countries on the European continent, industrialization had begun in the United States before the construction of the railroads, largely in New England and the states of New York and Pennsylvania. Various state governments were actively involved in building canals and turnpikes, as we saw with the Erie Canal. Despite a certain degree of similarity in developments in the United States and in Britain, the rapid expansion westward that occurred in the United States meant that an integrated market could not be created through canals and turnpikes alone as had happened in the much smaller country of Britain. The solution was to build a transcontinental network of railroads, but railroad construction could not move forward very quickly because of the longstanding tension between the federal government and the state governments, which was compounded by the conflict between the North and South. Such obstacles were cleared away by the Civil War, creating a perfect opportunity to extend a single market across the entire country [12].

By unifying and expanding the domestic market, the railroad contributed directly to the emergence of the modern corporation. The expansion of the market spurred the establishment of new manufacturing firms and encouraged market competition, leading to corporate investment in facilities and to the reorganization of the systems of production and distribution. The railroad companies themselves were huge corporations that would later pioneer changes in corporate organization.

There had been huge companies employing thousands of workers in Britain and the United States prior to this, of course, such as the Woolwich Dockyard and other manufacturers of war materials. But it was from the railroad companies that a new type of company began to emerge—companies that hired large number of workers and organized them into several stratified and specialized departments. Not only was more capital invested in the railroad companies than in previous companies, but an elaborate managerial hierarchy was required to maintain smooth operations throughout the railroad network. Given the high risk of accidents on American railroads in the mid-nineteenth century (when trains used the single-track system), railroad companies had to accurately plan and monitor train schedules according to information coming in over the telegraph wires, and they also had to manage a complicated pricing system that varied with the lines and the customers.

The railroad companies also needed a systematic way to manage their massive workforce (they employed about 5% of the total workforce in 1900), and they needed finance and accounting departments to handle the massive sums of invested capital and operating funds. The railroad companies were thus organized into a variety of departments, forming a hierarchy that stretched from the CEO to the lowest manager. There was a particular increase in the number of middle managers, the people responsible for day-to-day operations. In this sense, railroad companies were a precursor of the modern corporation [13].

The development of the railroads also had a major impact on the development of the capital market. A railroad company required an immense amount of invested capital. This capital, of course, largely came from investors in Britain and other European countries. During the mid-nineteenth century, Europeans were investing between 30 and 40 million dollars a year in American railroad companies. As a consequence, foreign investors' equity in American railroads reached 390 million dollars in 1874, while foreigners' stake in the major American railroad companies ranged from 50 to 75% in the early 1890s [14].

Raising capital on such a large scale required financial companies that could bring investment opportunities to the attention of foreign investors and could broker capital transactions, and this demand stimulated the development of the American financial industry. A number of measures were adopted to mitigate the risk of investing in new railroad companies and to gain investors' confidence. These measures included adopting the limited liability system, having the government set maximum and minimum interest rates to prevent excessive competition between railroad companies, and issuing preferred stock, which simultaneously had the characteristics of stocks and bonds. These measures, along with the American financial companies that emerged as a result of investment in railroad companies, contributed to the formation not only of the railroad industry but also of new corporations that required large amounts of capital [15].

In the 1880s, the American railroad network not only included the trunk lines that linked major cities around the continent but also belt lines and branch lines that were connected to the major roads. Once the entire country was connected with such a swift and reliable transportation network, the first innovation appeared in the distribution sector. The railroads made it possible for products shipped by manufacturers around the entire country to be delivered quickly and cheaply to the final consumer. In order to take advantage of this, however, companies had to distribute products on a scale large enough to secure discounts and other preferential treatment from railroad companies.

This demand was satisfied in a number of ways. New retail stores were built to satisfy mass consumer demand in densely populated cities, such as the department stores that appeared in major cities such as New York in the second half of the nineteenth century. Mail order and chain stores were also developed as ways of distributing mass-produced goods to consumers in the suburbs, towns, and even the countryside.

The development of the mass distribution sector brought about not only organizational development but also technological development in the distribution sector as a whole. In fact, the food processing industry (and particularly the meat processing industry, which was the origin of the integrated production system) pioneered the development of refrigeration technology such as refrigerator rail cars and food packing technology such as canning in an effort to achieve the economies of scale that mass distribution made possible [16]. To be sure, mass distribution and the market expansion made possible by the development of the railroad network were not the only factors driving profits. Indeed, they would not have been possible without the development of the production sector. That is to say, mass distribution went hand in hand with mass production. Thus, market expansion and mass distribution stimulated the development of the manufacturing sector.

The area in which the United States had long enjoyed a complete comparative advantage was agriculture, but there were constraints on how quickly the volume of agricultural production and distribution could be increased. Since there were basic biological constraints on when crops could be grown and how long they took to grow, the benefits resulting from continuous and rapid technological development were more limited in agriculture than in the manufacturing sector. This was true even when chemical fertilizer and farming equipment were adopted and when production units expanded on a large scale. To be sure, the food processing industry (including tobacco, whiskey, grain, and sugar) developed rapidly as a result of the distribution revolution in the second half of the nineteenth century. For the most part, though, the economies of scale made possible by mass production materialized in large-scale, capital-intensive heavy industries such as chemicals, steel, electricity, and machines [17].

The American system of mass production had several noteworthy characteristics. First, it developed in tandem with the spread of the factory system and the expansion of mechanization. We have already mentioned how industrialists responded to the American shortage of labor relative to natural resources by developing the American system of manufacturing, or the practice of manufacturing products on a large scale with standardized, interchangeable parts made by machine. Though this system was developed before the Civil War, mechanization did not really begin until the second half of the nineteenth century [18].

Second, the American system of mass production was resource-intensive and capital-intensive, based on the country's abundant natural resources. Although a plentiful supply of lumber in the United States caused the steam engine to be adopted there later than in Britain, the United States had become one of the world's leading producers of coal by the end of the nineteenth century. Furthermore, natural resources such as iron ore, copper, and petroleum were available for exploitation in several sectors of heavy industry. Furthermore, the producer goods and intermediate goods made by heavy industry also contributed to the development of the system of mass production in the consumer goods industry [19]. Thus, the great motive force provided by American's abundant coal and petroleum helped accelerate the adoption of machinery, increase the speed of machinery, and usher in a production system consisting of a series of uniform manufacturing processes. As a result, the utilization of capital and resources was much more important than the labor input in the American production system.

These two characteristics dovetail with the third characteristic of the American system of mass production, namely the transfer of control of the labor process to management. In order to ensure the smooth operation of a mechanized continuous production system and to maximize the profits derived from technological innovation, it was necessary to increase the speed and efficiency of production. This could be done by segmenting the manufacturing processes and introducing specialized power machines and tools into each of these processes.

But this provoked resistance from workers, and skilled workers in particular. There had been a long tradition of manual production in the United States, just as in Britain, and even after the factory system was introduced, skilled workers retained control of the labor process. Skilled workers considered the high wages and social status that their skills brought them as their most important assets, and to preserve those assets they organized strikes and other group actions. The periodic drops in prices and profits that began in the 1870s stoked the conflict between industrialists, who wanted to achieve economies of scale through the system of mass production, and workers, who wanted to preserve control of the labor process.

One attempt to resolve this dilemma was the theory of scientific management, advocated by Frederick W. Taylor and for that reason also called Taylorism. Scientific management, which is famous for its time and motion studies, called for the extreme segmentation of the labor process. After measuring the time and energy that workers needed to carry out each step of a given manufacturing process, companies calculated a standard output for each step and paid extra to workers who exceeded the standard output. This theory was perfected during experiments at Bethlehem Steel between 1898 and 1900, and it was widely promoted through various publications and societies. Taylorism was not often implemented strictly, of course, because of resistance from workers and skepticism on the part of managers, but scientific management symbolizes how control of the labor process was gradually shifting from skilled workers to managers. Because of the emergence of Taylorism, a consensus formed about the importance of management and consequently of the role that managers should play [20].

The fact that the American system of mass production began to develop after the Civil War can be deduced from changes in the average amount of capital invested in manufacturing companies, which increased from 4300 dollars in 1850 to 8400 dollars in 1870 and to 18,400 dollars in 1890 [21]. These figures show that the production units at manufacturing firms were increasing, but they do not show that the modern corporation had arrived on the scene. Big business began to appear in the 1890s, as companies responded to the Panic of 1893 by investing in cost-cutting measures and simultaneously carrying out mergers and acquisitions in order to limit competition.

In their efforts to reduce costs, companies of the time attempted on the one hand to implement scientific management by segmenting the labor process and speeding up machinery operation and on the other hand to achieve economies of scale and scope through vertical and horizontal integration. With economies of scale, companies attempted to use vertical integration (that is, having the company take over the entire production process, from acquiring raw materials to distributing the final product) to reduce the per-unit production cost. With economies of scope, they attempted to use horizontal integration (that is, pursuing a diverse line of products and acquiring or merging with companies that make the same kind of products) to profit from concentrated production and to control the market by limiting competition.

Horizontal integration was applied in the production and distribution of consumable goods such as tobacco and canned goods, durable consumer goods such as sewing machines and bicycles, and producer goods such as steel. In the area of consumer goods, producers implemented new techniques such as packaging, branding, and advertising. Since the 1880s, a substantial amount of horizontal integration had already been taking place, particularly in heavy industries such as steel. After the Panic of 1893, horizontal integration began to accelerate through mergers and acquisitions, leading to the formation of massive trusts such as Standard Oil and US Steel [22].

The conglomerates created through vertical and horizontal integration did not lead to monopolies. The "visible hand" of market control did give big business a way to limit competition and temporarily enjoy monopoly profits. But such profits could not be long maintained without continual innovation in the areas of technology and corporate organization. In fact, numerous conglomerates declined and failed, and the ones that survived had to innovate in order to fend off the challengers that were constantly entering the market. Furthermore, the Sherman Antitrust Act, which Congress passed in 1890, created a legal environment that prevented monopolies from controlling the market.

As a consequence, corporate competition in the United States became oligopolistic, with two or three powerful firms fighting for control of a specific sector of the market. In order to survive amid this ruthless competition, companies had to continuously invest in manufacturing, marketing, and the managers to supervise them—which Alfred D. Chandler, Jr., a leading scholar of business history, described as "three-pronged investment." This was the only way in which corporations could simultaneously achieve economies of scale by effectively operating large-scale productive facilities and economies of scope by diversifying product lines that could share manufacturing processes and intermediate goods [23].

Thus, the emergence of the conglomerate did not hinder competition but rather promoted it, forcing American companies to constantly engage in "three-pronged investment" and improve their organizational capabilities. This ultimately served to further accelerate the development of the American system of expansive reproduction. Amid such competition, American corporations eagerly explored new raw materials, manufacturing processes, machines, and products while continuing to pursue technological innovation, which ultimately sustained the virtuous cycle of the system of expansive reproduction.

Technological innovation did not only occur in big business, of course. As we have already seen in the chapters about Britain, technological development in Britain during the Industrial Revolution relied on experimental tinkering by untold numbers of craft workers, entrepreneurs, and amateur inventors. Starting in the mid-nineteenth century, technological advancement in the United States was also aided by the efforts of such inventors. Professional inventors like Thomas Edison frequently released new inventions as they devoted themselves not to specific areas but to industry as a whole. Thanks to their efforts, American industrial technology in the late nineteenth century was the most advanced in the world. This was the bedrock on which major American corporations built their own research institutes in the late nineteenth century, and they began to invest large amounts of capital into research at those institutes. This brought an end to the age of freewheeling and creative individual inventors, and R&D at corporations and universities began to make the United States' technological edge even more tangible [24].

During the final quarter of the nineteenth century, American big business placed the country's system of expansive reproduction on the basis of mass production and mass distribution. The social conflict that ensued was likely inevitable. As the popularity of the contemporary term "robber baron" suggests, most Americans of the time believed that the industrialists who ran the trusts were too preoccupied with lining their own pockets to remember their responsibility to society. They also believed that the industrialists were eroding equality of opportunity and individual liberties in the market, ideals that had traditionally defined political economy in the United States.

The country had been visited by periodic economic crises since the 1870s, and the Panic of 1893 was an especially hard time for workers and farmers. The financial crisis drove companies out of business, led to mass unemployment, and caused prices to plummet. Naturally, this intensified resentment against industrialists and conglomerates. This socioeconomic discontent inspired Populism and a belligerent labor movement and created a desire for reform of a political system that was plagued by corruption, including influence peddling and bribery. The calls for reform were not limited to farmers and workers, however. Middle managers at corporations also criticized political and economic inefficiency, and some politicians, believing the two-party system to be hopelessly corrupt, ended up forming their own political party. This wide-ranging demand for reform culminated in the Progressive movement.

During the Progressive Era that followed, more regulations were placed on economic activity, interest increased in the income tax and other forms of redistribution, and rudimentary forms of social insurance were put in place, including retirement pension and unemployment insurance. The tougher government regulations were a particularly important change in regard to the development of the American system of expansive reproduction. Just as the spread of new liberalism and socialism in Britain around the same time prompted more demand for "big government," the United States' federal government began to become more involved in economic activity during the Progressive Era [25].

There was a tendency at the time to expand the scope of government action to include protecting consumers, workers, and other vulnerable members of society. This tendency is exemplified by the Interstate Commerce Commission (ICC), which was established in 1887; the Pure Food and Drug Act, which became law in 1906; and the Adamson Act, which instituted an eight-hour workday for railroad workers. But the issue about which there was the strongest support for government regulation and intervention was monopolies. As we have already mentioned, the Sherman Antitrust Act (as well as the monopoly regulations that individual states enacted on their own) epitomized the demand to suppress monopolies. Under Theodore Roosevelt, one of the leading Progressive politicians, the Justice Department convinced the courts in 1911 that Standard Oil and American Tobacco should be dissolved under the Sherman Antitrust Act [26].

Opposition to monopolies was widely heard in the newspapers, magazines, elections, and various political gatherings, and the public stood behind the Sherman Antitrust Act. It is unclear, however, how effective the law actually was. Initially, the Justice Department (which was part of the federal government) was in charge of executing the law, while federal prosecutors were allowed to decide who to indict for monopolistic behavior as defined by the law. But aside from a few major cases like Standard Oil and the railroad companies, federal prosecutors for the most part only indicted loose vertical cartels composed of mid-sized companies.

Furthermore, since the act targeted any activity that interfered with the free market, collective action by labor unions also fell within its scope. Not only strikes but even demands for a closed shop or for collective bargaining rights could be interpreted as violating the rights of individual workers to make a contract with their employer. Though the law had been introduced to check the influence of big business, it was frequently used to bludgeon labor unions.

Nor was it easy to define monopolistic activity or to demonstrate that it had occurred. Was the market dominance of trusts like Standard Oil and US Steel that controlled more than three-quarters of the domestic market the result of deliberate attempts to keep competitors out of the market, or was it the result of aggressive three-pronged investment and technological innovation? It was hard to tell the two apart, and even harder to prove the point in court [27].

The emergence of huge corporations whose awesome manufacturing capacity and distribution systems enabled them to artificially manipulate market prices entailed the risk of creating monopoly markets that would make the economy less efficient. This made government regulations necessary. In the short term, of course, government regulations can impede the freedom of corporate activity, but in the long term, they help the system of industrial capitalism remain stable and the system of expansive reproduction continue developing.

It is not very surprising that a lively debate about the need for government regulation of monopolistic behavior and the methods of accomplishing this occurred in the United States, the country in which the modern corporation first appeared. But though this debate continued for several decades after the 1890s, no clear solution was found for regulating big business. In 1912, the energy behind reform helped Woodrow Wilson win the presidential election, ending the Republicans' long run in office. Even though bridling the influence of the conglomerates was a top priority for Wilson, who had run under the slogan of "New Freedom," he had to shelve his domestic reform agenda because of a series of more urgent developments overseas. Revolutions were ripping through parts of the Western Hemisphere that Americans had felt sure were under their control, and Europe was being swept into the maelstrom of war.

World War I and Its Consequences

While the major European powers were racing to seize colonies in Africa and Asia at the end of the nineteenth century, the United States was also expanding its territory with the acquisitions of Hawaii and Alaska. In 1898, the United States fought Spain to support the Cubans in their own war for independence against Spain's imperial rule. The American decision to go to war was based on the Monroe Doctrine, which had first been articulated by President James Monroe in 1823 and had later become official government policy. The war ended with relative swiftness —after less than a year—in American victory, and Spain ceded Guam, Puerto Rico, and the Philippines to the United States.

There were several reasons why the United States came to harbor expansionist ambitions at the end of the nineteenth century after refusing for so long to join the race for empire. As Frederick Jackson Turner expressed in the famous phrase the "end of the frontier," the United States' expansion in North America came to an end in the 1890s. This meant that there was no more room to practice the ideals of the "empire of liberty" that Thomas Jefferson had advocated long before—guaranteeing the public virtue of the free citizens of the republic and extending the republic's liberties throughout North America.

On an economic level, the end of the frontier was a troubling development for American industrialists, who were concerned that they might no longer be able to depend upon the markets, land, and resources that territorial expansion had provided. Those industrialists had started taking an interest in foreign markets in the second half of the nineteenth century, and the end of the frontier and the colonial rivalry between the nations of Europe pushed entrepreneurs and some politicians to urge the American government to adopt a more aggressive foreign policy [28].

But the American government and public believed that their assertive foreign policy was fundamentally different from the European powers' empire-building. The longstanding American antipathy for empire still persisted, and even those politicians and industrialists who called for aggressive expansion held an ambiguous attitude toward European imperialism. Those attitudes were evident in American policy in the Philippines, which the United States acquired in 1898 after its war with Spain. When the Filipinos demanded full independence, the American government offered instead to modernize their economy through bold investments in infrastructure and education. The government then had technocrats draft an elaborate plan for the modernization of the Philippines and allocated considerable money to make the plan a reality. But the Filipinos still wanted their independence, and they resisted American rule until 1902. During the Philippine-American War, 4300 American soldiers and 50,000 Filipinos lost their lives. This made it perfectly clear that not everyone welcomed American-style modernization [29].

Despite the fiasco in the Philippines, American government officials and politicians agreed that America had to maintain its dominance over the Western Hemisphere at the least. In 1904, Theodore Roosevelt, himself an ardent expansionist, went one step beyond the Monroe Doctrine with the Roosevelt Corollary, declaring that the United States reserved the right to intervene in the domestic affairs of nations in the Western Hemisphere, by force if necessary, to preserve regional stability and to protect American economic interests. The American government acted on this declaration the following year, when the American navy sent ships to Santo Domingo upon the Dominican Republic's failure to fulfill its obligations to foreign creditors. Even Wilson, who was skeptical of excessive expansionism, did not have the slightest doubt about the need for the United States to exert an influence on states in Central and South America [30].

Despite the vocal support for expansion, American foreign policy was limited to maintaining influence in Central and South America and ensuring equal access to Asian markets such as China, which stands in clear contrast to the aggressive colonial expansion of countries in Europe. The likely reason for this discrepancy is that the American system of expansive reproduction did not require colonies. When the system of expansive reproduction is in a virtuous cycle (as with Britain during the mid-nineteenth century), continuing technological innovation makes the manufacturing industry more competitive. This leads the state to focus on earning profit from trade rather than from more artificial and costly methods such as acquiring colonies.

In Britain, of course, the relatively small size of the domestic market meant that Britain had to compete fiercely with Germany and other late industrializers for the supply of raw materials and the demand for manufactured goods that were needed to fuel the system of expansive reproduction. When those late industrializers fought back with protectionist measures and colonial expansion, Britain had no choice but to follow suit. But the situation was different in the United States. The domestic market in the United States was large enough to sustain and develop the system of expansive reproduction, and the huge agricultural and resource extraction sectors supplied so many raw materials that industrialists did not need to look for them overseas.

Under such circumstances, it was reasonable for the American government to keep its distance from the conflict in Europe, with its web of alliances. When Europe stood on the brink of war at the end of the 1900s, the American government made clear that it would maintain a strict policy of neutrality. When the war began in 1914, the United States declared its neutrality and proclaimed the right to trade with all the belligerents. But as the war escalated, it became progressively harder for the United States to maintain its neutrality. Britain and France imposed a maritime blockade to cut off the flow of supplies to Germany and other members of the Central Powers, and Germany unleashed its U-boats in an attempt to break the blockade. Germany's submarine warfare represented not only a severe threat to Americans' economic interests but also an affront to their national pride [31].

The United States entered World War I in April 1917. Although it was only in the war for 19 months, it made a decisive contribution to the Allied victory by mobilizing 4.8 million troops altogether and by shipping over an immense amount of war supplies. To prosecute the war, the United States had to make huge economic expenditures. While it had spent a considerable amount of money on its military since the end of the nineteenth century—raising troops to fight a number of armed conflicts, including the war with Spain, and building the world's third largest navy—American defense spending between 1899 and 1916 only amounted to 0.8% of GNP. During the 19 months that the United States participated in World War I, in contrast, the American government spent 32.7 billion dollars. This was a huge sum, equivalent to 25% of GNP in 1919 [32].

In order to fund such an expensive war and to provide the materials needed for the war, the American government was forced to adopt experimental methods. The War Revenue Act, which was enacted in 1917, implemented an excess-profits tax. The act authorized the government to levy a progressive tax ranging from 20 to 60% on profit on capital exceeding a set rate. Income tax rates were raised sharply as well. Given a yearly income of 50,000 dollars, the tax rate was just 1.5% in the years 1913–1915 but increased to 22% in 1918.

Government bonds played an even more important role. While government income from taxes and other sources covered about 22% (7.3 billion dollars) of the cost of the war, the money that the government borrowed from the public in the form of government bonds covered 58% of the cost (24 billion dollars). Just as during the Civil War, the American government issued "liberty bonds" and promoted them through a big campaign in which it appealed to the patriotism of the American public. The government also offered a number of incentives to bondholders, waiving income tax on the bonds and making it possible to pay inheritance tax with them. Though these bonds' appeal as an investment was admittedly a more important factor than patriotic sentiment, they were extremely popular during the war [33].

As radical as the government's fiscal policies were, an even more radical change was the development of the command economy. World War I was history's first total war—the first war in which victory was determined by the state's industrial capacity. In order to wage such a war, it was necessary to produce and distribute an awesome amount of war supplies in a short period of time. Such a need simply could not be met by traditional methods such as military supply contracts with companies in the private sector. Instead, the government had to take action to temporarily suppress demand in the private sector and to switch over production and distribution facilities in the public and private sectors to satisfying wartime demand.

In other words, what was needed was a command economy in which the government would directly control prices and production. Immediately after announcing the United States' entry into the war, the Wilson administration set up the Council of National Defense along with a series of agencies charged with planning and monitoring production and distribution in each industry. As part of this, nearly 5000 federal agencies were established. Of course, neither the American government nor the private sector had the experience or expertise required for such a large command economy, and agencies such as the War Industries Board were not run very effectively. Nevertheless, the American government managed to supply an incredible amount of war materials to Europe, including around 4000 automobiles and about 2000 airplanes. This period also foreshadowed future developments by setting the precedent that a government could play an important role in production and distribution [34].

World War I demanded enormous fiscal expenditures, but it was also an opportunity for the American system of expansive reproduction to advance to the next level and for the United States to become the world's undisputed economic leader. One reason for the United States' sudden rise in status was that it had suffered less than the other belligerents in the war. In terms of the human toll, around 110,000 Americans were lost in World War I, while 1.3 million died in France, 900,000 in Britain and the British Empire, 2 million in Germany, 1.1 million in Austria, and 1.8 million in Russia.

Furthermore, the outcome of the war threatened the very existence of several European powers. After their defeat, Germany and Austria were forced to dissolve their empires, give up areas of critical strategic and economic value, and pay crippling reparations to the victors. The pressure of the war caused the implosion of the Tsarist government in Russia, which was soon replaced by the Soviet Union. Even the victors, Britain and France, had exhausted their energy in the long years of war [35].

While the European powers were focusing all their attention on fighting the war, the American system of expansive reproduction was experiencing an unprecedented boom. By 1913, the American manufacturing sector was already ahead of its British and German counterparts in terms of productive capacity and productivity. But the war allowed the United States to gain an even greater lead over its two Western European rivals in these two areas. In 1914, the United States accounted for 36% of global manufacturing production; by 1920, this had risen to 42%. The United

States' nominal GNP nearly doubled between 1914 and 1920, increasing from 46 billion dollars to 87.2 billion dollars [36].

The changing status of the United States is also evident in the capital market. From the time of its independence until just before World War I, the United States had always dealt with a shortage of labor and capital (in contrast with its plentiful land and resources), and it had achieved rapid industrialization since the mid-nineteenth century by attracting capital from overseas. But after the start of World War I, Britain and the other warring countries liquidated bonds and other securities to obtain the dollars they needed to buy war materials. They also raised funds in the New York capital market. As a result, the United States transformed from a net importer of capital to a net exporter of capital [37].

The contrast between the United States and Europe became even sharper in the 1920s. The various states of Europe plunged into extreme social chaos and political conflict that went far beyond the recession that tends to accompany the transition from a wartime to a peacetime economy [38]. Meanwhile, the United States quickly overcame the economic slowdown in 1920 and 1921 and entered a period of unprecedented prosperity.

The prosperity of the 1920s can be explained by two factors. First, technology had been accumulating in the automobile and electronics industries since the beginning of the twentieth century, and, backed by brisk capital investment in the 1920s, this technology was beginning to have an impact. Second, Americans' real income had increased during the wartime boom, and they used it in the 1920s to purchase automobiles and various other durable consumer goods.

There were other contributing factors, of course. It was around this time that various consumer finance programs, such as the installment plan, began to be fully implemented, and the expansion of three-pronged investment in the durable consumer goods sector made it possible to supply those goods even more cheaply. As a result, purchases of durable consumer goods grew at an average rate of 8.3% a year between 1922 and 1929, which was nearly double the GNP growth rate during this period. Because of increasing consumption, manufacturing production in the United States nearly doubled as well between 1921 and 1929 [39].

Without a doubt, it was the automobile that led the boom in the durable consumer goods sector during the 1920s. The development of the American automobile industry (epitomized by Ford and General Motors) during this period can be seen not only as the culmination of everything that the Second Industrial Revolution had achieved since the 1870s but also as the triumph of the American system of expansive reproduction, which had succeeded at combining mass production and mass consumption. The growth of the automobile industry depended on the development of heavy industries such as steel, machinery, chemicals, and oil refining, and the transformation of the automobile from an extravagant preference good for the wealthy into a mass commodity required the fall in prices resulting from the development of the integrated production system, which was itself made possible by vertical and horizontal integration and the principles of scientific management. The United States' abundant resources and its national market stretching across an entire continent were also favorable conditions for the development of the automobile industry [40].

At this precise moment in history, Henry Ford had the vision to understand the position of the American automobile industry. A mechanical engineer from Michigan, Ford entered the automobile industry in the 1890s by designing a race car. He set up the Ford Motor Company in 1903 and aimed from the outset to release models that were lightweight, affordable, and capable of being mass produced. Toward this end, Ford began to produce automobile parts inside the company with an eye toward vertical integration: by 1913, the company was making all the parts for its automobiles, including the engines and the chassis.

Next, Ford built a factory at Highland Park with an integration production system connected by a conveyor belt, which greatly reduced the time required to assemble automobiles. The automobile produced at this factory was none other than the Model T, which first debuted in 1908. The mass production system perfected in 1913 slashed the time it took to assemble a Model T by nearly five-sixths, which suggests how cheaply Ford Motor Company could supply this mass-produced automobile to the market. Indeed, the Model T cost 825 dollars in 1908, but the price had fallen to 290 dollars by 1927, when it was discontinued. By then, 15 million units of the car had been sold.

The production system that Ford Motor Company built adhered closely to the principles of scientific management that had been in vogue since the 1890s. Parts were standardized in order to increase the efficiency of production, the tools needed for production were designed to perform specific tasks, and the pace of production was directed not by skilled laborers but rather by the managers running the conveyor belt. As Ford explained it, the key of the company's production system was eliminating the need for workers to think and reducing their thoughts to a minimum.

This kind of production system stirred up discontent because it lowered workers' skill level and took away their control of the labor process. The result was a high turnover rate. In order to resolve these issues, the Ford Motor Company introduced the famous 8-h workday and the "five-dollar day"—nearly double the average wages at the time. Not all the workers at the company were paid five dollars a day, however. To receive this benefit, workers had to abide by a lifestyle code designed by the company and strictly enforced by its Sociology Department (renamed the Education Department in 1915).

Nevertheless, the five-dollar day created a major stir because it marked an important shift in attitude. Workers were no longer viewed merely as producers, but also as consumers. Automobiles had once been a luxury for the few, but they were now a mass commodity that could even be bought by workers at Ford Motor Company. This reflected a new awareness that consumers with purchasing power were a prerequisite for the development of the system of mass production [41].

Interestingly, the new systems of production and distribution pioneered by Ford were perfected not at Ford Motor Company but at General Motors. Struggling to win back the market share it had lost to the popular Ford Model T, General Motors hired Alfred Sloan, a management expert with a background in electrical engineering at MIT, as its vice president in 1918. With the help of Sloan's reforms,

General Motors became the world's largest automaker in the 1920s. Sloan retained the positive aspects of the company's integrated production system for automobiles while reorganizing the company into a divisional structure. This gave its managers more autonomy while making clear that they were responsible for performance and increased the organization's efficiency by standardizing accounting practices.

A more important factor in General Motors' success was its consumer research. The consumer preference survey that was launched in 1923 allowed the company to predict demand according to consumers' age, gender, and income and to use those predictions to determine inventory, the workforce, consumer credit, and pricing. While Ford Motor Company focused solely on improving the efficiency of the Model T, General Motors' strategy was to use its survey to satisfy consumers' preferences. It released a variety of models, ranging from the Chevrolet to the Cadillac, and introduced the concept of the model year, regularly improving its models' style, color, and finish. Some historians go so far as to describe this as "flexible mass production," arguing that General Motors' methods made mass production more flexible. In addition to this, General Motors was the first automaker to introduce installment payment plans as a new marketing tactic, stimulating mass consumption and thereby supporting mass production [42].

The series of innovations made by the Ford Motor Company and General Motors in the areas of technology, corporate organization, labor management, and marketing were the drivers behind a tremendous increase in the American automobile industry's productive capacity, which grew from 900,000 vehicles a year in 1919 to 26.7 million vehicles in 1929. That was eight times more than the total number of automobiles manufactured in Europe. The American automobile industry's overwhelming productive capacity helped American cars come close to taking over the entire global market. Before World War I, France had held the lead in the world automobile export market, followed by the United States, Britain, and Germany. By 1923, however, the United States controlled nearly 50% of the global automobile export market; by 1928, its market share had surpassed 70% [43].

In retrospect, the American automobile industry serves as a classic example of the virtuous cycle in the system of expansive reproduction. The combination of mass production, mass consumption, and managerial control of the labor process enabled the industry to take the lead in the global market, which supported technological innovation in the supply sector and brought about mass consumer spending. Known as Fordism, this system was widely adopted not only in the automobile industry but also in producer and consumer goods industries such as electricity, electronics, and chemicals. The system was a crucial driver of prosperity in the United States for the decade after World War I and in the global economy after 1945.

But the prosperity that the United States enjoyed in the years after World War I did not last for long. Falling stock prices on Wall Street in the fall of 1929 portended the beginning of the Great Depression, which would not only cause serious damage to the American system of expansive reproduction but also drive the entire global economy into a protracted slump.

From the Great Depression Until World War II

The American economic boom that began in 1921 seemed like it would last forever. After the signing of the Treaty of Versailles, the United States returned to isolationism, rejecting the idealism of Woodrow Wilson and his argument for a new liberal world system grounded in free trade and the self-determination of peoples. Running for president on the Republican ticket, Warren Harding won the 1920 election by a landslide. Under President Harding and his successor, Calvin Coolidge, Congress raised tariffs, and the Federal Reserve kept interest rates low to ensure that the period of economic expansion would continue. During the postwar readjustment, the United States steadfastly refused not only to write off the reparations owed by vanquished Germany but also the debts owed by Britain and the other victors [44]. The dilemma was that Europe did not have the money to pay back its debts, and the United States did not have the magnanimity or mercy to wait for Europe to do so.

With low interest rates in the United States coinciding with the financial demand in Europe for dollars to pay reparations and make debt payments to the United States, global capital began to converge in the United States in the 1920s. American capital that had been invested in Europe because of the high interest rates there flowed back into the United States through reparations and debt repayment, promoting investment and consumption inside the United States. But the rush of capital exceeded healthy investment levels and moved into speculation. A huge amount of speculative money was poured not only into the durable consumer goods industry but also into real estate, construction, and the stock market. Thus, the United States' GNP grew by 59% during the 1920s, but the Dow Jones Index soared by 400% [45].

It was inevitable that speculation's synergistic effect on the economy would come to an end. Concern that the economy was overheating led the Federal Reserve to start implementing austerity measures, and it raised the discount rate in the first half of 1928. Even so, stock prices on Wall Street continued to soar for some time afterward. It was not until September 1929 that they peaked and then crashed [46]. The collapse of the stock market led to a series of bank failures the following year and to a contraction in the manufacturing sector. Production in the American manufacturing sector in the early 1930s shrank to half of the level from the previous decade. The automobile industry had driven the boom of the 1920s, but the industry's yearly production declined by a full 75%, from 4.5 million units to 1.1 million units. International trade was also hit hard by the depression. American imports from Europe decreased from 1.3 billion dollars in 1929 to 390 million dollars in 1932, while American exports to Europe fell from 2.3 billion dollars to 780 million dollars during the same period. There was also a sharp increase in the unemployment rate. The manufacturing unemployment rate in the United States rose from 7.7% between 1921 and 1929 to 26.1% between 1930 and 1938 [47].

Historians and economists have long debated why and how the stock market crash on Wall Street in the fall of 1929 escalated into a worldwide depression in the early 1930s. The points we will mention here are conclusions from this debate about which there is some degree of scholarly agreement. The stock market crash of 1929 was a cyclical crisis caused by the economic overheating of the 1920s, and it ought not to have caused the Great Depression. The reason that the stock market crash resulted in a bank crisis and a contraction of the real economy was that the austerity measures that the United States had begun adopting in 1928 had taken a heavy toll on Europe, which relied upon American capital. But the immediate cause of the depression was that the United States maintained its austerity policy even after the stock market crash in an attempt to stay on the gold standard. The central banks of European states responded to American austerity with austerity measures of their own in a bid to remain on the gold standard. But with a complete interruption in the flow of American capital, those states could not maintain their posture for long.

With the financial crisis spreading and the downturn in the real economy becoming severe, a number of countries, including Britain, gave up the gold standard and devalued their currencies. But American policy makers left their austerity measures in place and did nothing to address the growing crisis in the real economy. They believed that the gold standard had to be preserved if employment and production were to recover. Of course, even the United States was eventually forced to abandon the gold standard in 1933, but it failed to take aggressive measures to stimulate the economy by expanding the currency supply because of lingering fears that devaluating the currency might cause inflation [48].

It is a puzzling fact that the country that suffered the most during the Great Depression was the United States, which had the advantages of an economic boom, the greatest industrial capacity in history, and extensive overseas assets in the 1920s. This enigma, scholars say, can ultimately be explained as policy failure, both in regard to the currency supply and in regard to creating effective demand. This explanation can be reinterpreted in terms of the virtuous cycle in the system of expansive reproduction as follows. The primary reason that government intervention was necessary was that the American system of expansive reproduction had failed to create enough domestic demand even as the United States was increasing its lead over its European competitors in the 1920s. Another problem was that the United States had failed to secure enough demand in Europe and elsewhere in the global market to absorb American productive capacity because of the rigidness of the gold standard and because of the fiscal imbalance between the United States and Europe caused by the postwar settlement. Simply put, American development after World War I was too fast, and the European recovery was too slow. It would have taken time for the innovation occurring in the American supply sector to create new demand, and the overheated American economy and the uncertainty in the European market did not provide enough time for innovation to do its work.

Obviously, the outcome would have been different if the United States had remained devoted to its role as the "lender of last resort" described by Charles Kindleberger. Ultimately, however, what was needed to keep the American system of expansive reproduction in a virtuous cycle was a new international division of labor that could reflect the gap in productive capacity and productivity between the

United States and Europe. The only way that the United States and Europe could have prevented a drastic crisis along the lines of the Great Depression was for them to manufacture products that were tailored to their unique positions and to promote the exchange of these products to constantly create new demand.

In this regard, the New Deal programs implemented by President Franklin D. Roosevelt could only bring about a limited amount of fundamental change. According to one scholar's categorization scheme, New Deal programs can be divided into relief, economic stimulus, and reforms, but there are no signs here of any interest in an international monetary or trade system that would support a new international division of labor. After the collapse of the gold standard, of course, the United States and the countries of Europe broke away from the global economic system and focused on protecting their own economies, and this was also the background of the New Deal.

This is not to say that the New Deal did not have any results. For example, the National Industrial Recovery Act (NIRA) encouraged organized labor and capital to compromise on working hours and wages. Even after the NIRA was ruled to be unconstitutional, the passage of the Wagner Act helped reinforce workers' rights and stabilize labor relations through compromises between capital and labor. The Wagner Act, a labor relations bill that was enacted in 1935 as part of the New Deal, recognized workers' rights to organize, engage in collective bargaining, and make collective agreements while also banning unfair labor actions. Even if government programs to bring electricity to the countryside, write off farmers' debts, institute social insurance, and help the unemployed did not have a long-term effect on the development of the American economy, they did provide immediate relief to millions of Americans who were struggling to find work.

An even more important product of the New Deal was the change that it brought to market expectations. If we may be forgiven a slight generalization, the Hoover administration held to the position that failing corporations would be allowed to go bankrupt, but the Roosevelt administration made it widely known that the state would take an active role in combatting the economic crisis. This inspired the expectation that the Great Depression would not last forever and helped trigger some degree of corporate investment and public consumption [49]. Indeed, the role of the state (and the federal government in particular) grew bigger during the New Deal period. As government expenditures increased sharply at the outset of the New Deal, the government budget grew from 12% of the national income to more than 20%. At the same time, more federal regulations were put into place, and the percentage of the total workforce that was employed by the federal government grew as well (from 0.3% in 1920 to about 0.8% in the mid-1930s).

But the Great Depression was not easily overcome. Unemployment would not drop below 10%, and even by 1937 industrial production had not returned to 1929 levels [50]. Ultimately, it was World War II that rescued the United States from the Great Depression. The economic recovery that took off in 1941 was fueled by wartime demand from Europe. This is illustrated by the fact that 81% of the increase of the real GNP in 1941 resulted from federal government fiscal policy connected with producing war supplies. After the United States decided to join the war, the wartime regime (including the production of war materials) accounted for more than half of the economic recovery and effectively brought about full employment [51].

After World War II began with Germany's invasion of Poland in September 1939, the United States tried to remain neutral. But when the war in Europe went poorly and Britain was left to fight the Axis Powers on its own, Winston Churchill repeatedly asked the United States to send war supplies and to join the fighting. In the end, the United States began rearming in 1940. In September 1940, Congress allowed peacetime conscription, and plans were laid to draft 16.4 million men. After Roosevelt declared the United States to be the "arsenal of democracy," Congress passed the Lend-Lease Act and allocated 7 billion dollars for the program. From March 1941 (when the act took effect) until June 1945, more than 50.2 billion dollars of war materials were exported to the Allied nations. As a result, American exports started rapidly increasing in 1941.

When the United States decided to enter World War II after the bombing of Pearl Harbor in December 1941, American wartime production and expenditures increased sharply. During the first half of 1942 alone, the federal government signed supply contracts worth more than 100 billion dollars, a huge amount that surpassed the GDP in 1940. Boosted by the massive military spending, the real GNP in the United States grew by 55% between 1939 and 1944. Military expenditures as a percentage of the real GNP ballooned from 1.4% in 1939 to 45% in 1944, but there was a certain decrease in the private sector's contribution from its 1939 level. In 1942, the production of durable consumer goods fell sharply and consumption in the private sector declined, but for the rest of the war, investment in the private sector decreased while total production steadily increased and consumption continued to increase as well [52].

Drawing upon its experience from World War I and the New Deal period, the federal government rapidly set up a wartime planned economy. Donald Nelson, executive vice president of Sears Roebuck, became the chairman of the War Production Board, which effectively categorized industry, collected information about each industrial sector, managed inventories, and planned production. Under the federal government's oversight, the United States' wartime production of military supplies increased at an astonishing rate. During the war, the United States produced 6500 naval vessels, 296,400 aircraft, 86,630 tanks, 12 million firearms of various kinds, and 47 million tons of munitions.

The total volume of war materials produced at Ford Motor Company alone was greater than the entire Italian economy. In 1944, Ford Motor Company's Willow Run manufacturing complex was rolling out one B-24 heavy bomber every 63 min. Henry J. Kaiser applied Ford's integrated production system to the shipping industry, which reduced the production period for a 7200-ton cargo ship from 244 to 42 days and enabled the United States to build a remarkable 2710 such ships during the war. There was also a dramatic increase in the production of raw materials. Production of aluminum increased by a factor of seven and magnesium by a factor of 100 between 1939 and 1943. In 1944, 5 million barrels of crude oil were being pumped out each day, which were used to extract 4000 tons of TNT, also on a daily basis [53].

Needless to say, the war entailed immense losses both of life and property. According to a recent estimate of the economic value of wartime casualties, the lives lost in World War II were worth 12.5 billion dollars, equivalent to about one-fourth of total consumption in 1940. But the war also gave the American system of expansive reproduction an opportunity to expand to an unprecedented degree. It is important to understand that this expansion did not result from the voluntarily behavior of corporations. This fact is illustrated by developments in the steel industry.

After the outbreak of the war in Europe, there was a dramatic increase in demand for munitions and other American manufactured goods, and the existing steel production facilities were not capable of meeting this demand. But the steel industry thought it was too risky to make massive facility investments on the grounds of temporary wartime demand. They believed that the excessive production capacity that would build up during the war would lead to painful restructuring after the war, just as during the Great Depression.

But the federal government relaxed its enforcement of antitrust and labor relations legislation, boosted the tax benefits of investing, and funded the construction of production facilities. At the same time, the government threatened to encourage the establishment of new steel companies if existing ones did not accept its demands. In 1941, the steel industry was at last forced to accept 1.2 billion dollars' worth of investment in facilities with a capacity of producing 13 million tons of steel. The fiscal burden for this investment, of course, was assumed by the federal government [54].

The war also afforded opportunities for technological innovation. Since the war was not fought at home, the United States did not suffer the physical destruction of its industrial facilities as the other belligerents did. Instead, there was a remarkable increase in R&D and investment in human capital at universities and companies in the private sector with the wholehearted support of the federal government. The number of workers and the amount of capital that the American government poured into R&D during World War II would have been inconceivable at ordinary times. This is exemplified by the Manhattan Project, which had a workforce of 130,000 people and a budget of 2 billion dollars.

When converted into 1930 dollars, the federal government's R&D spending increased from about 83 million dollars in 1940 to more than 1.3 billion dollars in 1945. The Defense Department alone spent 29 million dollars on R&D in 1940 and 423 million dollars in 1945. The Office of Scientific Research and Development played the most important role in R&D projects during the war. After its establishment in 1941, it assigned numerous research projects to universities and to the private sector. In this manner, Western Electric and similar companies received 17 million dollars in R&D funding during the war while MIT was given no less than 116 million dollars in research funding for 75 research projects [55].

The federal government's huge investment in R&D during World War II set an important precedent, and even after the war, R&D investment helped the United

States maintain its global edge [56]. Such investment was ultimately the most important force that enabled the American system of expansive reproduction to support the virtuous cycle of technological innovation, development of new products, and creation of new demand. Another noteworthy point is how common it was for R&D carried out for military purposes during the war to lead to technological innovation and the creation of new products in the private sector.

One example was the RCA Corporation, a leading electronics firm that signed 84 million dollars' worth of manufacturing contracts during the war and rapidly expanded its facilities to produce a variety of electronics parts, including radios and vacuum tubes. RCA ended up manufacturing 20 million vacuum tubes at the manufacturing plant that it built in Lancaster during the war. RCA was later able to use its military research into televisions to establish itself in the television manufacturing and broadcast services sector. Even amid increasing competition in the television production sector, RCA still made massive profits by producing vacuum tubes [57].

Another legacy of the war in the electronics sector was the computer. The American army commissioned a number of projects during the war aimed at developing a high-performance calculator. These projects culminated in the Harvard Mark I, which was developed through a partnership between Harvard University and IBM, and ENIAC, which was designed at the University of Pennsylvania in order to perform ballistics calculations. These two machines represented the birth of the computer industry. Furthermore, John von Neumann worked with the research team at the University of Pennsylvania that had developed ENIAC to build a computer that could carry out calculations using commands saved in memory. This constituted the basic framework for the modern computer, which is controlled by software [58].

Since multiple companies worked together on various supply contracts commissioned by the federal government, technology could be quickly transferred among the participating companies. In the case of synthetic rubber production, for example, the federal government invested 500 million dollars in a consortium consisting of Standard Oil and four major rubber companies. This kind of massive wartime capital investment completely transformed the American rubber industry. Synthetic rubber's share of the American rubber market increased from just 0.4% in 1940 to 85% in 1945, and synthetic rubber production increased by a factor of 100 over the same period [59].

Advancements were also made in the technology for producing fuel, which played a crucial role during the war. The basic technologies for fuel production had already been developed by Standard Oil in 1913, by Texaco in 1920, and by Sun Chemical in 1936. But the catalytic cracking technique that Standard Oil developed in 1940 made the cracking process for extracting gasoline from crude oil more effective and stable, which not only created a reliable supply of gasoline but also made it possible to freely convert gasoline into a raw material for TNT. Thanks to such technological innovations, the United States was able to maintain its lead in the petrochemical industry for long after the war. With the exception of Canada, it took competitors in other countries quite a long time to reach the level of American technology in this area [60].

World War II is said to be the first war in which air superiority had a decisive impact on the outcome. This meant that the ability to produce aircraft was essential for prosecuting the war, which spurred the development of key technology in the aviation industry. In 1939, the United States Air Force only had 26,000 employees, while Britain's Royal Air Force had 100,000 employees and Germany's Luftwaffe had 500,000 employees. After entering the war at the end of 1941, the Roosevelt administration and Congress began pushing to acquire and produce more military aircraft. This led to the building of new factories and the adoption of new technology. By the end of 1943, more than 2 million workers had been assigned to aircraft production, and when the war was coming to an end, the American aircraft industry had acquired the productive capacity to make 110,000 aircraft a year. Not only the navy and army's independent laboratories but also research facilities at universities and in the private sector were working on the development of aviation technology. With the support of the Office of Scientific Research and Development, which the United States established in 1941 to put technology specialists to work on military R&D, there was rapid innovation in aircraft design and flight technology. As a result of the wartime R&D that occurred in all sectors of the aviation industry —including radar, helicopters, jet engines, navigation systems, and long-range rockets—the American aviation industry managed to maintain its dominant position long after the war [61].

After World War I, the United States had already gained a definite advantage over its European rivals in terms of the productivity and productive capacity of the manufacturing sector. From approximately World War I until just before the Great Depression, the productivity of the American manufacturing sector steadily improved, growing at a rate of 5.4% a year. The improvement of the American manufacturing sector's productivity and productive capacity suffered a temporary setback during the long years of the Great Depression, but World War II proved to be a unique opportunity for American productive capacity to advance to the next level, as we have already discussed. Total war in industrial society demands the complete mobilization of a state's productive capacity, and the United States was able to improve its productive capacity without suffering any direct physical damage in its own territory and to take full advantage of the fact that it was acknowledged as an international hegemonic power [62].

But as the United States' experience in the Great Depression had shown, the disparity in productive capacity between the United States and Europe was not only propping up the United States' economic hegemony but also causing instability in the global economy. The growth of productive capacity in the American manufacturing sector had been based on the huge domestic market, but that productive capacity had already grown beyond the domestic market's ability to absorb it. Therefore, the United States had no choice but to turn to the overseas market, including its European rivals. In order for the overseas market to expand, the European economy (as the most important part of the overseas market) needed to quickly recover from the devastation of the war.

After the Industrial Revolution, Britain had possessed the world's greatest productive capacity, and so it had preached the doctrine of free trade and advocated the opening of markets around the world. In the same way, the United States also had to break from its long tradition of protectionism and isolationism and enter the era of free trade. This meant that the international role of the United States had to change after World War II.

The Postwar International Economic Order and the United States' Global System of Expansive Reproduction

The most important components of the American plan after World War II were preventing the chaos that had followed World War I and building an integrated world economy led by the United States. Whereas the interwar period was characterized by instability in the international monetary system resulting from the collapse of the gold standard, disequilibrium in the balance of payments, and the emergence of a system of protectionism, the global economy after World War II needed to be rebuilt on the foundation of a stable monetary system, free and open economies, and free international investment [63].

According to Cordell Hull, who served as Secretary of State in the Roosevelt administration, this meant that the first priority of the United States' postwar policy should be restoring the multilateral system of free trade. The reason that trade had to be expanded through a multilateral system instead of through bilateral agreements was that this would stimulate trade inside Europe, which had been devastated by the war, while simultaneously increasing the interdependence of major countries around the world to minimize the chance of another war breaking out [64].

The idea that this new international order should take shape under the leadership of the United States and that it should be subordinated to the interests of the American economy was expressed at an early point in World War II. Interestingly, this idea was developed into a detailed and sophisticated policy proposal not by the federal government but rather by the Council on Foreign Relations, a nongovernmental organization. Established in 1918 and reorganized in 1921 after merging with the American Institute of Foreign Affairs, the council was composed of leading government officials, politicians, industrialists, and academics. Through various study groups and a number of publications including the journal *Foreign Affairs*, the council advocated more free trade and international cooperation. Relying on a network of figures with close ties to politics and the government, the Council on Foreign Relations submitted a variety of reports and proposals about economic, diplomatic, and military policies and exerted a considerable influence on the policy-making process after the Roosevelt administration came to power.

Shortly after the beginning of World War II, the Council on Foreign Relations began to review how the war was affecting the United States' standing and interests through a project called War and Peace Studies. The main figures participating in this project were the key members of the Advisory Committee on Postwar Foreign Policy, which the State Department set up in December 1941. As the American plan for the postwar global economy gradually took shape through this process, the most important question to address was whether the United States could remain self-sufficient in isolation from the global economy. This question had grown in importance since Wilson's plans were thwarted by the rise of protectionism after World War I and by the Great Depression. The answer was clear: if the United States was to secure a stable supply of raw materials and to ensure the continuous growth of the manufacturing sector, it must not return to isolationism.

This view was elaborated in the concept of the "grand area." According to this concept, if Germany conquered Europe—and when this concept was developed in the early part of World War II, it seemed as if Germany would indeed conquer all of Europe, including Britain—the United States would have to promote economic exchange and integration over a large area that encompassed at least North and South America, the Pacific, the Far East, and Britain and the Commonwealth. It was because of this concept that the United States adopted a tough foreign policy stance in 1940, including its embargo on exports to Japan. As soon as the United States entered the war, this concept became the most important consideration behind its war planning. The concept dictated that the United States had to win the war and that, after winning the war, it had to reshape Europe, the Mediterranean, and the entire world into a sphere of American economic activity [65].

The United States was represented by Harry Dexter White (a member of an advisory committee for the Treasury Department who worked closely with members of the Council on Foreign Affairs) in discussions with John Maynard Keynes about the postwar global economic order during the 1940s. During talks on trade (which were conducted separately from those on the international monetary system), the chief American envoy was Myron Taylor, a steel magnate and a key member of the Council on Foreign Affairs. White and Keynes' negotiations took a great deal of time. While negotiators soon agreed that a stable international monetary system was essential for the stability of the global economy, they were deadlocked about whether that meant returning to the gold standard. International finance wanted the gold standard to be reinstated with limited adjustments, but the business world, labor unions, and governments were unwilling to accept the gold standard, since it precluded the use of exchange rate mechanisms to increase industrial competitiveness or to stimulate the economy.

White and Keynes came to an agreement on this issue in early 1944. According to their agreement, the exchange rate of each state's currency would be pegged to gold and the American dollar would be convertible to gold, while other states could adjust their exchange rate within a limited range as required for economic policy. This agreement also allowed states to engage in capital control to protect their domestic markets from speculative capital from overseas that would threaten monetary stability. Furthermore, it proposed an organization (called the International Monetary Fund) that could maintain the stability of international currency by monitoring each state's exchange rate adjustments and providing emergency funding to states facing a short-term liquidity crisis. The funding for the

International Monetary Fund was composed of contributions paid in gold and domestic currency by the member states (and chiefly the United States), and the member states received voting rights that were commensurate to the amount of their contribution. Since the United States contributed the most money to the fund, it was effectively able to shape the fund's policy [66].

Along with the international monetary system, another important aspect of the United States' postwar plan was international investment and international trade. White and Keynes predicted that a huge amount of capital would be needed to rebuild the various countries in Asia and Europe that had been ravaged by the war, with particularly large investments for infrastructure such as railroads and harbors. The solution that White and Keynes proposed was setting up the International Bank for Reconstruction and Development, commonly known as the World Bank. With political support from leading states around the world, the World Bank was charged with stimulating international investment by raising capital at low interest rates in capital markets in the private sector and supplying it to states that needed large investments of capital [67].

These breakthroughs in the international monetary system and international investment were formalized in the Bretton Woods agreement, which was signed in July 1944. The final matter that needed to be addressed was that of international trade. There had been hopes that the proposed International Trade Organization would launch a postwar era of free trade, but this organization was never established because of a concerted attack from protectionists and proponents of unrestricted free trade inside the United States.

As a consequence, the General Agreement on Tariffs and Trade (GATT), which had been proposed at the same time as the International Trade Organization, became the basic framework for the postwar trading regime. The GATT began to take concrete form when the United States agreed to decrease the tariff rate on a number of items by more than 50% and when Britain agreed to reduce the amount of imperial trade that was subject to preferential tariffs by 5%. GATT took effect in the spring of 1947 with about 20 signatory states. The GATT system was based on most-favored nation status, and disagreements between various countries blocked efforts to liberalize trade during the second and third GATT rounds held in 1949 and from 1950 to 1951. Even so, GATT served as the basic framework for international trade for a long time after the war [68].

With the adoption of the Bretton Woods agreement and GATT, the postwar international economic order envisioned by the United States had begun to take shape. But the situation was dire in Europe, which was both the United States' most important market and the key to its strategic interests. As Dean Acheson testified before Congress, the most important goals of the Bretton Woods agreement and GATT were advancing the economic interests of the United States. But while the new system was crucial for American exports and American exports were critical to American prosperity, there were not enough dollars in the European market to purchase those exports, even though Europeans wanted American products more than ever before [69].

Amid the grim economic circumstances, the efforts to set up an international political and economic order centered on the United States was being threatened both in Eastern Europe, which was under the sway of the Soviet Union, and in several countries of Western Europe such as France and Italy where socialist parties were gaining influence. This sense of crisis was reflected in the Harvard University commencement address delivered by Secretary of State George Marshall in 1947. During the address, Marshall argued for the need of the European Recovery Program (better known as the Marshall Plan) and spoke of "breaking the vicious circle and restoring the confidence of the European people in the economic future of their own countries and of Europe as a whole." [70]

American financial aid to Europe had already begun before the implementation of the Marshall Plan and remained available through a number of channels until 1953. Marshall aid was approximately matched in value by the assistance that the United States provided through the Government Aid and Relief in Occupied Areas program, the Mutual Defense Assistance Act, and the Mutual Security Act, while about 1.6 billion dollars were provided by the International Monetary Foundation and the World Bank [71]. The amount of assistance provided through the Marshall Plan between 1948 and 1951 amounted to around 12 billion dollars, which included about 9.2 billion dollars in grants, 1.55 billion dollars in conditional aid, and 1.1 billion dollars in loans.

The conditional aid in the Marshall Plan was intended to assist the Agreement for Intra-European Payments and Compensations, which was reached in 1948. Creditor countries that were party to this agreement provided debtor countries with foreign exchange bills and in exchange received an equivalent amount of aid from the United States. This was designed to address the dollar shortage while simultaneously promoting inter-European trade. Indeed, promoting trade was the most important economic goal of the Marshall Plan, as is evidenced by how Marshall aid was distributed among the beneficiary countries. Aid was distributed not according to the size of each country's economy but rather according to the amount of their trade deficit in dollars. Fifteen countries altogether were given aid in this manner, beginning with Britain [72].

Marshall aid was allocated to each country according to distribution and usage plans that were formulated by the Organisation for European Economic Co-operation (established in 1948), and the aid was used to redeem bonds and make investments. The United States was particularly interested in helping Europe replace its outdated production system with the American systems of scientific management and mass production so that Europe could improve its productive capacity and productivity. The ultimate goal was for Europe to move away from the class politics caused by the conflict between labor and capital and to move toward a "politics of productivity." While a number of OEEC programs aimed at improving productivity, including the Committee for Scientific and Technical Matters, were not immediately successful, they did spread American values and help reinforce American leadership [73]. Marshall aid was used in various ways according to the circumstances of the country in question. In Britain, the money was generally used to redeem state loans; in Germany, it was used to purchase foodstuffs and raw materials. Thus, it was not invested directly in rebuilding the infrastructure that had been destroyed by the war [74].

Even so, Marshall aid played a critical role in resolving the shortage of food and raw materials that had provoked severe social unrest after the war. The aid also prevented producers and consumers from abandoning the market economy and ultimately created an opportunity for stimulating production and investment in the private sector. The European country in the most trouble at this time was Germany, for example, but despite the enormous damage it had suffered during the war, Germany had more accumulated capital than it had before the war. After using American aid to defuse the market crisis, Germany was therefore fully capable of serving as Europe's most important exporter of industrial goods, just as it had done before the war. Thus, the Marshall Plan served to prime the pump, giving the European market economy a chance to resume normal operations [75].

In the end, the Marshall Plan helped the economies of Western Europe recover from the damage left by the war. Between 1947 and 1951, the GNP of Western Europe taken as a whole grew by more than 30%, and industrial production was up 41% from 1938. There was also rapid progress inside Europe toward liberalizing trade, as the United States desired. In October 1950, the OEEC resolved to liberalize 75% of imports between member states by the following February, and in 1955, it decided to increase this to 90%. The European Payments Union, which was established in 1959, decided to eliminate the restriction on current transactions and to resume specie payments, leading to the establishment of a kind of regional Bretton Woods system [76].

This new economic regime—centered on the United States and composed of a stable monetary system and free international trade—may at first remind us of the system that was in place in the middle of the nineteenth century, when Britain was at the zenith of its economic dominance. During this period (often called the first era of globalization), Britain used the overwhelming productive capacity that its manufacturing sector had acquired during the First Industrial Revolution to spread the doctrine of free trade around the world and to create a virtuous cycle in its system of expansive reproduction [77].

Just as with Britain, it was the overwhelming productive capacity and the high productivity of the United States' manufacturing sector that enabled it to concentrate on helping Europe rebuild after World War II (from the Bretton Woods agreement to the Marshall Plan) and on setting up an international monetary system and an international system of free trade and investment. Even after the major European powers returned to their prewar production levels in 1952, the American economy was still extremely powerful. The United States accounted for around 60% of the production of all the advanced industrial states and more than 50% of their capital accumulation, while Americans' per capita productivity was twice that of Britons and three times that of Germans [78].

Thus, the economic disaster suffered by the countries of Europe was not necessarily a desirable outcome for the United States. After the Cold War officially began in 1947, the United States had to continue providing Europe and Japan with military and diplomatic support in order to halt the spread of Communism and to defend the liberal order, and an economic recovery in Europe and Japan was essential for their political stability. If the European and Japanese economies did not grow stronger under these circumstances, they would continue to have a huge deficit to the United States in the balance of international payments, which would create a vicious cycle that would further prevent Europe and Japan from increasing production. Ultimately, the United States would be forced to keep providing them with economic aid. This would place a heavier burden on American taxpayers, prevent the government from balancing the budget, and hamper the development of the manufacturing sector, which was the pillar of the American economy. That is why American policy makers wanted a "Europe which can and will compete with us in the world markets and for that very reason will be able to buy substantial amounts of our products." [79]

This was the vision guiding the United States as it carried out the Marshall Plan to support the rebuilding of Europe and concentrated its energy on expanding international free trade and investment. The GATT system failed to establish multilateral free trade as the United States had hoped, but the United States demonstrated its commitment to free trade by liberalizing its domestic market, lowering the average tariffs from 60% in the 1930s to less than 20%. This made it possible for products from around the world to flow into the American market regardless of nationality for the first time in history.

But the United States did not unilaterally impose the market liberalization it had adopted on the countries of Europe or other countries around the world. At least in the short term, what was even more important to the interests of the United States and to the world order that it was planning was ensuring that Europe and Japan recovered. Therefore, the United States tolerated the rush by European countries to implement state planning in the postwar period and allowed them to adopt protectionist measures and industrial policy. For the same reasons, the United States not only provided economic aid to underdeveloped countries like South Korea and Taiwan but also stood by while their governments promoted the growth of infant industries using methods such as dumping and rigid protection of the domestic market [80].

While there are some superficial similarities between the United States' postwar policy of supporting free trade and Britain's pursuit of free trade after the mid-nineteenth century, there are a number of important differences. As we have already seen, the reason that Britain turned from protectionism to free trade was because of the economic and technological advantages brought by the First Industrial Revolution. But Britain's technology during the First Industrial Revolution was easy for late industrializing states to acquire, and they soon surpassed Britain's technological level through new technology of their own. As a result, the international division of labor between industrial states and agricultural states that Britain had dominated for a time led to stiff competition between several industrial states producing similar products, which greatly destabilized the international order.

In contrast, the international division of labor that the United States established after World War II was based on a vertical division of labor between advanced and late industrializing states. This vertical hierarchy was composed of the United States, the most advanced economy, at the top, Japan and a number of European countries in the middle, and a large number of developing countries that were largely specialized in primary industries at the bottom. Each country fit into this vertical division of labor by specializing in distinct products based on their productive capacity and their technological level, which reinforced complementary and cooperative relationships instead of the competition that had created instability in the global economy since the end of the nineteenth century.

Of course, the United States did not support the industrialization of Europe, Japan, and underdeveloped countries and work to establish a new international division of labor merely because the American government and people felt responsible as a hegemonic power for establishing world peace and harmony, any more than Britain had done so one century before. These feelings of responsibility were backed by the belief that orienting the development of the entire global economy on a vertical international division of labor was essential to sustaining the American system of expansive reproduction.

More specifically, this belief was grounded in two important facts. First, the country that would profit the most from the vertical international division of labor that the United States planned would ultimately be the United States itself, which had the most advanced productive capacity and technological level. One reason for this is that advanced industrial economies that make technology-intensive products with high added value will always profit more in the division of labor than late industrializing economies that specialize in labor-intensive products with less added value. Another reason is that if this division of labor persists, the disparity between the two sides will gradually increase because of the accelerating nature of the system of expansive reproduction.

The second fact supporting this belief was that the various consumer goods and intermediate goods that Europe, Japan, and underdeveloped countries produced with the help of their relatively cheap wages made the American manufacturing sector more competitive and brought benefits to American consumers. Cheap intermediate goods increased the competitiveness of American products by helping to mitigate the high-cost structure of the American manufacturing sector, while cheap imported consumer goods furthered the development of mass consumption society in the United States. Thus, the American postwar system of expansive reproduction is unique in the sense that it needed the simultaneous and global growth of the manufacturing sector and primary industry. That is what we mean by the global system of expansive reproduction.

Of course, this new vertical international division of labor led by the United States was the most important driver of the post-World War II economic boom. While the United States was not able to implement the system of completely free trade that it had planned, global trade during this long period of prosperity took a form that was much closer to free trade than the protectionism that suppressed the global economy during the interwar period. Global trade in manufactured goods in 1951–1953 and 1969–1971 grew by 349%, while exports of manufactured goods by advanced industrial states increased by 480% over the same period.

Trade barriers were rapidly broken down as well. Inter-European trade was liberalized even further with the establishment of the European Economic Community (ECC) in 1958, while the European Free Trade Association (EFTA), which was formed by Britain and six other states that did not belong to the EEC, also promoted the liberalization of trade. During the Kennedy Round in the second half of the 1960s, the average tariffs on industrial goods were reduced by more than 30%, while the average tariffs on machinery and automobiles were reduced by more than 50%. The Kennedy Round, which had been proposed by United States President John F. Kennedy, was the sixth round of GATT tariff negotiations. Held in Geneva with 54 nations participating, the negotiations culminated in an agreement to reduce tariffs on industrial goods by 33–35% [81].

During the postwar boom, the United States' gross production and per capita productivity steadily improved, and there was also a continuing surplus in trade. The country's economic performance between 1947 and 1960 was especially remarkable. Converted into 1954 dollars, the United States' GNP increased from 280 billion dollars in 1947 to 439 billion dollars in 1960, or in other words 56% of growth. Manufacturing production posted rapid growth as well. According to estimates by the Federal Reserve, the Industrial Production Index (IPI), which was just 58 in 1929, rose to 100 in 1947 and then to 163 in 1960.

As we have already noted, the postwar boom was accompanied by an explosive increase in mass consumption. Once again converted into 1954 dollars, personal consumption expenditures (PCE) increased from 195 billion dollars in 1947 to 298 billion dollars in 1960. Even accounting for the fact that the absolute population of the United States grew faster than ever before during the same period, it is undeniable that many Americans enjoyed the benefits of the postwar boom. During this period, per capita GNP increased by 24%, and per capita consumption expenditures increased by 22% [82].

But the most surprising results of the postwar boom were seen in Western Europe (especially Germany) and Japan. Comparing per capita productivity between 1960 and 1973, the growth rate of productivity per hour worked in the American manufacturing sector increased from 3.7% a year in the early 1960s to 3.9% in the early 1970s, while Europe posted 6.2 and 5.5% of growth, respectively. Productivity in Japan increased at an even faster clip, posting 8.6 and 9.5% of growth in the same period. A similar trend can be confirmed by comparing capital per capita. The per capita capital accumulation in the United States in the early 1960s only grew by an average of 0.9% a year, compared with 5.6% in Europe and a whopping 11.9% in Japan.

As an inevitable consequence, the share of the United States' economy shrank in relation to the global economy. The United States accounted for no less than 58% of the gross production of advanced economies in 1950, but this declined to 47% in 1970. The gap in the productivity of the manufacturing sector decreased as well. In 1950, the United States' manufacturing productivity surpassed that of Germany and Japan by a factor of 3 and 8.6, respectively, but by 1970 this had fallen to a factor of 1.7 and 2.4 [83].

It is generally known that growth in Germany and Japan resulted from the combination of military and economic aid from the United States, the expansion of a relaxed system of international free trade, the combination of non-tariff protectionism in the domestic market and the opening of markets (the American in particular), and government aid for corporations exporting manufactured goods. It is especially noteworthy that the German and Japanese governments consistently pursued a much more conservative and balanced fiscal policy than the United States or other European countries, which is unsurprising since both Germany and Japan had suffered from severe inflation during the interwar period and immediately after World War II. On the other hand, these two countries concentrated on using microeconomic policy support to increase the productive capacity and productivity of the manufacturing sector. It is well-known, for example, that Germany blocked foreign capital from flowing into the country and used export subsidies and various financial benefits to increase the competitiveness of its export companies, while Japan's Ministry of International Trade and Industry (MITI) played a leading role in promoting corporate investment, limiting the influx of foreign capital, and engaging in price discrimination (that is, dumping).

But yet another advantage shared by these two countries was that during World War II they had both carried out massive investment in facilities, technology, and human resources. Given the natural resources at their disposal and the shortfall in their productive capacity and productivity before the war, the German and Japanese governments also had to concentrate on increasing their industrial productive capacity, relying on much more oppressive measures than the United States. While such efforts did not lead to military victory, of course, they did help Germany and Japan acquire production facilities, technology, and a skilled workforce, which was ultimately what enabled the two countries to rise like a phoenix above the immense human and material losses they suffered during the war and to give chase to the United States [84].

Thus, the new global economic order that the United States build after World War II promoted not only the continuing development of the American system of expansive reproduction but also the rapid economic development of Europe, Japan, and a number of developing countries. When Britain called for the adoption of free trade and for the integration of the global economy based on the technological advantage and productive capacity acquired during the First Industrial Revolution, it did not receive a very positive response from the late industrializing states. In contrast, the postwar order led by the United States seemed to promise continuous economic growth, not only to the United States but to all the capitalist states.

To be sure, the driving force behind this striking success was the overwhelming economic advantage of the United States. The United States appeared to encompass the strengths of all the economic societies that had appeared until this point. The United States' abundant land and other resources continued to sustain its economy's powerful primary sector, while its commercial and financial sectors, which had been developing since the colonial period, both integrated the country's vast domestic market and seized control of the global market. On top of the United States' strengths with respect to the system of simple reproduction in agricultural society and the system of expansive reinvestment in commercial society, its manufacturing industry entered a period of full-fledged development after the Civil War and brought about the system of expansive reproduction. In the end, this was what enabled the United States' to rise as the hegemon in the global economy after World War I. Furthermore, the development of the American system of expansive reproduction accelerated the development not only of the manufacturing sector but also of the agricultural and commercial sectors. Thus, the "American century" was made possible by the productive capacity and the technological advantage of the American system of expansive reproduction.

References

1. Claudia D. Goldin and Frank D. Lewis, "The Economic Cost of the American Civil War: Estimates and Implications," *Journal of Economic History* 35 (1975), pp. 299–326; Jeremy Atack and Peter Passell, *A New Economic View of American History*, 2nd ed. (New York, 1994), pp. 360–363.
2. James McPherson, *Battle Cry of Freedom: The Civil War Era* (Oxford, 1988), pp. 442–450; Heather Cox Richardson, *The Greatest Nation of the Earth: Republican Economic Policies during the Civil War* (Cambridge, Mass., 1997), pp. 66–138.
3. McPherson, *Battle Cry of Freedom*, pp. 437–442. One scholar has even used the term "full-blown State socialism" to describe the Confederate government's increasing economic intervention during the war; Jeffrey Rogers Hummel, "The Civil War and Reconstruction," Price Fishback et al., *Government and the American Economy: A New History* (Chicago, 2007), p. 208.
4. Charles A. Beard and Mary R. Beard, *The Rise of American Civilization Vol. 2: The Industrial Era* (New York, 1927); Louis M. Hacker, *The Triumph of American Capitalism: The Development of Forces in American History to the End of the Nineteenth Century* (New York, 1940).
5. Atack and Passell, *A New Economic View*, pp. 360–363.
6. Robert E. Gallman, "Economic Growth and Structural Change in the Long Nineteenth Century," Stanley E. Engerman and Robert E. Gallman (eds.), *The Cambridge Economic History of the United States Vol. II: The Long Nineteenth Century* (Cambridge, 2000), p. 7.
7. Stuart Bruchey, *Enterprise: The Dynamic Economy of a Free People* (Cambridge, Mass., 1991), p. 256.
8. P. K. O'Brien, "The Pax Britannica and American Hegemony: Precedent, Antecedent or Just Another History?" O'Brien and Armand Clesse (eds.), *Two Hegemonies: Britain 1846–1914 and the United States 1941–2001* (Aldershot, 2002), pp. 28–29; Richard Sylla, "Experimental Federalism: The Economics of American Government 1789–1914," Engerman and Gallman (eds.), *The Cambridge Economic History of the United States, Vol II*, pp. 532–533. Tariffs were still the most important protectionist measure. From 1866 to 1883, the United States maintained high tariff rates at an average of 45%. Subsequently, there was a growing demand to lower tariffs in order to raise living standards for farmers and workers. Tariffs were even reduced on occasion, but even after World War I, the United States retained its protectionist stance. For more on this point, see Paul Bairoch, *Economics and World History* (Chicago, 1993), p. 36; Robert J. Gordon, "Two Centuries of Economic Growth: Europe Chasing the American Frontier," NBER Working Paper No. 10622 (August 2004), p. 21.
9. Lipsey, "U.S. Foreign Trade and the Balance of Payments, 1800–1913," Engerman and Gallman (eds.), *The Cambridge Economic History of the United States Vol. II*, p. 725.

10. Fishlow, "Internal Transportation in the Nineteenth and Early Twentieth Centuries," Engerman and Gallman (eds.), *The Cambridge Economic History of the United States Vol II*, pp. 583–584. It is instructive to compare American figures with British ones. In 1880, for example, the entire British railroad system was no more than around 25,000 kilometers in length; Alfred D. Chandler, Jr., *Scale and Scope: The Dynamics of Industrial Capitalism*, paperback ed. (Cambridge, Mass., 1994), p. 53.
11. For more on this point, see Stephen Broadberry and Kevin H. O'Rourke, *The Cambridge Economic History of Modern Europe Vol. I: 1700–1870* (Cambridge, 2010), Chap. 7.
12. It is widely known that the federal government—which was dominated by the Republican Party after the war—provided direct and indirect support to railroad construction. As with the Union Pacific Railroad, which was built in the 1860s, the federal government supplied the land that was necessary for building the railroad network or helped with capital by trading government bonds for stock or having state and local governments purchase shares in railroad companies. Richardson, *The Greatest Nation of the Earth*, pp. 171–208; Jonathan Barron Baskin and Paul J. Miranti, Jr., *A History of Corporate Finance* (Cambridge, 1997), pp. 146–164.
13. Alfred D. Chandler, Jr., *The Visible Hand: The Managerial Revolution in American Business* (Cambridge, Mass., 1977), Part 2; Bruchey, *Enterprise*, pp. 269–270.
14. Lance E. Davis and Robert J. Cull, "International Capital Movements, Domestic Capital Markets, and American Economic Growth, 1820–1914," Engerman and Gallman (eds.), *The Cambridge Economic History of the United States Vol. II*, pp. 750–755.
15. Naomi R. Lamoreaux, "Entrepreneurship, Business Organization, and Economic Concentration," Engerman and Gallman (eds.), *The Cambridge Economic History of the United States Vol. II*, p. 419; Baskin and Miranti, Jr., *A History of Corporate Finance*, pp. 146–164.
16. Chandler, Jr., *Visible Hand*, pp. 240, 289–290; William Leach, *Land of Desire: Merchants, Power and the Rise of a New American Culture* (New York, 1993), Part 1.
17. Chandler, Jr., *Visible Hand*, p. 241; Chandler, Jr., *Scale and Scope*, p. 62.
18. David A. Hounshell, *From the American System to Mass Production, 1800–1932: The Development of Manufacturing Technology in the United States* (Baltimore, 1984); Chandler, Jr., *Visible Hand*, pp. 240–283.
19. Gavin Wright, "The Origins of American Industrial Success 1879–1940," *American Economic Review* 80 (1990), pp. 651–668. Of course, natural resources in and of themselves do not fully explain the growth of the American manufacturing sector. The abundant supply of resources affected the specific way in which the American manufacturing sector developed, as we see in the development of the system of mass production. But we must not overlook the fact that the development and use of resources depended upon technological developments. In regard to the capital- and labor-intensive nature of the American manufacturing sector, see Table 1 on p. 656 of the same text.
20. Youngsoo Bae, *Miguk Yeoeronui Daeaneul Chajaseo* [In Search of Alternatives to American Exceptionalism], (Ilchokak, 2011), pp. 109–113.
21. Lamoreaux, "Entrepreneurship, Business Organization, and Economic Concentration," pp. 423–424.
22. Chandler, Jr., *Scale and Scope*, Part 2; Louis Galambos, "The U.S. Corporate Economy in the Twentieth Century," Stanley E. Engerman and Robert E. Gallman (eds.), *The Cambridge Economic History of the United States Vol. III: Twentieth Century* (Cambridge, 2000), pp. 927–959.
23. Chandler, Jr., *Scale and Scope*, pp. 14–31.
24. Richard R. Nelson and Gavin Wright, "The Rise and Fall of American Technological Leadership," *Journal of Economic Literature* 30 (1992), pp. 1931–1964; Thomas P. Hughes, *American Genesis: A Century of Invention and Technological Enthusiasm, 1870–1970*, 2nd ed. (Chicago, 2004).
25. The new liberalism that appeared in Britain at the end of the nineteenth century should not be confused with the similarly named neoliberalism that has come into fashion more recently.

Just as with the progressive movement in the United States, the new liberalism emphasized the failure of the market and the need for aggressive intervention from the state to prevent capital from monopolizing, to protect the rights of workers, and to expand social welfare.

26. Price Fishback, "The Progressive Era," Fishback et al., *Government and the American Economy*, pp. 288–322.
27. Mark Guglielmo and Werner Troesken, "The Gilded Age," Fishback et al., *Government and the American Economy*, pp. 267–273; Fishback, "The Progressive Era," pp. 309–310; Thomas K. McCraw, *Prophets of Regulation* (Cambridge, Mass., 1984), pp. 78–79 and *passim*.
28. For the "end of the frontier," see Jackson Lears, *Rebirth of a Nation: The Making of Modern America, 1877–1920* (New York, 2009), pp. 40–41.
29. Michael Adas, *Dominance by Design: Technological Imperatives and America's Civilizing Mission* (Cambridge, Mass., 2006), pp. 129–182.
30. Lears, *Rebirth of a Nation*, pp. 279–291 (for Roosevelt's aggressive foreign policy) and pp. 324–325 (for Wilson and American policy on Central and South America); Kris James Mitchener and Marc D. Weidenmier, "Empire, Public Goods, and the Roosevelt Corollary," NBER Working Paper No. 10729 (September 2004). According to the second paper, Roosevelt's announcement led to a major jump in the values of government bonds from Central and South American countries (74% after one year and 91% after two years), an increase in exports, and a decrease in regional conflict. The authors contend that this supports the hegemonic stability theory that was long ago espoused by Charles Kindleberger.
31. Lears, *Rebirth of a Nation*, pp. 325–326, 334–335, 337–338 (the Zimmermann Telegram); David Kennedy, *Over Here: The First World War and the American Society* (Oxford, 1980), pp. 5, 10. It is frequently said that the United States' entry into World War I was precipitated by the torpedoing of the RMS Lusitania, a British passenger liner, by a German submarine in May 1915, causing the death of a large number of Americans on board. But a more direct cause of the American decision was the Zimmermann Telegram in February 1917, which increased the American government's suspicions about Germany. In the telegram, which was allegedly sent to the Mexican government by German Foreign Secretary Arthur Zimmermann, Germany promised to force the United States to return the states of Texas, Arizona, and New Mexico to Mexico, provided that Mexico joined the war and Germany was victorious. While the authenticity of the telegram was doubtful since the American government had received it by way of a British intelligence agency, it played a major role in shifting American public opinion in favor of the war.
32. Hugh Rockoff, "Until It's Over, Over There: The U.S. Economy in World War I," Stephen Broadberry and Mark Harrison (eds.), *The Economics of World War I* (Cambridge, 2005), p. 334 Table 10.8; Michael Edelstein, "War and the American Economy in the Twentieth Century," Engerman and Gallman (eds.), *The Cambridge Economic History of the United States Vol. III*, p. 330, p. 342, Table 6.1 (estimated at 32.1 billion dollars).
33. Rockoff, "Until It's Over, Over There," pp. 316, 321, 322–327; Kennedy, *Over Here*, p. 105 (the campaign to promote sales of liberty bonds).
34. Rockoff, "Until It's Over, Over There," pp. 327–332; Kennedy, *Over Here*, pp. 126–136.
35. Stephen Broadberry and Mark Harrison, "The Economics of World War I: An Overview," Broadberry and Harrison (eds.), *The Economics of World War I*, p. 27 Table 1.9. It is worth remembering that Britain is estimated to have lost about 15% of its national wealth and that France and Germany are estimated to have both lost 55% of theirs during the war. See Table 1.10 on p. 28 of the same text.
36. Real GNP (converted into 1982 dollars) increased from about 400 billion dollars to 496 billion dollars during the same period. For these two figures, see Nathan S. Balke and Robert J. Gordon, "The Estimation of Prewar GNP: Methodology and New Evidence," NBER Working Paper No. 2574 (August 1988), p. 85, Table 10. According to another estimate that

examines changes in real GDP between 1914 and 1918, the United States' real GDP, assumed to be 100 in 1913, grew to 113.2 by 1918. See Broadberry and Harrison, "The Economics of World War I," p. 12, Table 1.4.

37. Rockoff, "Until It's Over, Over There," p. 335 Table 10.9. American foreign investment increased from 5 billion dollars in 1914 to 9.7 billion dollars in 1919, while foreign investment in the United States decreased from 7.2 billion dollars to 3.3 billion dollars during the same period. Even after the war, overseas capital investment by Americans continued for some time, and more than 1 billion dollars was exported every year between 1924 and 1928. Barry Eichengreen, "U.S. Foreign Financial Relations in the Twentieth Century," Engerman and Gallman (eds.), *The Cambridge Economic History of the United States Vol. III*, pp. 475–479. American government debt had been 3.7 billion dollars before the war, but by the end of the war the American government had loaned a similar amount of money to other countries. Kennedy, *Over Here*, p. 338.
38. For the chaos after the war, see Charles S. Maier, *Recasting Bourgeois Europe: Stabilization in France, Germany and Italy in the Decade after World War I* (Princeton, 1975).
39. Hughes and Cain, *American Economic History*, 6th ed., pp. 441, 443–444. According to these scholars, real wages rose by 17% between 1922 and 1929, and real income increased by about 60% between 1921 and 1929. As a consequence, the consumption of durable and semi-durable consumer goods increased from 12.5% of GNP in 1919 to 20% in 1929. It is also worth remembering that expenditures on durable producer goods and the construction sector also increased, from 5.5% and 6.3% in 1919 to 7.5% and 11.2% in 1929, respectively; Bruchey, *Enterprise*, p. 403, Table 37.
40. Of particular importance were the United States' abundant deposits of petroleum and iron ore. When the development of the automobile industry took off in the early 1910s (more specifically in 1913), the United States was producing 65% of the world's crude oil and 35% of its iron ore. Wright, "Origins of American Industrial Success," p. 661.
41. Hounshell, *From the American System to Mass Production*, pp. 217–261; Thomas K. McCraw and Richard S. Tedlow, "Henry Ford, Alfred Sloan, and the Three Phases of Marketing," McCraw (ed.), *Creating Modern Capitalism: How Entrepreneurs, Companies, and Countries Triumphed in Three Industrial Revolutions* (Cambridge, Mass, 1995), pp. 266–300.
42. McCraw and Tedlow, "Henry Ford, Alfred Sloan, and the Three Phases of Marketing," pp. 285–288.
43. Gordon, "Two Centuries of Economic Growth," p. 24.
44. The United States reinforced its protectionist stance after World War I. During Wilson's presidency, the United States reduced its average tariff rate from 19.3% to 9.1% with the Underwood-Simmons Act of 1913, but the Harding administration raised tariffs to 14% in 1922. American industrial sectors that had led the way in exports such as the finance sector, mining, petroleum, machinery, electricity, automobiles, rubber, and chemicals supported the Wilson administration's policies and called for the United States to reduce tariffs, to aid Europe's postwar reconstruction, and in particular to write off war reparations and wartime debt. But the agriculture sector and industrial sectors that had been traditionally labor-intensive were strongly in support of protectionism. Tariffs were raised again by the Smoot-Hawley Act immediately after the beginning of the Great Depression, and by 1932 the average tariff rate was 19.59%. For conflicting opinions inside the economic establishment and for the dispute between the Republican and Democratic Parties in the debate over raising tariffs and other aspects of economic policy during the interwar period, see Jeff Frieden, "Sectoral Conflict and Foreign Economic Policy, 1914–1940," *International Organization* 42 (1988), pp. 59–90; Barry Eichengreen, "The Political Economy of the Smoot-Hawley Tariff," NBER Working Paper No. 2001 (August, 1986), pp. 16–17; Colleen M. Callahan, Judith A. McDonald, and Anthony Patrick O'Brien, "Who Voted for Smoot-Hawley?" *Journal of Economic History* 54 (1994), pp. 683–684.
45. Requoted from O'Brien, "The Pax Britannica and American Hegemony," p. 51. For the speculative boom, see Gordon, *An Empire of Wealth*, p. 402; Dong-hyu Yang, *20 Segi*

Gyeongjesa: Daegonghwangeseo Segyehwakkaji [Economic History of the Twentieth Century: From the Great Depression to Globalization] (Ilchogak, 2006), p. 20.

46. Assuming that the value of stocks in July 1926 was 100, the index rose to 216 in September 1929. The index began to fall on "Black Tuesday" (October 29, 1929) and by July 1932 had dropped to 34.
47. Jonathan Hughes and Louis P. Cain, *American Economic History*, 6th ed. (New York, 2003), p. 460; Charles H. Feinstein, Peter Temin, and Gianni Toniolo, *Daegonghwang Jeonhu Segye Gyeongje* [The World Economy Between the World Wars], trans. Dong-hyu Yang, Bok-yeong Park, and Yeong-wan Kim (Dong-suh-Munhak-sa, 2008), p. 195, Table 7.2.
48. According to Dong-hyu Yang, this was a very unreasonable decision. The biggest problem facing the global economy at the time was not rising prices but falling prices. If expectation persisted that prices would continue to fall, people would keep postponing consumption and companies to keep postponing investment. The only way to overcome this was reversing people's psychological reluctance to spend and invest by moving away from the gold standard to reduce the value of currency and by greatly expanding the currency supply at the same time in order to raise prices. Dong-hyu Yang, *20 Segi Gyeongjesa* [Economic History of the Twentieth Century], pp. 28–42.
49. Dong-hyu Yang, *20 Segi Gyeongjesa* [Economic History of the Twentieth Century], pp. 43–45, 60–63, 125–161.
50. For the unemployment and industrial production indicators, see Dong-hyu Yang, *20 Segi Gyeongjesa* [Economic History of the Twentieth Century], pp. 19, 21.
51. J. R. Vernon, "World War II Fiscal Policies and the End of the Great Depression," *Journal of Economic History* 54 (1994), pp. 850–868.
52. Hugh Rockoff, "The United States: From Ploughshares to Swords," Mark Harrison (ed.), *The Economics of World War II: Six Great Powers in International Comparison* (Cambridge, 2000), pp. 81–121. When the per capita consumption of actual residents is estimated, the reduction in consumption in 1942 vanishes, and consumption steadily increases until reaching its highest point ever in 1943. When people at the time said that "Americans never had it so good," they were not exaggerating. For more on this point, see Table 3.5 in the same text.
53. Gordon, *An Empire of Wealth*, p. 453; Fred Aftalion, *A History of the International Chemical Industry* (Philadelphia, 1991), pp. 208–209.
54. Robert M. Collins, *More: The Politics of Economic Growth in Postwar America* (New York, 2000), pp. 11–12.
55. David Mowery and Nathan Rosenberg, "Twentieth-Century Technological Change," Stanley E. Engerman and Robert E. Gallman (eds.), *The Cambridge Economic History of the United States Vol. III*, p. 819.
56. For the role of the federal government in R&D investment after the war, see Mowery and Rosenberg, "Twentieth-Century Technological Change," pp. 820–823.
57. Alfred D. Chandler, Jr., *Inventing the Electronic Century: The Epic Story of the Consumer Electronics and Computer Industries*, paperback edition (Cambridge, Mass., 2006), pp. 27–29 (RCA), 83–84 (computers); Mowery and Rosenberg, "Twentieth-Century Technological Change," p. 886.
58. Chandler, Jr., *Inventing the Electronic Century*, pp. 83–84.
59. Mowery and Rosenberg, "Twentieth-Century Technological Change," pp. 856–857.
60. Aftalion, *A History of the International Chemical Industry*, pp. 209–212.
61. Ruth Schwartz Cowan, *A Social History of American Technology* (New York, 1997), pp. 256–258; Mowery and Rosenberg, "Twentieth-Century Technological Change," p. 842 (for the development of the jet engine).
62. Gordon, "Two Centuries of Economic Growth." There was a severe gap between the productive capacity of the United States and of Europe. While American industrial production just before the end of the war was 50% higher than before the war, the industrial production of the defeated countries of Germany and Japan had fallen to 20% of prewar industrial

production. Philip Armstrong, Andrew Glyn, and John Harrison, *Capitalism since 1945* (Oxford, 1991), p. 23.

63. Feinstein, Temin, and Toniolo, *Daegonghwang Jeonhu Segye Gyeongje* [The World Economy Between the World Wars], p. 278.
64. Eichengreen, *Globalizing Capital*, p. 99. For the Bretton Woods agreement, start reading at p. 93 in the same book and Kim Gi-su, *Gukje Tonghwa Geumyung Chejewa Segye Gyeongje Paegwon* [The International Monetary and Financial System and Global Economic Hegemony] (Sallim, 2011), Chap. 3.
65. For the origins of the Council on Foreign Relations and the postwar plan, see Youngsoo Bae, *Miguk Yeoeronui Daeaneul Chajaseo* [In Search of Alternatives to American Exceptionalism], pp. 431–432; Laurence H. Shoup and William Minter, *Imperial Brain Trust: The Council on Foreign Relations and United States Foreign Policy* (New York, 1977), see especially Chaps. 1 and 4.
66. Jeffry A. Frieden, *Global Capitalism: Its Fall and Rise in the Twentieth Century* (New York, 2006), pp. 255–257; Tony Judt, *Postwar: A History of Europe since 1945* (New York, 2006), pp. 107–108.
67. Frieden, *Global Capitalism*, p. 258.
68. Frieden, *Global Capitalism*, p. 270; Armstrong, Glyn, and Harrison, *Capitalism since 1945*, pp. 30–31.
69. Frieden, *Global Capitalism*, p. 265.
70. The United States was not worried, of course, that Communism would immediately sweep over Western Europe. Rather, the United States was concerned that socialism would grow in influence unless the economic conditions in Western Europe improved and that this would lead to increasing demand for socialization of the means of production and increased control by labor, all measures that conflicted with the free international economic order that the United States envisioned. Therefore, the objective of the aid provided through the Marshall Plan was not "to be the combatting of communism as such but to the restoration of the economic health and vigor of the European society," as George Kennan said (requoted from Armstrong, Glyn, and Harrison, *Capitalism since 1945*, p. 72); Judt, *Postwar*, pp. 88–90.
71. While Britain and France received the greatest portion of the 12 billion dollars of Marshall aid, this aid had an even greater effect on beneficiary countries with smaller economies. For example, the amount of aid that Austria received during the first year of the Marshall Plan was equivalent to 14% of Austria's national income. Judt, *Postwar*, pp. 90–91; Dong-hyu Yang, *20 Segi Gyeongjesa* [Economic History of the Twentieth Century], pp. 173–174, 261.
72. Dong-hyu Yang, *20 Segi Gyeongjesa* [Economic History of the Twentieth Century], pp. 174–175.
73. Dong-hyu Yang, *20 Segi Gyeongjesa* [Economic History of the Twentieth Century], pp. 185–186; for the "politics of productivity," see Charles S. Maier, *Among Empires: American Ascendancy and Its Predecessors* (Cambridge, Mass., 2006), pp. 191–237.
74. Dong-hyu Yang, *20 Segi Gyeongjesa* [Economic History of the Twentieth Century], pp. 176–177.
75. Dong-hyu Yang, *20 Segi Gyeongjesa* [Economic History of the Twentieth Century], pp. 202–212; Armstrong, Glyn, and Harrison, *Capitalism since 1945*, p. 3; Judt, *Postwar*, p. 86.
76. Dong-hyu Yang, *20 Segi Gyeongjesa* [Economic History of the Twentieth Century], pp. 191–198; Eichengreen, *Globalizing Capital*, pp. 106–107.
77. Findlay and O'Rourke, *Power and Plenty: Trade, War, and the World Economy in the Second Millennium*, Chap. 7.
78. Armstrong, Glyn, and Harrison, *Capitalism since 1945*, p. 151; Moses Abramovitz, "Catching Up, Forging Ahead, and Falling Behind," *Journal of Economic History* 46 (1996), p. 391, Table 1.
79. This remark by Allen W. Dulles, director of the CIA, is requoted from Judt, *Postwar*, p. 94.
80. Peter H. Lindert, "Twentieth-Century Foreign Trade and Trade Policy," Engerman and Gallman (eds.), *The Cambridge Economic History of the United States Vol. III*, pp. 444–455;

Judith Stein, *Pivotal Decade: How the United States Traded Factories for Finance in the Seventies* (New Haven, 2010), pp. 5–8.

81. Armstrong, Glyn, and Harrison, *Capitalism since 1945*, p. 154.
82. Collins, *More*, pp. 40–41; Stein, *Pivotal Decade*, pp. 1–2.
83. Armstrong, Glyn, and Harrison, *Capitalism since 1945*, pp. 177 (Table 11.5), 151 (Table 10.1). After the Kennedy Round (1962–1967), the average rate of tariffs fell to 8.7%; after the Tokyo Round (1973–1979), this rate dropped even further to 4.7%.
84. This can be conceptualized as the "phoenix factor." For more on this point, see Tai-Yoo Kim et al., "War, Peace and Economic Growth: The Phoenix Factor Reexamined," mimeograph.

Epilogue

The system of expansive reproduction revealed the potential of accelerating economic growth for the first time in history during the First Industrial Revolution in Great Britain, and this system was brought to maturity by the United States when it launched the Second Industrial Revolution. After 1945, the American system of expansive reproduction spread around the world through the international monetary and free trade systems known respectively as the Bretton Woods system and the General Agreement on Tariffs and Trade (GATT). In this way, a vertical international division of labor was forged that linked the United States at the top to the industrialized countries of Japan and Europe, the newly developing countries, and the agricultural states that still specialized in the primary sector of the economy.

This new international division of labor drove rapid economic growth not only in the United States but also in the late industrializing states that were trying to catch up with the United States, and as a result the global economy enjoyed a period of unprecedented prosperity. It was the Golden Age of Capitalism (as this period is called) that most clearly demonstrated the growth principle of the system of expansive reproduction, which is to say an endless cycle in which technological innovation in the supply sector leads to the development of new products, which in turn leads to the rapid creation of new demand. As the United States had promised in the wake of World War II, it appeared that accelerating economic growth driven by the improvement of productive capacity and productivity would permanently transcend the limits on growth faced by agricultural societies and commercial societies of the past as well as the ensuing societal and international conflicts over limited economic surplus. The people of the advanced capitalist states fully enjoyed the benefits of stable employment, high wages, and abundant consumption, and it looked as if the people of developing countries would be following in their footsteps before too long.

But while it had seemed as if the rapid economic growth would last forever, the postwar boom was not to last. As luck would have it, the first country to realize the precariousness of economic growth was the United States, which had laid the institutional foundation for the boom. In the early 1960s, American politicians had

T.-Y. Kim and D. Kim, *The Secrets of Hegemony*,
DOI 10.1007/978-981-10-4416-8

already started to notice that not only was the American economy growing much more slowly than the economies of Europe (and Germany in particular), but the economic planning of the Soviet Union was achieving remarkable results as well.

President Kennedy had proclaimed a "New Frontier," and in an episode that illustrates how circumstances were changing, he told his main economic advisor Walter Heller not to come back from economic consultations in Paris until he had "discovered the secret of European growth." Throughout the Kennedy and Johnson administrations, to be sure, the American economy was growing by 5% each year, while the unemployment rate dropped as low as 3.9% and the poverty rate stayed below 15% [1]. But compared to the record-breaking growth in Germany and Japan, even such remarkable accomplishments seemed inadequate. Furthermore, the Vietnam War, which began in 1965, demanded massive spending on the military [2].

Relatively slow economic growth and substantial military spending soon spelled trouble for the international monetary system controlled by the United States. Under the Bretton Woods system, the American dollar was in the privileged position of being the only convertible currency that was pegged to gold. Because of the expansion of international trade after the war and the development of the international currency market, demand for the dollar continued to increase, and Japan and European countries were more interested in acquiring dollars for their payment reserves than gold. During the postwar boom, when the United States posted a huge surplus in the trade in goods and when the interest and dividends paid on Americans' overseas assets continued to flow into the United States, various countries' demand for dollars was ultimately satisfied by the overseas outflow of American capital and the American government's overseas expenditures, including loans, aid, and military expenditures.

By the end of the 1960s, however, the latter had surpassed the former: more than 30 billion dollars were deposited at central banks in other countries, and the American gold reserves were running short. It was in such circumstances that the American government greatly expanded the currency supply in the early 1970s in an attempt to stimulate the economy, which caused domestic interest rates to fall and led to a large-scale exodus of speculative capital. This ultimately forced the Nixon administration in 1971 to take the extreme measure of suspending the convertibility of the dollar to gold. Despite this measure, speculation soon resumed, and the outflow of the dollar did not stop. In the end, the central banks of multiple countries abandoned the Bretton Woods principle of only allowing their currency's exchange rate to the dollar to fluctuate within a limited range. This meant the effective end of the Bretton Woods system in the strict sense and the beginning of the age of floating exchange rates [3].

Europe and Japan's attempts to overtake the United States, the breakdown of the Bretton Woods system, and the global economic crisis that began in 1973 increased doubts about the sustainability of the America-centered global economic order and about the decline of the United States. In an attempt to relieve the trade deficit and to stimulate sluggish global economic demand, the American government devalued the dollar, revalued the currencies of Germany and Japan, and took measures to increase American exports and promote the domestic market, but these measures achieved little.

Though the global economy contracted even further after the oil crisis, the export competitiveness of German and Japanese manufacturing companies became even stronger while the American manufacturing sector shrank substantially. The situation did not get much better even during the Reagan administration, which replaced the Keynesian economics that had held sway during the postwar boom with supply-side economics. But even in the late 1980s, there were no signs of a solution for the crisis of competitiveness in the American manufacturing sector, which was dramatically illustrated by the decline of the American automobile industry.

In an attempt to counteract this decline, the American government put pressure on the German and Japanese exchange rate policies and adopted a variety of protectionist measures, making American decline look even more obvious [4]. The debate over the decline of the American economy subsided for a time as the American and global economies enjoyed a time of prosperity in the 1990s, bolstered by the rise of the IT industry and the financial sector. This discussion has gained new momentum since the beginning of the twenty-first century, however, with the American fiscal deficit growing astronomically and the vulnerability of the American financial sector exposed during the global financial crisis.

To be sure, we must not jump to the conclusion that the American economy has entered a process of irreversible decline. In terms of the growth rate, it is undeniable that the American economy has grown more slowly than Europe, Japan, and the developing economies. During the 1970s and 1980s, when the decline of the American economy became a regular topic of discussion, the American real GDP posted a growth rate of 2.8%, which was lower than Europe's growth rate of 2.9% and Japan's growth rate of 4.3%. But it is worth bearing in mind that the growth rate of the American economy outpaced that of Europe in the 1980s and 1990s and that the American growth rate was faster not only than Europe's but also Japan's in the 1990s [5].

Perhaps even more important is the fact that the size of the American economy relative to the global economy has changed little since the 1980s. In the 1980s, the American economy made up about one-fourth of gross world product; in 2005, it still made up 20%. Compared with the fact that the United States accounted for more than half of gross world product in the early 1950s, it could be argued that the American economy has undergone a sharp decline. But from a different perspective, it could be said that the 1950s were an exceptional time when the productive capacity of most of the advanced industrialized countries had been exhausted by World War II [6].

When we examine not just the size of the economy or the growth rate but also the state's overall capacity, speculation about American decline looks even more premature. In *The Rise and Fall of the Great Powers*, which we examined in the prologue, Paul Kennedy offered a stern warning about the downfall of the United States, arguing that hegemonic states that engage in "military overstretch," or military spending that cannot be sustained by the state's economic resources, are doomed to failure. But as we have already seen, American military power has actually grown since the 1990s while military spending has soared alongside a huge fiscal deficit.

Even more important is the fact that, despite growing public opposition to the expansion of American military capability, there are no clear alternatives to this expansion. One study that ranks various countries according to their relative economic and military power confirms that the United States in the twenty-first century accounts for 60% of the world's military power and 40% of its economic power. In the end, this suggests that it is still too soon to be talking about American decline either in terms of its economic power or its overall national power [7].

Nevertheless, the debate over the relative decline of the American economy continues. The economic crises that have occurred with disturbing frequency since the end of the 1990s, the surge in productive capacity in emerging economies such as China and India and their huge financial holdings, and the record-breaking fiscal deficit in the United States are recurring themes in recent discussions of American decline. But the emphasis that this book has taken on the principles of economic development in its historical examination of the rise and fall of great powers shows that we are unlikely to reach a meaningful conclusion about American decline as long as we are fixated on short-term factors.

In our discussion of theory and our examination of how the system of expansive reproduction developed in Great Britain and the United States, we stated that the system of expansive reproduction is characterized by accelerating growth resulting from the new demand that is constantly created by expanding supply based on technological innovation. Since there can be a time lag between the expansion of supply and the creation of demand, of course, the system of expansive reproduction sometimes undergoes recessions and other crises. But such crises have been overcome by means of wars and government policy. Since the system of expansive reproduction is accompanied by continuous technological innovation, this innovation has been used to restart the virtuous cycle.

This is reaffirmed by the fact that it was Germany and Japan that provided the most serious challenge to American ascendancy after World War II. By waging total industrial war (needless to say, an immoral method), these two states were able to accumulate technology, largely in the area of heavy industry, and to greatly expand their accumulated capital. As a result, even though they were both defeated in World War II, they rapidly recovered their productive capacity and their productivity after the war with the help of the technology, manpower, and capital that they had accumulated during the war. This is what we call the phoenix factor.

Reexamining the position of the United States since the 1970s from this perspective prompts a question. The system of expansive reproduction is an economic system in which the economic growth rate gradually accelerates through a virtuous cycle that is launched by continuous technological innovation. Once the virtuous cycle in the system of expansive reproduction begins, therefore, there cannot be any limits on economic growth, at least theoretically. As we have repeated multiple times in this book, this is the most important feature that sets the system of expansive reproduction apart from the system of simple reproduction in agricultural society and from the system of expansive reinvestment in commercial society.

Thus, economic stagnation and a lack of rapid growth in productive capacity and productivity in a state that has established the system of expansive reproduction would imply that the virtuous cycle leading from technological innovation to the development of new products and to the creation of new demand has started to break down. The economic history of Britain since the late nineteenth century offers one plain example of the system of expansive reproduction deviating from this virtuous cycle, and the recent debate about the decline of the American economy is in the end prompted by suspicions that the American system of expansive reproduction is deviating from this virtuous cycle, too.

It would be impossible at the present moment to definitively answer whether the United States is deviating from this virtuous cycle and, if so, whether it will be able to restart the cycle as Germany and Japan did. Even if we narrowed our focus to R&D and technological innovation (which can fairly be described as the foundation of the system of expansive reproduction), we would have to carry out an exhaustive review of the R&D work carried out since the 1970s by the United States, the major industrialized countries, and emerging economies such as China; the successes they have achieved; and the corporate and government policies facilitating those successes. Since the American economic system is history's first global system of expansive reproduction, it would also be necessary to thoroughly examine the new aspects of competition and the rapid changes in global economic conditions since the 1970s.

While such a comprehensive study will have to wait for another day, just a few observations will be enough to show that the American economy is at a crucial juncture, just like Britain at the end of the nineteenth century or (looking further into the past) like the Netherlands in the seventeenth century. It is widely recognized that the most important asset of the American system of expansive reproduction since at least the first half of the twentieth century has been its major investment in R&D and the extensive knowledge accumulated in this manner. The United States continued to invest generously in R&D even in the 1950s and 1960s, when it had an overwhelming advantage in productive capacity and productivity, and it retains its advantage in this area today. On the other hand, American R&D investment has generally been directed by the state and concentrated in areas connected with the defense industry, where it has been applied to problems that cannot be immediately commercialized [8].

This situation began to change in the 1980s. The federal government's proportion of R&D investment gradually decreased, while the corporate sector began to account for an ever-greater share of R&D investment. An even bigger change involved the erosion of the American dominance of R&D investment around the world. In the 1980s, Japan and European countries such as Germany eagerly followed the American example and began to pour huge amounts of capital into R&D. Since the twenty-first century, emerging economies such as China have been making similar efforts. While the United States still retains its lead in R&D

investment and in accumulated technological knowledge, its edge over other countries is rapidly decreasing [9].

Another development that is provoking concerns about the future of the American system of expansive reproduction is the declining competitiveness of the American manufacturing sector and the shift toward deindustrialization. Signs of the sector's declining competitiveness began to appear as early as the postwar boom of the 1950s and 1960s. At the time, American companies neglected to make aggressive investments like their competitors in Germany and Japan. While German and Japanese corporations were making bold investments not only with their own earnings but also with big loans supported by government policy and by investment banks, American corporations were content to reinvest their earnings. This is known to have caused the collapse of the American automobile, steel, and electronics industries.

But we need to clearly understand that the collapse of the industries that had once led the American system of expansive reproduction is not the main problem that that system is facing. As we have repeatedly emphasized, the virtuous cycle in the system of expansive reproduction depends upon continuous technological innovation, and technological innovation not only improves the productive capacity and productivity of existing industries but also leads to the creation of new industries. In order to understand the problem facing the United States, therefore, we must go beyond the mere fact that traditional industries are in decline and examine the extent to which the new replacement industries are helping improve American productive capacity and productivity.

This is where it becomes clear that the American economy has reached an important turning point. The IT and biological engineering industries that led the American "New Economy" in the 1990s are still vital today, but the focus of the American economy is gradually shifting even further away from the manufacturing sector. This is evident from the historical observation that the service sector is gradually increasing relative to American GDP. The service sector accounted for about 30% of GDP in the 1960s, but this had increased to 46% by 2011, while the financial sector accounted for 8.4% of GDP in 2011 [10]. When the economic share of the real estate and construction sectors are also taken into account, it seems clear that the manufacturing sector is no longer the driver of the American economy in the twenty-first century.

Of course, the gradual decline of the manufacturing sector relative to the national economy is a phenomenon that can also be witnessed in Europe and Japan, so it need not be seen as strictly an American problem. Furthermore, financial services are necessary and indispensable for effectively distributing a country's economic resources, so the expansion of the financial sector does not in itself bring about the decline of the system of expansive reproduction. The problem is that the expansion of financial services in the United States largely led to investment not in industries that create added value but rather in the real estate industry and in speculative ventures, which tend to move added value around, as was starkly demonstrated by the subprime mortgage crisis of 2008. If this trend continues, it is inevitable that the American system of expansive reproduction will eventually deviate from the virtuous cycle—which is indisputably the most important lesson to be learned from the historical experience of Britain and the Netherlands.

In a narrative that begins with the rise of the Spanish Empire and concludes with the American Century, we have contended that the fate of powerful countries is ultimately determined by the characteristics of those countries' economic systems. As we have seen, Spain built the most powerful empire in the early modern period, but it was perpetually driven to conquer new territory and to appropriate economic surplus in order to overcome the decelerating growth that is an inherent constraint on the system of simple reproduction in agricultural society. This eventually provoked a vicious cycle that brought on Spain's economic decline.

After winning its independence from the Spanish Empire, the Netherlands developed the most advanced commercial system of its time and brought to perfection the system of expansive reinvestment, in which commercial profit is continually invested in new commercial activity. But the Dutch economy also ran into difficulties because of its fundamental reliance on the trade in luxury goods, which, being agricultural products, were subject to diminishing yields. The economic limitations of agricultural society and commercial society were overcome by the system of expansive reproduction, which opened up new potential for growth. The system of expansive reproduction came into being through the combination of the system of expansive reinvestment and innovation in the supply sector during the First Industrial Revolution in Britain, and that system was brought to maturity through the combination of production and technology that characterized the Second Industrial Revolution in the United States and Germany.

Compared to Britain, which was the first country to build the system of expansive reproduction, the United States had a peculiar economic system. The country's expansive territory, its abundant natural resources, and the commercial tradition dating back to the colonial period combined with the industrialization that got underway in the mid-nineteenth century to produce an economic system that seemed to contain only the best aspects of agricultural society, commercial society, and industrial society. While it is true that the United States transitioned from the system of expansive reinvestment to the system of expansive reproduction through the same process as Britain, the United States was much better positioned than Britain to take advantage of the economic strengths of agricultural society and commercial society.

Because of these advantages—advantages possessed by no other economic system in history—the United States was able to become the hegemonic power of the global economy, and it has remained in that position for a century so far. But as we have already seen, the American economy today stands at an important crossroads, just as the Netherlands and Britain did once before. In the past, the United States was able to use the two world wars to help facilitate the smooth operation of the virtuous cycle in the system of expansive reproduction. Germany and Japan were vanquished by the gargantuan economic power of the United States, but like a phoenix they revived the virtuous cycle in the system of expansive reproduction through the technological innovation they had achieved and the capital they had accumulated during the war.

With more and more of American capital invested in nonproductive economic activity and with the American system of expansive reproduction confronting ever-stiffer competition in the market, will another war prove the only way for this system to be rejuvenated? Or is there some other way for not only the United States but also the other developed and developing countries to enjoy the prosperity that continuous economic growth is supposed to bring? These are questions that we promise to tackle in subsequent research.

References

1. Collins, *More: The Politics of Economic Growth in Postwar America*, pp. 52 (for quoted passage), 53.
2. The American government spent 111 billion dollars on the Vietnam War through 1975. Converted to 2011 dollars, this amounts to 738 billion dollars, which is around 20% of the 4.1 trillion dollars spent on World War II.
3. Judith Stein, *Pivotal Decade: How the United States Traded Factories for Finance in the Seventies* (New Haven, 2010).
4. Stein, *Pivotal Decade.*
5. Alfred E. Eckes, Jr., and Thomas W. Zeiler, *Globalization and the American Century* (New York, 2003), p. 262, Table A.3. According to this table, the American GDP grew by 3.4% and 2.8% in 1980 to 1990 and 1990 to 1998, respectively, while Europe posted 2.5% and 1.8% in growth and Japan posted 4.1% and 1.2%.
6. For the quoted estimates and for a discussion of pessimistic and optimistic views, see Youngsoo Bae, *Miguk Yeoeronui Daeaneul Chajaseo* [In Search of Alternatives to American Exceptionalism] (Ilchokak, 2011), pp. 395–397.
7. For Paul Kennedy, see note 6 in the prologue. For Kennedy's retraction of his own warning about American decline and for the argument that powerful states derive their power less from the comprehensive capability of their economy and more from having a fiscal system that can efficiently fund long-term military spending, see Niall Ferguson, *Colossus: The Rise and Fall of the American Empire* (New York, 2004), particularly pp. 261–262. For a relative comparison of national power that combines economic power and military power, see William C. Wohlforth, "U.S. Strategy in a Unipolar World," G. John Ikenberry (ed.), *America Unrivaled: The Future of the Balance of Power* (Ithaca, 2002), pp. 98–118, requoted from Youngsoo Bae, *Miguk Yeoeronui Daeaneul Chajaseo* [In Search of Alternatives to American Exceptionalism], p. 397.
8. While Europe and Japan were investing 1.5% to 2% of their GDP in R&D in the 1960s, the United States invested 2.75%. According to another estimate, the United States spent 25.6 billion dollars on R&D in 1969, which was more than twice the combined R&D expenditures (11.3 billion dollars) of Germany, France, Britain, and Japan. While the defense industry accounted for a staggering 80% of R&D defense spending in 1949, it leveled off at 50% in the 1960s. Mowery and Rosenberg, "Twentieth-Century Technological Change," Stanley E. Engerman and Robert E. Gallman (eds.), *The Cambridge Economic History of the United States Vol. III: Twentieth Century* (Cambridge, 2000), pp. 819, 822.

T.-Y. Kim and D. Kim, *The Secrets of Hegemony*,
DOI 10.1007/978-981-10-4416-8

9. Also related to this is the fact that the quality of American trade is deteriorating. This point is clearly made (though in a somewhat exaggerated fashion) by Dambisa Moyo, *Migugi Pasanhaneun Nal: Seoguui Mollakgwa Sinheunggukui Bangyeok* [How the West Was Lost: Fifty Years of Economic Folly—and the Stark Choices Ahead], trans. Jong-su Kim (Joongang Books, 2011).
10. For estimates of the 2011 GDP, see http://www.bea.gov/newsreleases/national/gdp/2012/pdf/gdp4q11_3rd.pdf and http://blogs.wsj.com/economics/2011/12/10/number-of-the-week-finances-share-of-economy-continues-to-grow/.

The manufacturer's authorised representative in the EU is Springer Nature Customer Service Centre GmbH, Europaplatz 3, 69115 Heidelberg, Germany. If you have any concerns regarding our products, please contact ProductSafety@springernature.com

Printed and bound by CPI Group (UK) Ltd, Croydon, CR0 4YY
30/09/2026
02225447-0004